Meet the editor

Dr. Sudhakar Radhakrishnan is currently the professor and head of the Department of Electronics and Communication Engineering, Dr. Mahalingam College of Engineering and Technology, Pollachi, India. He is an editorial board member for 3 international journals and a reviewer of 14 international journals. He wrote two books titled *Research Issues in Image Compression Using Wavelet Variants* and *Practicing Signals and Systems Laboratory Using MATLAB*, both published by Lambert Academic Publishing (LAP), Germany (2010). He also wrote a book chapter titled "Wavelet-Based Image Compression" in the book titled *Computational Intelligence Techniques in Handling Image Processing and Pattern Recognition* published by Lambert Academic Publishing (LAP), Germany (2010). He edited two books titled *Effective Video Coding for Multimedia applications* and *Applications of Digital Signal Processing Through Practical Approach*, both published by InTech, Croatia (2011 and 2015). He has published 82 papers in international and national journals and conference proceedings. His areas of research include digital image processing, video coding, wavelet transforms and digital signal processing.

Meet the editor

RECENT ADVANCES IN IMAGE AND VIDEO CODING

Edited by **Sudhakar Radhakrishnan**

Recent Advances in Image and Video Coding
http://dx.doi.org/10.5772/62602
Edited by Sudhakar Radhakrishnan

Contributors

Chih-Peng Fan, Vladimir Lukin, Alexander N. Zemliachenko, Ruslan A. Kozhemiakin, Sergey Abramov, Mikhail L. Uss, Victoriya Abramova, Nikolay N. Ponomarenko, Benoit Vozel, Kacem Chehdi, Eduardo Quevedo, Gustavo Marrero, Félix Tobajas, Damon Chandler, Yi Zhang, Md Mushfiqul Alam, Amin Zribi, Clency Perrine, Yannis Pousset, Chou-Chen Wang, Yuan-Sing Chang, Ke-Nung Huang, Long Chen, Junwei Duan, C. L. Philip Chen, Weixing Wang, Liangqin Chen, Mario Mejia, Branimir Jaksic, Mile B. Petrovic, Lin Liqun

Published by InTech

Janeza Trdine 9, 51000 Rijeka, Croatia

Publishing Process Manager Martina Usljebrka

Technical Editor SPi Global

Cover InTech Design team

First published November, 2016

Printed in Croatia

Additional hard copies can be obtained from orders@intechopen.com

Recent Advances in Image and Video Coding, Edited by Sudhakar Radhakrishnan

p. cm.

Print ISBN 978-953-51-2775-8
Online ISBN 978-953-51-2776-5

Contents

Preface

Digital image processing and computer vision represent an exciting and important part of computer science. The last three decades have witnessed a significant growth of applications in the field of remote sensing, approach towards super resolution images, image analytics, scalable image and video coding, biomedical imaging and automatic surveillance due to Internet explosion.

Image processing is a technique to enhance raw images received from different sources such as satellites, biomedical field and pictures taken in normal day-to-day life for various applications. Various techniques have been developed in image processing during the last four to five decades. Image processing systems are becoming popular since image processing is used in various applications such as (a) remote sensing, (b) medical imaging, (c) forensic studies, (d) textiles, (e) mineral science, (h) film industry and (i) document processing.

Information and processing are the buzz words in the modern era. The demand for multimedia applications has increased enormously. Like many other recent developments, the tremendous growth of image and video processing is due to the contribution from major areas such as good network access, easy availability of powerful personal computers, large-size memory devices, availability of graphics software, good number of fast processors available in the market and evolution of pretty good signal processing algorithms.

The various image processing techniques are (1) image enhancement (2) image restoration, (3) image analysis, (4) image registration, (5) image segmentation, (6) image data compression, etc.

Image enhancement: Sometimes images obtained from satellites or conventional digital cameras lack in contrast and brightness (qualities of image) because of the shortcomings of imaging subsystems and poor illumination conditions. In image enhancement, the aim is to modify certain image features for subsequent analysis or for image display. Examples include contrast and edge enhancement, noise filtering, sharpening and magnifying. Image enhancement is useful in feature extraction, image analysis and image display. The enhancement process itself does not increase the inherent information content in the data.

Image analysis: This deals with taking quantitative measurements from an image to produce a description of the same. In the simple way, this could be reading a label on a grocery item, getting features from an image or measuring the size and orientation of cells in a medical image. More advanced image analysis systems measure quantitative information and use the same to make a sophisticated decision, such as navigating an aircraft with the aid of images acquired along its trajectory. Image analysis techniques require extraction of certain features that aid in the identification of the object.

Image segmentation: It is the process to subdivide an image into its constituent parts. In a simple understanding, this could be like locating countries in world map. The amount to which this subdivision is carried out depends on the problem, that is the segmentation should stop when the objects of interest in an application have been isolated, for example isolation of tumour from brain images. numbers of algorithms available such as image thresholding, watershed algorithm, atlas-based segmentation, region-based split and merge techniques and clustering-based segmentation which are used for image segmentation.

Image registration: It is the process of spatially aligning two or more images of a scene. The alignment process will determine the correspondence between points in the images, enabling the fusion of information in the images and the determination of scene changes. If identities of objects in one of the images are known, by registering the images, identities of objects and their locations in another image can be determined. Image registration is a critical component of remote sensing, biomedical and industrial image analysis systems.

Image restoration: This includes reduction of image degradation by different causes such as defects of optical lenses, relative motion between object and camera, wrong focus, turbulence in atmosphere and accumulation of noise. There are two main algorithms available for restoration: (1) deterministic methods and (2) stochastic methods in both spatial and frequency domains.

Image/video compression: Image and video data compression refers to a process in which the amount of data used to represent image and video is reduced to meet a bit rate (coding rate) requirement (below or at most equal to the maximum available bit rate), while the quality of the reconstructed image or video satisfies a requirement for a certain application, and the complexity of computation involved is affordable for the application. The required quality of the reconstructed image and video is application dependent. In still image compression, a certain amount of information loss is allowed and this is called lossy compression. Normally transform-based compression scheme removes interpixel correlation. The recent growth of data intensive multimedia-based web applications has not only sustained the need for more efficient ways to encode signals and images but has made compression of such signals central to storage and communication technology.

The first recommended international coding standard was Joint Photographic Experts Group (JPEG), and it completely relies on 8 X 8 block-based discrete cosine transform (DCT). The limitation of the JPEG standard comes from the introduction of blocking artefacts. A new standard called JPEG-2000 (using wavelets) was introduced because of the advancements in embedded quantization schemes and new transforms. Still, there is a need for the improvement in the image and video quality with an acceptable compression ratio.

The advancement of computer storage facility continues at a rapid pace so that a means of reducing storage requirements of an image and video has been evolved. Thus, the concept of digital video compression/coding emerged. This storage capacity seems to be more attractive when it is realized that the motive is to deliver very high quality video to the end user with as few visible artefacts as possible. Current methods of video compression such as Moving Picture Experts Group (MPEG) standard provide good performance in terms of retaining video quality while reducing the storage requirements.

Scope of this book: Many books are available for image and video coding fundamentals. This book is the research outcome of various researchers and professors who have contributed a might in this field. This book suits researchers doing their research in the area of image processing and video coding. The understanding of fundamentals of image processing and video coding is essential for the readers before reading this book. The book revolves around three different challenges, namely, (i) coding strategies (coding efficiency and computational complexity), (ii) video compression and (iii) error resilience. The complete efficient video system depends upon source coding, proper inter- and intra-frame coding, emerging newer transform, quantization techniques and proper error concealment. The book gives the solution of all the challenges and is available in different sections.

Structure of the book: The book contains eleven chapters grouped into five sections. The user of the book is expected to know the fundamentals of digital image processing which is available in the entire standard digital image processing books. Section 1 deals with image compression algorithms containing two chapters. Section 2 describes image segmentation and classification containing two chapters. Section 3 concentrates on image fusion algorithms containing two chapters. Section 4 deals with the role of artificial vision in mechanical applications, and the last section is devoted for video coding containing four chapters.

Acknowledgement

I thank the Almighty for showering me blessings and giving me intelligence and energy to complete this work. I thank all the professors and scientists who have contributed to this book with different chapters and their expertise. My sincere thanks to the management of Dr. Mahalingam College of Engineering and Technology and Prof. C. Ramaswamy, Secretary, NIA Institutions, for their encouragement and patronage rendered to carry out this work. I am indebted to my wife Mrs. Vinitha Mohan. Her support, encouragement, quiet patience and unwavering love undeniably led me to the successful completion of the work. No words to thank my son S.V. Hemesh for bearing my preoccupation and understanding and the love he gave me. I am grateful to InTech publishers especially the Publishing Process Manager Ms. Martina Usljebrka who constantly helped me in bringing out this book.

Prof. Dr. Sudhakar Radhakrishnan
Department of Electronics and Communication Engineering
Dr. Mahalingam College of Engineering and Technology
India

Section 1

Image Compression Algorithms

Chapter 1

Visually Lossless Perceptual Image Coding Based on Natural-Scene Masking Models

Yi Zhang, Md Mushfiqul Alam and
Damon M. Chandler

Additional information is available at the end of the chapter

http://dx.doi.org/10.5772/65362

Abstract

Perceptual coding is a subdiscipline of image and video coding that uses models of human visual perception to achieve improved compression efficiency. Nearly, all image and video coders have included some perceptual coding strategies, most notably visual masking. Today, modern coders capitalize on various basic forms of masking such as the fact that distortion is harder to see in very dark and very bright regions, in regions with higher frequency content, and in temporal regions with abrupt changes. However, beyond these obvious forms of masking, there are many other masking phenomena that occur (and co-occur) when viewing natural imagery. In this chapter, we present our latest research in perceptual image coding using natural-scene masking models. We specifically discuss: (1) how to predict local distortion visibility using improved natural-scene masking models and (2) how to apply the models to high efficiency video coding (HEVC). As we will demonstrate, these techniques can offer 10–20% fewer bits than baseline HEVC in the ultra-high-quality regime.

Keywords: HEVC, visual masking, contrast gain control, adaptive quantization

1. Introduction

Recent advancements in digital signal processing technologies have made available a wide variety of digital media for end use by consumers and practitioners. It is estimated that more than 100 billion digital photos and videos are recorded, transmitted, and viewed annually just in the United States. Today, the tremendous popularity of ubiquitously connected digital imaging devices has made the Internet the standard means by which to share imagery. Of course, digital images/videos have many uses beyond entertainment, including online education, video conferencing, remote medical diagnoses, and many others. Such widespread use of digital images and videos places a great demand on compression algorithms which are absolutely crucial for reducing the bandwidth requirements of storing and transmitting these images and videos.

To this end, state-of-the-art image/video compression algorithms exploit the fact that the human visual system (HVS) is an imperfect sensor. When a digital image/video is to be viewed by a human, an exact bit-for-bit reconstruction is unnecessary; rather, the data can be coded in a non-invertible or *lossy* fashion. Lossy compression is useful for applications where lower information fidelity can be tolerated, such as in consumer photography, computer vision, and machine vision applications. If the compression distortions are invisible, the compression is said to be *visually lossless*. Visually lossless compression techniques generally take advantage of a low-level psychophysical phenomenon such as visual masking. If, on the other hand, the compression distortions are visible, the compression is called *visually lossy*. Visually lossy compression techniques aim to generate the best-looking reconstructed version under the given bit-rate constraints. Both of these paradigms fall under the more general category of the so-called *perceptual coding*, owing to the need to model the human visual system (HVS), and in particular, how the HVS detects and perceives compression-induced distortions.

With the release of each new coding standard, the emphasis in perceptual coding research has largely shifted from the mid-quality regime toward the ultra-high-quality regime, with the aim of producing compressed images and videos which are visually equivalent to the originals. Thus, research in visually lossless compression has seen a recent resurgence in importance. In this chapter, we focus exclusively on visually lossless image compression. The key challenge in visually lossless compression is to automatically determine, on a per image basis, the maximum amount of compression that can be applied before the resulting image appears distorted. However, to tackle this challenge requires the ability to accurately and efficiently predict the visibility of local distortions in an image, a task which still remains elusive in the current research.

Perceptual coding strategies have long relied on well-known properties of the HVS largely derived from the visual psychophysics literature (e.g., see [1, 2]). Perhaps, the most well-known and widely used property is the *contrast sensitivity function* (CSF), which specifies the visibility of a narrowband spatial pattern (the *target* of detection) as a function of the pattern's spatial or temporal frequency. Previous psychophysical studies have shown that the minimum contrast needed to detect a visual target (e.g., distortions) varies with both the spatial frequency and the temporal frequency of the target. This minimum contrast is called the *contrast threshold,* and the inverse of this threshold is called *contrast sensitivity*. For targets consisting of spatial sine waves, the CSF is band-pass, indicating that we are least sensitive to very low-frequency and very high-frequency targets. The *temporal CSF* is an extension of the spatial CSF which takes into account sensitivity to time-varying targets, typically demonstrating a peak in sensitivity around 4–8 Hz.

The CSF can be thought of as a baseline visual sensitivity measure because the CSF is traditionally measured for targets shown against a blank background. However, for targets consisting of compression distortions, this blank-background scenario occurs only when the distortions happen to appear in very smooth regions such as in the sky. In other image regions, such as in structures, textures, and hybrids regions, the distortions are generally more difficult to detect (i.e., they exhibit higher contrast detection thresholds), and therefore, visual sensitivity to the distortions is said to be reduced in these regions. This concept of *visual masking* has served as the cornerstone of modern perceptual coding.

At the most general level, visual masking refers to a reduction or elimination in the visibility of one signal (called the "target") caused by the presence of another signal (called the "mask"). For image compression, the image serves as the mask, and the compression distortions serve as the targets of detection. There are various forms of visual masking which can occur and co-occur in images and video. For example, it is well-known that humans have a harder time seeing distortions in very bright regions of an image, an HVS property called *luminance masking*. To capitalize on this fact, modern coding schemes more coarsely quantize the coefficients corresponding to (devote fewer bits to) locations of higher luminance. A similar strategy can be used for very busy regions of an image (*contrast masking*) or during scene changes in video (*temporal masking*).

These low-level aspects of the HVS are so commonly used in image/video coding for two simple reasons: (1) they are easy to incorporate and (2) such low-level aspects have been well-documented in the visual psychology literature with accompanying computational models. However, most existing models of masking (and thus, existing perceptual coding techniques) are largely based on findings using artificial stimuli rather than on a true database of natural scenes. The advantage of these artificial masks is that they have well-defined features and parameters, which allows one to investigate the effects of specific mask properties on the detection thresholds. However, in image compression, the mask is necessarily an image, and thus, it remains unclear whether the results obtained using artificial masks can be used to predict the results obtained using natural scene masks. There are some studies using natural scenes as masks, but these studies either employed only a limited number of tested images, or the thresholds were limited to select spatial locations within images (e.g., [3–5]).

In this chapter, we present our latest research in visually lossless image compression which operates based on the concept of *masking maps* predicted from a natural-scene masking model built upon a large local masking database [6]. Specifically, we recently published the results of a large-scale psychophysical study designed to obtain local contrast detection thresholds (masking maps) for a database of natural images [6]. This database can serve as crucial ground-truth data for investigating on how local image content affects the visual masking thresholds. Using this database, we present an high efficiency video coding (HEVC)-based quantization scheme which uses the contrast gain control (CGC) with structure facilitation model trained on the database of local masking thresholds to predict a masking map for the to-be-compressed image. The masking map is then used to guide a spatially adaptive quantization scheme, which more coarsely quantizes the blocks that can induce greater masking, and vice-versa. Using this approach, our technique can generate compressed images in which the contrasts of the local compression artifacts are much closer to their masked visibility thresholds than when using standard HEVC.

This chapter is organized as follows: Section 2 provides a brief review of current visually lossless perceptual image compression algorithms. In Section 3, we describe the computational models used to predict the masking map for any given input image. In Section 4, we describe how to incorporate the masking map to perform spatially adaptive compression using HEVC. In Section 5, we analyze and discuss the performance of the proposed visually lossless compression method. General conclusions are presented in Section 6.

2. Previous work on perceptual image compression

As we mentioned, the goal of visually lossless image compression is to generate images containing distortions at or just below the visual detection threshold. To this end, previous work in this area has exploited properties of the HVS (most notably the CSF and visual masking) and has taken a variety of approaches toward incorporating these visual properties into the transform, quantization, and/or encoding stages. In this section, we briefly review previous work on perceptual (HVS-based) image compression.

Perceptual image compression techniques can be dated back as early as 1990s when Safranek et al. [7] published one of earliest attempts at incorporating HVS properties into compression through a system called perceptually tuned subband image coder (PIC). Three properties of low-level vision were modeled in PIC: (1) contrast sensitivity, (2) luminance masking, and (3) contrast masking. These properties were used to guide the selection of per-subband quantization step sizes designed to yield visually lossless results. Although PIC was initially designed for visually lossless compression, Pappas et al. [8] reported that this system can also be used for visually lossy compression, and high performance can be achieved when the perceptual thresholds are properly scaled. Also, Hontsch et al. [9] extended PIC by exploiting visual masking; they proposed a locally adaptive perceptual coder, which discriminates between image components based on their perceptual relevance.

Later research on compression has exploited the properties of the HVS and employed the CSF to regulate the quantization step size in order to minimize the visibility of compression artifacts. For example, Nadenau et al. [10] incorporated HVS properties into a wavelet-based coding algorithm via a noise-shaping filtering stage which preceded quantization. Albanesi [11] proposed a method for incorporating HVS characteristics directly into the transform stage of a wavelet-based coder via the design of analysis and synthesis filters based on the CSF. Antonini et al. [12] introduced a wavelet coder which employed a CSF-weighted distortion criterion during bit allocation. O'Rourke et al. [13] proposed a wavelet-based image compression technique based on two properties of the HVS: orientation sensitivity and contrast sensitivity. Specifically, the diamond-shaped frequency passband of the HVS was exploited for the design of the compression scheme, and the logarithm of the contrast sensitivity was employed for bit allocation. Lai et al. [14] presented an image compression scheme in which contrast-sensitivity and visual masking adjustments were performed within a wavelet-based coder using a low-pass model of the CSF and a local measure of visual distortion. In two similar approaches, Beegan et al. [15] used a "CSF mask" to adjust transform coefficients prior to the quantization, and Wei et al. [16] used a "visual compander." Also, in [17], Zhang et al. proposed luminance and chrominance CSF-based weighting in the discrete-wavelet-packet-transform domain to reduce perceptible information of the high-dynamic-range images.

There are also some researchers who conducted psychophysical experiment to measure visibility thresholds for compression artifacts in unnatural images and/or on natural scenes. For example, Watson et al. [18] measured visual detection thresholds for both individual wavelet basis functions and simulated wavelet subband quantization distortions presented against a gray background. The thresholds were modeled as a function of the spatial frequency of the distortions, and the model was then used to compute quantizer step sizes for each wavelet subband. In [19], Watson's approach was extended to lower rate coding via models of visual masking and summation. Nadenau et al. [5] measured the visibility thresholds of quantization noise in natural scenes and compared five visual masking models to predict the visibility thresholds. They concluded that a masking model considering local activity of the wavelet subbands performed better than point-wise contrast masking models.

In a recent study, Chandler et al. [3] proposed a new kind of masking called the *structural masking* by psychophysically measuring the visibility thresholds of wavelet distortions placed on small patches categorized in three groups: texture, structure, and edges. The authors have also proposed different set of values of parameters of contrast-gain control model [20] for three different categories and have shown that the category-specific masking model showed better compression results for wavelet-type compression schemes. Similarly, in [21], Chandler et al. proposed a visually lossless compression algorithm based on psychophysical detection experiments of wavelet distortion on radiograph images.

Several other studies have specifically focused on the visually lossless compression of JPEG and JPEG2000 compression schemes. For example, Oh et al. [22] developed a visually lossless compression model which allocates the code streams of the JPEG2000 encoder by measuring visibility thresholds via a wavelet statistics-based quantization distortion model and a visual masking model. In [23], Ponomarenko et al. pointed out that the visual quality of input (to-be-compressed) image has a large effect on the compression performance. Thus, they adaptively adjusted the scaling factor of the JPEG quantization matrix based on the estimated blur and noise content of the input image and showed that such a compression scheme gives larger compression ratio compared to super-high quality mode of consumer digital cameras. Leung et al. [24] proposed a JPEG2000-based visually lossless compression scheme for CT images in which the visibility thresholds varied according to the viewing window/display size of the CT image.

3. Computational models of local masking

This section describes the computational masking models that we developed to predict the masking map for the given input (to-be-compressed) image. First, we describe the ground-truth database used to train the models. Next, we describe a modified version of the model put forth by Watson and Solomon, which operates by simulating V1 neural responses with contrast gain control (CGC). Here, we have modified the model and optimized its parameters to provide the best predictions for the aforementioned database. In addition, we describe an extension of the model to deal with structural facilitation which we earlier reported in [3]. Structural facilitation refers to the reduction in threshold (increased distortion visibility) in parts of the image containing highly recognizable structure.

3.1. Database of local masking in natural scenes

In [6], we performed a large-scale psychophysical experiment in which we measured thresholds for detecting simulated distortions placed within each 85 × 85 block of every image from the CSIQ database [25]. The simulated distortion was a narrowband log-Gabor noise target whose center frequency was chosen to be near the peak of visual sensitivity (3.6 cycles/degree of visual angle). The thresholds were obtained using a three-alternative forced-choice procedure [26]; we employed at least three subjects per image, with at least two trials per subject. The end result of the experiment was a masking map for each of the 30 CSIQ images; each entry in each map denotes the minimum contrast required for a human subject to detect distortions at that location in the image.

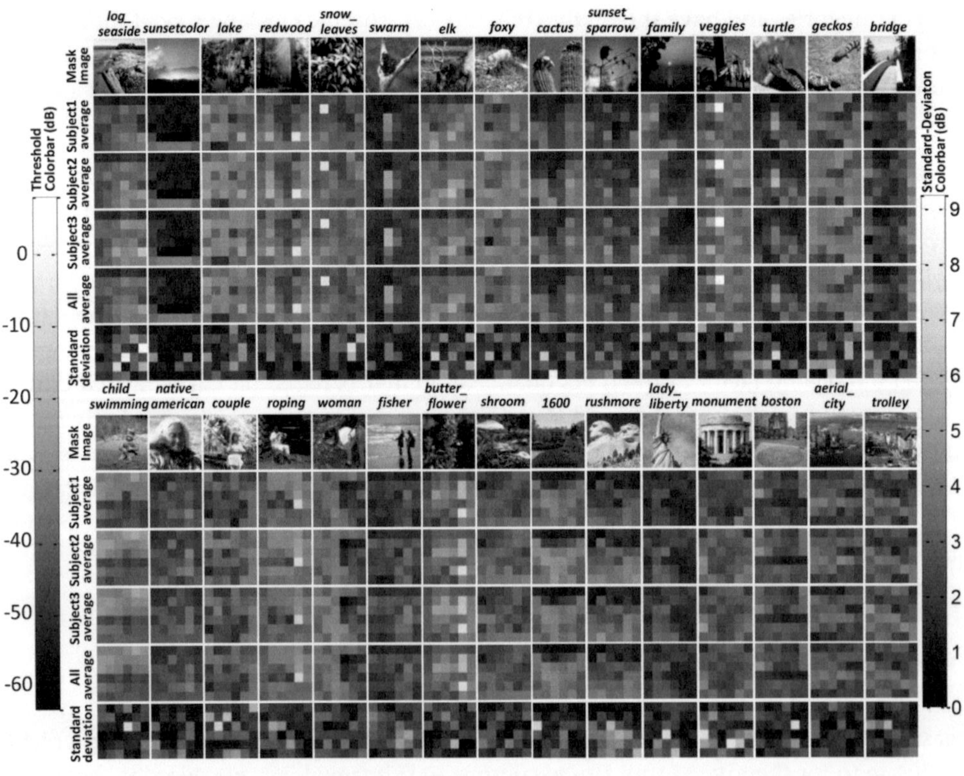

Figure 1. Masking maps and the corresponding standard deviation maps for all 30 images in the CSIQ database. See text for details.

Figure 1 shows the masking maps from the database. Each map consists of 36 values corresponding to the 36 blocks of the associated image. Brighter map values denote higher thresholds (i.e., more masking); darker maps values denote lower thresholds (less masking). The first and seventh rows of **Figure 1** show the 30 mask images. Below the mask images, the first, second, and third images show the average maps of the two trials of Subject 1, Subject 2, and Subject 3. The remaining rows show the average maps (taken across all six trials; 2 × 3 subjects), and the corresponding maps of the standard deviations of each average. Note that the averages and standard deviations are on different scales; please refer to the respective color bars shown in **Figure 1**. Overall, the subjects were in high agreement with each other and with themselves across separate trials.

In the following subsection, we describe the contrast gain control with structure facilitation model which operates by simulating V1 neural responses to predict these masking maps.

3.2. Contrast gain control with structure facilitation (CGC+SF) model

Contrast masking [27] has been widely used for predicting distortion visibility in images and videos [28, 42–44]. Among the many existing models of contrast masking, those which simulate the contrast gain-control response properties of V1 neurons are most widely used. Although several *contrast gain control* (CGC) models have been proposed in previous studies (e.g., Refs. [20, 27, 30, 31, 41]), in most cases, the model parameters are selected based on results obtained using either unnatural masks [20] or only a very limited number of natural images. Thus, in this chapter, we describe two approaches to improve the current CGC model: (1) the CGC model parameters are optimized by training on the large dataset of local masking in natural scenes; and (2) the CGC model is incorporated by a structural facilitation (SF) model which better captures the reduced masking observed in structured regions.

3.2.1. Watson-Solomon contrast gain control (CGC) model

The Watson and Solomon model [20] is a model of V1 simple-cell responses that includes CGC from neighboring neurons. **Figure 2** shows a block diagram of the model. The model takes two images as input: (1) the mask image (original image), and (2) the mask+target image (distorted image). Both of these images are then subjected to the following stages:

1. A spatial filter designed to mimic the human contrast sensitivity function (CSF).
2. A local spatial-frequency decomposition designed to mimic the initially linear response properties of individual V1 neurons.
3. Excitatory and inhibitory nonlinearities designed to mimic the nonlinear response properties of individual V1 neurons.
4. Divisive inhibition designed to mimic the interactions among groups of V1 neurons.

***Steps* 1 *and* 2**: For Step 1, we use the CSF filter specified in [32, 33]. For Step 2, we use a log-Gabor filterbank consisting of six scales and six orientations. The center radial frequencies of the filters are 0.3, 0.61, 1.35, 3.22, 7.83, 16.1 c/deg, each with a radial-frequency bandwidth of

2.75 octaves. The center orientations of the filters are 0°, $\pm 30°$, $\pm 60°$, 90°, each with an orientation bandwidth of 30°.

Steps 3 and 4: Let $c(x_0, y_0, f_0, \theta_0)$ denote the output of the log-Gabor filter with a center of radial frequency f_0, an orientation θ_0, and at the spatial location (x_0, y_0). This filter output represents the initially linear response of the neuron. To obtain the nonlinear neural response, $R(x_0, y_0, f_0, \theta_0)$, we perform Steps 3 and 4 via the following equation:

$$R(x_0, y_0, f_0, \theta_0) = g \cdot \frac{c(x_0, y_0, f_0, \theta_0)^p}{b^q + \sum_{(x,y,f,\theta)\in I_N} (c(x,y,f,\theta))^q} \quad (1)$$

Here, g is an output gain factor (we use $g = 0.1$). The parameters p and q are the exhitatory and inhibitory exponents which impose the nonlinearities (we use $p = 2.4$ and $q = 2.35$). The parameter b is a constant designed to prevent division by zero (we use $b = 0.035$). The division simulates inhibition from neighboring neurons; these neurons constitute the so-called inhibitory pool, and they are neighbors in space, radial frequency, and orientation. In Eq. (1), the inhibitory pool is represented by the set of spatial and spatial frequency coordinates I_N. The neighbors come from a 3 × 3 surround in space, a ±0.7 octave bandwidth surround in radial frequency, and a $\pm 60°$ bandwidth surround in orientation.

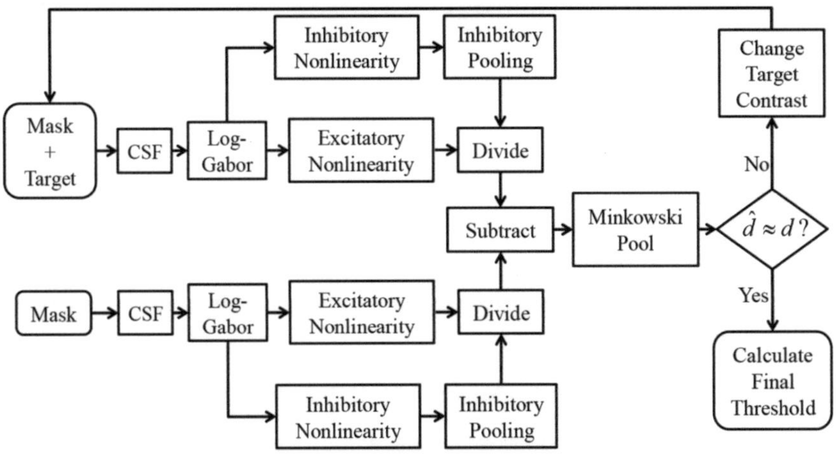

Figure 2. Flow of Watson and Solomon contrast gain control model.

All of the abovementioned parameters (g, p, q, b, and I_N) were chosen via a brute-force search to provide the best overall fit to the thresholds from our database, under the condition that the parameters remain within biologically plausible ranges [3]. The radial frequency bandwidth and center radial frequencies were chosen in this way as well. The other parameters of the model were either set as specified in [20] or were chosen based on our prior related modeling efforts [3].

http://dx.doi.org/10.5772/65362

Comparing the responses: Step 4 results in two collections of responses: One collection of responses to the mask, and another set of responses to the mask+target. The target is deemed visible if these collections of responses are sufficiently different from each other; thus, indicating a visible difference in the two stimuli (i.e., that the distortions are visible). To determine whether this condition is met, the collections of responses are subtracted from each other, then collapsed via Mikowski sum [20], and then this scalar difference ($\hat{d}$) is compared to a predefined "at-threshold" difference value ($d = 1$). We used a Minkowski exponent of 2.0 to collapse across space, and an exponent of 1.5 to collapse across radial frequency and orientation. The contrast of the target is iteratively adjusted until $\hat{d} \approx d$. When this condition is met, the contrast of the target is deemed to be the at-threshold contrast (i.e., the contrast detection threshold).

We refer interested readers to [6] for more specific details of the database and model.

3.2.2. Structure facilitation (SF) model

Using the optimized parameters described in the previous subsection, our implementation of the Watson and Solomon CGC model is quite accurate in predicting detection thresholds. On our database, the model is able to achieve a Pearson correlation coefficient (PCC) of 0.83 between the ground-truth and predicted thresholds. Generally, the model works best on regions containing textures and is worst on regions containing more complex structure. In particular, the model tends to overestimate thresholds for regions containing recognizable structure. This notion is demonstrated in **Figure 3**, which shows the ground-truth and predicted thresholds for two images; observe that the model predict the thresholds to be higher than ground-truth near the top of the gecko's body and in the child's face.

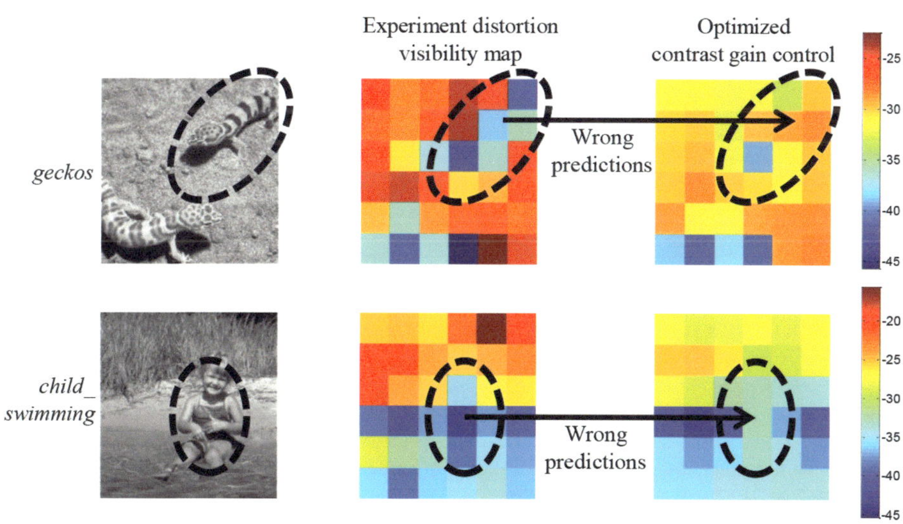

Figure 3. Examples of the Watson and Solomon model overestimating thresholds for distortion in some image regions that contain recognizable structures.

As we mentioned in [3], recognizable structures within the local regions of natural scenes facilitate (rather than mask) the distortion visibility. Thus, to model this "structure facilitation," we employ an inhibition modulation factor (λ_s) in the gain control equation:

$$R(x_0, y_0, f_0, \theta_0) = g \cdot \frac{c(x_0, y_0, f_0, \theta_0)^p}{b^q + \lambda_s \sum_{(x,y,f,\theta)\in I_N} \left(c(x, y, f, \theta)\right)^q} \tag{2}$$

where we adjust λ_s depending on the strength of structure within an image. Although the specific amount of inhibition modulation remains an open area of research, we have found the following sigmoidal relationship between λ_s and estimated structure strength to be quite effective (shown in **Figure 4**):

$$\lambda_{s,i} = \begin{cases} 1 - 80 \sum_{x,y=1,1}^{M,N} \left[1 \Big/ \left(1 + \exp\left(-\dfrac{S_i(x,y) - p(S,80)}{0.005} \right) \right) \right], & \max(S) > 0.04 \ \& \ \mathrm{Kurt}(S) > 3.5 \\ 1, & \text{otherwise} \end{cases} \tag{3}$$

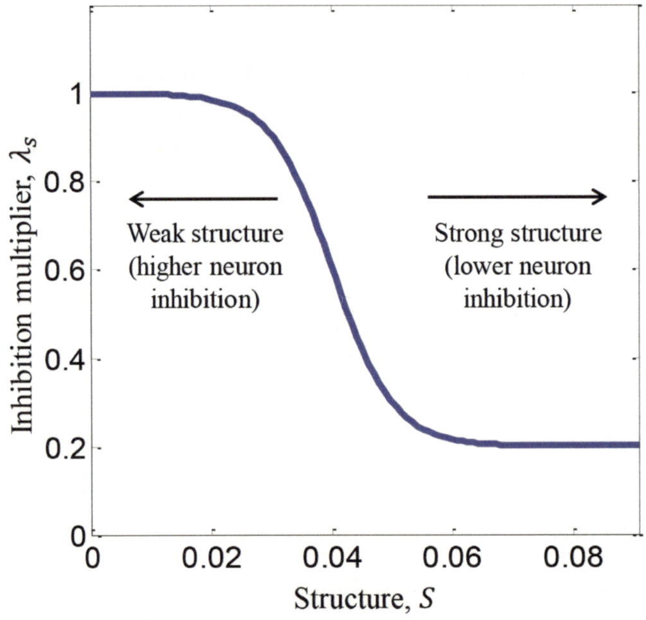

Figure 4. The inhibition multiplier λ_s varies depending on structure strength. Strong structures give rise to lower inhibition to facilitate the distortion visibility.

Observe that the inhibition modulation is applied in a block-based fashion. Here, $\lambda_{s,i}$ denotes the inhibition modulation factor for the ith block of size $M \times N$.

The variable S in Eq. (3) is a map which denotes the local structure strength (described next), and S_i is a block of S corresponding to the ith block of the image. The inhibition modulation for each block is further adjusted based on 80% largest values of S, denoted by the variable $p(S, 80)$. Furthermore, if the largest value of S is small, or if the kurtosis of S is small, then there is either no sufficient structure (e.g., the image is mostly textured or smooth), or the structure is not locally concentrated. In this case, no inhibition modulation is applied (i.e., $\lambda_{s,i} = 1$, for all blocks) (**Figure 4**).

The structure map S of an image is generated via the following equation which uses different feature maps:

$$S = L_n \times Sh_n \times E_n \times \left(1 - D_{\mu n}\right)^2 \times \left(1 - D_{\sigma n}\right)^2. \tag{4}$$

Here, L_n, Sh_n, and E_n denote maps of local luminance, local sharpness [29], and local first-order Shannon entropy, respectively. The values $D_{\mu n}$ and $D_{\sigma n}$ denote, respectively, maps of the average and the standard deviation of fractal texture features [34] computed for each local region. All features were computed for 32 × 32 blocks with 50% overlap between neighboring blocks. Each feature map was then normalized to the range [0, 1] and then resized to match the input image's dimensions. **Figure 5** shows some examples.

Figure 5. Structure maps of two example images. The color bar at right denotes the structure strength at each spatial location of the structure map.

The prediction performance of the Watson and Solomon CGC model can be greatly improved when the structure facilitation is taken into account [as specified in Eq. (2)]. As demonstrated in **Figure 6**, the proposed SF model was able to improve the CGC model's prediction performance in local image regions that contain recognizable structures, while not adversely affecting the prediction results of the others. For example, near the top of the gecko's body and in the child's face, the contrast detection thresholds predicted using the combined CGC+SF model match the ground-truth thresholds better than using the CGC model. Furthermore, the Pearson correlation coefficients between the CGC+SF model predictions and ground-truth thresholds also improved as compared to using the CGC model alone.

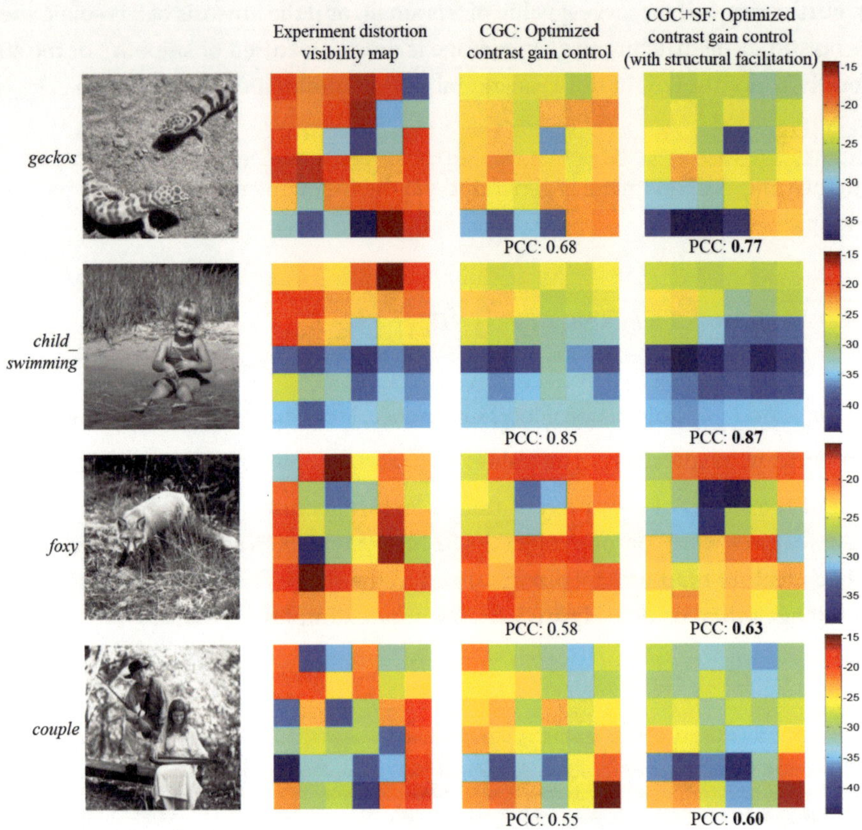

Figure 6. Structural facilitation improves the distortion visibility predictions in local regions of images containing recognizable structures. Pearson correlation coefficient (PCC) of each map with the experiment map is shown below the map.

4. Application of the masking model to compression

The masking model described in the previous section provides a way of predicting a masking map for any given input image. In this section, we show how to use this masking map to achieve visually lossless compression. In particular, we describe two different ways of incorporating the masking maps into an HEVC image coder: (1) by adjusting the QP values in HEVC on a per-block basis; and (2) by pre-adjusting the image's pixel values prior to the HEVC compression, and post-adjusting the pixel values of the decompressed image following HEVC decompression.

Similar to H.264/AVC, HEVC employs a uniform reconstruction quantizer for the transform coefficients. It is the quantization stage that introduces distortions; thus, to generate visually lossless results requires direct or indirect modification of the quantization step sizes (Q_{step} values) or quantization parameters (QP values). Previous efforts toward improved quantization have aimed at achieving higher PSNR values (e.g., [35, 36]) or other visual quality measures (e.g., [37, 38]). However, for visually lossless compression, we argue that the use of masking maps is a much better and logical alternative.

Our approach assumes that each local area within an image should have its own QP based on the amount of masking induced in that region. Note that the larger QP value is, the greater the contrast of the distortions. Therefore, the first step of our method is to predict a QP map consisting of block-based QP values, such that the resulting distortions in each corresponding block exhibit a contrast at the contrast threshold C_T. Furthermore, as we mention later in Section 5, because the predicted C_T values are underestimates of thresholds for normal viewing conditions (as opposed to the highly controlled viewing conditions used in the psychophysical experiment), we aim for QP values required to generate slightly greater than C_T (greater by at most 10 dB).

4.1. Local QP estimation from the masking map

Let QP_i denotes the QP value for the ith block, and let C_i denotes the contrast of the resulting distortions. Our objective is to employ a QP_i for the ith block such that the C_i for that block is given by $C_i = C_{T,i}$, where $C_{T,i}$ denotes the contrast threshold for the ith block. That is, we seek the QP_i value for each block required to make the block's distortions at the threshold of visibility.

The primary difficulty in determining the relationship between C and QP is that the relationship changes depending the patch. In our previous work [39], we used a regression model to predict the relationship between QP and C on a per-block basis using statistical properties of each block as regressors. Although that approach was extremely fast, it suffered from a significant number of mispredicted QP values and thus induced distortions with incorrect contrasts. Here, we present a much more accurate solution based on the use of a pre-compression lookup table.

Specifically, prior to using HEVC, we perform the following steps:

STEP 1. Divide the image into 32 × 32 blocks (the maximum block size for HEVC).

STEP 2. Compute the 2D DCT of each block.

STEP 3. Iterate over a QP range from 1 to 51…

a. Quantize the block using a corresponding Q_{step} value given by $Q_{step} = (2^{1/6})^{QP-4}$ as specified in [40].

b. Perform an inverse 2D DCT of each block.

c. Measure and record the contrast of the resulting distortions.

In this way, for each block, we record a table that can be used to look up the closest QP_i value required to achieve $C_i = C_{T,i}$. **Figure 7** shows the lookup table values in the forms of plots (QP vs. C) for eight different image blocks. Generating the lookup table requires only a small fraction of the total time required to encode the image because only a series of inverse 2D DCTs and contrast measurements in required. Most importantly, this technique provides extremely accurate selection of the QP values.

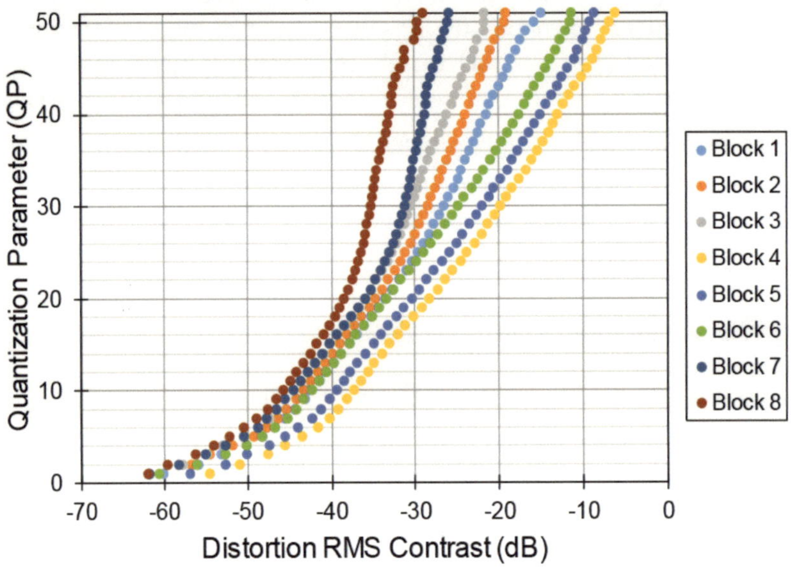

Figure 7. The relationship between distortion contrast C (in dB) and the QP used to generate that distortion for eight blocks from an image. Observe that the QP vs. C relationships are patch-specific; thus, we generate these curves (in the form of lookup tables) for all blocks prior to the compression.

4.2. Spatially adaptive quantization using the QP map

Given the QP map, we present two approaches to implement the compression. The first approach, which is the more direct approach, assigns different QP values for each 64 × 64 block. This approach was implemented by modifying the reference HEVC profile to explicitly use a separate QP value for each 64 × 64 coding unit. This approach is straightforward to implement, but it lacks some flexibility.

The other approach, which can be used with any lossy compression algorithm, effects the spatially adaptive quantization using pre-processing and post-processing stages. Let x_1 and x_2 denote the two image pixels and their corresponding quantization step sizes are denoted by Q_{s1} and Q_{s2}, respectively. The quantized values of the two pixels (denoted by $\hat{x}_1$ and $\hat{x}_2$) are then given by

$$\hat{x}_1 = \left\lfloor \frac{x_1}{Q_{s1}} + \frac{1}{2} \right\rfloor \cdot Q_{s1} = \beta \cdot \left\lfloor \frac{x_1/\beta}{Q_{s1}/\beta} + \frac{1}{2} \right\rfloor \cdot \frac{Q_{s1}}{\beta} \tag{5}$$

$$\hat{x}_2 = \left\lfloor \frac{x_2}{Q_{s2}} + \frac{1}{2} \right\rfloor \cdot Q_{s2} = \left\lfloor \frac{x_2 \cdot \frac{Q_{s1}}{Q_{s2}}}{Q_{s1}} + \frac{1}{2} \right\rfloor \cdot \frac{Q_{s2}}{Q_{s1}} \cdot Q_{s1} = \frac{1}{\alpha} \cdot \left\lfloor \frac{x_2 \cdot \alpha}{Q_{s1}} + \frac{1}{2} \right\rfloor \cdot Q_{s1} = \frac{\beta}{\alpha} \cdot \left\lfloor \frac{x_2 \cdot \alpha/\beta}{Q_{s1}/\beta} + \frac{1}{2} \right\rfloor \cdot \frac{Q_{s1}}{\beta} \tag{6}$$

where $\alpha = Q_{s1}/Q_{s2}$ is a scaling factor; β is a factor that normalizes the scaled pixel value (e.g., $x_2 \cdot \alpha$) into [0, 255]. Eqs. (5) and (6) indicate that different local image areas can have different quantization parameters even though the whole image is quantized using one uniform QP, as long as different image pixels are scaled properly.

For standard HEVC, the quantization step sizes relate to the QP values via $Q_{step} = \left(2^{1/6}\right)^{QP-4}$. However, in our second approach, because pixel values are quantized, we relate the quantization step to QP value through

$$Q_{step} = f(QP) = A \cdot QP^t + B, \tag{7}$$

where t is a nonlinear coefficient which aims at increasing/decreasing the QP value range within a QP map; A and B are the ratio and offset parameters which adjust the quantization step size after the nonlinear transform. The block diagram of the second approach is shown in **Figure 8**. Specifically, in the pre-processing stage, the luma channel of an image is first multiplied by a scaling map (dented by U) and then divided by β to have a range of [0, 255]. The scaling map is given by

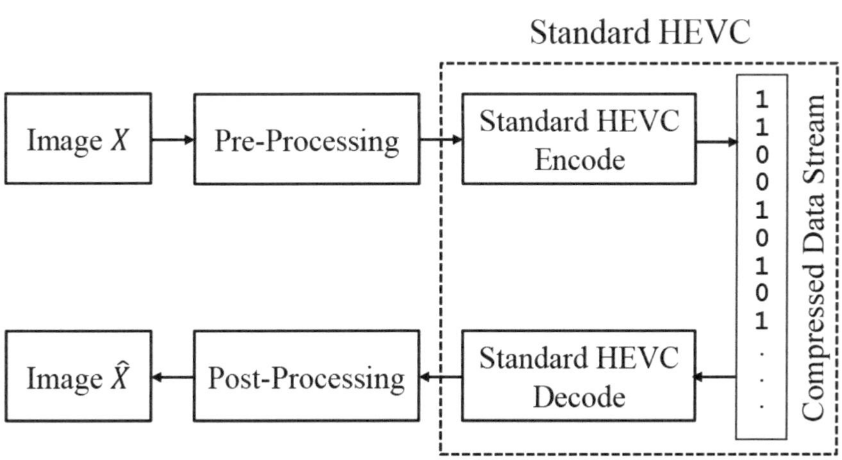

Figure 8. Block diagram of the second approach to achieve spatially adaptive quantization. Although in this chapter, we show results using HEVC as the encoder and decoder, this second approach can be used with any image compression algorithm.

$$U = \left[\frac{A \cdot Q_m + B}{A \cdot Q_1^t + B}, \frac{A \cdot Q_m + B}{A \cdot Q_2^t + B}, \ldots, \frac{A \cdot Q_m + B}{A \cdot Q_N^t + B} \right], \tag{8}$$

where $Q_1, Q_2, ..., Q_N$ denote the QP values for N different local image areas; Q_m denotes the average value of $Q_1^t, Q_2^t, \cdots, Q_N^t$ [i.e., $Q_m = \left(Q_1^t + Q_2^t + \cdots + Q_N^t\right)/N$];$\beta$ is given by

$$\beta = \max \left\{ \frac{A \cdot Q_m + B}{A \cdot Q_1^t + B} \cdot x_1, \frac{A \cdot Q_m + B}{A \cdot Q_2^t + B} \cdot x_2, \ldots, \frac{A \cdot Q_m + B}{A \cdot Q_N^t + B} \cdot x_N \right\} / 255. \tag{9}$$

In this chapter, we set $t = 2/3$, $B = 0$. Thus, U and β can be written as

$$U = \left[\frac{Q_m}{Q_1^t}, \frac{Q_m}{Q_2^t}, \ldots, \frac{Q_m}{Q_N^t} \right], \tag{10}$$

$$\beta = \max \left\{ \frac{Q_m}{Q_1^t} \cdot x_1, \frac{Q_m}{Q_2^t} \cdot x_2, \ldots, \frac{Q_m}{Q_N^t} \cdot x_N \right\} / 255. \tag{11}$$

In the post-processing stage, an inverse scaling map (dented by V) is applied to convert the scaled luminance to the original value:

$$V = \left[\frac{\beta \cdot Q_1^t}{Q_m}, \frac{\beta \cdot Q_2^t}{Q_m}, \ldots, \frac{\beta \cdot Q_N^t}{Q_m} \right]. \tag{12}$$

In standard HEVC stage, the global QP is computed by

$$QP = round \left[\left(\lambda_1 \frac{Q_m}{\beta} + \lambda_2 \right)^{\frac{1}{t}} \right], \tag{13}$$

where λ_1 and λ_2 are the linear coefficients which adjust the RMS contrast of the distortions in the compressed image to be near or below the threshold. We estimated their values by fitting the model to the 30 images in the CSIQ database, and thus, we set $\lambda_1 = 0.8$, $\lambda_2 = 2.4$.

Two problems can occur with this approach. First, the QP map may possibly contain zero values, in which case the above equations are not valid. Second, the predicted block-based QP maps often contain abrupt changes of QP values on the patch edges, which may possibly deteriorate the qualities of the compressed images by producing the ringing or blocking artifacts especially at lower bit compression. To solve these two problems, we first set the local zero QP values to be the minimum value among all the extra QP values within the image and then applied a Gaussian filter to the modified QP maps. As we have observed, for most natural images, the image contrast should change smoothly, not abruptly, and consequently, the resulting QP maps should also be smooth. **Figure 9** shows the *1600* image compressed using the QP map with and without the Gaussian filtering. Observe that the blocking artifacts occur in the compressed image (**Figure 9a**) if the original QP map was used; these blocking artifacts disappear when the QP map is smoothed by a Gaussian filter (**Figure 9b**).

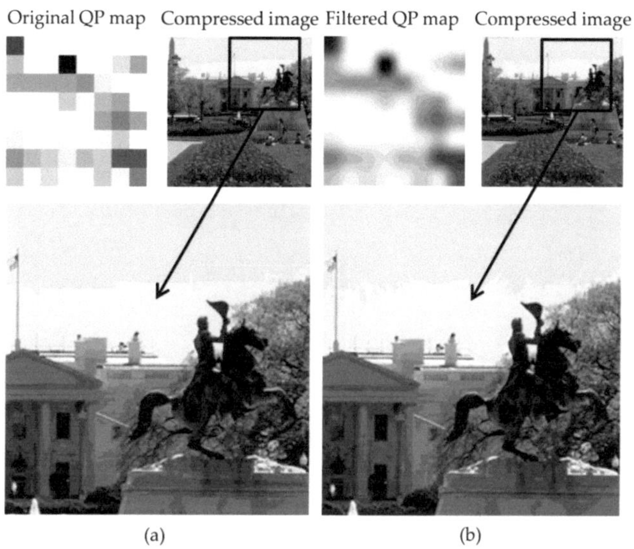

Figure 9. Gaussian filtering of the QP map improves the perceived quality of the compressed image.

In the following section, we show qualitative and quantitative results of using these two schemes with HEVC.

5. Results and discussion

In this section, we analyze the performance of the proposed visually lossless image coding algorithm. For this task, all 30 reference images in the CSIQ database were compressed at visually lossless rates using the proposed method and compared against standard HEVC. The main difference is that standard HEVC employs a uniform QP for coding the whole image, whereas our approach uses spatially adaptive QP values based on masking.

Furthermore, we have found that it is possible to induce distortions at up to 10 dB above the predicted C_T values while still yielding images which are visually lossless under normal viewing conditions. The contrast thresholds measured in the aforementioned experiment and thus the contrast thresholds predicted by the CGC+SF model are accurate for the highly controlled viewing conditions; yet, they are quite conservative for normal, everyday viewing.

5.1. QP maps

The CGC+SF model takes the 64 × 64-pixels image patch as input and predicts the distortion contrast threshold (C_T) and the corresponding threshold QP map. **Figure 10** shows the QP maps generated from the CGC+SF model for eight images in the CSIQ database.

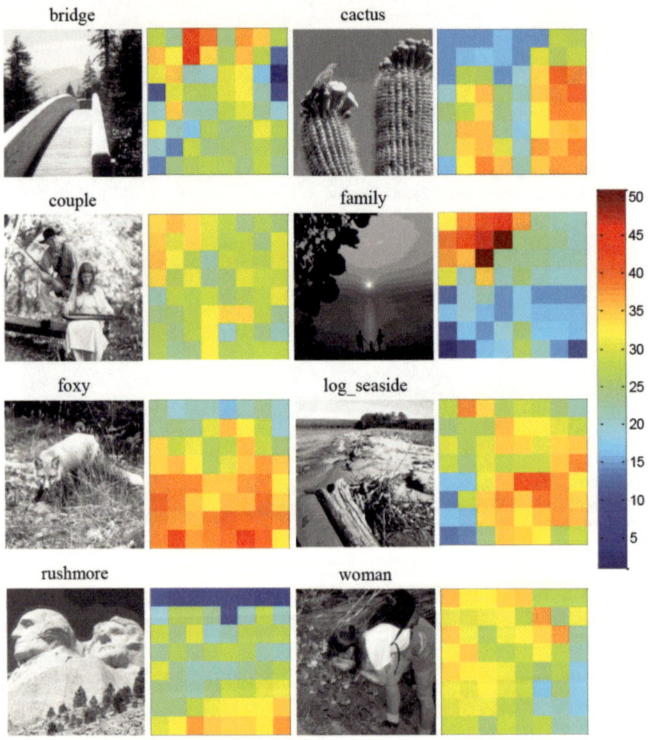

Figure 10. Eight sample reference images in CSIQ and their corresponding QP maps estimated based on CGC+SF model.

Observe that the QP maps are indeed image-adaptive; that is, the pattern of how quantization step sizes are varied across space adapts based on the image content (which is itself based on the masking model and the relationships between QP and C). In general, the QP maps specify larger quantization step sizes for regions that can mask the resulting distortions, and small quantization step sizes for regions with less masking. For example, in the *cactus* image, the bodies of the cacti impose great masking, the bird and boundaries of the cacti impose much

http://dx.doi.org/10.5772/65362

less masking, and sky has almost no masking. Accordingly, the QP values are smallest for the sky, larger for the bird and cacti boundaries, and largest for the bodies of the cacti.

Again, we remind the reader that the QP maps alone can provide only a rough gauge of how the distortions will be distributed across space. Recall from **Figure 7** that the relationship between QP and the contrast of the resulting distortion C is very much patch-specific. The same QP applied to two different blocks can give rise to vastly different distortion contrasts.

5.2. Distortion contrast maps

The proposed coding approach assumes that to compress an image in a visually lossless manner, the RMS contrast of the distortion in any compressed image region should be near or below the ground truth RMS contrast threshold. Thus, to verify the effectiveness of our proposed approach, **Figure 11** shows the contrast threshold maps (masking maps) for four sample images (as predicted by the CGC+SF model), as well as the resulting distortion contrast maps of the corresponding images coded with standard HEVC and the two proposed approaches. Note that the displayed contrast threshold maps are all 10 dB greater than predicted by the CGC+SF model due to the fact that the experimental contrast thresholds are overly conservative for normal viewing conditions. As we have found in our research, distortions with a contrast up to 10 dB above threshold can still remain visually undetectable under normal viewing conditions. Observe from **Figure 11** that images coded by standard HEVC have quite different contrast patterns with the ground truth, whereas images coded by the proposed approaches appear quite similar in pattern to the masking maps. These figures demonstrate that it is possible to achieve better compression performance than standard HEVC if using QP maps and the proposed adaptive coding scheme. We will quantify the compression performance of each method in the following section.

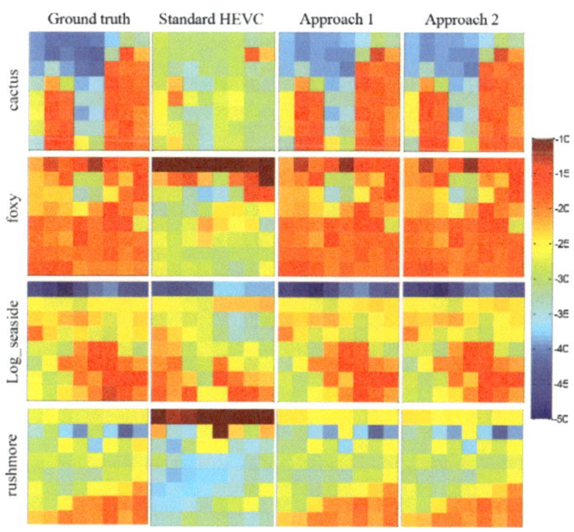

Figure 11. The ground truth RMS contrast threshold maps for four sample images, as well as the RMS contrast maps of their corresponding compressed images coded by standard HEVC, and two proposed approaches.

Image	Standard HEVC				JPEG			JPEG2000			Approach 1			Approach 2		
	QP	bpp	PSNR	Error	bpp	PSNR	Error	bpp	PSNR	Error	bpp	PSNR	Error	bpp	PSNR	Error
1600	24	1.98	40.21	733.48	3.31	45.83	563.06	2.21	45.88	594.24	1.88	39.21	676.20	1.49	41.94	786.39
Aerial_city	23	1.75	40.29	794.63	2.52	42.29	841.94	2.21	45.05	692.72	2.09	38.36	716.19	2.10	46.09	653.83
Boston	20	2.41	43.02	502.98	2.61	42.31	712.80	2.34	45.43	534.92	1.81	38.53	699.00	1.61	44.37	703.05
Bridge	22	1.73	41.97	706.05	1.46	38.41	1017.83	2.09	46.57	575.40	1.85	39.83	689.23	1.67	43.35	645.30
Butter_flower	23	1.13	42.10	1036.55	2.17	47.32	1153.96	0.60	41.29	890.83	0.87	35.58	1005.51	0.71	42.64	1282.70
Cactus	21	2.14	42.64	638.78	1.75	39.16	876.22	2.20	46.97	651.90	1.55	33.40	757.97	1.65	47.20	642.46
Child_swimming	25	2.17	38.35	577.45	3.32	43.14	438.94	2.49	43.83	426.37	1.74	33.67	715.74	1.67	43.80	641.40
Couple	25	1.60	39.22	460.92	2.74	45.07	323.70	1.47	42.61	431.27	1.21	34.76	618.40	1.45	42.21	375.91
Elk	29	1.02	35.60	740.88	1.94	40.37	616.10	1.23	39.80	665.91	1.38	34.09	660.53	1.47	42.92	521.01
Family	22	0.94	42.60	962.12	1.15	43.74	966.63	1.13	47.04	794.78	1.65	45.80	586.11	0.74	51.36	845.01
Fisher	21	1.27	42.25	936.04	1.41	43.27	1034.82	1.16	44.84	953.55	1.63	43.02	789.65	0.93	46.91	995.65
Foxy	26	2.43	37.42	415.59	3.00	39.33	427.49	2.48	42.08	434.99	1.62	29.47	680.18	2.14	42.65	374.69
Geckos	28	1.57	35.70	546.44	2.03	37.41	593.12	2.48	43.83	242.22	1.48	31.78	696.98	2.05	39.93	294.62
Lady_liberty	22	0.70	43.55	948.07	2.36	50.94	691.58	0.52	44.55	1027.35	1.26	39.56	767.69	0.58	50.48	932.29
Lake	23	3.14	40.59	433.81	2.26	34.64	937.05	3.99	48.82	420.27	2.24	31.84	634.87	2.42	39.93	517.14
Log_seaside	25	2.53	38.40	582.71	2.34	36.49	867.01	3.99	50.95	359.16	2.15	33.74	651.16	2.52	41.75	462.66
Monument	22	1.49	41.51	687.93	2.01	43.03	741.39	1.52	44.17	692.42	1.48	36.64	696.29	1.12	42.84	737.65
Native_american	23	1.57	40.63	801.26	1.60	41.28	911.87	1.98	46.68	633.27	1.70	38.14	713.70	1.62	43.99	676.87
Redwood	22	1.97	41.59	675.00	1.57	38.18	942.47	2.34	46.40	539.17	1.81	35.81	710.60	1.33	46.47	778.18
Roping	23	1.67	41.63	573.60	1.57	40.85	737.25	1.47	43.79	682.79	1.10	32.22	653.10	1.42	40.88	586.43
Rushmore	21	2.88	42.16	558.05	3.34	42.79	627.87	2.48	43.70	622.51	2.29	34.39	726.84	2.89	44.70	461.22
Shroom	19	2.35	43.94	410.47	1.52	42.36	630.61	1.28	43.89	549.87	1.25	36.79	610.10	0.79	43.71	683.36
Snow_leaves	28	1.08	37.26	675.15	1.58	38.92	787.26	1.47	41.99	612.13	1.31	35.25	548.25	1.35	40.54	519.24
Sunset_sparrow	23	1.56	40.27	1012.00	1.37	40.27	1142.99	1.52	45.13	907.72	2.04	40.10	721.38	0.91	44.04	1052.54
Sunsetcolor	22	0.32	44.57	1165.65	0.50	46.37	1166.02	0.26	47.32	1137.51	1.42	48.35	810.06	0.60	49.00	1061.84
Swarm	21	1.03	42.60	1001.60	1.42	44.85	1014.01	0.91	45.19	1024.93	1.59	41.05	813.39	0.67	44.27	1066.44
Trolley	22	2.57	41.14	482.71	3.17	41.55	589.34	3.31	47.75	387.67	1.95	34.47	668.14	1.94	43.13	581.13
Turtle	19	1.49	44.15	839.82	0.97	42.85	1038.58	1.16	46.64	866.72	1.46	40.26	778.86	1.06	44.96	880.51
Veggies	24	1.64	40.83	497.75	1.96	41.98	696.02	1.72	44.79	602.85	1.01	31.49	584.03	1.23	41.48	616.87
Woman	24	1.72	39.61	654.98	2.09	41.17	730.93	1.98	44.55	538.89	1.51	36.76	710.15	1.45	43.25	655.77
Average	23	1.73	40.86	701.75	2.03	41.87	793.96	1.86	45.05	649.81	1.61	36.81	703.01	1.45	44.03	701.07

Table 1. Performance comparison of standard HEVC, JPEG, JPEG2000, and the two proposed CGC+SF model based approaches in terms of coded rate (bpp), PSNR, and the absolute RMS contrast error.

http://dx.doi.org/10.5772/65362

5.3. Compression performance

Table 1 shows the compression results of 30 images using standard HEVC, JPEG, JPEG2000, and the two proposed approaches. To compare with the standard HEVC, JPEG, and JPEG2000 coding methods, a visual quality matching experiment was performed by three experienced subjects. The purpose of the experiment was to find at which compression rate, the three reference coding methods (i.e., HEVC, JPEG, and JPEG2000) yielded images with just detectable distortions; the corresponding bit-rates of these "at-threshold" compressed images were then recorded. Note that all these five coding methods only add near or below-threshold distortions, and thus judging the quality of the images is quite difficult. Although the human subjective judgment is a more reliable way for assessing the intensities of the near/below threshold distortions, we also report the PSNRs and the absolute RMS contrast errors between the reference images and the coded images for reference.

From **Table 1**, observe that the second approach of the CGC+SF model demonstrates a reduction in coded rate (bpp) by an average factor of about 16% as compared with standard HEVC, while still maintaining relatively higher PSNR values and equivalent RMS contrast errors. In comparison, the first approach seems to work less effectively. This might due to the fact that fixed local QP values are applied to the local image areas, but some local QP values are improperly estimated because of the much complex image patches and potential model limitations. However, this straightforward approach still performs competitively well, considering the relatively smaller errors it produces. For the second approach, we employed additional parameters, which indirectly adjust the coded rate to meet the visually lossless requirement. Note that for each method, the average total error is around 700 dB, which means that for each block there is an approximately 10 dB RMS contrast error (each image contains 64 blocks) compared with the ground truth. This is also attributed to the three-alternative forced-choice procedure that has been used in the experiment and mentioned in Section 5.2. Also, it should be noted that we generated the QP maps mainly from contrast masking and structural facilitation. Thus, if an image does not contain areas that can sufficiently mask the distortions, using the QP map yields no gain.

6. Conclusion

This chapter described a computational model which predicts masking maps for any given input images, and two approaches which employ the predicted masking map to achieve visually lossless compression. The proposed computational model consists of a contrast gain control model, which was trained on a database of local masking thresholds in natural images, and a structural facilitation model, which was incorporated to take into account the effects of recognizable structures on distortion visibility. Compared with standard HEVC, our approach shows an average of 16% improvement in bit-rate when testing on the CSIQ database

Author details

Yi Zhang[1], Md Mushfiqul Alam[2] and Damon M. Chandler[1*]

*Address all correspondence to: chandler.damon.michael@shizuoka.ac.jp

1 Department of Electrical and Electronic Engineering, Shizuoka University, Hamamatsu, Shizuoka, Japan

2 mPerpetuo, Inc., San Francisco, CA, USA

References

[1] R. L. DeValois and K. K. DeValois. *Spatial Vision*. Oxford University Press, 1990.

[2] D. Regan. *Human Perception of Objects: Early Visual Processing of Spatial Form Defined by Luminance, Color, Texture, Motion, and Binocular Disparity*. Sinauer Associates, Inc., Publishers, Sunderland, Massachusetts, 2000.

[3] D. M. Chandler, M. D. Gaubatz, and Sheila S. Hemami. A patch-based structural masking model with an application to compression. *J. Image Video Process.*, 2009:1–22, 2009.

[4] S. Winkler and S. Susstrunk. Visibility of noise in natural images. *Electronic Imaging*. International Society for Optics and Photonics, pp 121–129, 2004.

[5] M. J. Nadenau, J. Reichel, and M. Kunt. Performance comparison of masking models based on a new psychovisual test method with natural scenery stimuli. *Signal Process.: Image Commun.*, 17(10):807–823, 2002.

[6] M. M. Alam, K. P. Vilankar, D. J. Field, and D. M. Chandler. Local masking in natural images: A database and analysis. *J. Vis.*, 14(8):22–22, 2014.

[7] R. J. Safranek and J. D. Johnston. A perceptually tuned sub-band image coder with image dependent quantization and post-quantization data compression. *Proc. ICASSP*, 3:1945–1948, 1989.

[8] T. N. Pappas, T. A. Michel, and R. O. Hinds. Supra-threshold perceptual image coding. *Proc. ICIP*, vol. 1, pp 237–240, 1996.

[9] I. Höntsch and L. Karam. Locally adaptive perceptual image coding. *IEEE Trans. Image Process.*, 9:1472–1483, 2000.

[10] M. Nadenau, J. Reichel, and M. Kunt. Wavelet-based color image compression: Exploiting the contrast sensitivity function. *IEEE Trans. Image Process.*, 12:58–70, 2003.

[11] M. G. Albanesi. Wavelets and human visual perception in image compression. *Proc. ICPR*, II:859–863, 1996.

[12] M. Antonini, M. Barlaud, P. Mathieu, and I. Daubechies. Image coding using wavelet transforms. *IEEE Trans. Image Process.*, 1:205–220, 1992.

[13] T. P. O'Rourke and R. L. Stevenson. Human visual system based wavelet decomposition for image compression. *J. Visual Comm. Image Repr.*, 6:109–121, 1995.

[14] Y. K. Lai and C-C. J. Kuo. Wavelet image compression with optimized perceptual quality. *SPIE's International Symposium on Optical Science, Engineering, and Instrumentation*, International Society for Optics and Photonics, pp 436–447, 1998

[15] A. P. Beegan. Wavelet-based image compression using human visual system models. *PhD dissertation*, Virginia Tech, 2001.

[16] Z. Wei, Y. Fu, Z. Gao, and S. Cheng. Visual compander in wavelet-based image coding. *IEEE Trans. Consumer Elec.*, 44:1261–1266, 1998.

[17] Y. Zhang, E. Reinhard, and D. R. Bull. Perceptually lossless high dynamic range image compression with jpeg 2000. In *2012 19th IEEE International Conference on Image Processing*, IEEE, pp 1057–1060, 2012.

[18] A. B. Watson, G. Y. Tangand, J. A. Solomon, and J. Villasenor. Visibility of wavelet quantization noise. *IEEE Trans. Image Process.*, 6:1164–1175, 1997.

[19] Z. Liu, L. J. Karam, and A. B. Watson. JPEG2000 encoding with perceptual distortion control. *IEEE Trans. Image Process.*,15(7):1763–1778, 2006.

[20] A. B. Watson and J. A. Solomon. A model of visual contrast gain control and pattern masking. *J. Opt. Soc. Am. A*, 14:2379–2391, 1997.

[21] D. M. Chandler, N. L. Dykes, and S. S. Hemami. Visually lossless compression of digitized radiographs based on contrast sensitivity and visual masking. In M. Eckstein and Y. Jiang, editors, *Proceedings of SPIE Medical Imaging 2005: Image Perception, Observer Performance, and Technology Assessment*, vol 5749. pp 359–372, 2005.

[22] H. Oh, A. Bilgin, and M. W. Marcellin. Visually lossless encoding for JPEG2000. *IEEE Trans. Image Process.*, 22(1):189–201, 2013.

[23] N. N. Ponomarenko, V. V. Lukin, K. O. Egiazarian, and L. Lepisto. Adaptive visually lossless jpeg-based color image compression. *Signal, Image Video Process.*, 7(3):437–452, 2013.

[24] T. Leung, M. W. Marcellin, and A. Bilgin. Visually lossless compression of windowed images. In *Data Compression Conference (DCC), 2013*, IEEE, pp 504–504, 2013.

[25] D. J. Field. Relations between the statistics of natural images and the response properties of cortical cells. *J. Opt. Soc. Am. A*, 4:2379–2394, 1987.

[26] N. Graham. *Visual Pattern Analyzers*. Oxford University Press, New York, 1989.

[27] G. E. Legge and J. M. Foley. Contrast masking in human vision. *J. Opt. Soc. Am.*, 70:1458–1470, 1980.

[28] Y. Jia, W. Lin, and A. A. Kassim. Estimating just-noticeable distortion for video. *IEEE Trans. Circuits Syst. Video Technol.*, 16(7):820–829, 2006.

[29] C. T. Vu, T. D. Phan, and D. M. Chandler. A spectral and spatial measure of local perceived sharpness in natural images. *IEEE Trans. Image Process.*, 21(3):934–945, 2012.

[30] J. M. Foley. Human luminance pattern mechanisms: masking experiments require a new model. *J. Opt. Soc. Am. A*, 11:1710–1719, 1994.

[31] J. Lubin. A visual discrimination model for imaging system design and evaluation. *Vision Models for Target Detection and Recognition 2*, World Scientific Publishing Co. Pte. Ltd. pp 245–283, 1995.

[32] S. Daly. Visible differences predictor: an algorithm for the assessment of image fidelity. In A. B. Watson, editor, *Digital Images and Human Vision*. pp 179–206, 1993.

[33] E. C. Larson and D. M. Chandler. Most apparent distortion: full-reference image quality assessment and the role of strategy. *J. Electron. Imaging*, 19(1):011006, 2010.

[34] A. F. Costa, G. Humpire-Mamani, and A. J. M. Traina. An efficient algorithm for fractal analysis of textures. In *2012 25th SIBGRAPI Conference on Graphics, Patterns and Images*, IEEE, pp 39–46, 2012.

[35] E.-H. Yang and X. Yu. Rate distortion optimization for H. 264 interframe coding: a general framework and algorithms. *IEEE Trans. Image Process.*, 16(7):1774–1784, 2007.

[36] M. Karczewicz, Y. Ye, and I. Chong. Rate distortion optimized quantization. *ITU-T Q*, 6, 2008.

[37] Y. Mo, J. Xiong, J. Chen, and F. Xu. Quantization matrix coding for high efficiency video coding. In *Advances on Digital Television and Wireless Multimedia Communications*. Springer, pp 244–249, 2012.

[38] J. Chen, J. Zheng, F. Xu, and J. Villasenor. Adaptive frequency weighting for high-performance video coding. *IEEE Trans. Circuits Syst. Video Technol.*, 22(7):1027–1036, 2012.

[39] M. M. Alam, P. Patil, M. T. Hagan, and D. M. Chandler. A computational model for predicting local distortion visibility via convolutional neural network trainedon natural scenes. In *2015 IEEE International Conference on Image Processing (ICIP)*. Institute of Electrical & Electronics Engineers (IEEE), 2015.

[40] V. Sze, M. Budagavi, and G. J. Sullivan. High efficiency video coding (HEVC). *Integrated Circuit and Systems, Algorithms and Architectures*. Springer, pp 1–375, 2014.

[41] P. C. Teo and D. J. Heeger. Perceptual image distortion. *Proc. SPIE*, 2179:127-141, 1994.

http://dx.doi.org/10.5772/65362

[42] A. B. Watson. DCTune: A technique for visual optimization of DCT quantization matrices for individual images. *SID International Symposium Digest of Technical Papers*, vol. 24. Society for Information Display, pp 946-946, 1993.

[43] Z. Wei and K. N. Ngan. Spatio-temporal just noticeable distortion profile for grey scale image/video in DCT domain. *IEEE Trans. Circ. Syst. Video Technol.*, 19(3):337-346, 2009.

[44] X. H. Zhang, W. S. Lin, and P. Xue. Improved estimation for just-noticeable visual distortion. *Signal Process.*, 85(4):795-808, 2005.

Chapter 2

Automatic Adaptive Lossy Compression of Multichannel Remote Sensing Images

Vladimir Lukin, Alexander Zemliachenko,
Ruslan Kozhemiakin, Sergey Abramov, Mikhail Uss,
Victoriya Abramova, Nikolay Ponomarenko,
Benoit Vozel and Kacem Chehdi

Additional information is available at the end of the chapter

http://dx.doi.org/10.5772/64944

Abstract

In this chapter, we consider lossy compression of multichannel images acquired by remote sensing systems. Two main features of such data are taken into account. First, images contain inherent noise that can be of different intensity and type. Second, there can be essential correlation between component images. These features can be exploited in 3D compression that is demonstrated to be more efficient than component-wise compression. The benefits are in considerably higher compression ratio attained for the same or even less distortions introduced. It is shown that important performance parameters of lossy compression can be rather easily and accurately predicted.

Keywords: adaptation, automation, lossy compression, multichannel, remote sensing, image processing

1. Introduction

Remote sensing (RS) is an application area where compression of images acquired on-board of an aircraft or a spacecraft is a very important task [1]. Its actuality is explained by continuous tendencies of improving sensor spatial resolution, more frequent observation of sensed terrains, larger number of exploited channels (e.g., in multi- and, especially, hyperspectral sensing), etc. [2]. Meanwhile, the communication channel bandwidth and time of data transferring can be limited [1, 3, 4]. Facilities of data processing on-board can be restricted.

Possibilities of image compression in a lossless manner are often limited as well [4]. Even the best existing methods of lossless compression applied to hyperspectral data and fully exploiting interband correlation inherent for such images provide a compression ratio (CR) of about 4.5 [4, 5], and this is often not enough. Thus, there is a need in efficient methods for lossy compression of acquired multichannel images.

There are several peculiarities of lossy compression with application to multichannel remote sensing images. First, if it is performed on-board, full or partial automation is required [1, 6]. Second, lossy compression is reasonable and useful only if introduced losses do not have essential impact on the value of compressed data, i.e., if accuracy and reliability of information extracted from compressed images are approximately at the same level as from original (uncompressed, compressed in a lossless manner) data. In this sense, introduced losses should be smaller, or in the worst case, comparable to the original image distortions due to noise [7]. This means that image-processing (compression) methods should be adaptive to noise characteristics. Meanwhile, noise in images acquired by modern multichannel RS sensors is not additive and has more complicated nature [8–11]. Thus, either blind estimation of its characteristics or attraction of available *a priori* information is needed. Third, adaptation to other specific properties of subband images is desired. Here, we mean that images in channels might have considerably different dynamic ranges, signal-to-noise ratios, and interchannel correlation factors [8, 12, 13].

All these influence efficiency of lossy compression and open perspectives of its improvement. Meanwhile, all or some of the aforementioned peculiarities of multichannel RS images are often ignored in the design of lossy compression techniques.

On the one hand, it is well understood that high interchannel correlation should be exploited for more sparse representation of data and reaching higher CR than for component-wise compression [14–16]. On the other hand, there are many different ways to realize this. Different transforms can be used [17–20]. Component image grouping can be organized in different manner [15, 21, 22] and till the moment there are no strict rules what is the best way to do this and what benefit can be maximally achieved compared to component-wise compression in the sense of CR under condition of the same or smaller distortions introduced.

Noise characteristics and different dynamic ranges of data in component images are often not taken into account in lossy compression as well. Little attention has been paid to these aspects in the design of lossy compression techniques for the considered application although it is clear that they are important and restrict applicability of methods designed for other types of multidimensional data [3, 20, 23].

Requirements to lossy compression of multichannel images and their priority have to be taken into consideration as well. The main requirements [1, 3, 20] are the following. First, introduced distortions should not negatively influence the efficiency of solving further tasks of multichannel image processing such as classification, object detection, visual inspection, etc. Only under aforementioned condition, the compressed data remain to be practically of the same value as original images. This means that introduced distortions should be less or of the same order as noise in each component (channel) image. Second, there can be a necessity to provide

CR not smaller than some limit value or a desire to provide as large CR as possible. Third, lossy compression and operations associated with it (preliminary analysis of data, some transformations, and/or normalizations, etc.) have to be quite simple, especially if one deals with lossy compression on-board. Fourth, there can be some recommendations or restrictions imposed on standardization of lossy compression or mathematical basis. Currently, there are no standards for lossy compression of multichannel RS images although special efforts are put toward its creation [3]. In addition, it is understood that most of the aforementioned requirements can be met on the basis of 2D or 3D orthogonal transforms under condition of proper preparation of multichannel images to compression [20].

In this chapter, we focus on the aspects of automation and adaptation of lossy compression with application to multichannel image processing. First, we show that noise is signal dependent where its signal-dependent component is either of the same order as signal independent (additive) or is dominant [6, 8, 9]. Second, we show how this property can be taken into account at lossy compression stage by applying proper variance stabilizing transform (VST) in component-wise manner [20, 24]. Third, we analyze peculiarities of lossy compression in the neighborhood of the so-called optimal operation point (OOP) where introduced losses characterized by mean square error are of the same order as equivalent noise variance [25]. Fourth, we demonstrate that there is quite strict relation between OOP existence and compression ratio (CR) in it and some statistical parameters of noisy images [25, 26]. Moreover, there are quite easy methods to provide a desired CR by exploiting this statistics [27]. Fifth, we discuss and compare component-wise and 3D compression. Advantages of the latter approach have been paid special attention [28, 29] and more discussion on group size is provided.

2. Image and noise models and their parameters

While 10–20 years ago, it was usually assumed that noise is additive in all components of multichannel remote sensing data [30], studies carried out by different researchers [9, 10] indicate that the following image/noise model is more adequate

$$I_{kij}^{\text{noisy}} = I_{kij}^{\text{true}} + n_{kij}(I_{kij}^{\text{true}}),\ i = 1,...,I, j = 1,...,J, k = 1,...,K \tag{1}$$

Here, $I_{k\,ij}^{\text{noisy}}$ denotes the ijth sample of the kth component for a considered multichannel image, $n_{k\,ij}$ is the ijth value of the signal-dependent noise in the kth component image. To indicate that noise is signal dependent, we use notation $n_{k\,ij}(I_{kij}^{\text{true}})$ where I_{kij}^{true} is the true value for the kijth voxel, I and J define the data size, and K denotes the number of components. For multi- and hyperspectral images, model (1) transforms to

$$I_{kij}^{\text{noise}} = I_{kij}^{\text{true}} + N_{kij}^{\text{SI}} + N_{kij}^{\text{SD}}, \tag{2}$$

where N_{kij}^{SD} and N_{kij}^{SI} denote signal-dependent (SD) and signal-independent (SI) noise components. SI is usually associated with dark and electronic noise and is assumed zero mean, white, and Gaussian. The situation with the SD component is more complicated since it is associated with wave power estimation by sensors and system calibration. For photon-counting detectors it can be assumed that this noise component is also zero mean, white, and its variance is proportional to I_{kij}^{true}. Thus, one gets the following model for the noise variance:

$$\sigma_{kij}^2 = \sigma_k^2 + \gamma I_{kij}^{true}, \tag{3}$$

where σ_k^2 denotes the SI noise variance and γ is the SD noise proportionality factor. Then, it becomes possible to determine the input MSE for each component images as

$$\text{MSE}_k^{\text{inp}} = \sum_{i=1}^{I}\sum_{j=1}^{J}(I_{kij}^{\text{noise}} - I_{kij}^{\text{true}})^2 / (IJ), k = 1,...,K$$

and the input PSNR

$$\text{PSNR}_k^{inp} = 10\log_{10}(D_k^2 / \text{MSE}_k^{inp}), k = 1,...,K, \tag{4}$$

where D_k determinates image dynamic range.

One can estimate equivalent noise variance for SD component as

$$\hat{\sigma}_{\text{eq SD}}^2(k) = \sum_{i=1}^{I_{\text{Im}}}\sum_{j=1}^{J_{\text{Im}}}\gamma(k)I_{kij}^{true} / (I_{\text{Im}}J_{\text{Im}}) \approx \sum_{i=1}^{I_{\text{Im}}}\sum_{j=1}^{J_{\text{Im}}}\hat{\gamma}(k)I_{kij}^{\text{n}} / (I_{\text{Im}}J_{\text{Im}}) = \hat{\gamma}(k)I_{\text{mean}}(k) \tag{5}$$

where $I_{\text{Im}}, J_{\text{Im}}$ denotes the image size, $\hat{\gamma}(k)$ is the SD noise component parameter estimate assumed accurate enough, and $I_{\text{mean}}(k)$ is the image mean. If there is also an estimate of SI component variance σ_k^2, then one can obtain an estimate of the input MSE as

$$\hat{\text{MSE}}_k^{\text{inp}} \approx \hat{\sigma}_{\text{eq SD}}^2(k) + \hat{\sigma}_k^2, \tag{6}$$

where $\hat{\sigma}_k^2$ denotes the SI noise variance estimate (assumed accurate enough) for a kth component of multichannel image.

It is important to know how large is relative contribution of SD noise component into the input MSE. To get imagination about this, the values $\hat{\sigma}_{eq\,SD}^2(k)$ have been derived and graphically compared to $\hat{\sigma}_k^2 = \hat{\sigma}_0^2(k)$ [25]. The plots for AVIRIS [31] (224 subbands in optical visible and infrared ranges) and Hyperion [32] (242 subbands in the same ranges, for some very noisy subbands the estimates have not been obtained) sensors are represented in **Figure 1** in logarithmic scale (since there is a very wide limit of variation for these estimates). The values of $\hat{\sigma}_{eq\,SD}^2(k)$ for subbands for which negative estimates of $\hat{\gamma}(k)$ have been obtained by the method [10] are assigned unity values (zero values in logarithmic scale).

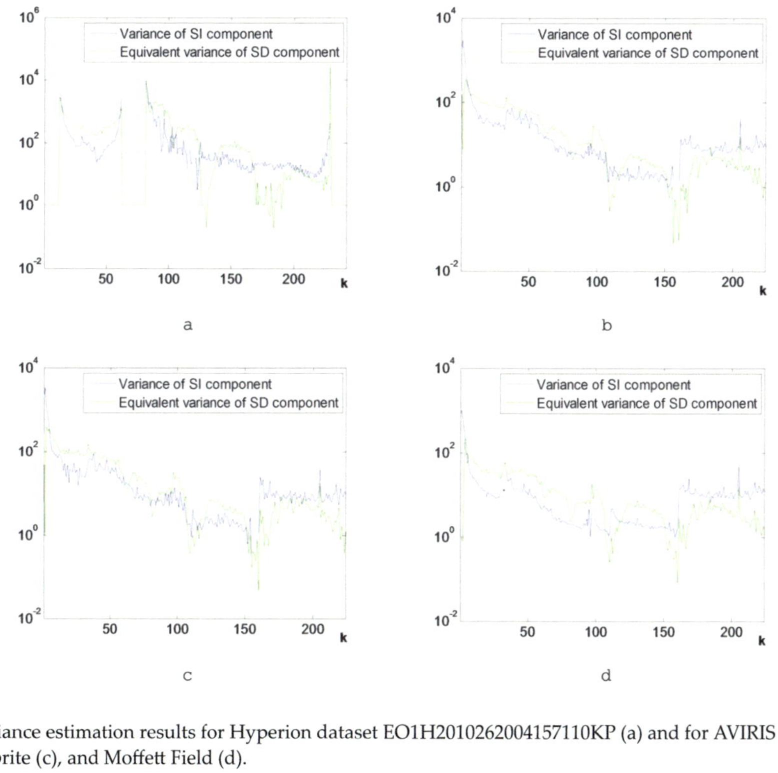

Figure 1. Variance estimation results for Hyperion dataset EO1H2010262004157110KP (a) and for AVIRIS images Lunar Lake (b), Cuprite (c), and Moffett Field (d).

Analysis of data presented in **Figure 1** shows the following. For Hyperion data (**Figure 1a**), in most subbands of visible and near infrared ranges (these are subbands with indices from 13 to 61), $\hat{\sigma}_{eq\,SD}^2(k)$ Is larger than $\hat{\sigma}_0^2(k)$, i.e., the SD component contribution is prevailing. In infrared range (these are subbands with indices from 78 to 230; **Figure 1a**), there is approximately equal percentage of subbands where the influence of SD or SI components is dominant. According to our experiments, similar conclusions can be drawn for other real-life images acquired by the Hyperion sensor.

The results for three widely known test datasets acquired by the sensor AVIRIS are given in **Figure 1(b)–(d)**. Their analysis allows concluding the following. All three dependences of the same type (for instance, $\hat{\sigma}_0^2(k)$) are very similar to each other. Then, if hyperspectral images are acquired during the same session, one can assume that noise characteristics do not change. In addition, $\hat{\sigma}_{eq\,SD}^2(k)$ are larger than $\hat{\sigma}_0^2(k)$ for most images acquired by visible range AVIRIS sensor (spectrometer A, indices 1, ..., 32). The same conclusion is valid for most subbands of the second AVIRIS spectrometer (B, indices 33, ..., 96). Contributions of the considered noise components are comparable for the third spectrometer images (C, indices 97, ..., 160). SI noise is dominating for most subband images acquired by the fourth AVIRIS spectrometer (D, indices 161, ..., 224). Thus, contributions of noise components depend upon wavelength and sensor used in a hyperspectral system. But in any case, assumption on additive character of the noise is not valid. Moreover, for hyperspectral imaging, there is a tendency to increasing the relative contribution of SD component [33].

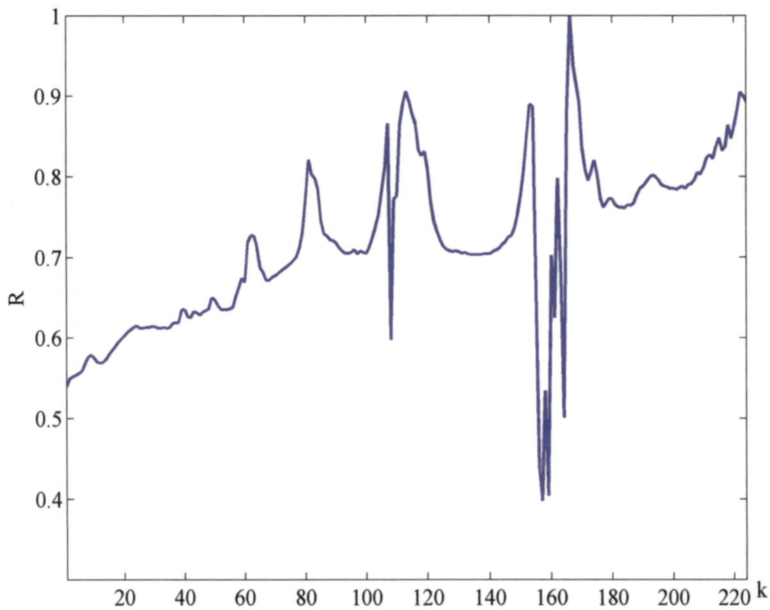

Figure 2. Dependence of cross-correlation factor R on k for the 166th subband image.

One more important property of multichannel RS images is that signal components in them are often cross-correlated. Meanwhile, the cross-correlation factor also depends upon noise intensity in both images and decreases if noise is intensive in one or both component images. Keeping this in mind, we have chosen for analysis the subband image with k = 166 that corresponds to far-infrared range and is acquired by the fourth spectrometer of AVIRIS. This image is quite noisy and the input PSNR for it is less than 30 dB (dynamic range of this image is small and this is the second reason of low input PSNR). The dependence of the cross-correlation factor R on k is presented in **Figure 2**.

The factor $R(166) = 1$ and for this subband image the signal-independent noise component is prevailing with the input MSE about 11. But we are more interested in $R(k)$ for other subbands. Analysis of data presented in **Figure 2** shows that $R(k)$ varies in rather wide limits. On average, values of $R(k)$ are the largest for the subband images acquired by the fourth spectrometer of AVIRIS imager for which $k > 160$. Meanwhile, cross-correlation factors are large enough for subbands relating to other ranges as well.

Although cross-correlation of images in multichannel images is often high, there can also be sufficient variation in the dynamic range D_k usually defined as $D_k = I_k^{\max} - I_k^{\min}$ where $I_k^{\max}$ and $I_k^{\min}$ are maximal and minimal values in the kth subband image, respectively. For hyperspectral data, the values D_k and D_{k+1}, i.e., for neighbor subbands, are usually close enough. As it follows from analysis of noise components in **Figure 1**, neighbor channels commonly have quite close values of input MSEs (equal to noise variance σ_k^2 if the noise is pure additive). Thus, input PSNR values determined as $\mathrm{PSNR}_k^{\mathrm{inp}} = 10\log_{10}(D_k^2/\mathrm{MSE}_k^{\mathrm{inp}})$ are usually close to each other for neighbor images of hyperspectral and multispectral data.

3. Considered performance criteria and peculiarities of lossy compression of noisy images

After lossy compression of a multichannel image, one obtains $\{I_{k\,ij}^c, i = 1, \ldots, I, j = 1, \ldots, J, k = 1, \ldots, K\}$. If one deals with lossy compression of a noise-free image, then quality of compressed image is worse for a larger compression ratio (smaller bpp, larger quantization step or scaling factor for DCT-based coders). The reason is that more distortions are introduced for larger CR.

Meanwhile, many researchers [34–36] have stressed that there are peculiarities in lossy compression of noisy images. Lossy compression leads to a specific noise removal effect that can be large enough under certain conditions. Due to this, it might be possible that MSE for compressed image

$$\mathrm{MSE}_k^c = \sum_{i=1}^{I}\sum_{j=1}^{J}(I_{k\,ij}^c - I_{kij}^{\mathrm{true}})^2 / (IJ), k = 1, \ldots, K \tag{7}$$

is less than MSE_k^{inp} and MSE_k^c be minimum for some value of a parameter that characterizes compression for a given method. This can be quantization step (QS), scaling factor (SF), or bits per pixel (bpp)—this depends on a coder used. Then, such a parameter is associated with the so-called optimal operation point (OOP). **Figure 3** presents dependences of

$$\mathrm{PSNR}_k^c = 10\log_{10}(D_k^2 / \mathrm{MSE}_k^c), k = 1, \ldots, K \tag{8}$$

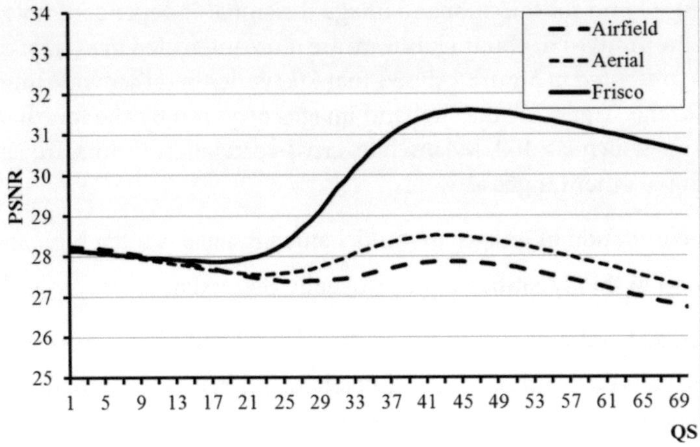

Figure 3. Dependences $\text{PSNR}^c(\text{QS})$ for the coder AGU and test images Airfield, Aerial, and Frisco corrupted by AWGN with noise variance equal to 100.

on QS for the lossy DCT-based coder AGU [37] applied to three standard grayscale test noisy RS images, Airfield, Aerial, and Frisco. All three images were corrupted by additive white Gaussian noise (AWGN) with variance 100. Note that the test image Frisco has a simpler structure while the test images Aerial and Airfield have more details. This is the reason why the denoising effect of lossy compression is considerably greater for the image Frisco and the dependence for it has an obvious global maximum. This is OOP according to the metric PSNR^c that coincides with OOP according to the metric MSE^c—see **Figure 8**. For the test image Aerial, the OOP is not so "obvious" although it exists. Finally, for the test image Airfield, there is no OOP formally but the dependence $\text{PSNR}^c(\text{QS})$ has local maximum. Note that in all cases maxima occur $\text{QS}_{\text{OOP}} \approx 4\sigma$. This is the choice recommended for the coder AGU [24] and for a more complex coder ADCT [38]. This recommendation allows compressing lossy images by the aforementioned DCT-based coders component-wise in one iteration under assumption that noise characteristics for component images are known or preestimated with an appropriate accuracy. Note that there are many modern methods for blind estimation of parameters of additive noise [39, 40] and signal-dependent noise [41–43]. Availability of these techniques gives rise to fully automatic compression based on noise parameter estimation [20, 44].

For the recommended $\text{QS}_{\text{OOP}} \approx 4\sigma$(or $\text{QS}_{\text{OOP}} \approx 4\sigma_{\text{equiv}}, \sigma^2_{\text{equiv}} = \text{MSE}^{\text{inp}}$, used if noise is signal dependent and VST is not applied before compression), it can be interesting to study such parameters as $\text{PSNR}_k^{\text{OOP}}$ and $\delta\text{PSNR}_k^{\text{OOP}}$ determined as

$$\delta\text{PSNR}_k^{\text{OOP}} = \text{PSNR}_k^{\text{OOP}} - \text{PSNR}_k^{\text{inp}} \tag{9}$$

where positive $\delta\mathrm{PSNR}_k^{\mathrm{OOP}}$ means that OOP exists according to a corresponding metric. Such a study has been carried out recently [26]. It has been established that $\delta\mathrm{PSNR}_k^{\mathrm{OOP}}$ can vary in rather wide limits, from about –3 to 5–6 dB. Negative values show that OOP does not exist and this happens if a compressed image has a rather complex structure and/or noise is not intensive. On the contrary, positive values indicate that there is OOP and it takes place for quite simple structure images and/or quite intensive noise. It has also been shown in [26] that $\delta\mathrm{PSNR}_k^{\mathrm{OOP}}$ can be quite accurately predicted before compression using different statistics of DCT coefficients determined for a limited number of 8 ×8 pixel blocks.

Let us consider dependences of CR on QS for the same test noisy images as in **Figure 3**. These dependences are represented in **Figure 4**. The first observation is that lossy compression with the recommended QS leads to sufficiently different compression ratios for different images. Recall that the recommended QS is equal to 40 for σ^2=100 and to 56 for σ^2=200. Simpler structure and/or noisier images are compressed with larger CR. For QS=40 (σ^2=100), one has CR about 17 for the image Frisco and about 7 for two other test images. If noise intensity is greater (QS=56, σ^2=200), larger CR values are attained: about 26 for Frisco and 14 for other two images. Thus, noisier images are compressed in OOP with larger CR. This means that image complexity and noise intensity should be taken into account in practice. Some ways to do this will be described in the next section.

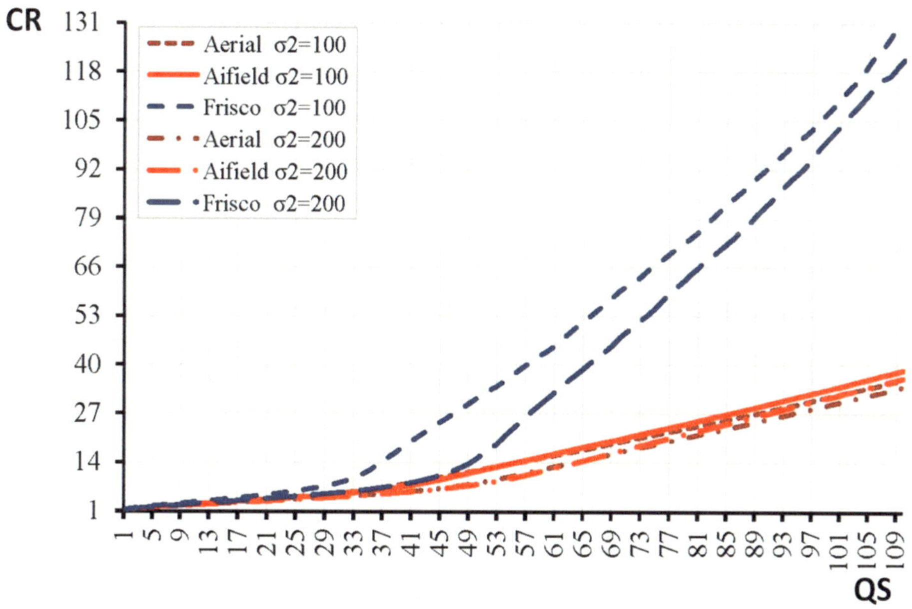

Figure 4. Dependences of CR on QS for three test images of different complexity for two values of noise variance σ^2 (100 and 200).

4. Efficiency for 3D compression

4.1. Main dependences and benefits

As mentioned above, the compression of multichannel RS images can be carried out component-wise and using variants of 3D approach. In the former case, there are certain benefits. First, it is easier to handle data. For example, QS or bpp can be set individually for each component image. Second, a part of operations can be performed in parallel. For example, orthogonal transforms and quantization of coefficients can be performed separately for each component image and, thus, this part of processing can be parallelized. In the latter case, 3D compression can be applied to multichannel image as a whole [14] or as to a set of component image groups [15, 22]. Each variant has its own positive features and drawbacks. If groups are used, it is easier to parallelize computations (since processing can be partly performed separately in each group) and adjust compression parameters.

Figure 5. Noise-free (a) and noisy (b) three-channel test image in pseudocolor representation.

Let us analyze some peculiarities of 3D compression for a rather simple three-channel test image (presented in **Figure 5a**). This image has been considered noise free and it has been composed from three channels of visible range of Landsat RS data associated with red, green, and blue components for visualization. The noisy image with artificially added AWGN having the same variance equal to 130 in all components is shown in **Figure 5(b)**. Noise is seen well in quasihomogeneous regions.

The plots of MSE_k^c (QS) are presented in **Figure 6(a)**. Notation 2d relates to two-dimensional, i.e., component-wise compression. For all three components, the plots almost coincide and, therefore, we present the averaged dependence. In turn, notation 3d concerns 3D compression using 3D version of AGU coder [15]. Again, the dependence averaged for all three components is given.

http://dx.doi.org/10.5772/64944

There are several interesting observations for these plots. If QS is rather small, e.g., less than 2σ, the dependences MSE_k^c (QS) practically coincide, i.e., there is almost no difference between 2D (component-wise) and 3D (volumetric) compression. Then, for larger QS, differences start to appear. And they become quite large for QS about 4σ, i.e., when OOP can be observed. First, OOP is observed (see **Figure 6a**) for both 2D and 3D compression. But MSE_k^c (QS) in OOP for 3D compression is considerably (by almost two times) smaller. This means that noise-filtering effect due to 3D compression is sufficiently better compared to 2D compression. This can be noticed in **Figure 7** that presents images compressed in OOP for 2D and 3D AGU coder versions. Second, OOP in the case of 3D compression is observed for the same conditions as for 2D compression. More examples confirming this can be found in the paper [29].

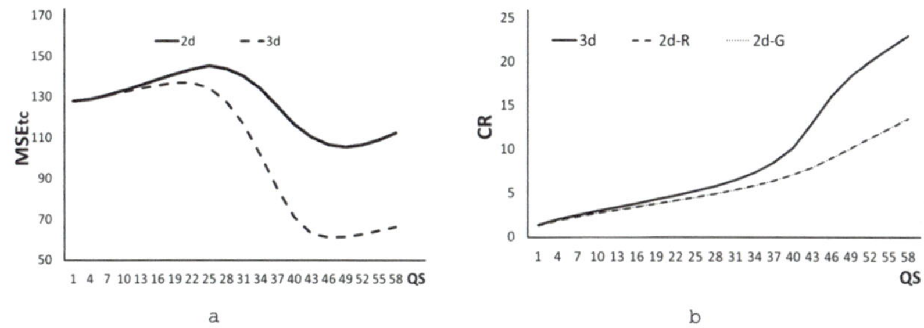

Figure 6. Averaged dependences $\text{MSE}^c(\text{QS})$ (a) and $\text{CR}(\text{QS})$ (b) for 2D and 3D compression.

Figure 7. Images compressed in OOP for 2D (a) and 3D (b) compression.

Consider now the plots of CR(QS) represented in **Figure 6(b)**. For QS less than 2σ there are almost no benefits of 3D compression. However, for larger QS, the benefits become obvious. CR provided by 3D compression occurs to be almost twice larger than for component-wise processing. A question is why this happens? Another question is can we predict CR and situations when 3D compression might be beneficial compared to component-wise coding.

4.2. Prediction of compression parameters

There are two main compression parameters for which prediction is desirable for compression in OOP neighborhood, namely, $\delta \mathrm{PSNR}_k^{\mathrm{OOP}}$ and CR. An approach to predict $\delta \mathrm{PSNR}_k^{\mathrm{OOP}}$ for component-wise compression has been recently proposed [26]. Its essence is the following. Suppose that one has a parameter that is able to jointly characterize complexity of image to be compressed and noise intensity in it. Suppose also that this (input) parameter can be calculated easily (quickly, considerably faster than compression is performed) and it is tightly connected to output (predicted) parameter (indicator) that characterizes compression from a desired viewpoint. This connection is expressed either as some analytical dependence allowing to determine (predict) output parameter easily and quickly. Then, it becomes possible to estimate the input parameter for a considered image, to use it as argument for calculating the output parameter, and to carry out some decision based on this prediction [26].

Having described the general strategy of prediction, let us give some details. First of all, there are many parameters that can be used as inputs [45–47]. Under condition that noise parameters (variance) are known in advance or preestimated with appropriate accuracy, statistical parameters of the family $P_{\alpha\sigma}$ can be used. These are mean probabilities that absolute values of DCT coefficients calculated in N_{bl} blocks of size 8 × 8 pixels are less than a threshold $\alpha\sigma$ where α is the parameter (in our experiments it has been equal to 0.5, 1.0, 1.5, or 2.0). The input parameter $P_{\alpha\sigma}$ is indirectly connected with number of zeroed DCT coefficients in image filtering [45] that influences denoising efficiency performed by lossy compression applied to noisy images. There is also parameter P_{0q}—mean probability that DCT coefficients calculated in N_{bl} blocks of size 8 × 8 pixels are equal to zero after quantization with a used QS.

Obtaining dependence between output and input parameters is a special stage performed in advance (offline). This stage presumes getting a scatterplot where the horizontal axis corresponds to an input parameter and vertical relates to a predicted output parameter. Scatter-plot points correspond to a test image corrupted by AWGN with a certain variance compressed in a specified way. An example of the scatterplot is shown in **Figure 8**. $P_{2\sigma}$ serves as an input parameter and $\delta \mathrm{PSNR}^{\mathrm{OOP}}$ as an output parameter.

Having such a scatterplot, curve fitting is applied to obtain a desired dependence. At this substage, several subtasks should be solved. They can be, in general, treated as providing good fit and include choice of proper type and parameters of approximating functions, accounting for restrictions, etc. Different criteria of fitting quality can be used [48] where R^2 (goodness of fit that has to approach unity for good fit) is one of the commonly employed parameters. The example for 2D image compression presented in **Figure 8** shows that the scatter-plot points are not spread a lot and it can be assumed that the dependence is a smooth function. Then, polynomials of the fourth and fifth orders and some other functions provide appropriate results (the fitted polynomial expression is presented in **Figure 8**). The performance of prediction for different input parameters should be analyzed and compared since considerably different values of R^2 can be potentially and practically produced [27]. Some analysis has been already carried out [27] but this study is far from completeness.

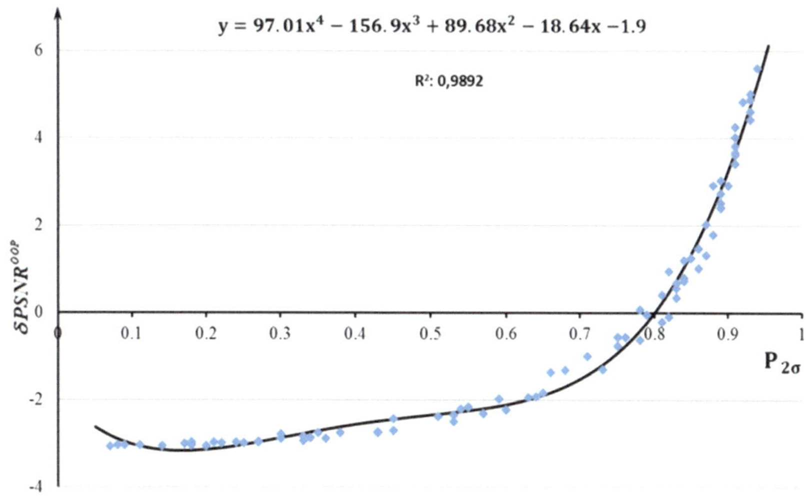

Figure 8. Scatterplot of $\delta\text{PSNR}^{\text{OOP}}$ on $P_{2\sigma}$ and the fitted fourth-order polynomial.

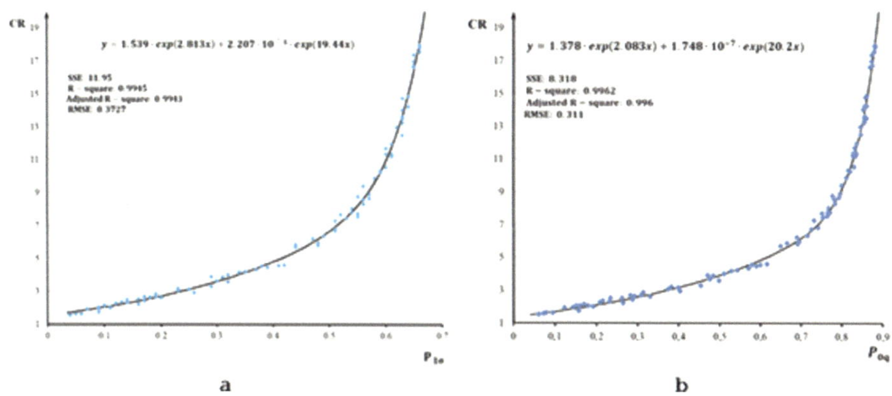

Figure 9. Scatterplots of CR vs $P_{1\sigma}$ (a) and P_{0q} (b) and the fitted curves.

Similar strategy has been applied in the prediction of CR for 2D compression. The first attempt to predict CR for lossy compression of noisy images in OOP for AGU and ADCT [38] coders has been made in 2015 [26] using two input parameters, $P_{2\sigma}$ and $P_{2.7\sigma}$. A more thorough study has been carried out later [27]. Below we present two scatterplots from the aforementioned paper (**Figure 9**). As it can be seen, both scatterplots have small spread and, according to their visual inspection, CR has the tendency to increase if the input parameters $P_{1\sigma}$ or P_{0q} (considered here as example) become larger. Fitting is excellent in both cases although the results for P_{0q} are slightly better. Here, tight connection of CR with P_{0q} is easily understood. A larger P_{0q} shows that there are more zeros in a sequence to be coded and this in turn [49] leads to a larger CR.

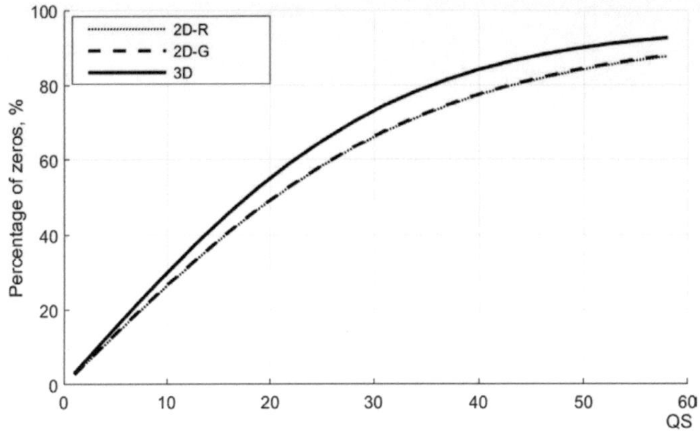

Figure 10. Dependences P_{0q} on QS for 2D and 3D compression.

Thus, we can expect that benefits of 3D compression compared to 2D deal with more zeros after 3D DCT (better decorrelation of the data) than in component-wise compression. To check this hypothesis, we have determined P_{0q} for 3D compression and for 2D component-wise compression for the test image in **Figure 5(b)**. The results are given as dependences of P_{0q} on QS for 3D AGU (notation 3D) and for two components, red and green (notations 2D-R and 2D-G, respectively). As it can be seen, the curves for "red" and "green" channels practically coincide. In 3D compression, more zeros are observed for any QS. For optimal QS=56 one has P_{0q} about 0.87; the predicted CR is about 13 (see **Figure 9b**) and this practically coincides with the value of practically attained CR (**Figure 6b**). In turn, for 3D compression, P_{0q} is about 0.92; the predicted CR is over 20 (see **Figure 9b**), and this is in good agreement with the value of practically attained CR (**Figure 6b**). Certainly, a more thorough study is needed. However, we can expect that the prediction of CR using P_{0q} can work for 3D DCT-based compression as well (**Figure 10**).

4.3. Experimental data

The observations described above have also been verified for two types of multichannel images. The first type is Landsat TM data [50]. Different variants of uniting eight images of the same resolution into groups for further 3D compression have been considered. It has been shown that there are benefits in CR (it sufficiently increases for the same level of introduced distortions) only if images combined into a group are highly correlated and have similar dynamic range [50]. Then, there is an increase in the percentage of zeros P_{0q} for 3D coder compared to P_{0q} for component images within this group. This increase can serve as an indicator of expedience to apply 3D compression. Meanwhile, there are component images (e.g., in channel nine, wavelength 1360–1390 nm) for which separate compression is expedient since adding it to any group does not improve the compression performance.

The second type of analyzed data is hyperspectral images acquired by the Hyperion sensor (the dataset EO1H1800252002116110KZ). Hyperion produces bad-quality (very noisy) data in some bands (for example, in subbands with indices q=1–12). These component images are usually discarded in analysis and we have not processed them too.

Hyperspectral data can be compressed with and without utilizing VST to take into account signal-dependent nature of the noise. Below we consider data obtained for the procedure that employs VST for both 2D and 3D compression. In both cases, after determining the parameters of the noise in all subbands (if needed), the generalized Anscombe transform and/or normalization is carried out [20]. Note that original data are presented as 16-bit values and this is taken into account in CR calculation and prediction.

We have considered four variants to compress the data. The first variant is to perform component-wise compression. The second is to divide this hyperspectral image into two groups. The first group includes subbands with indices from 13 to 57 while the second one contains subband images with indices from 83 to 224. The third variant is to use groups of size eight subbands. The fourth is to apply 16-channel groups. Some subbands left in both ranges formed groups of smaller size. CR for all subbands of each group is assumed to be the same since all images are compressed jointly.

The obtained results are presented in **Figure 11**. Their analysis shows several interesting facts. First, CR for component-wise compression is, on average, sufficiently smaller than for any of 3D compression variants. If component-wise compression is applied, CR for neighbor subbands are close to each other although the total range of CR variation is rather wide—from about 4 to about 27. In general, there is correlation between CR values for 2D and 3D compression. If CR for 2D compression is larger, CR for variants of 3D compression is usually larger too. However, there are a few exceptions when CR for a particular subband image compressed separately is larger than for 3D compression. This happens for subband images with low-input SNR and low correlation with data in neighbor subbands [50].

It is difficult to understand from visual inspection of plots (see **Figure 11**) what variant of 3D compression is preferable. More thorough analysis has shown that the CRs for groups of size 8 (18.34 and 12.72) and 16 (20.81 and 14.65) subbands are quite close. CRs for the case of using only two large unequal size groups are slightly smaller (17.43 and 13.00).

We have also determined the percentage of zeros for 3D compression in groups of size 8 and 16 subbands. The results are presented in **Figure 12**. As can be seen, there is tight correlation between CR for a group and the corresponding percentage. This allows expecting that it is possible to predict CR for 3D compression in groups by analyzing P_{0q} for these groups. Note that P_{0q} varies from 0.3 (30%) for subbands compressed with small CR till almost 0.9 (90%) for subbands compressed with very large CR.

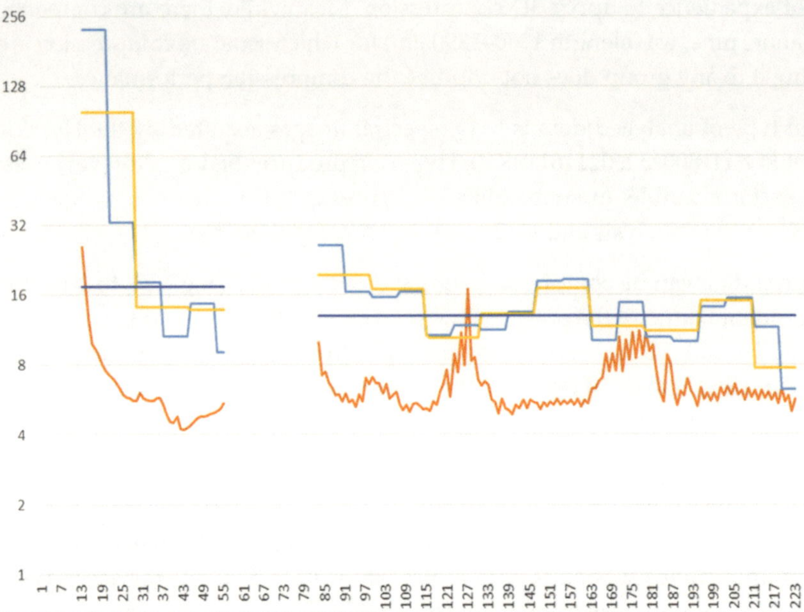

Figure 11. CR values for subbands of hyperspectral Hyperion data for component-wise and 3D lossy compression, 8 channels (blue), 16 channels (yellow), and all channels in group(violet) and component-wise (red).

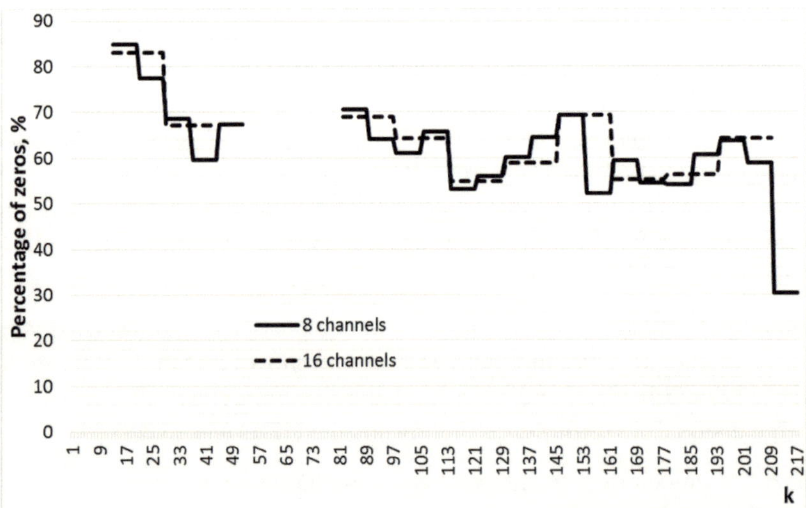

Figure 12. Percentages of zero values for quantized DCT coefficients for hyperspectral data compression in groups of size 8 and 16 channels.

Examples of real-life images before and after compression for particular subbands can be found in the paper [22]. If noise intensity is high and noise is visible, lossy compression provides noticeable filtering effect. If noise is invisible, original and compressed images look almost the same.

5. Conclusions

The task of lossy compression of multichannel remote sensing images is considered. It is shown that this type of data has some peculiarities to be taken into account in compression. The main peculiarities consist in signal-dependent nature of the noise, wide limits of variation of data dynamic range and SNR in subband images, and sufficient correlation of data in neighbor channels. Lossy compression should be carried out in automatic manner especially if it has to be performed on-board. Then, it has to adapt to noise properties where the simplest adaptation mechanism is to set QS proportional to noise standard deviation (before or after VST depending upon whether it is applied or not). A good decision in compression of noisy images is to perform compression in the neighborhood of optimal operation point. It is shown that OOP exists for both component-wise and 3D compression where the latter approach is preferable since it produces better denoising and considerably larger CR. Parameters of compression can be predicted rather easily before execution compression with quite high accuracy. This allows adapting compression to image and noise properties and to undertake decision does compression performance meet requirements.

Meanwhile, there are several tasks to be solved in the future. The main of them could be adaptive grouping. Another task is QS adjusting to provide a desired CR.

Author details

Vladimir Lukin[1*], Alexander Zemliachenko[1], Ruslan Kozhemiakin[1], Sergey Abramov[1], Mikhail Uss[1], Victoriya Abramova[1], Nikolay Ponomarenko[1], Benoit Vozel[2] and Kacem Chehdi[2]

*Address all correspondence to: lukin@ai.kharkov.com

1 Dept of Transmitters, Receivers and Signal Processing, National Aerospace University, Kharkov, Ukraine

2 University of Rennes 1, Institute of Electronics and Telecommunications of Rennes, UMR CNRS 6164, School of Applied Sciences and Technology, Lannion, France

References

[1] Christophe E. Hyperspectral Data Compression Tradeoff in Optical Remote Sensing. In: Prasad S., Bruce L.M., Chanussot J., editors. Advances in Signal Processing and Exploitation Techniques. 8th ed. Springer; Berlin Heidelberg 2011. pp. 9–29.

[2] Schowengerdt R. Remote Sensing: Models and Methods for Image Processing. 3rd ed. Academic Press; Orlando USA 2006. p. 560.

[3] Blanes I., Magli E., Serra-Sagrista J. A tutorial on image compression for optical space imaging systems. IEEE Geoscience and Remote Sensing Magazine. 2014;2(3):8–26.

[4] Yu G., Vladimirova T., Sweeting M.N. Image compression systems on board satellites. Acta Astronautica. 2009;64(9–10):988–1005.

[5] Magli E., Olmo G., Quacchio E. Optimized onboard lossless and near-lossless compression of hyperspectral data using CALIC. IEEE Geoscience and Remote Sensing Letters. 2004;1(1):21–25.

[6] Lukin V., Abramov S., Ponomarenko N., Krivenko S., Uss M., Vozel B., Chehdi K., Egiazarian K., Astola J. Approaches to automatic data processing in hyperspectral remote sensing. Telecommunications and Radio Engineering. 2014;73(13):1125–1139.

[7] Aiazzi B., Alparone L., Barducci A., Baronti S., Pippi I. Estimating noise and information of multispectral imagery. Journal of Optical Engineering. 2002;41:656–668.

[8] Abramov S., Uss M., Abramova V., Lukin V., Vozel B., Chehdi K. On Noise Properties in Hyperspectral Images. In: Proceedings of IGARSS;; Milan, Italy; July 2015. pp. 3501–3504. http://ieeexplore.ieee.org/stamp/stamp.jsp?tp=&arnumber=7325672)

[9] Meola J., Eismann M.T., Moses R.L., Ash J.N. Modeling and estimation of signal-dependent noise in hyperspectral imagery. Applied Optics. 2011;50(21):3829–3846.

[10] Uss M.L., Vozel B., Lukin V., Chehdi K. Image informative maps for component-wise estimating parameters of signal-dependent noise. Journal of Electronic Imaging. 2013;22(1). DOI: 10.1117/1.JEI.22.1.013019 (see http://electronicimaging.spiedigitallibrary.org/article.aspx?articleid=1568204)

[11] Uss M., Vozel B., Lukin V., Chehdi K. Maximum likelihood estimation of spatially correlated signal-dependent noise in hyperspectral images. Optical Engineering. 2012;51(11). DOI: 10.1117/1.OE.51.11.111712 see http://opticalengineering.spiedigitallibrary.org/issue.aspx?journalid=92&issueid=24230

[12] Lukin V., Ponomarenko N., Fevralev D., Vozel B., Chehdi K., Kurekin A. Classification of pre-filtered multichannel remote sensing images. In: Escalante-Ramirez B., editor. Remote Sensing—Advanced Techniques and Platforms. In-Tech, Austria; 2012. pp. 75–98.

[13] Zhong P., Wang R. Multiple-spectral-band CRFs for denoising junk bands of hyperspectral imagery. IEEE Transactions on Geoscience and Remote Sensing. 2013;51(4): 2269–2275.

[14] Khelifi F., Bouridane A., Kurugollu F. Joined spectral trees for scalable SPIHT-based multispectral image compression. IEEE Transactions on Multimedia. 2008;10(3):316–329.

[15] Ponomarenko N., Zriakhov M., Lukin V., Kaarna A. Improved grouping and noise cancellation for automatic lossy compression of AVIRIS images. In: Editors Jacques Blanc-Talon, Don Bone, and Wilfried Philips Proceedings of ACIVS, Springer, Heidelberg, Australia. LNCS-6475, Part II; 2010. pp. 261–271.

[16] Valsesia D., Magli E. A novel rate control algorithm for onboard predictive coding of multispectral and hyperspectral images. IEEE Transactions on Geoscience and Remote Sensing. 2014;52(10):6341–6355.

[17] Shoba L.L., Mohan V., Venkataramani Y. Landsat image compression using lifting scheme. In: Proceedings of International Conference on Communication and Signal Processing; India; April 2014. pp. 1963–1968.

[18] Thayammal S., Silvathy D. Multispectral band image compression using adaptive wavelet transform—tetrolet transform. In: Proceedings of 2014 International Conference on Electronics and Communication Systems; Coimbatore, India; February 2014. pp. 1–5. DOI: 10.1109/ECS.2014.6892610

[19] Wang L., Jiao L., Bai J., Wu J. Hyperspectral image compression based on 3D reversible integer lapped transform. Electronic Letters. 2010;46(24):1601–1602. DOI: 10.1049/el.2010.1788

[20] Zemliachenko A.N., Kozhemiakin R.A., Uss M.L., Abramov S.K., Ponomarenko N.N., Lukin V.V., Vozel B., Chehdi K. Lossy compression of hyperspectral images based on noise parameters estimation and variance stabilizing transform. Journal of Applied Remote Sensing. 2014;8(1):25. DOI: 10.1117/1.JRS.8.083571

[21] Shinoda K., Murakami Y., Yamaguchi M., Ohyama N. Multispectral image compression for spectral and color reproduction based on lossy to lossless coding. In: Proc. SPIE Image Processing: Algorithms and Systems VIII; SPIE 75320H; February 2010. DOI: 10.1117/12.838843

[22] Zemliachenko A.N., Abramov S.K., Lukin V.V., Vozel B., Chehdi K. Prediction of optimal operation point existence and parameters in lossy compression of noisy images. In: Proceedings of SPIE, Vol. 9244, Image and Signal Processing for Remote Sensing XX; SPIE 92440H; October 15, 2014. DOI: 10.1117/12.2065947

[23] Aiazzi B., Alparone L., Baronti S., Lastri C., Selva M. Spectral distortion in lossy compression of hyperspectral data. Journal of Electrical and Computer Engineering. 2012;20(12):850637. DOI: 10.1155/2012/850637

[24] Zemliachenko A.N., Kozhemiakin R.A., Uss M.L., Abramov S.K., Lukin V.V., Vozel B., Chehdi K. VST-based lossy compression of hyperspectral data for new generation

sensors. In: Proceedings of SPIE Symposium on Remote Sensing; Dresden, Germany; September 2013. SPIE Vol. 8892; p. 12. DOI: 10.1117/12.2028415

[25] Zemliachenko A., Abramov S., Lukin V., Vozel B., Chehdi K. Compression ratio prediction in lossy compression of noisy images. In: Proceedings of IGARSS; Milan, Italy; July 2015. pp. 3497–3500.

[26] Zemliachenko A.N., Abramov S.K., Lukin V.V., Vozel B., Chehdi K. Lossy compression of noisy remote sensing images with prediction of optimal operation point existence and parameters. Journal of Applied Remote Sensing. 2015;9(1):095066. DOI: 10.1117/1.JRS.9.095066

[27] Zemliachenko A., Kozhemiakin R., Vozel B., Lukin V. Prediction of compression ratio in lossy compression of noisy images. In: Modern Problems of Radio Engineering, Telecommunications and Computer Science (TCSET); Lviv-Slavske, Ukraine; February 2016. pp. 693–697.

[28] Kozhemiakin R., Abramov S., Lukin V., Djurović I., Vozel B. Peculiarities of 3D compression of noisy multichannel images. In: Proceedings of MECO; Budva, Montenegro; June 2015. pp. 331–334.

[29] Lukin V., Abramov S., Kozhemiakin R., Vozel B., Djurovic B., Djurovic I. Optimal operation point in 3D DCT-based lossy compression of color and multichannel remote sensing images. Telecommunications and Radio Engineering. 2015;20:1803–1821.

[30] Christophe E., L´eger D., Mailhes C. Quality criteria benchmark for hyperspectral imagery. IEEE Transactions on Geoscience and Remote Sensing. 2005;43(9):2103–2114.

[31] Green R.O., Eastwood M.L., Sarture C.M., Chrien T.G., Aronsson M., Chippendale B.J., et al. Imaging spectroscopy and the airborne visible/infrared imaging spectrometer (AVIRIS). Remote Sensing of Environment. 1998;65:227–248.

[32] Pearlman J.S., Barry P.S., Segal C.C., Shepanski J., Beiso D., Carman S.L. Hyperion, a space-based imaging spectrometer. IEEE Transactions on Geoscience and Remote Sensing. 2003;41(6):1160–1173. DOI: 10.1109/TGRS.2003.815018

[33] Gao L., Du Q., Zhang B., Yang W., Wu Y. A comparative study on linear regression-based noise estimation for hyperspectral imagery. IEEE Journal of Selected Topics in Applied Earth Observations and Remote Sensing. 2013;6(2):488–498.

[34] Al-Chaykh O.K., Mersereau R.M. Lossy compression of noisy images. IEEE Transactions on Image Processing. 1998;7(12):1641–1652.

[35] Bekhtin Y.S. Adaptive wavelet codec for noisy image compression. In: Proceedings of the 9th East-West Design and Test Symposium; Sevastopol, Ukraine; September 2011. pp. 184–188.

[36] Lukin V., Bataeva E. challenges in pre-processing multichannel remote sensing terrain images. In: Djurovic I., editor. Importance of GEO Initiatives and Montenegrin Capaci-

ties in This Area. The Section for Natural Sciences Book No 16 ed. The Montenegrin Academy of Sciences and Arts Book. No 119; 2012. pp. 63–76.

[37] Ponomarenko N.N., Lukin V.V., Egiazarian K., Astola J. DCT based high quality image compression. In: Proceedings of 14th Scandinavian Conference on Image Analysis; Joensuu, Finland; 2005. pp. 1177–1185.

[38] Ponomarenko N., Lukin V., Egiazarian K., Astola J. ADCT: a new high quality DCT based coder for lossy image compression. In: CD ROM Proceedings of LNLA; Switzerland; August 2008. p. 6.

[39] Liu C., Szeliski R., Kang S.B., Zitnick C.L., Freeman W.T. Automatic estimation and removal of noise from a single image. IEEE Transactions on Pattern Analysis and Machine Intelligence. 2008;30(2):299–314.

[40] Vozel B., Abramov S., Chehdi K., Lukin V., Ponomarenko N., Uss M., Astola J. Blind methods for noise evaluation in multi-component images. In: Wiley-ISTE Multivariate Image Processing; France; 2009. pp. 263–295.

[41] Abramov S., Zabrodina V., Lukin V., Vozel B., Chehdi K., Astola J. Methods for blind estimation of the variance of mixed noise and their performance analysis. In: J. Awrejcewicz, editor. Numerical Analysis—Theory and Applications. Austria: In-Tech; 2011. pp. 49–70. ISBN 978-953-307-389-7

[42] Anfinsen S.N., Doulgeris A.P., Eltoft T. Estimation of the equivalent number of looks in polarimetric synthetic aperture radar imagery. IEEE Transactions on Geoscience and Remote Sensing. 2009;47(11):3795–3809.

[43] Colom M., Lebrun M., Buades A., Morel J.M. A non-parametric approach for the estimation of intensity-frequency dependent noise. In: IEEE International Conference on Image Processing (ICIP); Paris, France; 27–30 October 2014. pp. 4261–4265. DOI: 10.1109/ICIP.2014.7025865

[44] Lukin V., Abramov S., Ponomarenko N., Uss M., Zriakhov M., Vozel B., Chehdi K., Astola J. Methods and automatic procedures for processing images based on blind evaluation of noise type and characteristics. SPIE Journal on Advances in Remote Sensing. 2011;5(1):27/053502. DOI: 10.1117/1.3539768

[45] Abramov S., Krivenko S., Roenko A., Lukin V., Djurovic I., Chobanu M. Prediction of filtering efficiency for DCT-based image denoising. In: Proceedings of MECO; Budva, Montenegro; June 2013. pp. 97–100.

[46] Kozhemiakin R.A., Zemliachenko A.N., Lukin V.V., Abramov S.K., Vozel B. An approach to prediction and providing of compression ratio for DCT-based coder applied to remote sensing images. Ukrainian Journal of Earth Remote Sensing. Forthcoming. No 9, 2016, pp. 22-29.

[47] Rubel O.S., Kozhemiakin R.O., Krivenko S.S., Lukin V.V. A method for predicting denoising efficiency for color images. In: Proceedings of 2015 IEEE 35th International

Conference on Electronics and Nanotechnology (ELNANO); Kiev, Ukraine; April 2015. pp. 304–309.

[48] Cameron C., Windmeijer A., Frank A.G., Gramajo H., Cane D.E., Khosla C. An R-squared measure of goodness of fit for some common nonlinear regression models. Journal of Econometrics. 1997;77(2):1790–1792. (see http://www.irbis-nbuv.gov.ua/cgi-bin/irbis_nbuv/cgiirbis_64.exe?I21DBN=LINK&P21DBN=UJRN&Z21ID=&S21REF=10&S21CNR=20&S21STN=1&S21FMT=ASP_meta&C21COM=S&2_S21P03=FILA=&2_S21STR=ukjdzz_2016_9_5), No 9, 2016, pp. 22–29.

[49] Rissanen J. Modeling by shortest data description. Automatica. 1978;14(5):465–471. DOI: 10.1016/0005-1098(78)90005-5

[50] Kozhemiakin R., Abramov S., Lukin V., Djurović B., Djurović I., Vozel B. Lossy compression of Landsat multispectral images. In: Proceedings of MECO; Bar, Montenegro; June 2016. pp. 104–107.

Section 2

Image Segmentation and Classification

Chapter 3

Mineral Froth Image Classification and Segmentation

Wang Weixing and Chen Liangqin

Additional information is available at the end of the chapter

http://dx.doi.org/10.5772/65028

Abstract

Accurate segmentation of froth images is always a problem in the research of floating modeling based on Machine Vision. Since a froth image is with the characteristic of complexity and diversity, it is a feasible research idea for the workflow of which the froth image is firstly classified and then segmented by the image segmentation algorithm designed for each type of froth images. This study proposes a new froth image classification algorithm. The texture feature is extracted to complete the classification. Meanwhile, an improved method based on the original valley-edge detection algorithm is also proposed in the study. Firstly, the fractional differential is introduced to design the new valley-edge detection templates which can extract more information on bubble edges after the enhancement of the weak edges, and finally the close bubble boundaries are obtained by carrying out the improved deburring and gap connection algorithms. Experimental results show that the new classification method can be used to distinguish the types of small, middle and large bubble images. The improved image segmentation algorithm can well reduce the problems of over-segmentation and under-segmentation, and it is in higher adaptability.

Keywords: froth image, bubble, classification, segmentation, valley-edge detection

1. Introduction

In the conventional mineral processing, froth flotation is the most widely used method [1]. Based on the difference between the physical and chemical properties of mineral surfaces, flotation is a separation method by making the mineral particles selectively attached to the bubbles [2]. The froth flotation is a continuous physical and chemical process occurring in the solid, liquid and gas-phase interface [3], in which the froth layer is a key factor. The visual feature of the surface of the froth layer is a direct indicator of flotation process conditions and production performance [3–7]. The flotation operation process is controlled by workers' visual observation of the surface condition of the foam layer [8–10]. Clearly, this traditional way of working has many disadvantages, such as strong subjectivity, randomness and huge errors [11]. It seriously affects the flotation efficiency and performance. Since the 1990s of the last century, Machine Vision is introduced into the flotation process monitoring. Machine Vision flotation monitoring and control system is on the research about obtaining quantitative characteristics of the visual surface of the foam layer by using a computer, cameras and other industrial equipments, and applying digital image processing and artificial intelligence and other advanced technologies [12]. And further, by studying the relationship between these features and the flotation performance the flotation modeling can be realized, and accordingly the automatic monitoring and optimization control of the flotation process can be achieved [13]. Machine vision is a nonintrusive, cost-effective, reliable technique for monitoring and controlling flotation systems [14–17].

In recent years, with the rapid development of computer and digital image processing technology, the bubble image analysis attracts more and more attention. The University of Queensland, Australia, the United States of Process Technology Co., Ltd., UK, Sweden, Finland, Italy, Chile and other countries have been joined the research of the flotation process by computer vision. Efforts continues to be directed into how to measure accurately the physical and dynamic features of froth, and linking concentrate grade with these measurable attributes of the froth phase, although this is creating difficult [5, 12, 18]. The physical features of froth are the bubble size distribution, bubble shapes and colors. These features can be measured directly from digitized images of the froth, in which the image is segmented in order to explicitly identify individual bubbles on the froth surface [5]. Edge detection algorithm and Watershed algorithm are commonly used for bubble image segmentation and edge delineation. Reference [19] has proposed the use of valley-edge detection and valley-edge tracing to segment froth images. The method firstly uses Otsu threshold algorithm to extract the white spot areas on bubbles, under which the froth images are classified as the large, medium, small and mix-sized bubble images; then based on the different gray scale distribution characteristics for each class, a set of valley-edge detection algorithms are designed to extract the bubble edges. For each category, the filtering parameters and the threshold used in valley-edge detection are set separately, which can obtain good segmentation results for different classes of images. Hence, before the image segmentation the froth image must be classified correctly, otherwise the segmentation result will be unsatisfactory. In the end, a cleanup procedure based on valley-edge tracing is carried out to complete the gap connection between the valley edges. The advantage of such methods based on the edge detection algorithm is the fast calculation speed, but it is sensitive to noise in large bubble images, and the rough areas of the bubble surface always result in a large number of false boundary information, which are difficult to be completely removed. Watershed-based algorithms are morphological approaches based on a simulation of water rising from a set of markers [5].Watershed algorithm can obtain good segmentation results when they are used to process the froth images of bubble size distributed more uniform, but for the images with the large variation of the bubble sizes, it is easy to encounter the over-segmentation or under-segmentation problems.

Around these two categories, many improved methods and other algorithms have been studied [20–25]. However, to a certain degree these improved algorithms suffer the same problem that the balance of the accuracy of bubbles extraction and the high adaptability of algorithms is difficult to achieve in the application. Measuring the bubble size distribution is an intricate process [26]. No algorithm can obtain good segmentation result for all types of froth images. Currently, there are several commercial froth image processing systems, such as FrothMaster (Outokumpu), SmartFroth (UCT) and VisioFroth (Metso). About the bubble size and shape measurement, each of the systems is only available in some special cases, not for all the cases. The implementation of a long-term fully automated flotation control system is difficult due to the image segmentation problem [12, 18].

In this study, a new classification algorithm and a new image segmentation algorithm of froth images are proposed. The new classification algorithm combines the size feature of white spot and the texture feature. And the new image segmentation algorithm is improved based on the original valley-edge detection algorithm.

2. Flotation and froth image

2.1. Flotation mechanism and process

Flotation process is described as in **Figure 1**: A flotation agent is added to the pulp and mixed mechanically, while air is blown to create bubbles; under certain operating conditions of flotation, the hydrophobic mineral particles are adhered to the surface of bubbles during the floating of the air bubbles, and eventually rise to the surface of the flotation cell mineral to enrich and form a froth layer, while the hydrophilic particles are primarily retained in water and are discharged with the tailings finally. The flotation process circuit includes grinding, classification and flotation roughing, cleaning and scavenging operations. Each flotation bank includes dozens of flotation cells. **Figure 2** shows a concise flowchart of the flotation circuit. The rough concentration from the rougher cell should be processed by the subsequent flotation procedures to improve the concentration grade. The first operation in which the slurry is fed is called rougher operation. The froth obtained from the rougher operation is again in the flotation process, which is called the cleaner operation. The tailing output from the rougher operation is again in the flotation process, which is called the scavenger operation. The outputs, including the tailing from the cleaner operation and the froth from the scavenger operation, are called the middle minerals. After the slurry is fed into the rougher cell, the useful mineral particles are adhered to the bubbles and floated to overflow the flotation cell and then fed into the cleaner operation from the pipe. The froth output from the cleaner operation is fed into the total fine groove and processed to get the final concentration production by settling and filtration operations. The underflow slurry of the rougher cells is put into the scavenger operation. The froth from the scavenger operation is back as middle mineral into the rougher cell to be processed again. The underflow slurry of the scavenger cells is converged into the total end groove. In the end groove, the tailing is discharged after the final operation. The flotation process is a continuous and complex industrial production process in which each subprocess is interrelated and interacted with each other.

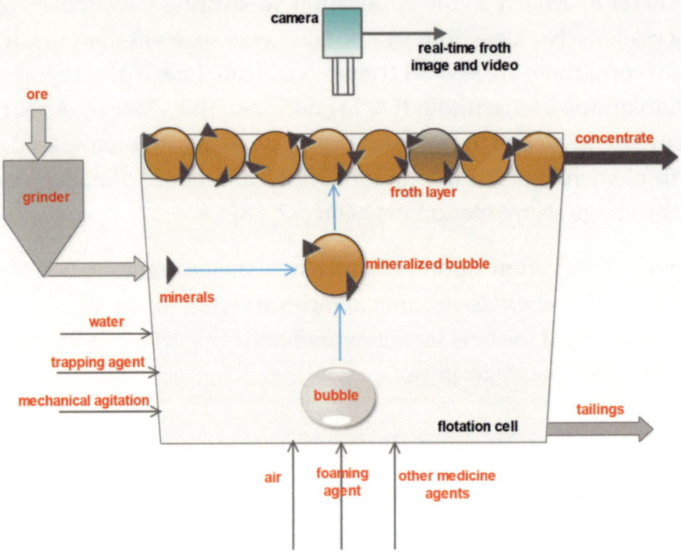

Figure 1. Principle of flotation cell.

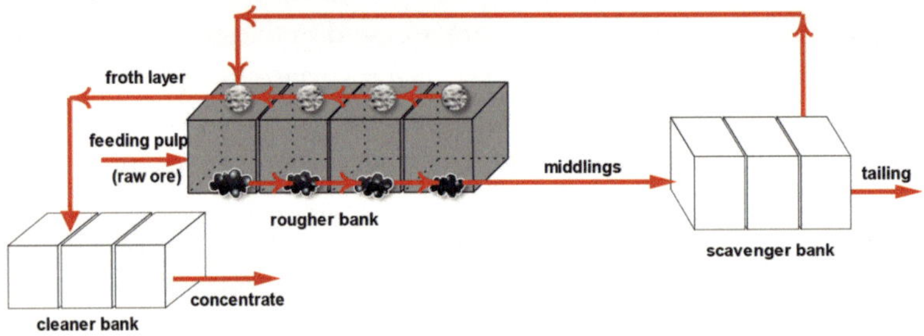

Figure 2. Schematic of flotation circuit.

2.2. Flotation image characteristic analysis

In the flotation system based on image analysis and machine vision, a CCD video camera is mounted vertically above a flotation cell to capture froth images. The froth image is a special kind of professional image. **Figure 3** shows a lead froth image. A typical flotation image has the following characteristics: (1) A large number of bubbles stick together to form the foreground of an image without background; (2) The bubbles sizes are different, and there is a high-light area (or more) on the top of each bubble, and the boundaries of bubbles are in low gray value; (3) The contrast is low, and there is noise on the surface of bubbles, and the illumination is uneven. In addition, there are often some black holes of different sizes on some bubble surfaces, and the colors of bubbles of different mineral flotation images are very different. Flotation is a dynamic and continuous process, and therefore the bubble will be a growth, burst and merger process.

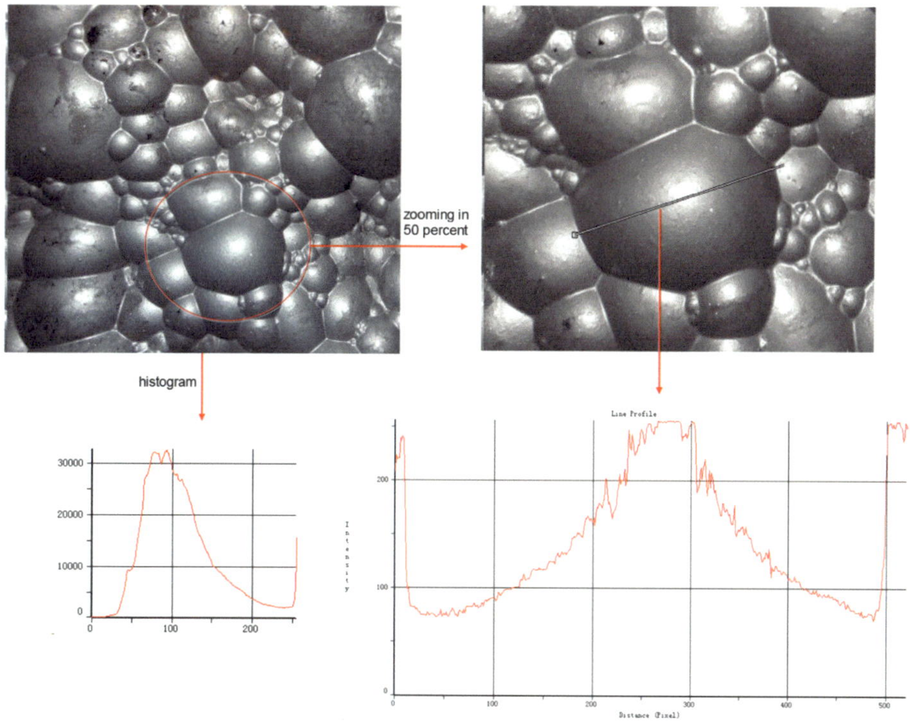

Figure 3. A froth image and its gray characteristic analysis.

All the characteristics of froth images make bubble delineation hard. Therefore, how to achieve an efficient froth image segmentation method has become a major task in this research field. Since a flotation image is with much noise and without background at all, the flotation image processing is very difficult. In order to achieve fast and efficient image processing results, it is necessary to classify froth image first, then the image segmentation is carried out.

3. Froth image classification

As described above, before image segmentation, a froth image should be classified into accurate categories based on the bubble size. Previous studies have shown that in most of the cases, each of the bubbles in a froth image includes one or more high light areas, called white spots, the size of a white spot is proportional to the bubble size and the average size of the white spots is inversely proportional to the number of the bubbles in a froth image. The white spots are generated by the artificial illumination in a froth cell.

3.1. Classification method on the white spot

One kind of bubble classification method is based on the size of the white spot area of bubble. Firstly, the white spot is extracted by an image segmentation method such as a method on threshold. And then the average size of the white spot is used to classify the bubble image category. Similarly, it can also determine the category based on the number distribution of white spots. **Figure 4** presents three froth image binarization results, which can be used for image classification.

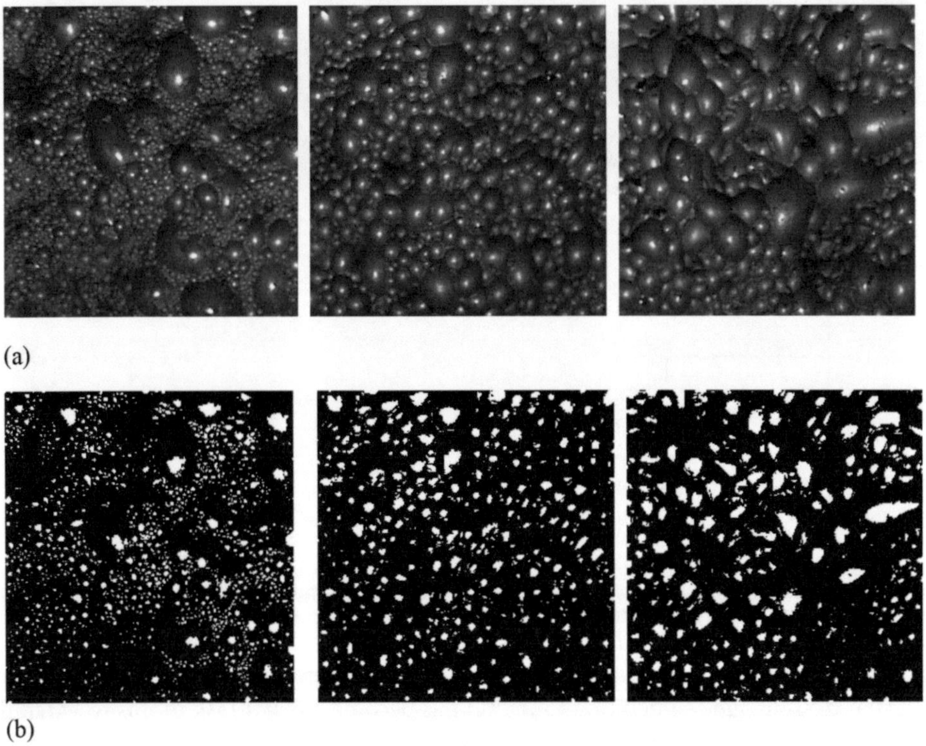

Figure 4. Image classification based on the white spot. (a) Three types froth images, from left to right are mixed, middle and large bubble image. (b) Extracted white spot using Otsu threshold segmentation method.

3.2. Classification method on bubble surface texture feature

3.2.1. Bubble surface texture feature based on GLCM

In this section, a new classification method is proposed.

Based on the above-mentioned information, for the correct bubble segmentation results, we believe that the froth images should be classified into four classes: (1) images with small size bubbles (or mixed with a few middle/large size bubbles), which is called "small bubble;" (2) images in which most of the bubbles have a medium size, which is called "middle bubble;" (3)

http://dx.doi.org/10.5772/65028

images, where, most of the bubbles have a relatively large size, which is called "large bubble"; and (4) a few white spots can be detected or the detected white spots with a very large size, which is called "super-large bubble."

For class 1 images, a bubble consists of a few pixels, it is difficult to detect the contours of bubbles, but it is enough to estimate the bubble size distribution property by detecting white spots; for class 2, 30–60 pixels are contained in a bubble, a rough contour location can be detected by using a morphological segmentation algorithm; therefore, just the size distribution and texture information can be obtained; for class 3, where the contours of bubbles are clear, a small miss-location of bubble contours cannot affect shape analysis results, thereby, the size, shape distribution can be obtained exactly with an image segmentation algorithm based on bubble contour tracing; and for class 4, the white spots information is less useful, only valuable information of bubbles is of bubble edges, so the valley-edge detection algorithm was developed and used for estimation of size and texture information.

Texture is about the pixels collection with a certain size and shape. It is used to express the properties of the surface or structure of an object. Texture provides a measure of roughness, smoothness, regularity and other features of an image in an intuitive manner. The methods commonly used to extract texture can be summed up in two categories: the method on the spatial domain and the method on the frequency domain. In the space domain method, the brightness variation, relevance and direction of adjacent pixels are calculated, and then the characteristics of image texture are obtained using a statistical method. The analysis of power spectrum is a method widely applied to extract the texture of the frequency domain. The fine texture is reflected in the higher frequency, and the rough texture is reflected in the low frequency. For that, the texture features can be extracted from the spectral distribution of an image. However, the Fourier transformation should be calculated for the power spectrum, which leads to the large amount of computation.

In this paper, gray-level co-occurrence matrix (GLCM) is used to describe the texture feature of a bubble image. GLCM is a method based on the space domain. It provides the probability of a certain gray value variation between adjacent pixels. GLCM is different to histogram of an image. The histogram gives the statistical result. GLCM is a function of distance and direction. Given the condition and the size of window, the numbers of pixel pairs that meet with the condition are calculated. For an image of $M \times N$ size, given a predetermined direction θ (0°, 45°, 90°, 135°, etc.) and a distance value d, the element of $P(i, j|d, \theta)$ describes the probability of appearances of a pixel pair with the gray value i and j, of which the two pixels are along θ direction and at a distance of d.

Once the co-occurrence matrix is calculated, the texture features can be described using the matrix. The most used ones are the following:

1. Energy, the formula is as:

$$FT_1 = ASM = \sum_i \sum_j \left[P(i, j \mid d, \theta) \right]^2 \tag{1}$$

Energy is the square values of the element of GLCM. The texture changes more regular, the value of energy becomes greater.

2. Contrast, the formula is expressed as follows:

$$FT_2 = CON = \sum_i \sum_j P(i,j \mid d,\theta)(i-j)^2 \tag{2}$$

The clarity of an image is higher, the value of contrast is greater.

3. Entropy, the formula is:

$$FT_3 = \sum_i \sum_j P(i,j \mid d,\theta) \log_2 P(i,j \mid d,\theta) \tag{3}$$

Entropy is a measure of irregularities of texture in an image. The distribution of the gray value of the image is messier and more disordered, and the value of entropy is greater.

4. Evenness, the formula can be expressed as:

$$FT_4 = IDM = \sum_i \sum_j \frac{P(i,j \mid d,\theta)}{1+(i-j)^2} \tag{4}$$

The change and distribution of the local area of an image is less and more uniform, the value of evenness is greater.

5. Correlation, the formula is as follows:

Correlation is the expression of the degree of similarity of GLCM elements between each column and row.

$$\begin{aligned} FT_5 = C\,O\,R &= \sum_i \sum_j \frac{ijP(i,j \mid d,\theta) - \mu_x \mu_y}{\sigma_x \sigma_y} \\ \mu_x &= \sum_i j \sum_j P(i,j \mid d,\theta) \\ \mu_y &= \sum_i j \sum_j P(i,j \mid d,\theta) \\ \sigma_x^2 &= \sum_i (i-\mu_{x)}^2 \sum_j P(i,j \mid d,\theta) \\ \sigma_y^2 &= \sum_j (i-\mu_{y)}^2 \sum_i P(i,j \mid d,\theta) \end{aligned} \tag{5}$$

In the experiment, four froth images are chosen to carry out GLCM calculation. Based on human eyes, the chosen four images are classified into small, middle, large and super large bubble images, as shown in **Figure 5**. Energy, entropy, contrast and correlation are obtained from GLCM, and the results are shown in **Table 1**. In the calculation of GLCM, the distance *d* is 1, and for each texture feature, the average value in 0°,45°,90°,135°four directions is calculated as the final value.

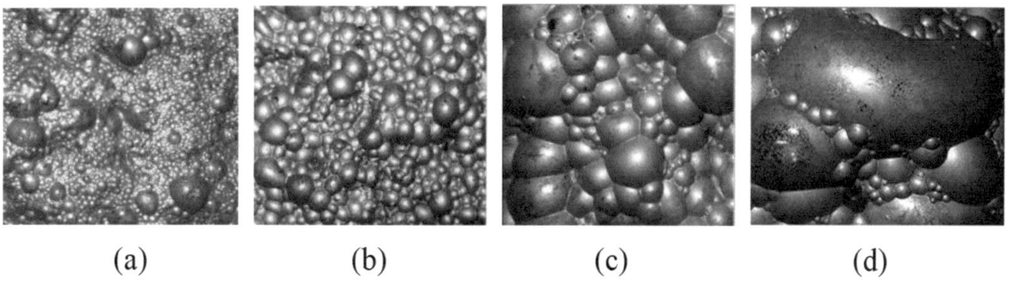

Figure 5. Four types of bubble images. (a) Small, (b) middle, (c) large and (d) super-large.

Image type	Energy	Entropy	Contrast	Correlation
Small	0.0512	3.6108	1.9535	0.1227
Middle	0.0382	3.7851	1.5868	0.1113
Large	0.0644	3.3802	1.0884	0.1366
Super-large	0.0596	3.5659	1.6412	0.1284

Table 1. GLCM texture features of four images in **Figure 5**.

Tests are carried out on 50 images, including the four types of bubble images. The statistical data show that for the small, middle and large bubble images, the value of the contrast parameter of each type has a significant difference distribution area. The value of the small bubble images is the maximum one, and the area is about 1.9–2.1; and The value of the small bubble image is the maximum one, and the corresponding area is about 1.9–2.1; and the contrast value of the middle bubble image is about 1.4–1.6. The only exception is the super-large bubble image. The value of the super-large bubble image is not distributed at a fixed interval.

Based on the above analysis, a method combining the size of the white spot area and the texture feature is proposed to classify the bubble images. The input image is firstly segmented to extract the white spots. If the average size of the white spot areas is greater than a given threshold, the input image is classified into a super-large bubble image. If not, GLCM of the input image is calculated to extract the contrast feature, and then the image is classified into the small, middle and large bubble image based on the difference distribution area of the value of the contrast feature.

3.2.2. *Classification experiments and results based on SVM*

After the texture features are extracted based on GLCM, these features can be used to design and train the classifier. And the classifier can be used to classify the froth images.

Support vector machine (SVM) was proposed based on the structural risk minimization principle. It means that the design principle of SVM is based on the maximization of the accuracy of both training and testing, or the minimization of the risk of both experience and expectation. For the traditional classifiers, the insufficient samples always lead to the imbalance between the training samples and the testing samples, and it affects the performance of the classifiers. SVM can overcome this shortcoming, and is one of the better machine learning algorithms. In this chapter, SVM method is used to classify the froth images.

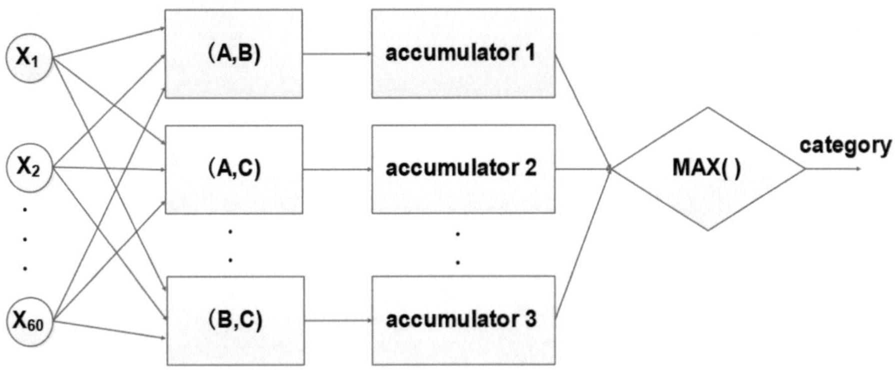

Figure 6. The voting and the decision process.

In the experiment, one-to-one way (two kinds of classifier) is used to design the classifier. Let class A denote the large froth image, class B for the middle froth image, and class C for the small froth image. Each two classes of A, B and C is composed to design and train the classifier. That's to say, there are total three classifiers, that is, classifier **(A, B)**, classifier **(A, C)** and classifier **(B, C)**. During the testing phase, the test sample x_i is sequentially fed into these three classifiers, and then the voting way is used to decide the category. The specific voting procedure is described as follows:

1. The initialization process: set these variables as in initial value 0, that is, ***vote(A)*** = ***vote(B)*** = ***vote(C)*** = **0**;

2. The voting process: If the test sample x_i is judged as class A in the classifier **(A,B)**, then ***vote(A)*** = ***vote(A)*** **+ 1**, otherwise ***vote(B)*** = ***vote(B)*** + **1**;

   If the test sample x_i is judged as class A in the classifier **(A,C)**, then ***vote(A)*** = ***vote(A)*** + 1, otherwise ***vote(C)*** = ***vote(C)*** + ***1;***

   If the test sample x_i is judged as class B in the classifier **(B,C)**, then ***vote(B)*** = ***vote(B)*** + **1**, otherwise ***vote(C)*** = ***vote(C)*** + ***1;***

3. The final decision process: Find the category corresponding to the maximum based on the following formula, and the test sample x_i is classified into the corresponding class.

   Max(vote(A),vote(B),vote(C))

If there are two maximum values, the class corresponding to the first maximum is generally taken as the selected class. **Figure 6** gives the demonstration of the voting and decision process.

In the following section, we take the classifier **(A,B)**, that is, the classifier of the large froth image and the middle froth image, as an example to describe the design procedure. The designs of the other two classifiers are similar.

We chose the radial basis function (**RBF**) with the strong generalization ability as the kernel function of **SVM**. The formula of RBF is as follows:

$$K\left(x,x_i\right)=\exp\left(-\gamma\left|x-x_i\right|^2\right) \tag{6}$$

where $\gamma = \frac{1}{\sigma^2}$, and in our experiment, γ is set as 0.07.

In the experiment, 35 large froth images and 35 middle froth images are chosen as the datasets. Among the datasets, 15 samples of each class are selected as a training set and the remaining 20 samples of each class as a test set. That is, there are 30 training samples and 40 testing samples in total. Eight dimensions of the texture features based on GLCM of each sample are used including the mean and the standard deviation of the energy, entropy, moment of inertia and correlation feature.

The model of the classifier is obtained after the training of 30 samples, and then 40 testing samples are fed into the classifier to complete the prediction classification. **Figure 7** gives the classification results, of which ***label 1*** represents the large froth image and ***label -1*** for the middle froth image.

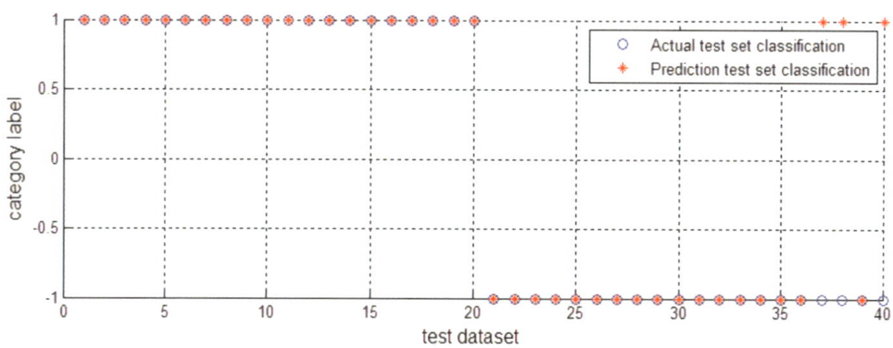

Figure 7. Forty test samples classification results of classifier **(A,B)**.

As shown in **Figure 7**, 20 large froth image test samples were all classified correctly and three samples were classified into the false class in 20 middle froth image test samples.

Classifier **(A,C)** and classifier **(B,C)** are designed as the above procedure. When the three classifiers are available, each test sample is fed into the classifier by turn and judged to the corresponding class by the voters. For 60 test samples, the classification results are shown in **Figure 8**, where ***label* 2** represents the large froth image test sample, ***label* 1** the middle froth image test sample and ***label* -1** the small froth image test sample. **Table 2** shows the statistical result corresponding to the figure. The statistical result shows that the probability of misclassification of the middle froth image test samples is highest. It leads to a higher misclassification rate for the reason that the texture feature of some middle froth images is possibly close to the large froth image or small froth image. However, the overall average correct classification rate, 83.3%, can basically meet the application requirements.

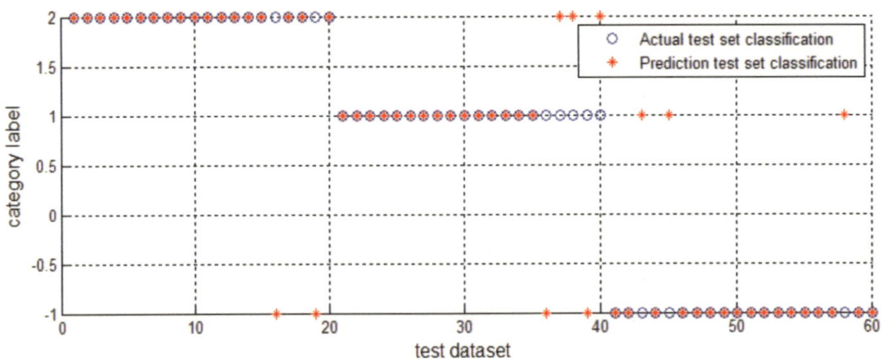

Figure 8. Sixty test samples classification results.

Froth image category	Number of test samples	Number of correct classification test samples	Correct classification rate (%)
Large	20	18	90
Middle	20	15	75
Small	20	17	85
Total amount	60	50	83.3

Table 2. The statistical data corresponding to **Figure 8**.

4. Froth image segmentation

Bubble image segmentation and delineation are the key to extract the morphological characteristics of froth. Classical image segmentation methods, such as methods on threshold and on edge detection, can only detect the highlighted areas of some bubbles. These methods fail to extract the edges of bubbles. Actually the practice has proved that the better methods are the ones based on valley-edge extraction and Watershed. Around these two categories, many improved methods have been proposed.

4.1. Segmentation method based on valley-edge extraction

Segmentation method based on valley-edge extraction was purposed by Wang et al. [19]. The algorithm includes valley-edge detection and valley-edge tracing. The detection process was designed on the gray value distribution feature of a cross-section of a froth image. It detects each pixel to see if it is the lowest valley point in a certain direction. If it is, then the pixel is used as the valley-edge candidate, and both its direction and location are marked. The above-mentioned search process is performed in the 0°, 45°, 90° and 135° four directions of the current pixel respectively. A threshold is set to find the greatest value, and then the detected point is marked as a valley-edge candidate point.

Valley-edge tracing is performed on the result image of valley-edge detection after simple denoising. First, the significant endpoints of curves are detected, and then the direction is estimated, and finally the contour is traced according to the information of direction of each new detected point and an intensity cost function.

It should be noted that good segmentation results could be obtained only if the input froth image is classified into the exact type. **Figure 9** gives the valley-edge extraction results of the four types of bubble images in **Figure 5**. We can see that over-segmentation or under-segmentation problem cannot be avoided in the four types of bubble images.

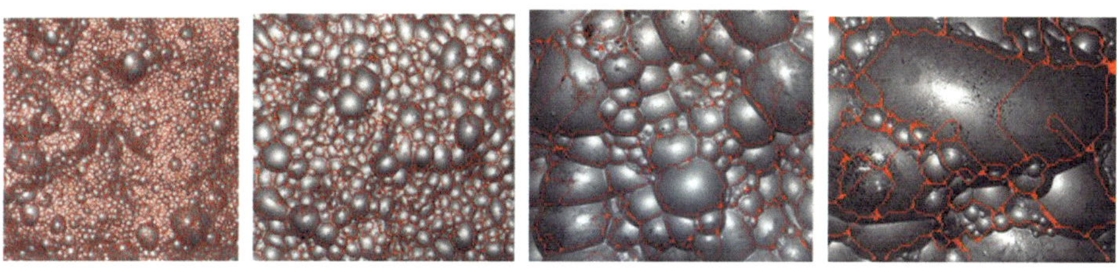

Figure 9. Segmentation results on the valley-edge extraction.

4.2. Segmentation method based on watershed

Watershed is a kind of segmentation method based on mathematical morphology. The watershed algorithm is used to find the local maximal values (Watersheds) of an image. Vincent and Soille [27] proposed and described the algorithm in detail. An image is seen as a topographical surface, with holes pierced at the location of the minima. As this surface is lowered into a lake, the water level within the surface will start to rise within each of the catchment basins. When the water from two catchment basins is about to merge, a dam is built to prevent this. At the end of the process, each minimum is surrounded by a dam, with the dams corresponding to the watershed of the image. In order to obtain the good segmentation result, minimal location of each object should be found to be as a marker, see Ref. [28]. **Figure 10** shows the watershed segmentation results of the four types of bubble images in **Figure 5**. The same problems with the valley-edge extraction method can be seen in the watershed segmentation results.

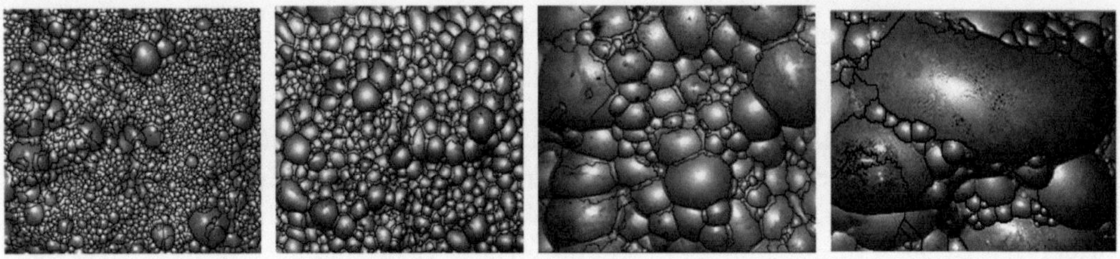

Figure 10. Segmentation results on Watershed.

4.3. New segmentation method based on valley-edge extraction

The main reason for that the froth image is hard to segment accurately is in the very weak boundaries of bubbles. Based on the original valley-edge extraction algorithm, we propose an improved segmentation method on the fractional integral. The valley-edge detection mask is designed based on the fractional integral in the improved method. The new mask helps to extract more details on the bubble edges.

The fractional integral of signal ***f(x)*** is defined as:

$$
\begin{aligned}
I^{v} f(x) \approx f(x) + vf(x-1) + \frac{v(v+1)}{2} f(x-2) + \frac{v(v+1)(v+3)}{6} \\
f(x-3) + \ldots + \frac{\Gamma(v+1)}{n!\Gamma(v-n+1)} f(x-n)
\end{aligned} \tag{7}
$$

And each factor is defined as follows:

$$
\begin{cases}
a_0 = 1,\ a_1 = v,\ a_2 = \dfrac{v(v+1)}{2} \\
a_3 = \dfrac{v(v+1)(v+2)}{6} \\
\vdots \\
a_n = \dfrac{\Gamma(v+1)}{n!\Gamma(v-n+1)}
\end{cases} \tag{8}
$$

The first three coefficients, i.e. a_0, a_1, a_2, are taken to define the eight detection templates of the valley-edge detection algorithm. The eight templates are defined as shown in **Figure 11**.

http://dx.doi.org/10.5772/65028

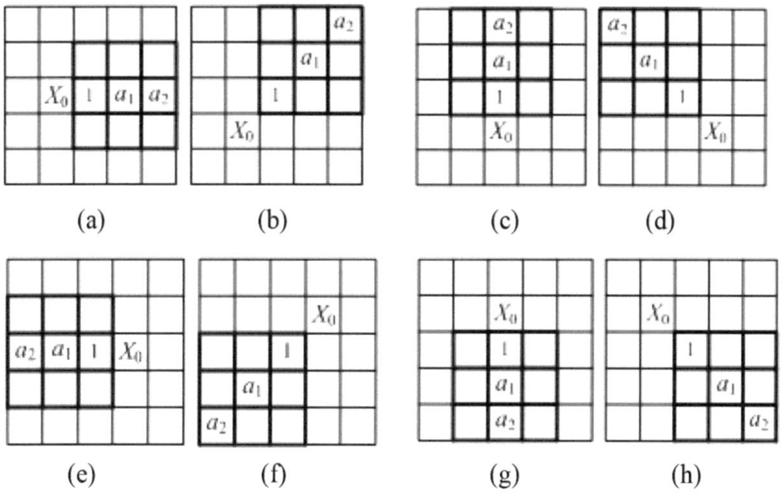

Figure 11. Eight directions templates. (a) X_1, (b) X_2, (c) X_3, (d) X_4, (e) X_5, (f) X_6, (g) X_7 and (h) X_8.

Based on the eight direction templates, the convolution operation is carried out on the image. For each pixel ***f(i,j)***, eight operation results can be obtained, each of which is marked with $G_1 \sim G_8$. The convolution operation rules of the eight directions are defined as:

$$G_1 = \frac{1}{1+a_1+a_2}\sum_{s=-b}^{b}\sum_{t=-b}^{b} X_1^* f(s,t) \tag{9}$$

$$G_2 = \frac{1}{1+a_1+a_2}\sum_{s=-b}^{b}\sum_{t=-b}^{b} X_2^* f(s,t) \tag{10}$$

$$G_3 = \frac{1}{1+a_1+a_2}\sum_{s=-b}^{b}\sum_{t=-b}^{b} X_3^* f(s,t) \tag{11}$$

$$G_4 = \frac{1}{1+a_1+a_2}\sum_{s=-b}^{b}\sum_{t=-b}^{b} X_4^* f(s,t) \tag{12}$$

$$G_5 = \frac{1}{1+a_1+a_2}\sum_{s=-b}^{b}\sum_{t=-b}^{b} X_5^* f(s,t) \tag{13}$$

$$G_6 = \frac{1}{1+a_1+a_2}\sum_{s=-b}^{b}\sum_{t=-b}^{b} X_6^* f(s,t) \tag{14}$$

$$G_7 = \frac{1}{1+a_1+a_2} \sum_{s=-b}^{b} \sum_{t=-b}^{b} X_7^* f(s,t) \tag{15}$$

$$G_8 = \frac{1}{1+a_1+a_2} \sum_{s=-b}^{b} \sum_{t=-b}^{b} X_8^* f(s,t) \tag{16}$$

In the above-mentioned formula, ***b*** is the size of the template, and in this chapter we take, ***b*** = 3.

In accordance with the detection rules of the original valley-edge extraction algorithm, if the values of the two directions of each pair are both greater than the value of the given threshold *T*, then the value of the current center pixel ***f(i,j)***, the pixel ***f(i,j)***, would be marked as a valley point of the current direction. And the new values of the four directions are set as follows:

$$g_m(i,j) = \begin{cases} \dfrac{G_m + G_{m+4}}{2}, & G_m - f(i,j) \geq T \,\&\&\, G_{m+4} - f(i,j) \geq T \\ 0, & other \end{cases} \tag{17}$$

where ***m*** = 1, 2, 3, 4. Take the maximum value of the four directions as the final value of valley point ***g(i,j)***. Finally, the valley-edge image is binarized based on the selected threshold ***T2***.

$$f(i,j) = \begin{cases} 255, & g_m(i,j) \geq T2 \\ 0, & other \end{cases} \tag{18}$$

Figure 12 shows the bubble edges obtained by the improved valley-edge extraction method. The original images are from **Figure 5**.

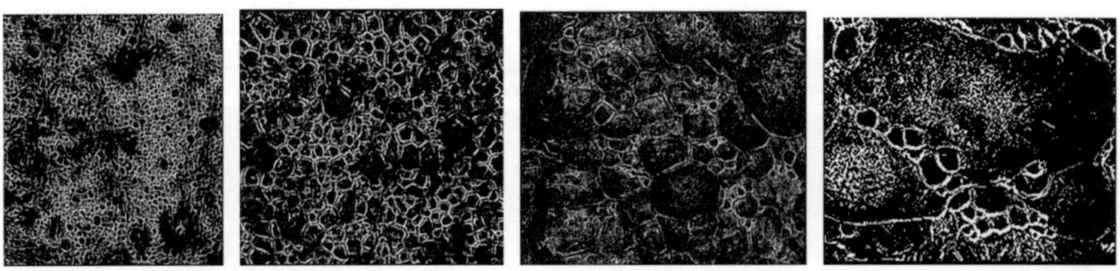

Figure 12. Bubble edge extracted by improved valley-edge extraction method.

In the bubble edge image, as shown in **Figure 12**, there are many isolated point noise, short lines and gaps. A series of post-processing functions must be applied to get clean and complete closure of the boundaries of bubbles. The post-processing procedure includes denoising, burr removal and gap connection.

(1) Denoising processing

The first step is for the expansion procedure on eight-neighbor, and the second step is for the corrosion procedure on four-neighbor. The expansion processing can be used to connect the small gaps, and the corrosion processing can eliminate the small glitches, and the boundaries can become smoother after the expansion and corrosion processing. **Figure 13** gives the structural elements of the expansion and corrosion.

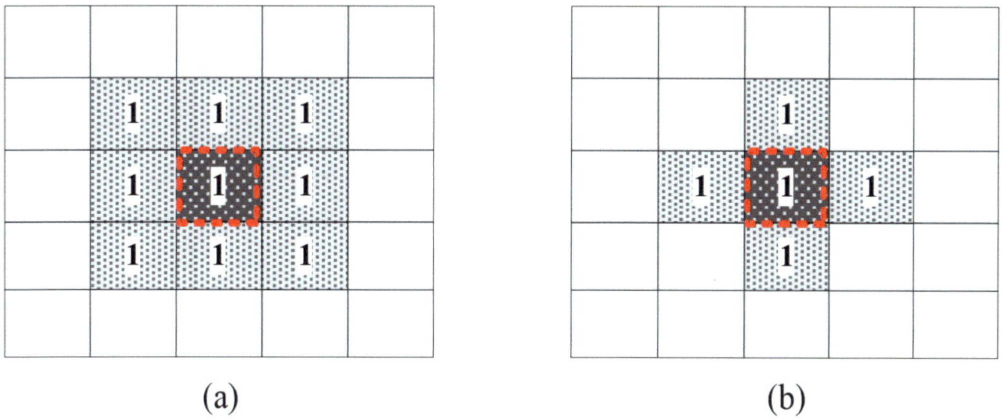

Figure 13. Structural elements of expansion and corrosion. (a) Expansion structure on 8-neighbor. (b) Corrosion structure on 4-neighbor.

(2) Deburring process

For the short line noise, the traditional method is to eliminate them based on a given length threshold. In order to maintain more information of bubble boundaries as possible while removing the glitch noise, an improved deburring algorithm is designed, and it is shown in **Figure 14**.

(3) Gap connection processing

There are some boundary gaps after the deburring process. A normal method for the gap connection is to find the endpoints of the fracture gaps firstly and then to search other candidate endpoints in the surrounding area of the current pixel. If the candidate endpoints are found, the connection is carried out or not based on the condition of the distance and angle difference between the current endpoint and the candidate endpoint.

Since the bubble boundary is complex, an improved gap connection algorithm combined the long connection and the short connection is studied. **Figure 15** shows the workflow of the improved algorithm.

In the above algorithm, the processing of the short connection is described as follows. When the distance between the two endpoints is less than a given value (here it is taken as 4 pixels), the two endpoints are connected directly.

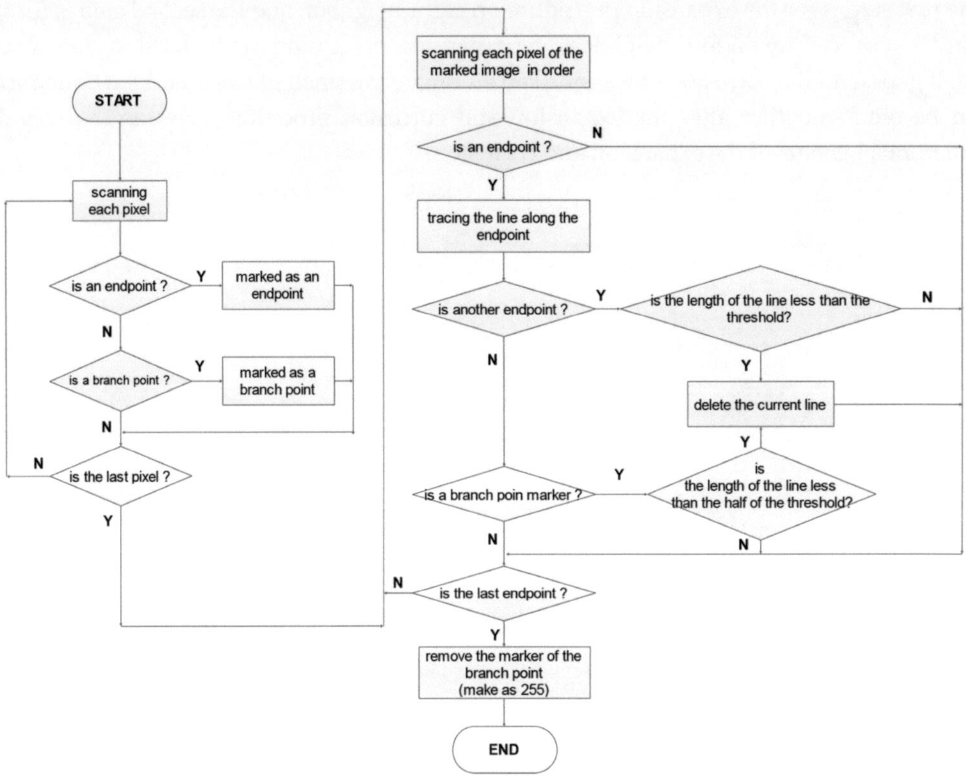

Figure 14. Workflow of improved deburring algorithm.

The long connection processing is a connection method based on the maximum entropy threshold method. The processing steps are shown as follows:

a. Take the original froth image as a reference image.

b. Calculate the threshold value of the original froth image based on the maximum entropy threshold. There is a fact that the gray value of bubble boundary is less than the threshold.

c. Use the current endpoint and the candidate endpoint to locate the positions in the original image. If there is boundary information (the gray value is less than the threshold value of step b), the two endpoints can be connected.

For the four types of bubble images in **Figure 5**, the proposed improved segmentation method is tested on them. The segmentation results are shown in **Figure 16**. Compared with the results of the original valley-edge extraction and the watershed methods, the improved algorithm has the advantage of restraining the over-segmentation and under-segmentation problems.

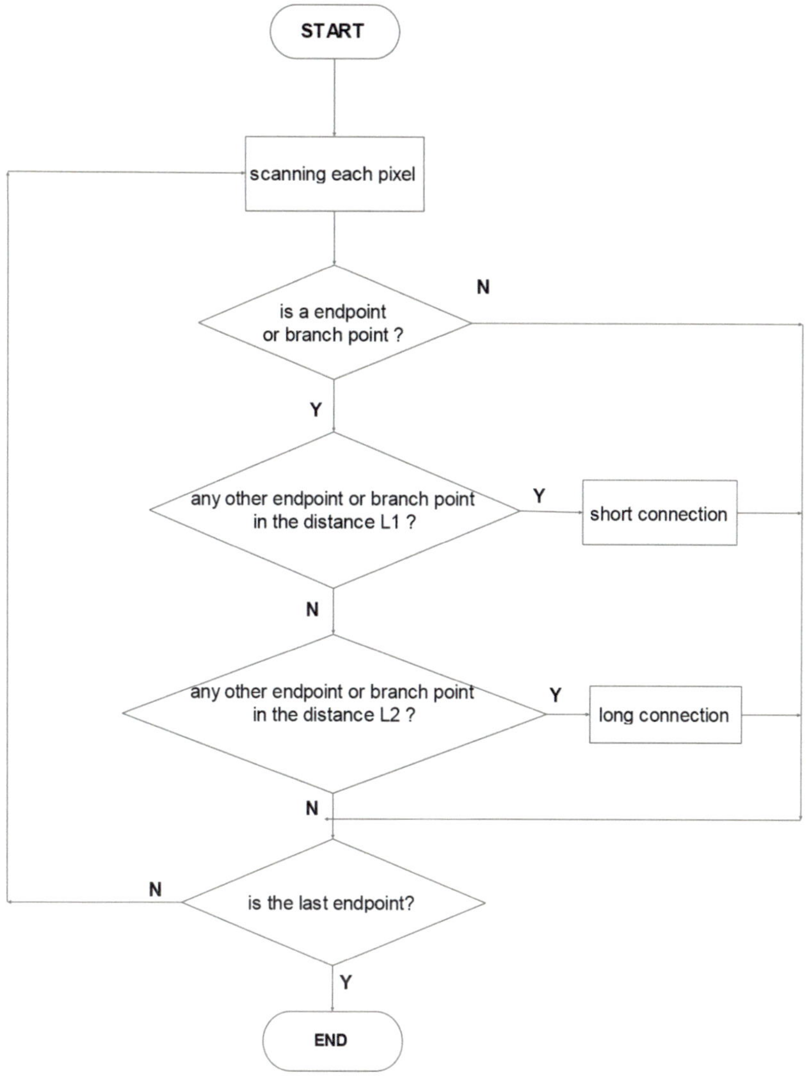

Figure 15. Workflow of improved gap point connection algorithm.

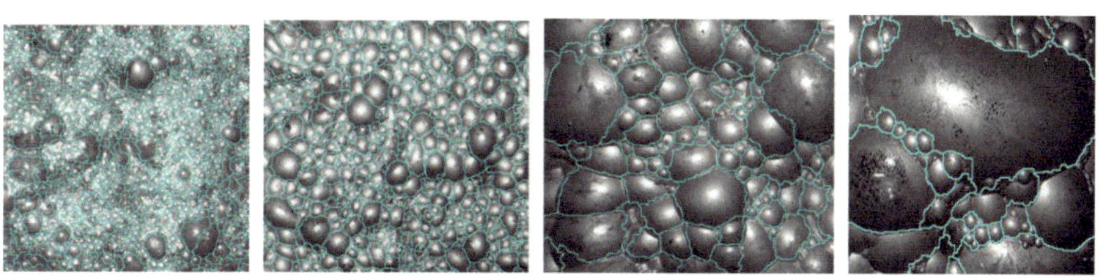

Figure 16. Final segmentation results on improved valley-edge extraction algorithm.

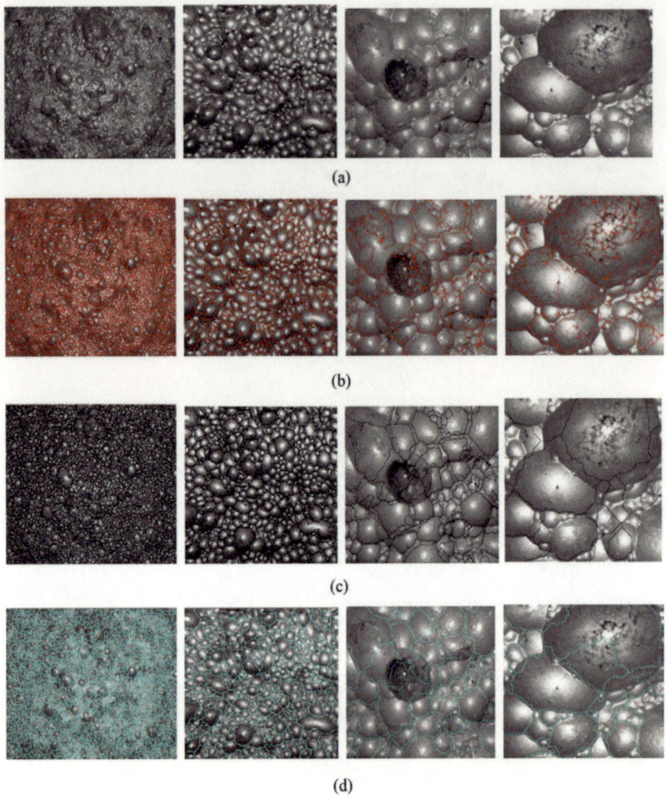

Figure 17. Comparison between improved algorithm and other segmentation algorithms. (a) Original froth images belonging to the four types. (b) Results of the original valley-edge detection algorithm. (c) Results of the watershed algorithm. (d) Results of our improved algorithm.

Another experiment is carried out on the other four types of froth images as shown in **Figure 17**. The experimental results demonstrate again that no algorithm can always obtain good segmentation result for all types of froth images. For the froth image with the uniform bubble size distribution, the segmentation result is always satisfactory. The black hole areas and the raised mineral particle areas always lead to the over-segmentation problem. And for the super large type of the froth image, the segmentation results of the four algorithms are all not satisfactory. The noise and the uneven gray value distribution become more obvious for the super large type of the image, so the position deviation of the extracted bubbles edges, over-segmentation and other problems become more serious.

5. Conclusion

The classification and the segmentation of froth images are discussed and analyzed in this paper. And for each of the two questions, a new method is proposed.

1. The existing classification and segmentation methods are discussed firstly.

2. A new froth image classification method is proposed. It adopts GLCM to extract the contrast texture feature, and based on the difference distribution area of the contrast feature, the froth image can be classified into small, middle or large bubble image. The classification experiments and results based on SVM show that the supposed method is feasible for the application.

3. An improved froth image segmentation method is suggested based on the original valley-edge extraction algorithm. Firstly, the fractional differential is introduced to design the new eight direction templates used to extract the bubble boundary. Secondly, the mathematical morphology methods including expansion and corrosion are used to denoise. Thirdly, an improved deburring algorithm is used to remove burrs. Finally, an improved gap connection combined the long connection and the short connection is applied to form the close and integral bubble boundary.

4. The experimental results demonstrate the effectiveness of the two improved algorithms. A froth image can be correctly classified using the new classification method. The improved segmentation algorithm can reduce over-segmentation and under-segmentation.

However, because of the complexity, particularity, diversity, randomness and dynamic of froth images, it should be noted that the difficulties of the classification and segmentation of froth images are still not completely overcome.

Author details

Wang Weixing* and Chen Liangqin

*Address all correspondence to: znn525d@qq.com

College of Physics and Information Engineering, Fuzhou University, Fuzhou, Fujian, China

References

[1] Nissinen A, Lehikoinen A, Mononen M, et al. Mint: Estimation of the bubble size and bubble loading in a flotation froth using electrical resistance tomography. Minerals Engineering. 2014; 69: 1–12. DOI:

[2] Napier-Munn T, Wills BA. Wills' Mineral Processing Technology: an Introduction to the Practical Aspects of Ore Treatment and Mineral Recovery. Butterworth: Heinemann. 2011.

[3] Farrokhpay S. Mint: The significance of froth stability in mineral flotation—a review. Advances in Colloid and Interface Science. 2011; 166: 1–7.

[4] Nunez F, Cipriano A. Mint: Visual information model based predictor for froth speed control in flotation process. Mineral engineering. 2009; 22: 366–371.

[5] Aldrich C, Marais C, Shean B J, et al. Mint: Online monitoring and control of froth flotation systems with machine vision: a review. International Journal of Mineral Processing. 2010; 96(1–4): 1–13.

[6] Kistner M, Jemwa G T, Aldrich C. Mint: Monitoring of mineral processing systems by using textural image analysis. Mineral Engineering.2013; 52: 169–177.

[7] Neethling S J, Cilliers J J. Mint: Modelling flotation froths. International Journal of Mineral Processing. 2003; 72: 267–287.

[8] Moolman DW, Eksteen JJ, Aldrich C, et al. Mint: The significance of flotation froth appearance for machine vision control. International Journal of Mineral Processing. 1996; 48 : 135–158.

[9] Reddick J F, Hesketh A H, Morar S H, et al. Mint: An evaluation of factors affecting the robustness of colour measurement and its potential to predict the grade of flotation concentrate. Minerals Engineering. 2009; 22: 64–69.

[10] Tan J K, Liang L, Peng Y L, et al. Mint: The concentrate ash content analysis of coal flotation based on froth images. Minerals Engineering. 2016; 92: 9–20.

[11] Zhang J, Tang Z, Liu J, et al. Mint: Recognition of flotation working conditions through froth image statistical modeling for performance monitoring. Minerals Engineering. 2016; 86: 116–129.

[12] Jovanovic I, Miljanovic L, Jovanovic T. Mint: Soft computing-based modeling of flotation process—A review. Minerals Engineering. 2015; 84: 34–63.

[13] Morar S H, Harris M C, Bradshaw D J. Mint: The use of machine vision of predict flotation performance. Minerals Engineering. 2012; 36–38:31–36.

[14] Mehrabi A, Mehrshad N, Massinaei M. Mint: Machine vision based on monitoring of an industrial flotation cell in an iron flotation plant. International Journal of Mineral Processing. 2014; 133: 60–66.

[15] Moolman D W, Aldrich C, Schmitz G, et al. Mint: The interrelationship between surface froth characteristics and industrial flotation performance. Minerals Engineering. 1996; 9: 837–854.

[16] Bonifazi G, Massacci P, Meloni A. Mint: Prediction of complex sulfide flotation performances by a combined 3D fractal and colour analysis of the froths. Minerals Engineering. 2000; 13: 737–746.

[17] Vanegas C, Holtham P. Mint: On-line froth acoustic emission measurements in industrial sites. Minerals Engineering. 2008; 21: 883–888.

[18] Jahedsaravani A, Marhaban M, Massinaei M, et al. Mint: Froth-based modeling and control of a batch flotation process. International Journal of Mineral Processing. 2016; 146: 90–96.

[19] Wang WX, Bergholm F, Yang B. Mint: Froth delineation based on image classification. Minerals Engineering. 2003; 16(11): 1183–1192.

[20] Banford AW, Aktas Z. Mint: The effect of reagent addition strategy on the performance of coal flotation. Minerals Engineering. 2004; 17: 745–760.

[21] Yang CH, Xu CH, Mu XM, et al. Mint: Bubble size estimation using interfacial morphological information for mineral flotation process monitoring. Transaction of Nonferrous Metals Society of China. 2009; 19: 694–699.

[22] Wang WX, Chen LQ. Mint: Flotation bubble delineation based on Harris corner detection and local gray value minima. Minerals. 2015; 5(2): 142–163.

[23] Vinnett L, Alvares-Silva M. Indirect estimation of bubble size using visual techniques and superficial gas rate. Minerals Engineering. 2015; 81: 5–9.

[24] Jahedsaravani A, Marhaban M H, Massinaei M, et al. Mint: Development of a new algorithm for segmentation of flotation froth images. Minerals and Metallurgical Processing. 2014;31(1):66–72.

[25] Liu JP, Gui GH, Tang ZH, et al. Mint: Recognition of the operational statuses of reagent addition using dynamic bubble size distribution in copper flotation process. Minerals Engineering. 2013; 45: 128–141.

[26] Kracht W, Emery X, Paredes C. Mint: A stochastic approach for measuring bubble size distribution via image analysis. International Journal of Mineral Processing. 2013; 121: 6–11.

[27] Vincent L, Soille P. Mint: Watersheds in digital spaces: An efficient algorithm based on immersion simulutions. IEEE Transactions on Pattern Analysis Machine Intelligence. 1991; 13(6): 583–598.

[28] Vincent L. Mint: Morphological grayscale reconstruction in image analysis: Applications and efficient algorithms. IEEE Transactions on Image Processing. 1993; 2(2): 176–201.

Chapter 4

Segmentation of Fuzzy and Touching Cells Based on Modified Minimum Spanning Tree and Concave Point Detection

Wang Weixing and Lin Liqun

Additional information is available at the end of the chapter

http://dx.doi.org/10.5772/65029

Abstract

In order to segment fuzzy and touching cell images accurately, an improved algorithm is proposed based on minimum spanning tree (MST) and concave point detection. First, the cell images are smoothed and enhanced by a Gaussian filter. Then, the improved minimum spanning tree algorithm is used to segment the cell images. The MST algorithm is modified from three aspects, namely, weight function of edges, difference function of internal and inter region, and threshold function and parameter *k*. Furthermore, the problem of cell touching is solved by means of concave point detection. According to the rugged topography of touching cells, the concave points are found from the concave regions in the touching cell images, which are used to find the separation points quickly and accurately. Experimental results indicate that the new algorithm is ideal and effective.

Keywords: image segmentation, touching cell, MST, concave

1. Introduction

Nowadays, the medical image segmentation has a wide range of applications and researches in the medical research field, such as clinical diagnosis, pathological analysis, surgical planning, computer-aided surgery, and so on. Especially in recent years, the global incidence of cancer is increasing, and the early diagnosis of cancer is particularly important. Accurate segmentation is an important part in computer-aided analysis of blood cell image. And the blood cell image has the characteristics of cell touching, frequent severe adhesion, varying sizes of the cells, unclear cell boundary, and so on. It is difficult to accurately segment them. In particular, it has become a hot and difficult topic to study how to extract the cell region and achieve good segmentation of cell adhesion in the complex background.

Li et al. [1] and Al-Kofahi et al. [2] proposed that the cell touching is the most difficult problem in the field of cell segmentation, which easily leads to undersegmentation, and a plurality of cells adhered together is regarded as a cell detection and segmentation, eventually leading to cell density calculation, spatial distribution, and morphological analysis error. In the field of the concave point detection, Anand et al. [3] used the color as the feature for the segmentation of adhesion cells, the algorithm can be highly segment irregular images, and has high segmentation accuracy. To segment fuzzy and touching cell images accurately, Micko et al. [4] used fast radial symmetry transform (FRST) algorithm to extract target and background markers, an improved watershed algorithm based on FRST was proposed for the cell touching segmentation. Aymen et al. [5] put forward improved watershed algorithm based on gradient distance transform combined with concave detection. It can split touching cells, and oversegmentation phenomenon has been partially improved.

The image segmentation method based on graph theory is widely used in recent years [6–10]. Zhang et al. [11] proposed an image segmentation method based on watershed and graph theory. Wang et al. [12] adopted a new image segmentation algorithm based on graph theory and mathematical morphology. Fabijanska et al. [13] used an improved algorithm based on minimum spanning tree, which can increase the speed of image segmentation by reducing the number of vertices in the graph. Song et al. [14] made graph theory combined with the method of multiscale convolution network (MSCN) to segment the cervical cell touching images, and achieved good results. Other methods such as Hough circular detection [15] and adaptive template matching [16] are also used for the segmentation of cell images, but there is more error localization and they cannot effectively isolate the touching cells.

From the study, it is found that the segmentation accuracy rate of the above algorithms is not high, the main reason may be the effect of the complex image background, and the dividing lines of the touching cells cannot be accurately obtained [17]. Hence, the most critical is to split the touching cells.

In addition, Felzenszwalb and Huttenlocher algorithm (FH algorithm) [18] suggested an improved minimum spanning tree segmentation algorithm, namely, when the regional internal differences are larger than the pixel differences between regions, it identifies two regions belonging to a homogeneous region and then merges them. According to the different characteristics of the images, it can work with high efficiency. But it also has its own shortcomings; when the threshold is set too large, it is easy to produce oversegmentation problem, and if the threshold is set too small, the phenomenon of undersegmentation will appear, so the segmentation scale is difficult to be grasped.

Based on this, a new blood cell image segmentation algorithm is studied which is based on the graph theory and concave point detection.

2. Image segmentation based on graph theory

2.1. Graph theory

Let $G = (V, E)$ be an undirected graph with vertices $v_i \in V$, and edges $(v_i, v_j) \in E$, which are corresponding to pairs of neighboring vertices. Each edge $(v_i, v_j) \in E$ as a corresponding weight $w(v_i, v_j)$, which is a nonnegative measure of the dissimilarity between neighboring elements v_i and v_j. In the case of image segmentation, the elements in V are pixels and the weight of an edge is some measure of the dissimilarity between the two pixels connected by that edge (e.g., the difference in intensity, color, motion, location, or some other local attributes).

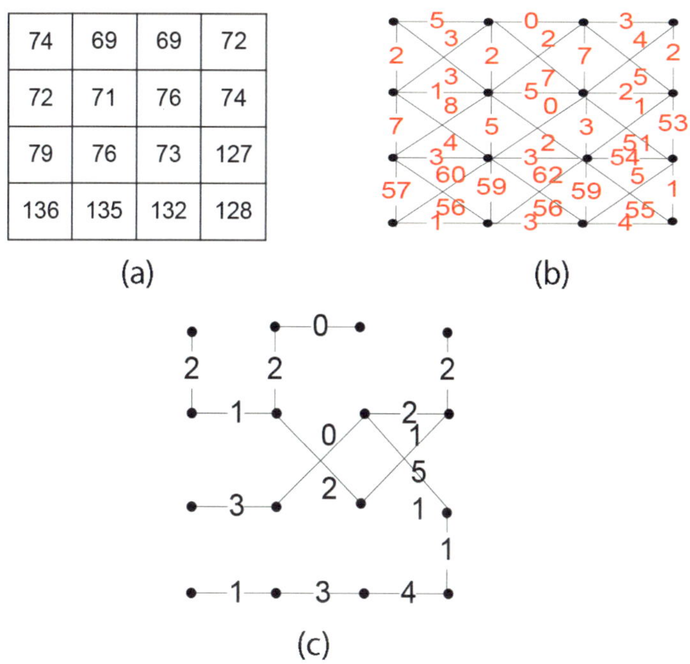

Figure 1. Minimum spanning tree: (a) pixel matrix of an image; (b) mapping diagram; **(c)** minimum spanning tree generated by graph.

By using the MST to segment images, the image information might be grasped from the overall situation, the growth process of MST can keep details of a region, and the process of looking for the smallest weight is adaptive, thus the global performance of an image meets the needs of the human visual characteristics. The algorithm can guarantee a good segmentation result in general, and it is of the high efficiency and has the simple data structure. So this paper uses the improved MST algorithm to conduct the cell image segmentation.

Using the MST algorithm, **Figure 2** is the segmentation result of **Figure 1(c)**. The threshold is greater than or equal to 51, and the segmentation result is shown in **Figure 2(a)**, which is the red region and the blue region; if the threshold is 4, then the image is divided into three parts, as shown in **Figure 2(b)**.

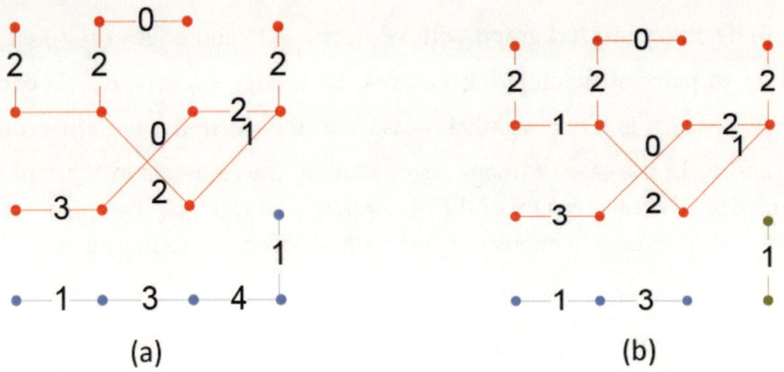

Figure 2. Minimum spanning tree segmentation: (a) segmentation results of threshold 51; (b) segmentation results of threshold 4.

Using the MST algorithm, **Figure 2** is the segmentation result of **Figure 1(c)**. The threshold is greater than or equal to 51, and the segmentation result is shown in **Figure 2(a)**, which is the red region and the blue region; if the threshold is 4, then the image is divided into three parts, as shown in **Figure 2(b)**.

Thus, the threshold K selection is very important for the segmentation results.

2.2. Modified MST algorithm

In this paper, the image is mapped into a weighted graph $G(V, E)$, and using Kruskal algorithm based on merged strategy. It is mainly related to three kinds of parameters: Gaussian filter parameter sigma; threshold function parameters of K used to control the extent of segmentation; and the parameters of minimum size, if the two neighboring region size is less than minimum size, the two regions are merged. The algorithm has the advantages of simple structure and high computational efficiency. For the algorithm, the following points of its improvement are presented.

2.2.1. Improved weight function of edges

According to Felzenszwalb and Huttenlocher algorithm (FH algorithm), the edge weights of MST only represent absolute difference of color information between two pixels, without considering their spatial position information. If the space position (distance) of the two pixels is farther away, their relevance in general will also become weak, we should increase the edge strength. Only the edge weights of gray level images are redefined in the literature [19]. It can be redefined as the weight function.

For gray level images, the edge weight is defined as:

$$\omega(i,j) = e^{\frac{\sqrt{(f_i-f_j)^2}}{2} \cdot \sqrt{(x_i-x_j)^2+(y_i-y_j)^2}} \tag{1}$$

where f_i and f_j are two pixel gray level values. x_i, x_j, y_i, and y_j are the horizontal and vertical coordinates for f_i and f_j correspondingly. The definition for the weight is made by the difference of image pixel gray level values and spatial distance between the pixels.

For color images, the edge weight is defined as:

$$\omega\,(i,j) = e^{\frac{\sqrt{(H_i-H_j)^2+(S_i-S_j)^2+(I_i-I_j)^2}}{2} * \sqrt{(x_i-x_j)^2+(y_i-y_j)^2}} \tag{2}$$

Among them, H_i, H_j, S_i, S_j, I_i, and I_j are the pixel components. x_i, x_j, y_i, and y_j are the horizontal and vertical coordinates of the point.

2.2.2. *Improved difference function of internal and inter region*

We redefine the internal difference, Int (*C*), such that it gives a more accurate description of component *C*. Formally,

$$Int(C) = 1/N * \sum_{e \in MST(C,E)} w(e) \tag{3}$$

where *N* is the number of the MST edges, namely $N = |C| - 1$. It can reduce the sensitivity to a certain extent, and control segmentation scale by adjusting the parameter *K*, mainly inhibit the effect of noise. It is more stable than the original definition. More importantly, it does not increase the time complexity.

The definition of Diff (C_1, C_2) is as the following merge condition:

$$Diff(C_1,C_2) \le Int(C_1) + T(C_1) \quad \text{and} \quad Diff(C_1,C_2) \le Int(C_2) + T(C_2) \tag{4}$$

where Diff(C_1, C_2) is the difference between components C_1 and C_2; Int(C_1) and Int(C_2) are respectively the internal differences of C_1 and C_2; $T(C) = k/|C|$ is the threshold function. Parameter *k* controls the size of the components in the image segmentation.

2.2.3. *Improvement of threshold function and parameter k*

Felzenszwalb et al. pointed out that a large *k* was conducive to large areas, but the quantitative relationship between the *K* and the size of the region was not given. Therefore, an appropriate value is difficult to provide users with a parameter *k* for the expected component size. For example, two different *k* values of 150 and 300 are used. But they do not explain why 150 or 300 is selected, rather than the other values. For each particular image, this approach becomes infeasible in real-time applications if the value of *k* is determined by trial and error. Therefore, the expressions of the improved threshold and parameter *k* are as follows:

$$T(c) = (w_{\max} - w_{\min} / |c|) * (Num_c / k) \tag{5}$$

In the formula (5), Num_c is the region number, the initial value is the number of pixels, *k* is a constant. The larger the *k* is, the more obvious the boundaries of the two regions can be distinguished. Note that *k* is not for the region numbers of the segmentation; the bigger the *K* value is, the lager the producing area is. Based on this, the stop-merge condition for the component *C* becomes:

$$k > ((w_{\max} - w_{\min})Num_c) / |c| (Diff(c_1, c_2) - Int(c)) \tag{6}$$

In the formula (6), for a given image, $(w_{max} - w_{min})$ is fixed. Num_c is monotonically decreasing, while $(Diff(c_1, c_2) - Int(c))$ is not decreasing.

3. Separation of touching cells based on concave point detection

3.1. Determination of cell adhesion and the extraction of core coordinate

Cell touching can be divided into three types: parallel, series, and serial-parallel, as shown in **Figure 3**. In parallel, the cell is enclosed in a closed area, as shown in **Figure 3(a)**. Series cells are end-to-end cells, as shown in **Figure 3(b)**; and the third is both cells connected in series and parallel cell, as shown in **Figure 3(c)**.

3.1.1. Principle of cell touching

When the cells are stuck together, the boundaries will become more complex, usually concave regions will appear in the touching areas. The shape factor can describe the complexity of cell boundaries, and its formula is defined as follows:

$$PE = \frac{4\pi A}{C^2} \tag{7}$$

In the formula, *C* is the circumference of the object, and *A* is the area of the object.

By scanning the image, the total numbers of pixels in the same marked area are the area of the target. The accumulation of the distances between adjacent edge points in the closed curve is the perimeter of the target. The distance between the two adjacent edge points in any horizontal direction or vertical direction is 1, while the distance between the two adjacent edge points in the tilt direction is $\sqrt{2}$.

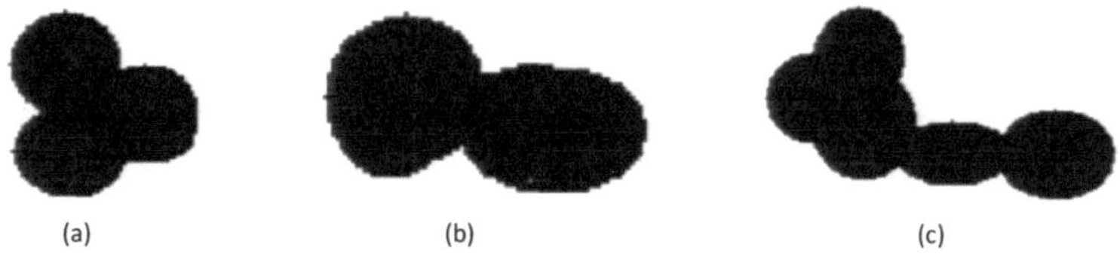

Figure 3. Cell touching categories: (a) parallel cells; (b) serial cells; (c) serial-parallel cells.

The range of shape factor is less than 1. When the target is close to the circle, the shape factor is close to 1. If cells are stuck together, their boundaries are complex. In the case of the same area, the circumference of the target with a concave object is larger than that of the target without a concave target, resulting in a corresponding smaller size of the shape factor. After learning and training to determine a threshold P_0, when $P_E > P_0$, the cell touching does not exist. When P_E is less than or equal to P_0, the cell touching exists. With this constraint, the shape factor can prevent the error of separation.

3.1.2. Extraction of the cell core coordinates

The core of the cell is the central pixel of the cell, which is the core of each cell that is touched together. As long as the touching cells are split into single cells, you can simplify the problem into the calculation of the core of a single cell. The algorithm flow chart is shown in **Figure 4**.

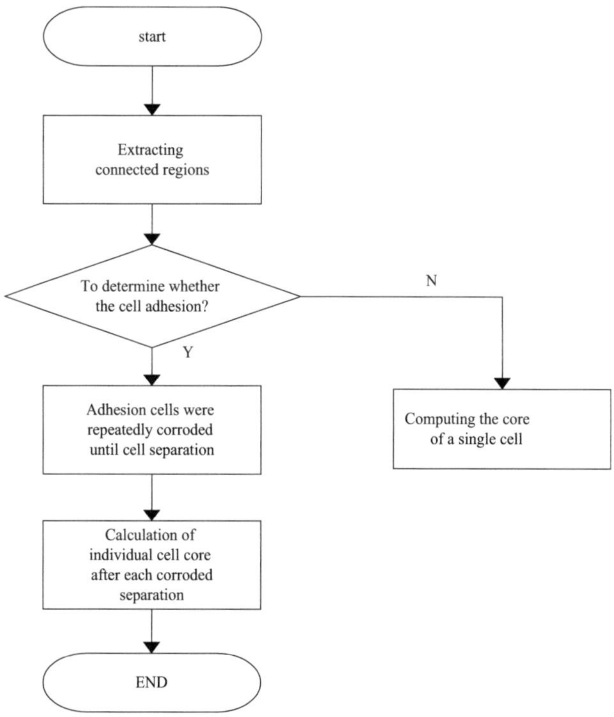

Figure 4. Algorithm flow chart.

3.1.3. Experimental results and analysis

Fu et al. [21] used the drawing software to generate cell images. After repeated experiments and training, the threshold of the best shape factor is $P_0 = 0.5$. When P_E is greater than P_0, there is no cell adhesion, and when P_E is less than or equal to P_0, there are cell adhesion. However, for the cells of some complex shape, the threshold of the shape factor may cause the misjudge phenomenon. After a number of experimental training, it is found that the value of P_E is generally distributed in the range of 0.4–0.6, so a spinner control is added, as shown in **Figure 5**.

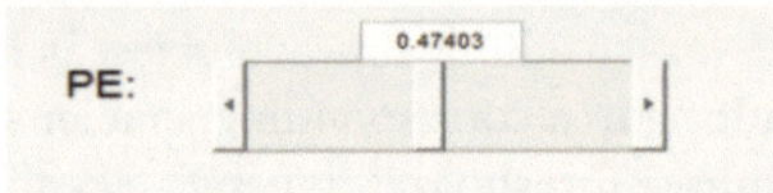

Figure 5. Spinner control.

The experimental results of adhesion cell core extraction are shown in **Figures 6–9**. From the above experimental results, we can see that the number of cell cores extracted by the algorithm in this paper is consistent with the actual cell numbers, and the core position is also basically accurate.

Figure 6. Two cell series: (a) origin image; (b) core extraction.

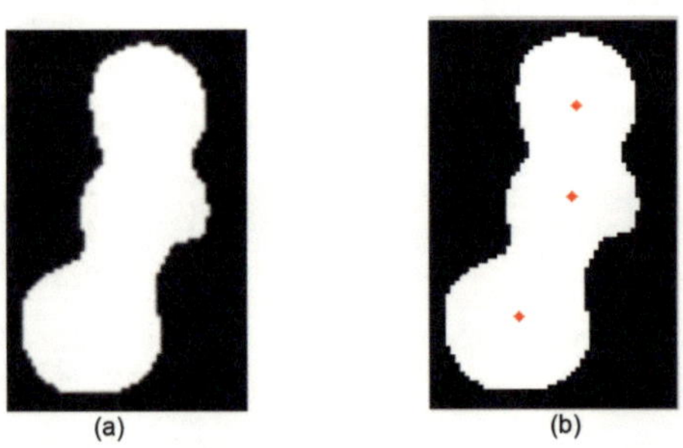

Figure 7. Three cell series: (a) origin image; (b) core extraction.

http://dx.doi.org/10.5772/65029

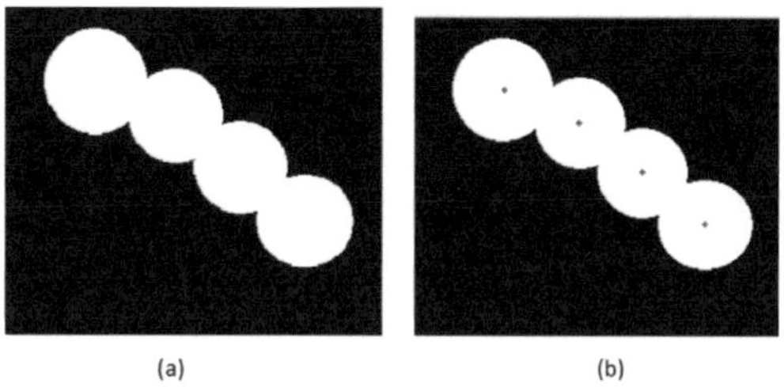

Figure 8. Four cell series: (a) origin image; (b) core extraction.

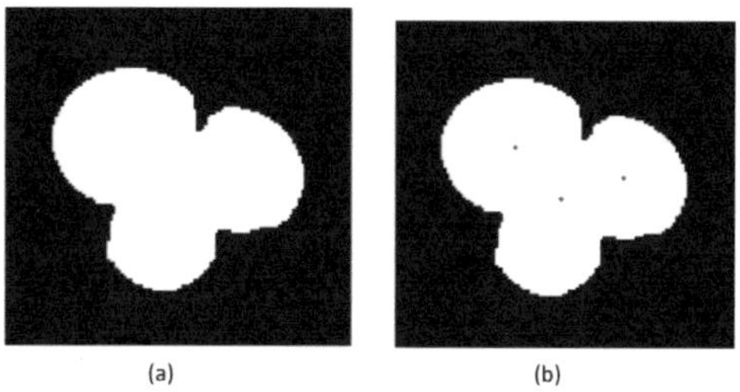

Figure 9. Three cell parallel: (a) origin image;. (b) core extraction.

3.2. Principle and method of searching adhesion cell concave point

The angle and curvature may be the most widely used in the concave point separation algorithm. However, angle and curvature are susceptible to the effect of noise, especially when the cell image has a complex background and uneven cells in the outer nuclear region, the cell division will not produce the correct cell profile. Hence, considering the simplicity and robustness of the algorithm, the best concave points are found through detecting the concave points in major concave regions. How to search and extract the main concave points on the edges is described as follows.

3.2.1. Search for concave points

The concave point is a very important parameter in the study of cell shape. If the number of concave points is more, then there are many touching cells. If there are a large number of concave points in a single cell, then the probability of cell mutation is higher. So it is a very meaningful work to study the concave points.

A cell image is generally characterized by concave pattern. The pixel value of the image background is 0, and the foreground pixel value is 1. There is no pixel value 0 on the line connecting any two pixel value 1, and the image is a convex figure; otherwise, it is concave. Therefore, the main problem of the algorithm is to determine the location relationship between the line connecting two edge points and the cells. It is observed that only the local concave points are the concave points on the cell edge, and the local convex points are not the concave points on the cell edge. Based on this, the algorithm first finds out the local concave points of the cell edge and then selects a concave point from the concave point group as the main concave point of the concave region.

As shown in **Figure 10**, set L_i for the edge of the cell adhesion profile, p_j represents a point on the L_i. P_{j-h} and p_{j+h} are the locations of h pixel points before and after p_j pixel point. After a number of experimental tests, when h is equal to 10, the results will be better. If the line connecting p_{j+h} and p_{j-h} is more than 60% outside of the adherent cell, p_j is considered as a concave point [22]. In order to enhance the robustness of the algorithm, discarding the concave regions that only contain two or fewer local concave points, and only retaining the main concave points, and finally the main concave point is the central point of the corresponding concave region.

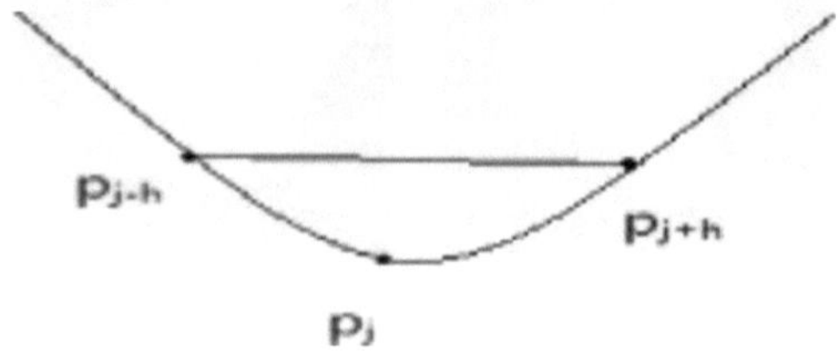

Figure 10. Concave points searching.

Specific implementation steps are as follows:

1. Select a point p_j on the cell edge;
2. To determine whether p_j is J (horizontal) direction change or I (vertical) direction change;
3. In accordance with the direction of step 2, to find adjacent points p_{j+h} or p_{j-h} in the 8 neighborhood of p_j, if not found adjacent point, return to step 1;
4. To determine whether to find the first h point, if not, then p_{j+1} or p_{j-1} as the starting point, return to step 2, if there is, step 5 is executed;
5. To connect point p_{j-h} and p_{j+h}, getting the percentage of the connection located in the outer region of the adhesion cells, if it is greater than or equal to 60%, then p_j is a concave point, if less than 60%, p_j is not a concave point;
6. To determine whether the edge pixels are extracted, if not, return to step 1, if there is, the algorithm ends.

3.2.2. Extraction of the main concave point

After all the local concave points of the cell edge are extracted, find out the main concave points from them. First, the local concave points are classified, finding the concave points that are in the concave regions, because the local concave point distance is relatively close in a concave region, so just find out a local threshold D_h. The concave points on the cell edge are divided into k classes, then the classes that contained only less than or equal to two local concave points are removed, and finally, the intermediate point in concave point group is taken as the main concave point of the concave area.

3.2.3. Design of adhesion cell separation method

Due to the diversity of the cell itself and the complexity of cell adhesion, there are many difficulties in the design of the separation algorithm, the difficulty and the key point is how to find the separation point. When the cells are stuck together, a pair of matched points can be found out on the edge of the cell profile, and a straight line that connects the two points can divide the touching cell into two parts. This pair of matching points satisfies the following properties:

1. Located in the cell junction.

2. The distance between them is locally the shortest.

According to the concave and convex of the adhesion cells, the concave area is calculated from the cell adhesion area, and the main concave point is found to be the separation point.

(a) Tandem cell separation

For cells that are connected in series, the separation points are all located on the edge of the touching region, because the cell series connection will form a pair of concave region. According to this characteristic, as long as the main concave points are found from the concave areas, connecting a pair of concave points, the tandem cells will be reasonably separated. Assuming that the number of the concave points is A, and the number of cells is M, then:

$$A = 2M - 2 \quad (8)$$

If there are only two touching cells, then the number of the main concave points is 2, which can be directly connected to split the touching cells. However, for more than three touching cells, the main concave points will be greater than or equal to 4, and then you need to determine which of the two main concave points are paired. As shown in **Figure 11**, the green dots are the main concave points of the cells, and the red spots are the center of the cells.

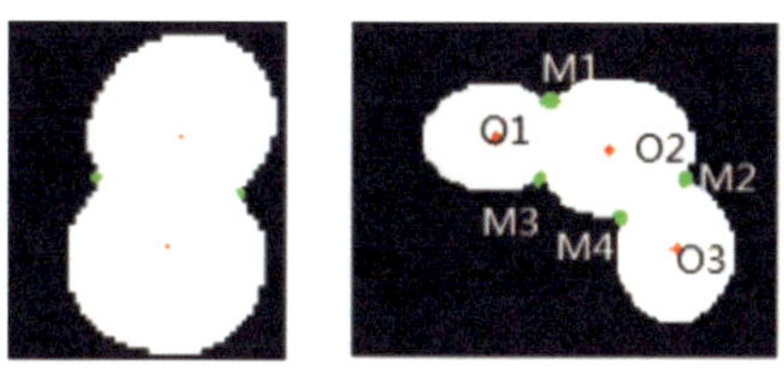

Figure 11. Main concave pairing.

According to the geometric relationship between the cell core and the main concave point, the distance between the main concave point and the core of the cell is close to each other. As shown in **Figure 11**, $M1O1 \cong M1O2$, $M3O1 \cong M3O2$. However, the distance between *M*1 and *M*3 to *O*3 is much larger than that of *O*1 and *O*2.

$$|M1O1\text{-}M1O2| < \{|M1O1\text{-}M1O3|,|M1O2\text{-}M1O3|\} \tag{9}$$

$$| M2O2 - M2O3 |< \{| M2O1 - M2O2 |,| M2O1 - M2O3 |\} \tag{10}$$

In conclusion, the distance between *M*1 to *O*1 and *O*2 is minimal, and the distance between *M*3 to *O*1 and *O*2 is minimal, so *M*1 and *M*3 and *M*2 and *M*4 are paired. The experimental results are shown in **Figure 12**.

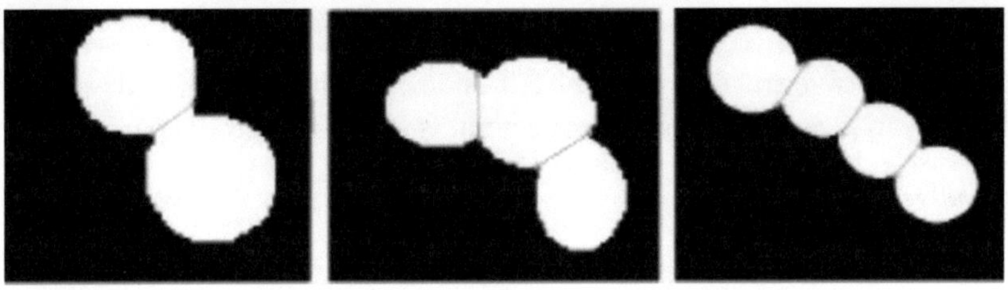

Figure 12. Separation of cell series.

(b) Separation of parallel cells

In parallel, the pairing of the main concave points is relatively easy, because the adhesion of the parallel cells is located in the internal of the adhesion area, so the central point of the adhesive cells can be connected with the main concave point to split the touching cells. Assuming that the number of cells is parallel to *M*, the number of concave points is *A*, and it should satisfy:

$$A=M \tag{11}$$

The experimental results are shown in **Figure 13**.

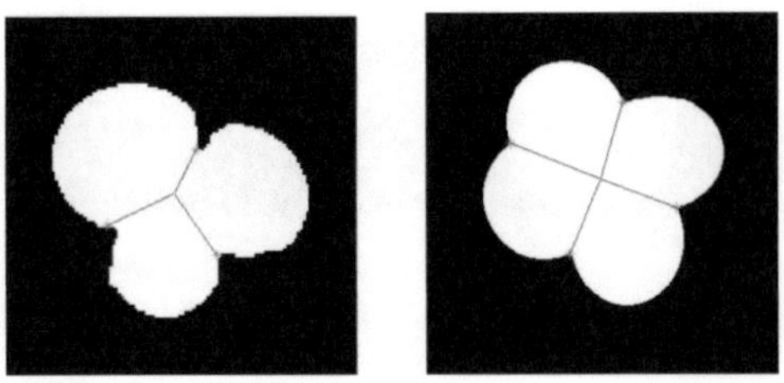

Figure 13. Separation of cell parallel.

3.3. Experimental results and analysis

The blood cell image of this paper comes from the First Affiliated Hospital of Fujian Medical University, and a total of 35 different types of blood smear cell images were collected. In order to verify the practicability of the algorithm, the experiments are carried out on 35 images, and selects some representative images to do further analysis. In **Figure 14**, the algorithm can efficiently split the touching cells. The segmentation result is stable and controllable.

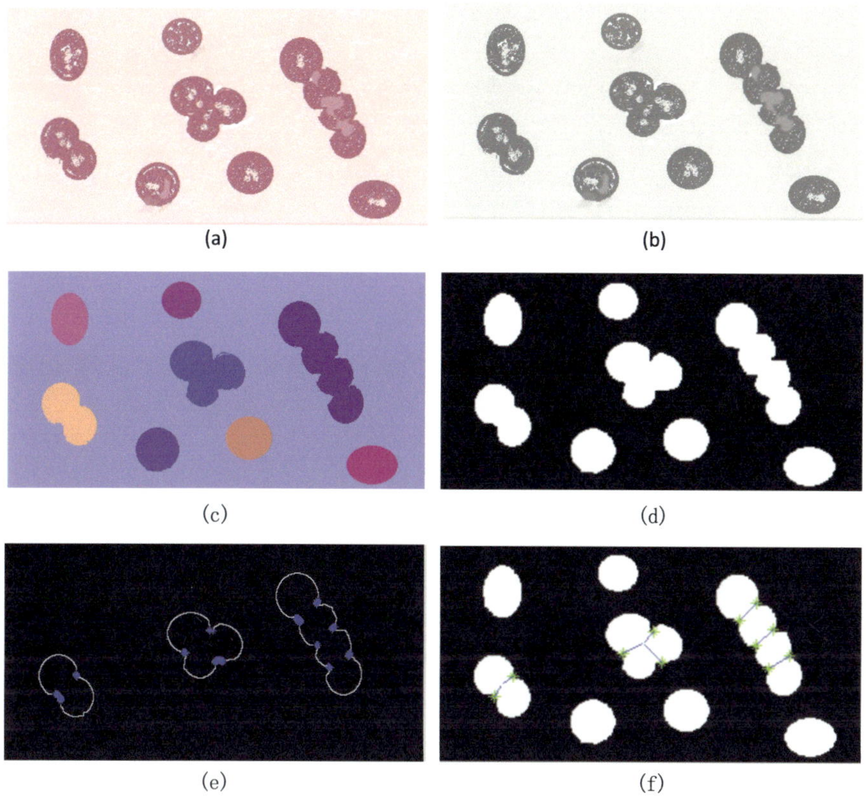

Figure 14. Split process of touching color cell image: (a) origin image; (b) bilateral filtering; (c) improved graph; (d) binarization; (e) main concave point extraction; (f) separation of adherent cells.

4. Flow chart of new algorithm

Through the above analysis, the general flow chart of this algorithm (including two partial operation based on graph theory segmentation and adhesion separation) is shown in **Figure 15**. The red digital label 1 is the improved image segmentation algorithm based on the MST, and the mark 2 is the part of touching cells split based on concave point detection.

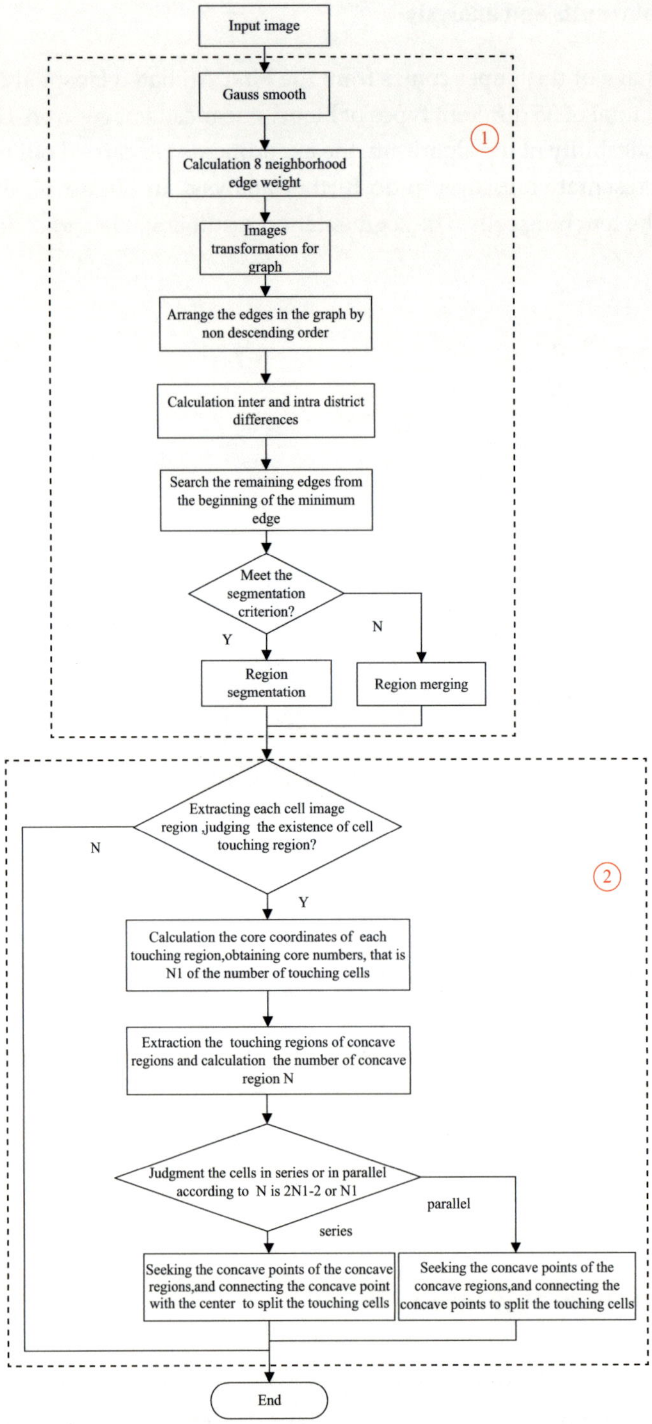

Figure 15. Flow chart of the proposed algorithm.

5. Experiments and analysis

5.1. Experimental result analysis

The original gray cell image is shown in **Figure 16(a)**. The background is clear. In addition to red blood cells, there are some small particles and cell nucleus in the cells and the gray value of the nucleus is relatively large. It has a large difference of gray value compared with the cytoplasm, so using ordinary methods are difficult to segment them. The overall cell is of regular shape, except for a small number of touching cells. For the original MST algorithm, there are many rough edges in the segmentation result. Because of the defects in the algorithm, dyeing pollution, particle noise, and the more redundant areas will be produced, with nonideal effect, and the segmentation result is shown in **Figure 16(b)**. In order to control region merging, the size of the area is introduced in the construction process of MST in the FH algorithm, which can reduce the generated redundant region segmentation results. So the holes of the segmentation results are eliminated and the cell surface becomes smooth, as shown in **Figure 16(d)**. The watershed algorithm is intuitive, fast, and accurate, which is widely applied in medical image segmentation. It is more effective for segmenting touching cell images, but it is prone to produce oversegmentation phenomenon. The watershed segmentation results are shown in **Figure 16(e)**, and the oversegmentation phenomenon is very obvious. The split results of FCM and mean shift are shown in **Figure 16(f)** and **(g)**; they are not ideal. For **Figure 16(d)**, the split result of the touching cells is shown in **Figure 16(h)**.

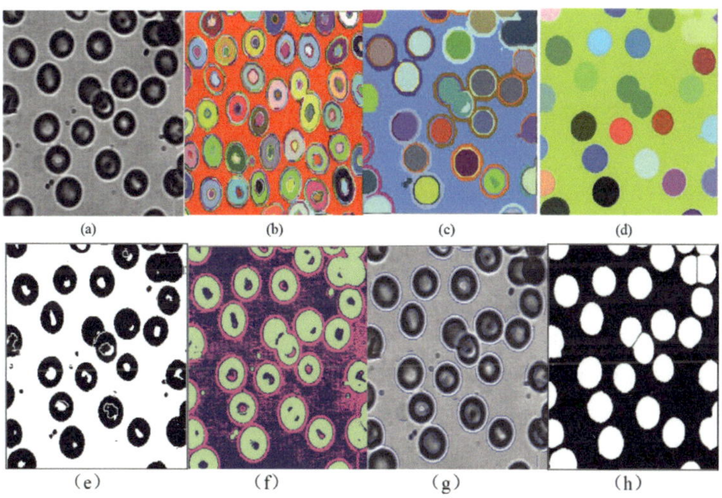

Figure 16. Split process of touching gray cell image: (a) original image; (b) result of MST; (c) result of reference [13]; (d) result of improved MST; (e) result of watershed algorithm; (f) result of FCM; (g) result of mean shift; and (h) result of applying concave point searching in (d).

Figures 17 and **18** are more complex than **Figure 16**, in which the gray value of the target is close to background. These two images have more holes caused by uneven light, and there are a lot of touching cells. In **Figure 17**, the contrast of the object and background is relatively obvious and has also more holes caused by uneven light, so the normal segmentation algorithms are difficult to segment this kind of images. There are a lot of rough edges in the segmentation results and the similar areas have not been well merged in **Figures 16(b), 17(b),** and **18(b)**. The rough edges reduce and region merging are good, but there are still some redundancies in **Figures 16(c), 17(c),** and **18(c)**. In comparison with the results of Ref. [18], the results are more ideal in **Figures 16(d), 17(d),** and **18(d)**. It is found from the split results of each algorithm that, in comparison with several commonly used classical algorithms, the segmentation result of the proposed algorithm is ideal.

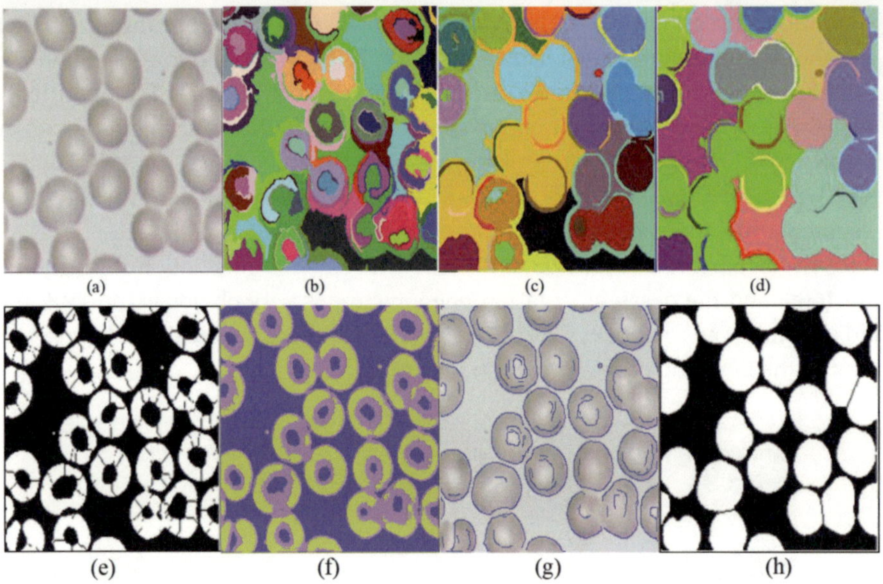

Figure 17. Split process of fuzzy and touching color cell image #1: (a) original image; (b) result of MST; (c) result of Ref. [18]; (d) result of improved MST; (e) result of watershed algorithm; (f) result of FCM; (g) result of mean shift; and (h) result of applying concave point searching in (d).

From the above segmentation results, for the adhesion separation part of a medical cell image, the algorithm proposed in this paper is ideal, and the algorithm can also be used for other separating adhesion target images with more effective effect. **Figure 19** is a land flow particle image, in which the discrimination of the object and the background is very clear. Because the viewing distance is farther, the rock surface information is vague. And the contour is relatively clear, but the individual parts have adhesion phenomenon. In **Figure 19(b)**, the segmentation results based on MST have not only good separation of target and background, but also increasing the adhesion degree of rock blocks. In **Figure 19(c)**, it exsits a lot of rough edges and holes. In **Figure 19(d)**, the rough edges are removed, and different regions are distinguished. As shown in **Figure 19(e)**, the watershed segmentation is able to handle some adhesion part, but it is easy to cause the oversegmentation phenomenon. The segmentation effect based on FCM algorithm is unable to handle the adhesive part of the rock mass, as shown in **Figure 19(f)**. **Figure 19(g)** is also not ideal.

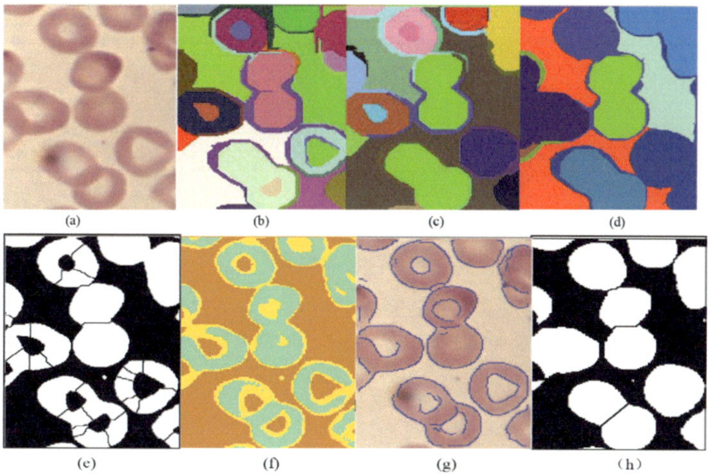

Figure 18. Split process of fuzzy and touching color cell image #2: (a) original image; (b) result of MST; (c) result of Ref. [18]; (d) result of improved MST; (e) result of watershed algorithm; (f) result of FCM; (g) result of mean shift; and (h) result of applying concave point searching in (d).(e) Concave searching in (d) (f) Watershed (g) Canny (h) Ostu **Figure 5.** Split process of fuzzy and touching color cell image #2

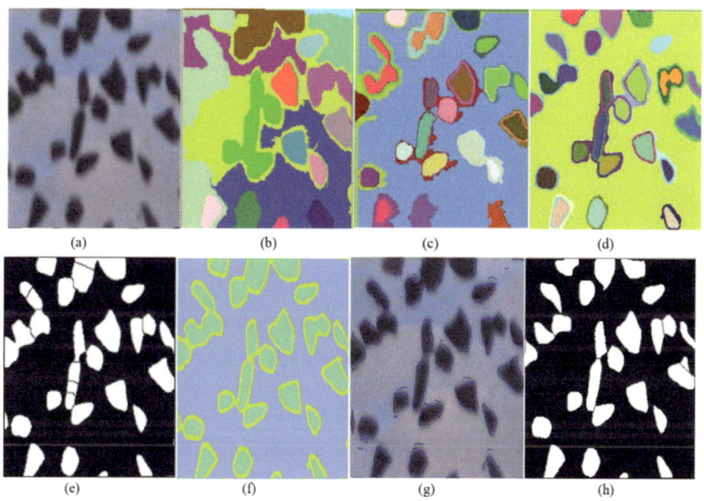

Figure 19. Split process of the land flow particle image: (a) original image; (b) result of MST; (c) result of Ref. [13]; (d) result of improved MST; (e) result of watershed algorithm; (f) result of FCM; (g) result of mean shift; and (h) result of applying concave point searching in (d).

5.2. Location analysis

In this paper, the author uses the proposed method to segment these images, and then the final segmentation results are located to verify the accuracy of the algorithm. The positioning results are shown in **Figures 20** and **21**.

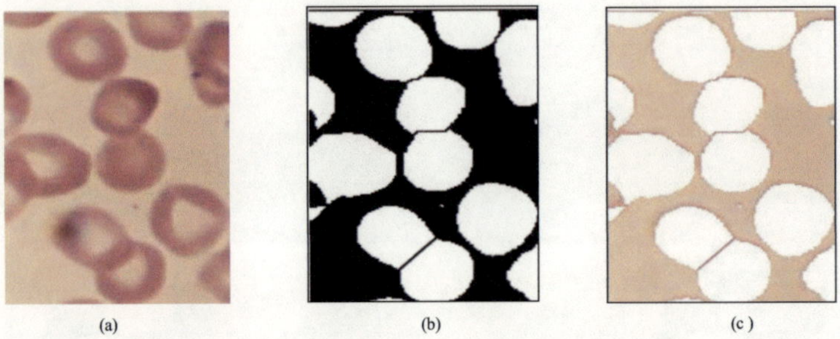

Figure 20. Result of fuzzy and touching color cell image #1: (a) original image; (b) result of the proposed algorithm; and (c) result of (b) diagram located in (c).

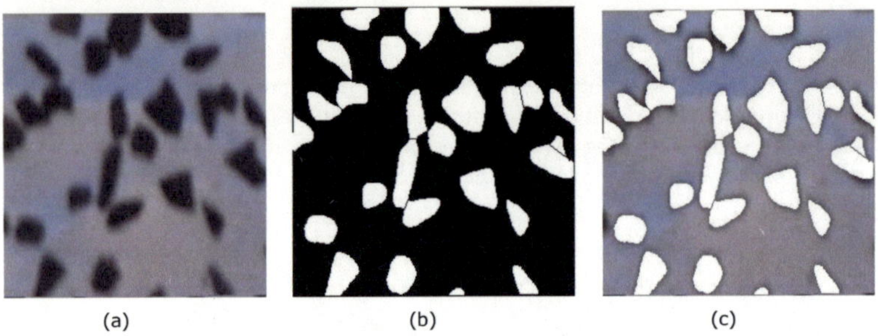

Figure 21. Result of the land flow particle image: (a) original image; (b) result of the proposed algorithm; and (c) result of (b) diagram located in (c).

Image ID	Number of cells	Undersplit	Oversplit
1	32	1/2	0/23
2	25	0/0	0/much
3	14	0/0	0/19
4	75	2/0	0/much
5	71	6/2	0/0
6	83	3/1	0/much
7	52	1/0	0/22
8	45	3/2	0/much
9	67	8/5	0/35
10	78	4/3	0/10
Ave.	54	2.5/1.3	0/much

Table 1. Evaluation of splitting performance based on the proposed segmentation algorithm and watershed algorithm.

5.3. Performance analysis

In order to illustrate the differences of the new algorithm and others, comparative analysis data are listed in **Table 1**. The data include the number of objects with oversplit and undersplit, and the total number of cells. The new algorithm has the minimum value in the above statistic data. In **Table 1**, in comparison with other algorithms, the new algorithm presents a better result. For this kind of the touching cell images, the watershed algorithm is better in comparison with other algorithms, but it causes an oversegmentation problem.

6. Conclusion

In order to solve the segmentation problem of the medical cell images with fuzzy and touching characteristics, this paper proposes an algorithm combing with modified MST and concave point detection. The MST method is improved from the following three aspects, namely, regional difference function, edge weight function, and the threshold function and parameter *k*, which can reduce the effect of noise on the segmentation result and improve the segmentation accuracy. But the improved MST cannot solve the cell touching problem. For splitting the touching cells, the concave point detection is adopted to find out the separation points. In comparison with the results of several commonly used image segmentation algorithms, the segmentation results of the proposed algorithm do not have many small areas, the oversegmentation phenomenon does not appear basically, and the touching cells can be split accurately, which is helpful to improve cell counting and recognition. A large number of tests show that the new algorithm is more ideal, undersegmentation and oversegmentation numbers are less, and the error rate is relatively low.

Author details

Wang Weixing[1,2*] and Lin Liqun[1]

*Address all correspondence to: wxwwx@fzu.edu.cn

1 College of Physics and Information Engineering, Fuzhou University, Fuzhou, Fujian, China

2 Royal Institute of Technology, Stockholm, Sweden

References

[1] Li G, T Liu, J Nie, et al. Mint: Segmentation of touching cell nuclei using gradient flow tracking. Journal of Microscopy. 2008;231(1):47-58.

[2] Al-Kofahi Y, Lassoued W, Lee W, et al. Mint: Improved automatic detection and segmentation of cell nuclei in histopathology images. IEEE Transactions on Biomedical Engineering. 2010; 57(4): 841-852.

[3] Anand Raj Ulle, T N Nagabushan, Dr Vijaya Basavaraj. Mint: Clump Splitting in Histopathological images based on Concave points. Cognitive Computing and Information Processing. 2015;3(4):1-6.

[4] Veta M. Mint: Automatic nuclei segmentation in H&E stained breast cancer histopathology images. Plos 0ne. 2013;8(7): e70221.

[5] Mouelhi A, Sayadi M, Fnaiech F, et a1. Mint: Automatic image segmentation of nuclear stained breast tissue sections using color active contour modeI and an improved watershed method. Biomedical Signal Processing and Control. 2013;8(5):421-436.

[6] Pin W, Xian-Ling H, Yong-Ming L, et al. Mint: Automatic cell nuclei segmentation and classification of breast cancer histopathology images. Signal Processing. 2016;122(2): 1-13.

[7] Wang S, Siskind JM. Mint: Image segmentation with ratio cut.IEEE Trans on PAKI. 2003;25(6):675-690.

[8] Sirmacek B. Mint: Graph theory and mean shift segmentation based classification of building facades. Urban Remote Sensing Event (JURSE). 2011;2010:409-412.

[9] Pham VH, Byung Ryong Lee. Mint: An image segmentation approach for fruit defect detection using k-means clustering and graph-based algorithm. Vietnam J Comput Sci. 2015; 2:25–33.

[10] Vanhamel I, Sahli H, Pratikakis I. In: Nonlinear Multiscale Graph Theory based Segmentation of Color Images. In:IEEE conferences. 2011;2(2):409-412.

[11] Yan Z, Xiao-Ping C. Mint: Medical image segmentation based on watershed and graph theory. Image and Signal Processing. 2010;3:1419-1422.

[12] Wei-Xing W, Li-Ping T, et al. Mint: Segmentation of cell images based on improved graph MST and skeleton distance mapping. Opt. Precision Eng.2013; 21(9):2464-2470.

[13] Fabijanska Anna, Jarosław Gocławski. Mint: New accelerated graph-based method of image segmentation applying minimum spanning tree . IET Image Processing. 2014; 8(4):239-250.

[14] You-Yi S, Ling Z, Si-Ping C, et al. Mint: Accurate Segmentation of Cervical Cytoplasm and Nuclei Based on Multiscale Convolutional Network and Graph Partitioning. IEEE TRANSACTIONS ON BIOMEDICAL ENGINEERING.2015; 62(10):2421-2433.

[15] Filipczuk P, Fevens T, Krzyzak A, et a1. Mint: Computer-aided breast cancer diagnosis based on the analysis of cytological images of fine needle biopsies.IEEE Transactions on Medical Imaging. 2013;32(12): 2169-2178.

[16] Alilou M, Kovalev V, Taimouri V. Mint: Segmentation of cell nuclei in heterogeneous microscopy images.Computerized Medical Imaging and Gmphics. 2013;37(7):488-499.

[17] Ping W, Xian-Ling H, Wen-Bin H, et al. Mint: Image segmentation of breast cells based on multi-scale region-growing and splitting model. Chinese Journal of Scientific Instrument. 2015; 36(7): 1653-1658.

[18] Felzenszwalb PF; Huttenlocher DP. Mint: Efficient Graph-Based Image Segmentation. International Journal of Computer Vision. 2004;59(2) :167-181.

[19] Wei-Xing W, Xin Z, Ting C, et al. Mint: Fuzzy and Touching Cell Extraction on Graph Minimize Spanning Tree and Skeleton Distance Mapping Histogram. Journal of Medical Imaging and Health Informatics. 2014; 4(3) :350-357.

[20] Felzenszwalb PF, Huttenlocher DP. Mint: Efficient Graph-Based Image Segmentation. International Journal of Computer Vision. 2004;59(2) :167-181.

[21] Rong F. Mint: Technical Study on the Separation and Segmentation for Cell Overlap and Fusion Image[D]. Doctoral Dissertation of First Military Medical University.2007.

[22] Rong F, Shen Hong, Chen Hao. Mint: Research of automatically separating algorithm for over lap cell based on searching concave spot. Computer Engineering and Applications. 2007; 43(17):21-23.

Section 3

Image Fusion Algorithms

Chapter 5

Approach to Super-Resolution Through the Concept of Multicamera Imaging

Eduardo Quevedo, Gustavo Marrero and
Félix Tobajas

Additional information is available at the end of the chapter

http://dx.doi.org/10.5772/65442

Abstract

Super-resolution consists of processing an image or a set of images in order to enhance the resolution of a video sequence or a single frame. There are several methods to apply super-resolution, from which fusion super-resolution techniques are considered to be the most adequate for real-time implementations. In fusion, super-resolution and high-resolution images are constructed from several observed low-resolution images, thereby increasing the high-frequency components and removing the degradations caused by the recording process of low-resolution imaging acquisition devices. Moreover, the proposed imaging system considered in this work is based on capturing various frames from several sensors, which are attached to one another by a $P \times Q$ array. This framework is known as a multicamera system. This chapter summarizes the research conducted to apply fusion super-resolution techniques to select the most adequate frames and macroblocks together with a multicamera array. This approach optimizes the temporal and spatial correlations in the frames and reduces as a consequence the appearance of annoying artifacts, enhancing the quality of the processed high-resolution sequence and minimizing the execution time.

Keywords: super-resolution, multicamera, camera array, video enhancement, fusion

1. Introduction

The limitations of imaging devices directly affect the spatial resolution of images and video. The super-resolution (SR) reconstruction concept is considered in the literature as the process of combining information from multiple low-resolution images with subpixel displacements to obtain a higher resolution image. Even though numerous methods have been developed to this end, there are still multiple future research challenges [1]. SR arises in several fields, such as remote sensing, surveillance, and an extensive set of consumer electronics applications [2–4].

This chapter proposes an imaging system in which high-resolution (HR) images are generated from low-resolution (LR) sensors through a SR image reconstruction process. In order to get several LR images minimizing the local motion, several digital cameras are attached to each other by a $P \times Q$ array frame. This framework is known as a multicamera (MC) system. The image reconstruction problem using an MC system applying an SR process could be stated as follows: *Given a set of multiview low-resolution frames of size M × N pixels taken with a multicamera system, and a scale factor s, reconstruct a higher resolution frame of size sM × sN pixels that accomplishes the definition of resolution enhancement.*

After a comprehensive review of the state of the art [5–21], it has been concluded that the application of SR to an MC system involves some preceding and subsequent steps. These steps are summarized in the proposed block diagram shown in **Figure 1**. However, in some cases, many steps could be skipped. For instance, the previous steps: MC system prototyping and construction and sometimes the MC system adjustment are not applicable if a commercial camera array is used [5], image capture is almost always considered, and pre- and postprocessing are sometimes omitted.

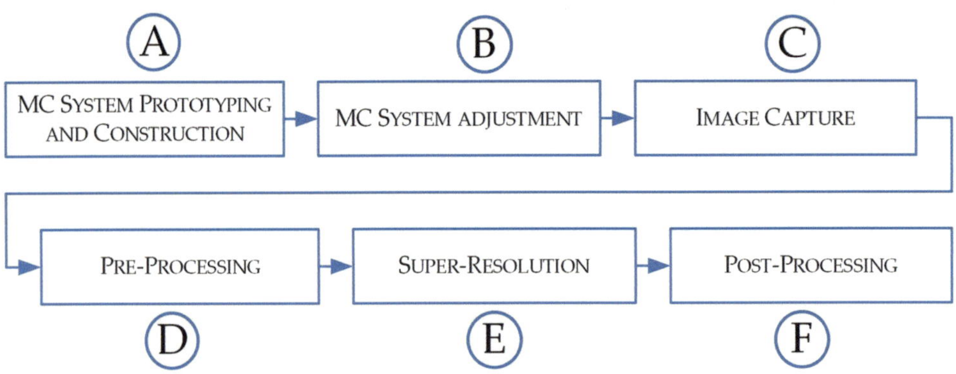

Figure 1. Block diagram of SR applied to an MC system.

This chapter is organized as follows: the state of the art of the steps described in **Figure 1** is discussed in Section 2, whereas Section 3 shows dedicated preprocessing schemes implemented together with three different methods which maximize the combination between SR and MC, proposed by the authors. These methods exploit the temporal correlation of the recorded videos and the spatial correlation among cameras. Finally, the conclusions are highlighted in Section 4.

2. Applying SR to an MC system

2.1. Multicamera system prototyping and construction

The prototyping of the MC system mainly depends on the application. One of the most used approaches is image-based rendering [4]. Using a MC array for this purpose can allow a device to process a higher quality frame in real time by means of multiple observations recorded simultaneously.

Some advisable factors to consider in any prototype of MC system are the following [4]:

- *User-friendliness*: The system should be designed to be easily created, i.e., cameras should require minimal setup and time-consuming calibration procedures should be avoided.
- *Flexibility*: Addition or removal of cameras according to their participation in the network and to a certain extent the flexibility in placing the cameras physically.
- *Off-the-shelf components*: It is desirable to keep reduced costs.

SR through the concept of MC imaging has been considered in the literature:

- Fanaswala [5] introduced in his thesis a commercial camera array of 25 cameras arranged on a 5 × 5 grid (ProFUSION25) of the commercial brand Pointgrey.
- Park et al. [6] used a prototype of a MC system based on a 3 × 3 array composed of nine digital cameras, CCD (charged coupled device).
- In Agrawal et al. [7], an implementation using four PointGrey Dragonfly2 cameras, each one equipped with 12 mm lens and triggering the cameras with a microcontroller (PIC) is presented.
- Finally, Firoozfam [8] presented a stereo MC conical system with 6 and 12 cameras, showing that increasing the number of cameras makes it possible to take advantage of several scenes observations at each time instant.

All these camera array systems are illustrated in **Figure 2**. In real-time applications, there is a compromise between the number of cameras and the computational cost, so it is useful to have a flexible architecture in order to select the cameras to be used, often in a N^2 configuration: 4, 9, 16, 25, … [5].

2.2. Multicamera system adjustment

The success of SR recovery from multiple views in real applications mainly depends on two factors [9]:

- The accuracy of multiple view registration results.
- The accuracy of the camera and data acquisition model.

Hence, in order to have a good level of SR, it is very important to perform a detailed adjustment of the MC system. The approach of using software located in a central server for the system adjustment is usually taken into account. For instance, Park et al. [6] developed a software that shows previews and the status of the images, grabbing them simultaneously. The intensity and focusing indexes are also included in the implementation in order to adjust the lenses for the purpose of intensity and blur uniformity.

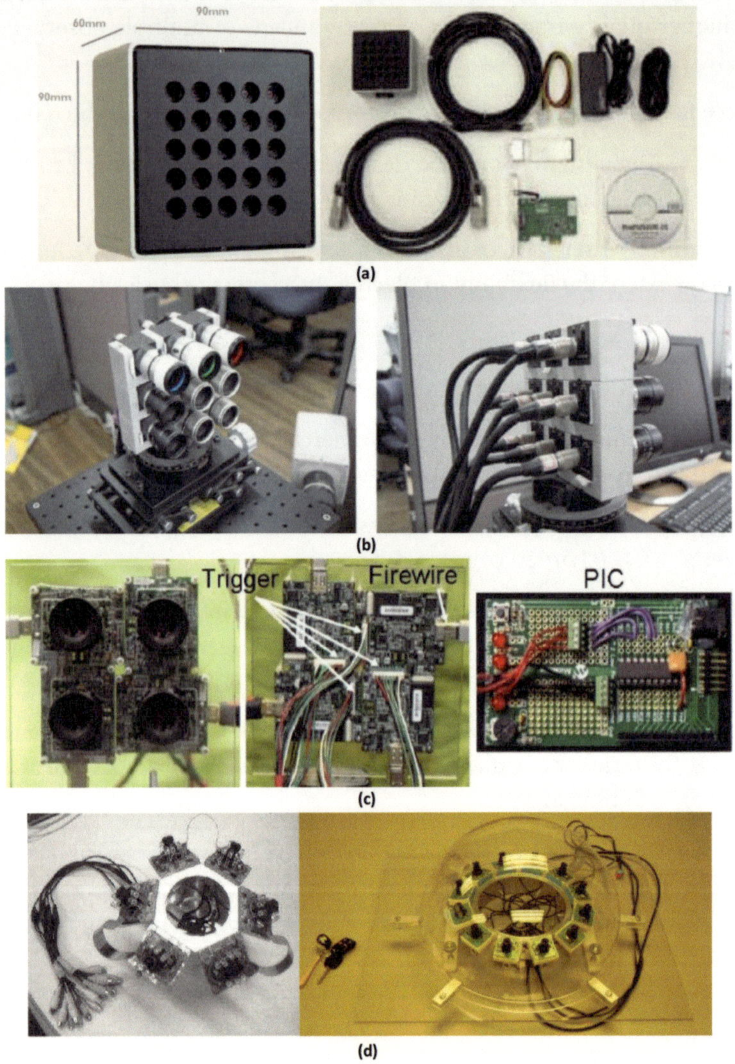

Figure 2. MC systems used for SR: (a) Fanaswala [5], (b) Park [6], (c) Agrawal et al. [7], and (d) Firoozfam [8].

There are also calibrations based on other elements, for example, Agrawal et al. [7] assumed that the scene is planar and perform geometric calibration using a checkerboard. Meanwhile color calibration is done using a Macbeth chart by computing a 3 × 3 color transformation for every camera. Finally, in this system, all cameras are triggered using microcontrollers, which avoid temporal synchronization issues. In the same way, both determining the camera parameters and rectifying the images for lens distortion are achieved by intrinsic calibration with a checkerboard by Firoozfam [8].

The adjustment process of the MC system is a basic step to settle a solid basis for the rest of the steps in the multicamera-super-resolution (MC-SR) approach. If a commercial system is used (as for instance Fanaswala in [5]), this process is simplified, but the calibration step is limited by the system performance; however, this makes the comparison between SR algorithms easier.

2.3. Image capture

Low-resolution images are captured by cameras generally using software implemented in a central server. The variation between researches depends on where the software is included: in an external computer, in the MC system, or sharing both systems.

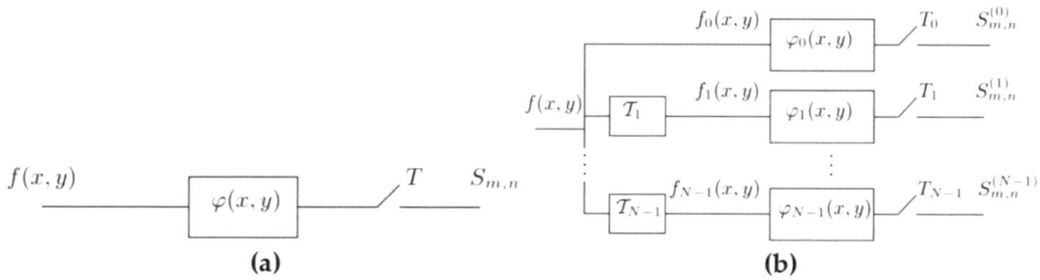

Figure 3. Classic VS distributed acquisition device [11]. a) Classic device, b) Distributed device.

- *Using an external computer*: Directo et al. [10] uses a vision server as the core of the SR system. It organizes the image capture from camera nodes, and processes the images using a high-resolution image reconstruction algorithm. In order to capture low-resolution images, three image transmission protocols, are used. In a similar way, Baboulaz et al. [11] introduced a distributed acquisition system. **Figure 3** shows a classic versus a distributed acquisition device. On the one hand, in the classic case of a single acquisition device, see **Figure 3(a)**, the incoming 2D projection $f(x, y)$ of the 3D scene is first filtered with a smoothing kernel modeling the point spread function of the lens of the camera and returning the set of samples $S_{m,n}$. On the other hand, in a distributed acquisition system, N cameras P_i, $i = 0,\ldots, N - 1$, are observing the same 3D scene from different unknown locations. Therefore, the incoming 2D projections $f_i(x, y)$ at each sensor will differ. Every projection $f_i(x, y)$ is the result of a transformation with T_i of the projection of reference $f(x, y)$. By choosing a camera as a reference (e.g., $i = 0$) the distributed acquisition system can be modeled as depicted in **Figure 3(b)**. Examples of transformations T are translation, rotation, or affine transformation according to the observed scene and to the locations of the cameras. Similarly to the single camera case, each sensor outputs a set of samples $S^{(i)}_{m,n}$. Finally, Park et al. [6] proposed a system in which low-resolution images of the same scene with different subpixel displacements from each other, are taken simultaneously by frame grabbers and a controlling software within the computer of the MC system.

- *Using the MC system*: Agrawal et al. [7] used a dedicated device, a microcontroller, to trigger all the cameras of the system, since they found that this was more stable than using a PC's parallel port [12], which could have triggered variations of 1 ms.

- *Using a shared approach with the MC system and a computer*: This approach utilizes the MC system to perform part of the multiimaging capture process. In Ref. [5], the ProFUSION25 camera array outputs raw 8-bit gray-scale images of pixel resolution 640 × 480 using one-shot mode to restrict the possibility of temporal motion of objects in the scene. In such a way, the multiview images captured by this system are well fitted for SR applications. The small baseline between each camera in the array allows the multiple views to sample the high-resolution image appropriately. Then, the images are ready to be sent to a PC using a PCI Express external cable. This connection provides more than 200 MB/s effective bandwidth and transfers 25 images at 25 FPS to the PC. In Ref. [12], a mapping between a conical view and the MC realization is performed by forming overlapping areas on the images of neighboring cameras. Unlike a rotational conical camera, a MC configuration can have multiple observations for some points of the scene. This allows recovering 3D information for these points from multiple view cues using the computational power of external software in a PC. **Figure 4** shows a sample image taken by the six-camera prototype system.

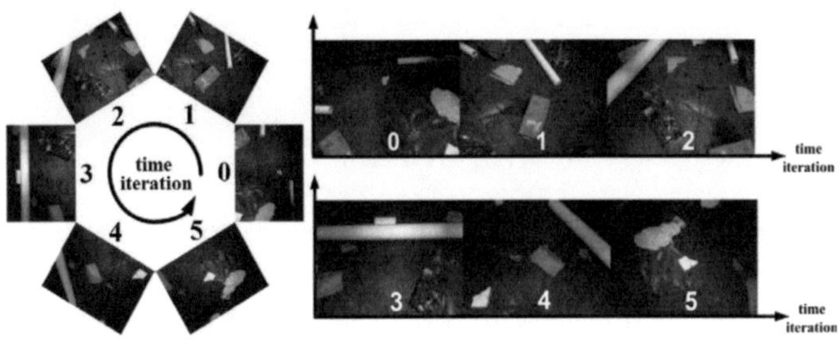

Figure 4. A sample-image taken from a MC conical system [8].

2.4. Preprocessing steps

In an MC set-up, low-resolution images are acquired by different cameras, which have different positions in space and are possibly not synchronized [9]. This causes some spatial and temporal misalignments among the sequences. On the one hand, the temporal misalignment results as a result of the possible frame rate and time offset differences among the cameras and can be modeled by a 1D affine transformation. On the other hand, the spatial misalignment between the two sequences results from the fact that the two cameras could have different internal and external parameters and has been mainly described by one of next two different models:

- *Homography*: Describes the exact image motion of an arbitrary planar surface between two discrete uncalibrated perspective views. The spatial transformation among the low-resolution sequences can be approximated by a homography when a planar scene assumption can be made [9, 10].

- *Fundamental matrix*: Homography assumption is no longer valid when there are a significant amount of camera translations and nonplanar depth variations. Such scenarios require 3D motion models, which consist a set of local parameters (per pixel) for the representation of the 3D structure and global parameters for the camera motion.

In Ref. [11], the use of the continuous moments, instead of the discrete moments, together with the approach described in Ref. [13], allowed to perform an affine registration of very low-resolution sampled images with the accuracy of the original image.

In Ref. [7], coded sampling is used, demonstrating that it is optimal by considering a linear invertible combination of time samples.

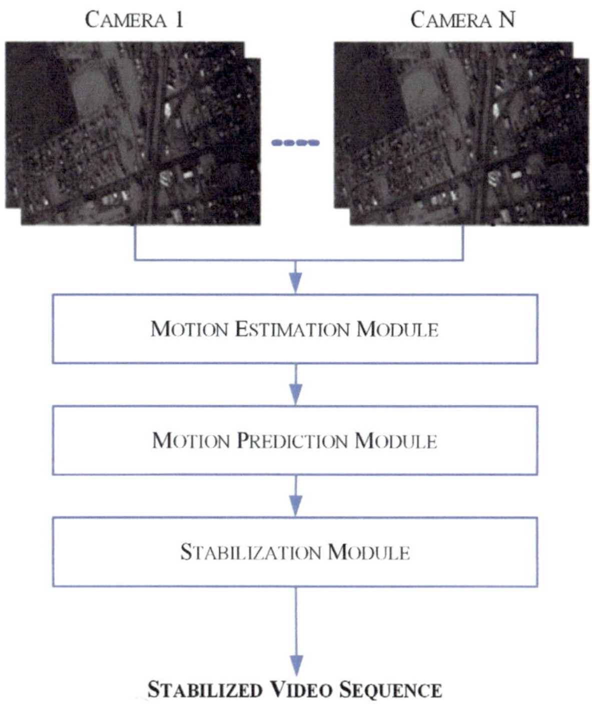

Figure 5. Video stabilization algorithm flow chart [14].

In Ref. [6], preprocessing steps consist of selecting one of the frames to be the referenced, meanwhile the contrast and lightness of the other frames are accordingly adjusted with the reference image by histogram specification. As a result, the relative global motions of the other images are calculated in accordance with the reference frame.

Images rendered by remote sensing MC platforms are basically considered to contain jitter caused by decoding timing delays, target movement and platform motion. The problem of stabilizing large-frame and low-frame rate imagery acquired from a multicamera array system for persistent surveillance and monitoring is dealt with in Ref. [14] with an algorithm based on temporal coherence properties between the cameras, thus eliminating the need to perform motion estimation on every individual camera sequence. The video stabilization algorithm is shown in **Figure 5** and consists of the following three steps:

1. *Motion estimation module*: It computes the interframe or frame-to-frame (F2F) transformation between adjacent frames for the primary camera(s).
2. *Motion prediction module*: It predicts the F2F transformations for the video frames from the secondary set of cameras, which relies on a prior knowledge of the camera-to-camera transformations and the outputs from the motion estimation module.
3. *Stabilization module*: It temporally aligns the final image sequence from each camera so that the jitter is reduced.

There are also techniques to reduce motion blur as presented in Ref. [15], where the main idea is to capture the same static scene with a hand-held MC array by keeping different exposure settings for different cameras and subsequently reconstruct high-resolution space time volume to get less motion blur image frames.

2.5. Super-resolution

In order to apply SR, many different approaches have been adopted in the literature. A good classification for all of them could be established depending on the approach to the real conditions of the MC system: first, in some cases, a popular technique is used without introducing any modification; second, one of these techniques could be slightly adapted to the camera array; finally, the algorithm may be prepared to be adjusted to the MC system, using an observation model.

- *Using a well-known technique*: There are several approaches to the SR reconstruction of a reference image from multiple still images or video sequences. Among the popular SR recovery, techniques are the projection onto convex sets (POCS) approach [10, 16] and the Bayesian approach [17]. These techniques assume global motion between successive frames of video, as in the case of camera motion with static scenes.
- *Modifying a well-known technique*: In order to consider the MC system, Eren et al. [18] extended POCS method to object-based super-resolution from video by proposing segmentation and validity maps. In the same way, the formulation used in Ref. [6] is an extended form of the SR algorithms in Refs. [19, 20] to estimate the local accuracy of the motion estimation results and incorporate it in the minimization functional as a local regularization parameter. According to the research in Ref. [19], the result of inaccurate motion estimation is proportional to the partial derivatives of the image, which can be interpreted as the amount of high-frequency data.
- *Adjusting the algorithm to the MC system*: In this approach, real conditions of the camera array are assumed. The exposure time, for example, is critical in order to achieve a good quality super-resolved image. In Ref. [17], a Bayesian SR algorithm based on an imaging model is

shown. It includes camera response function, exposure time, sensor noise, and quantization error in addition to spatial blurring and sampling. SR reconstruction is then presented as an inverse problem, where the input q is estimated from a set of observations z_i, as shown in **Figure 6**.

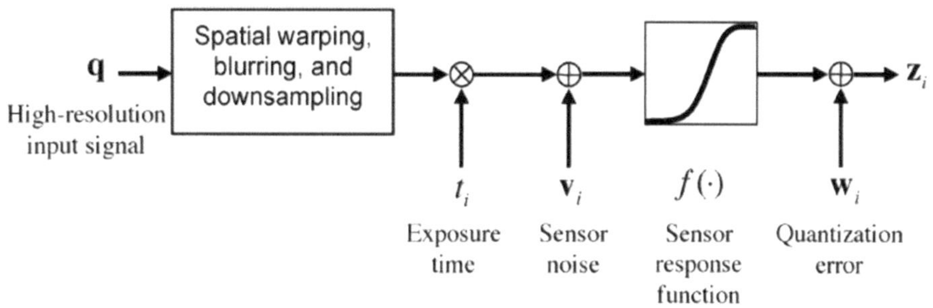

Figure 6. SR algorithm proposed in Ref. [20].

Including characteristics of the camera array in the SR process is also considered in Ref. [5] (see **Figure 7**), where a detailed observation model is integrated in the SR restoration method (see **Figure 8**). This model is sometimes referred to as the forward model to emphasize the fact that SR is an inverse problem (as shown in **Figure 6**). The accurate description of the observation model is vital for the success of the SR process. This involves characterizing the imaging sensor as fully as possible and making appropriate assumptions about the type of scene being imaged.

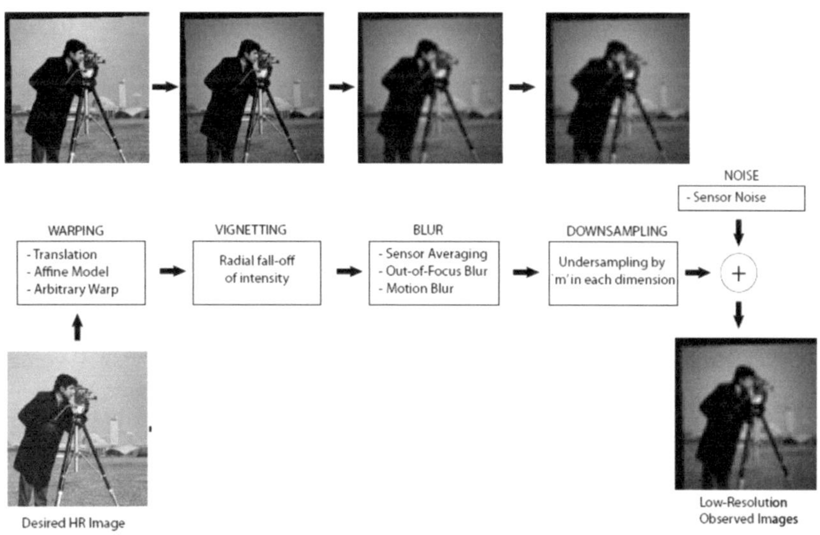

Figure 7. General observation model proposed in Ref. [5].

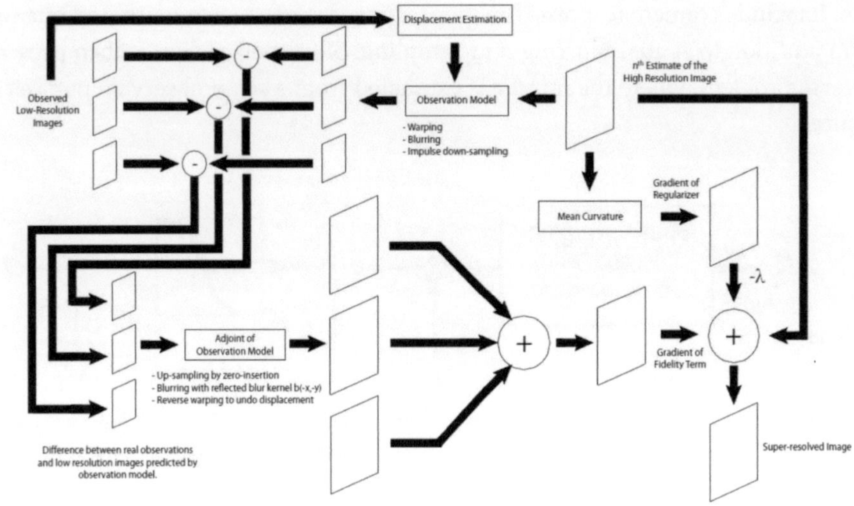

Figure 8. Single iteration in regularized super-resolution restoration [5].

The idea of the observation model is well presented in **Figures 6** and **7**. Including an observation model in the SR restoration minimizes the preprocessing steps. The fundamental components comprise the warp operator, the blur operator, and the downsampling operator:

- *Warp operator*: It describes the existing displacement between two images in a sequence, which could arise from camera motion, object motion in the scene, or a combination of both.
- *Blurring operator*: It defines the cumulative blurring effects from sensor averaging, motion blur, and out-of-focus blur.
- *Downsampling operator*: It applies a magnification factor "*m*" in each dimension (undersampling).

It is also important to consider the noise that is directly added by the system once an image is captured. This is the reason why the sensor noise is added directly in a typical observation model. Besides these fundamental components, there are some specific parameters such as the sensor response function in **Figure 6** or the vignetting operator in **Figure 7**, which are introduced due to the characteristics specific to every system. The observation model is flexible enough to include many different applications. For example, in Ref. [8], a similar observation model, which is represented in **Figure 9**, is presented for a 3D-SR application, only including geometric projection, which is based on the 3D model of the scene and position of every camera. The geometric transformation of X (3D SR scene) to the coordinates of each image (Y_n^L, low-resolution image) is computed using the camera projection model. In this situation, the accuracy of the 3D model and the camera positions are critical to the performance of the 3D-SR algorithm.

The method to measure the quality of the reconstructed image should also be considered. It is demonstrated [21] that although the image quality is usually measured by the expected and the actual mean squared error (MSE), an alternative performance measure might be based on edge errors, since edges are often the first step in more complex image analysis for both image processing systems and biological systems. Finally, the use of MC commercial applications, as in Ref. [5], is interesting since it can be exploited by different researchers in order to compare the suitability of the SR algorithm.

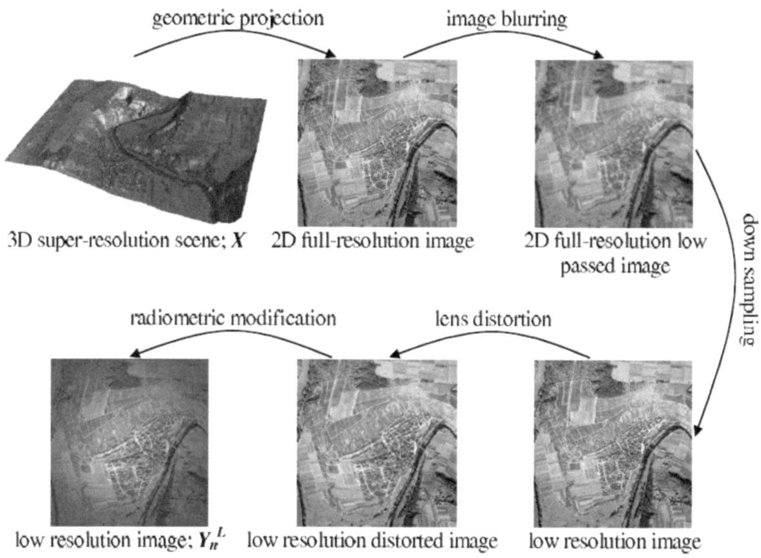

Figure 9. 3D-SR observation model [9].

2.6. Postprocessing

The implementation of postprocessing steps is not very common in the literature. In fact, SR is usually the last link in the chain of SR applied to MC systems. However, there are some researchers that continue working with the images once the SR step has concluded.

- In Ref. [6], the quality of the SR solution can be enhanced with the application of spatially adaptive regularization parameters. Also an image fusion algorithm is applied for merging the high-resolution image reconstructed by the SR algorithm and color channel resolution images. By combining image fusion with the color difference domain, which is widely used in color interpolation, the proposed image fusion algorithm can produce clearer multispectral images, even when the spectral low-resolution channels are not perfectly registered one to another.

- In Ref. [8], as it was explained in Subsection 2.5, it is demonstrated that when an accurate 3D model of the scene is available, or can be estimated, perspective projection of the scene can be exploited in place of the image alignment/warping step in the 2D super-resolution technique, so the 3D adaptation could be considered as part of the observation model or a postprocessing step.

3. Spatial and temporal SR through a MC system

It has been shown in the previous section that, there are several methods where either temporal information between frames captured by a single camera or spatial information between cameras when using a camera array is used to obtain an HR sequence using SR. Accordingly, these method are named in the literature as spatial SR and temporal SR. In this section, the implementation of algorithms to enhance video sequences combining spatial and temporal SR with an MC approach is presented, together with some associated preprocessing steps [22, 23]. According to the block diagram of **Figure 1** this corresponds to Subsections 2.4 and 2.5. The video SR algorithm used as a basis in this work belongs to the "fusion" category. The *baseline super-resolution* (BSR) algorithm execution can be divided into three independent stages: *Motion Estimation, Shift & Add* and *Fill Holes*:

- The *Motion Estimation* stage determines the motion between two or more frames with subpixel accuracy; depending on the selected *scale factor* (i.e., obtaining an output frame whose size is twice the vertical and horizontal size of the input frame would mean *a scale factor* of 2). In order to obtain the motion vectors of each MB, a block-matching method is considered.

- The second stage, known as *Shift & Add*, is executed once the motion vectors have been calculated. A grid is filled with the contributions given by the estimated motion vectors.

- Finally, the *Fill Holes* stage considers that it is possible that there could be some empty positions in the grid for the current frame, as the candidate frames do not contain information enough to fill all the locations. These empty positions are denoted as *holes* in the scope of this work. In this case, a bilinear surface interpolator is used to fill each empty pixel. For each one of the frames, the whole process is repeated. As a result, a HR super-resolved image is obtained and the SR sequence is stored.

Figure 10 summarizes a general scheme using LR frames captured by multiple cameras to generate an HR sequence from a user selected camera. It includes the following steps:

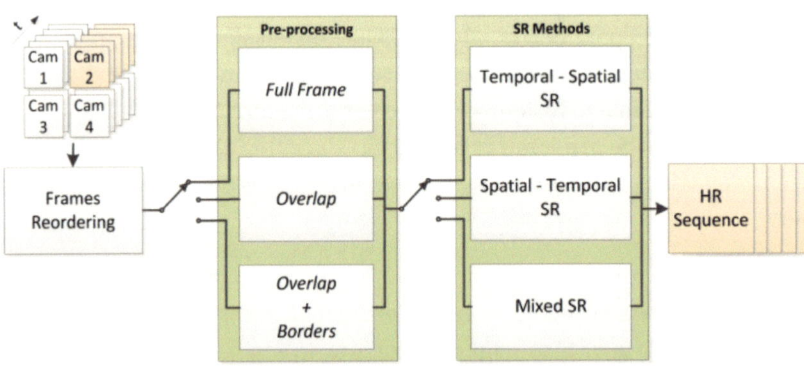

Figure 10. General scheme showing preprocessing modes and SR methods [22].

http://dx.doi.org/10.5772/65442

- First, the frames captured by the cameras are lexicographically reordered.
- Second, a preprocessing step is considered, including three possible options: *Full Frame*, *Overlap + Borders* and *Overlap*.
- Finally, the SR process is applied considering three methods: *temporal-spatial SR* method, *spatial-temporal SR* method, and *mixed SR* method. These methods combine spatial and temporal information.

3.1. Preprocessing

After reordering the frames recorded from the different cameras of the MC array, the first stage of the algorithm implementation is based on preprocessing algorithms. The target consists on deciding whether some regions of the captured frames should be discarded in order to enhance quality by avoiding artifacts and/or reducing the execution time. Some constraints to the MC array configuration are considered:

- A rectangular geometry.
- Location of the cameras in the same plane.
- Common parts from the same global scene are recorded by the cameras from different locations.

Considering a MC system which complies with these constraints, as the one shown in **Figure 11(a)**, a common region (or *overlap*) of the recorded information by the cameras of the MC system could be available (or a subset of cameras). Surrounding the *overlap*, there will be a *border*, as presented in **Figure 11(b)**. The separation and geometry between cameras of the MC system affects the way to obtain the borders and the *overlap* as shown in **Figure 11(b)**.

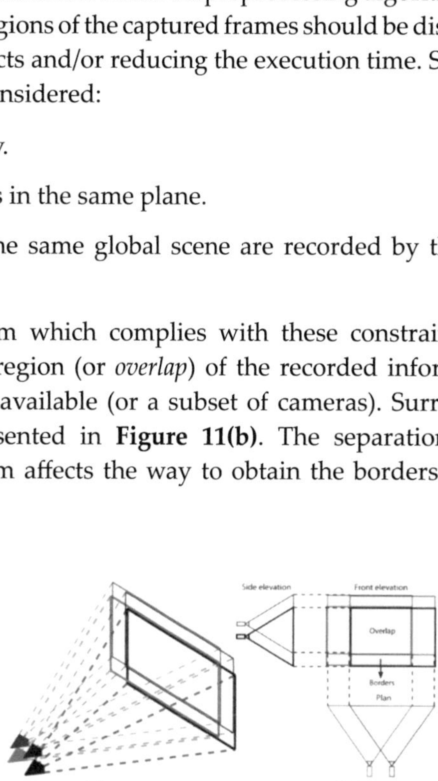

Figure 11. Borders and overlap in an MC array. (a) Frames recorded by an MC array in perspective. (b) Side and front elevations, and plan views of the recorded frames [22].

From this analysis, several ways to process the frames captured by the MC array arise:

- Considering the whole frame information (*Full Frame* mode). This is the basic mode, in which the full frame is captured by every camera.
- Considering the *overlap* between cameras (*Overlap* mode). In order to obtain the *overlap*, it is necessary to know the *offset* in pixels between cameras.

- Considering dividing the frame between the *overlap* and the *borders* (*Overlap* + *Borders* mode). As shown in **Figure 12**, this method provides 9 different parts to be super-resolved: 4 *sides*, 4 *corners*, and the *overlap*.

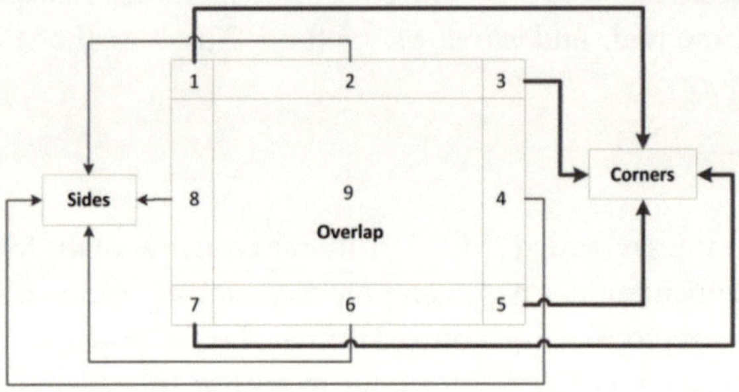

Figure 12. Frames division of the MC array in Overlap + Borders mode [22].

3.2. Temporal-spatial SR method

This method considers information provided by the MC array in order to obtain an HR sequence in two phases. In the first phase, only temporal information is considered, while in the second phase spatial information is processed. **Figure 13** presents this method. First, temporal SR is applied to the LR frames of each camera of the MC system. This SR process considers a *temporal working window* (TWW), which determines the number of frames used in the SR process. The output of this phase consists on a sequence of a resolution named *Medium Resolution*$_{temporal}$ (MR_t) determined by the MC array dimensions: $P \times Q$.

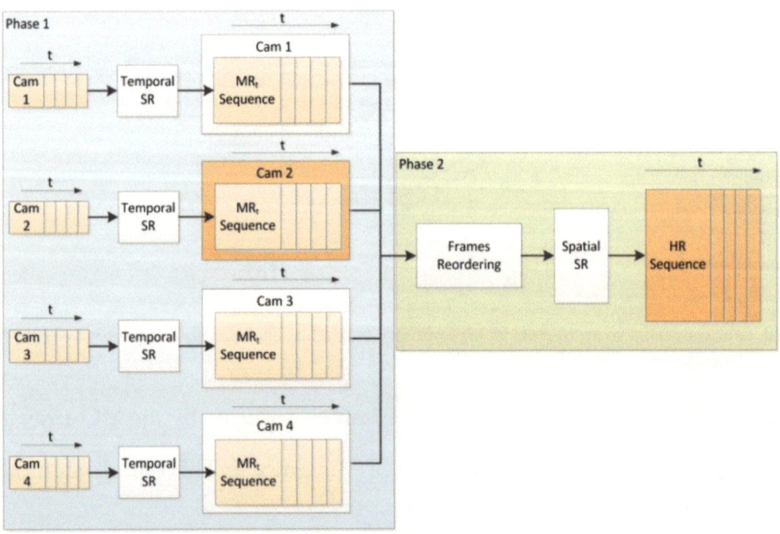

Figure 13. Temporal-spatial SR method [22].

http://dx.doi.org/10.5772/65442

The second phase begins with a *frame* reordering process, storing the frames in lexicographical order, from left to right and top to bottom, as shown in **Figure 14**. Then, the spatial information of the MR_t sequences is used to obtain a super-resolved HR output sequence. In order to perform the *spatial SR*, the working window considers the frames p_f the *spatial SR* process (*spatial working window*, SWW).

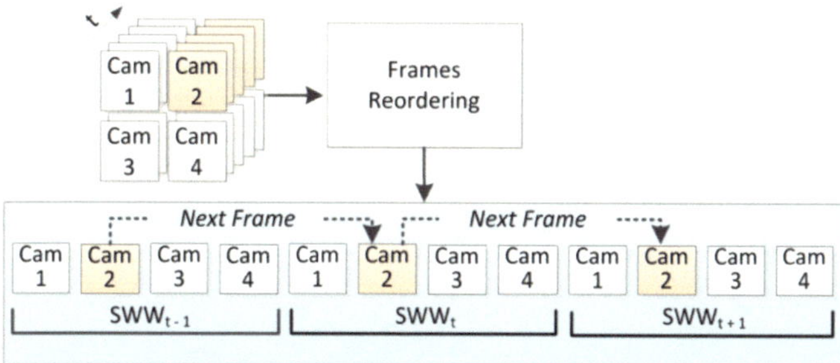

Figure 14. Frames reordering process [22].

The computational cost of this method is high, since the dimensions of the MC array directly affect the number of SR processes to be applied in the first phase, plus a *Spatial SR*, determining a total of $(P \times Q) + 1$ SR processes.

3.3. Spatial-temporal SR method

The *spatial-temporal SR* method, presented in **Figure 15**, is similar to the *temporal-spatial SR* method but reversing the order of the SR processes. In this case *Spatial SR* is applied first. As a result, the output sequence resolution is named *Medium Resolution*$_{spatial}$ (MR_s). After applying *Spatial SR* a *Temporal SR* process is applied considering a *temporal working window* as in BSR, and obtaining as output an HR sequence.

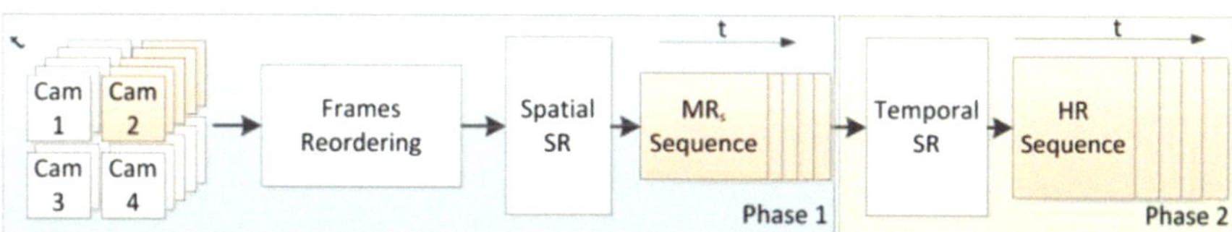

Figure 15. Spatial-temporal SR method [22].

In this case, only two SR processes are applied to obtain the HR output, which reduces considerably the computational cost.

3.4. Mixed SR method

After analyzing the characteristics of the previous methods, the *mixed SR* method was considered. The advantage of this method consists on integrating the spatial and the temporal information in a combined SR process way to generate the HR output. In this scope, a new WW is defined (*mixed working window*, MWW). The frames selection process is performed in a smart way in the *block matching* process of the *motion estimation* stage, widening the possibilities to find more appropriate information in the SR process.

An example of how MWW is defined is shown in **Figure 16**. A 2 × 2 MC array is selected and SR is applied to camera #2. As it is shown, MWW considers the information of a backward time slot and a forward time slot from the frame to be processed. For instance, the time slot "*t*" considers a WW including both the frames of the MC system captured in the time slots "*t* − 1," "*t*," and "*t* + 1." After processing the frame of the camera #2 in the time slot "*t*," SR is applied to the same frame in the time slot "*t* + 1." In this case, a similar MWW is generated, but considering the time slots "*t*," "*t* + 1," and "*t* + 2" and proceeding in the same way for the subsequent frames.

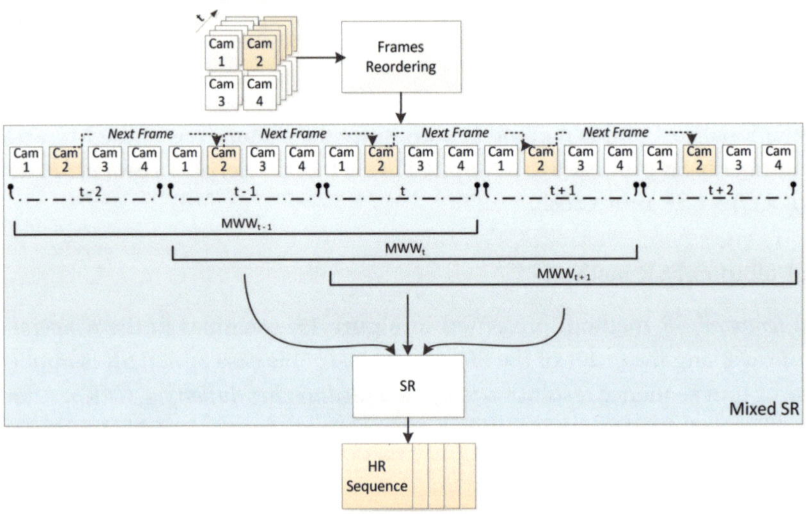

Figure 16. Mixed SR method [22].

This method reduces the computational cost of the previous presented methods, as it only consists on one SR, but the memory requirements of the algorithm are higher.

3.5. Results

In this section, significant results based both on test sequences adapted for comparison and on real MC acquisition systems are shown. The *Water Cooler* sequence [24] was recorded by using a 5 × 5 MC system. The selected cameras for this sequence are the *leftmost center, topmost center, bottommost center*, and *rightmost center*, forming a rhomboid. Additionally, several tests were completed by using a rectangular 3 × 3 camera array, to demonstrate the versatility of the proposed methods. As the rhomboid configuration of *Water Cooler* has no information of the corners, no results for the preprocessing mode *Overlap + Borders* can be shown.

http://dx.doi.org/10.5772/65442

Sequence/method	Water cooler		Mobcal		Stockholm		Shields		Parkrun	
	PSNR(dB)	SSIM	PSNR(dB)	SSIM	PSNR(dB)	SSIM	PSNR(dB)	SSIM	PSNR(dB)	SSIM
TS SR	*28.33*	*0.879*	26.55	0.879	27.05	0.901	26.92	0.927	19.82	0.825
ST SR	27.85	0.868	26.51	0.879	26.64	0.895	26.61	0.923	19.57	0.820
Mixed SR	27.67	0.869	*27.26*	*0.920*	*28.32*	*0.939*	*27.73*	*0.952*	*20.47*	*0.900*
BSR	27.66	0.868	26.47	0.891	26.31	0.891	25.91	0.903	19.30	0.808
INT	27.20	0.858	26.32	0.858	25.47	0.834	25.44	0.870	18.67	0.736

Table 1. PSNR and SSIM results for full frame preprocessing mode (best values are represented in italics).

Sequence/method	Water cooler		Mobcal		Stockholm		Shields		Parkrun	
	PSNR(dB)	SSIM	PSNR(dB)	SSIM	PSNR(dB)	SSIM	PSNR(dB)	SSIM	PSNR(dB)	SSIM
TS SR	*27.73*	*0.871*	26.28	0.848	26.70	0.844	27.24	0.885	*19.52*	0.717
ST SR	27.03	0.855	26.07	0.847	26.26	0.830	26.83	0.872	19.20	0.690
Mixed SR	27.31	0.867	*27.34*	*0.893*	*28.26*	*0.912*	*27.51*	*0.905*	19.31	*0.746*
BSR	26.94	0.858	25.82	0.842	25.82	0.826	26.03	0.850	18.65	0.656
INT	26.06	0.838	26.03	0.829	25.06	0.761	25.57	0.809	18.32	0.613

Table 2. AVG PSNR and SSIM results for Overlap preprocessing mode (best values are represented in italics).

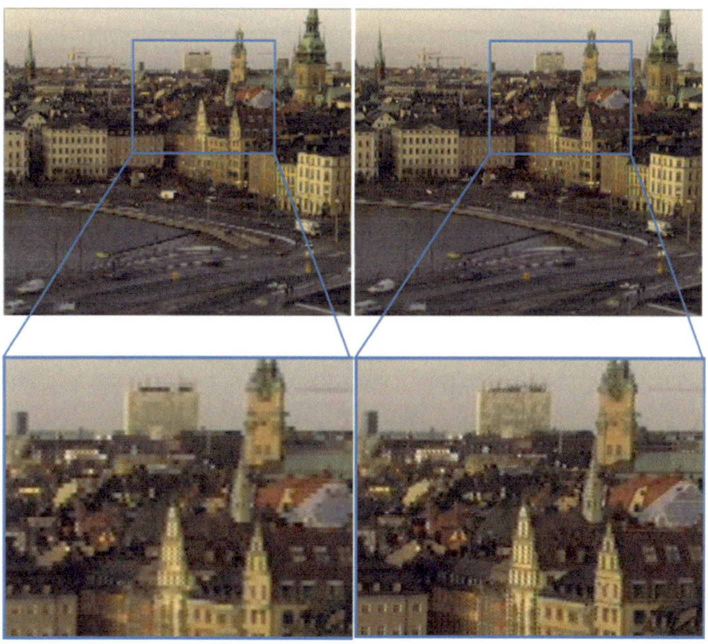

Figure 17. Complete and detailed view of a frame of *Stockholm* sequence [22]. BSR; (left); *Mixed* SR method (right).

Tables 1 and **2** show the results for the sequences under test: *Water Cooler, Mobcal, Stockholm, Shields,* and *Parkrun*. The three presented methods are evaluated using the *peak signal-to-noise ratio* (PSNR) and *structural similarity index* (SSIM) metrics: *temporal-spatial* SR (TS SR), *spatial-temporal* SR (ST SR), and *mixed SR*, together with BSR and interpolation (INT) as a reference. Each table represents the results for the preprocessing modes: *Full Frame* mode (**Table 1**) and *Overlap* mode (**Table 2**). As it can be seen from these tables, the preprocessing modes *Full Frame* and *Overlap* follows a similar behavior. It can be concluded from the results in **Table 2**, that the *mixed SR* method outperforms the other methods in the majority of the cases. In terms of subjective comparison, two sets of frames are shown for the *Stockholm* sequence and the *Water Cooler* sequence in **Figures 17** and **18**, respectively. In **Figure 17**, there is a relevant enhancement in the roofs and the facades of the buildings in the *mixed* SR method. **Figure 18** shows that a higher definition is provided by the TS SR method versus the BSR, minimizing the number of artifacts in the items on the table [22].

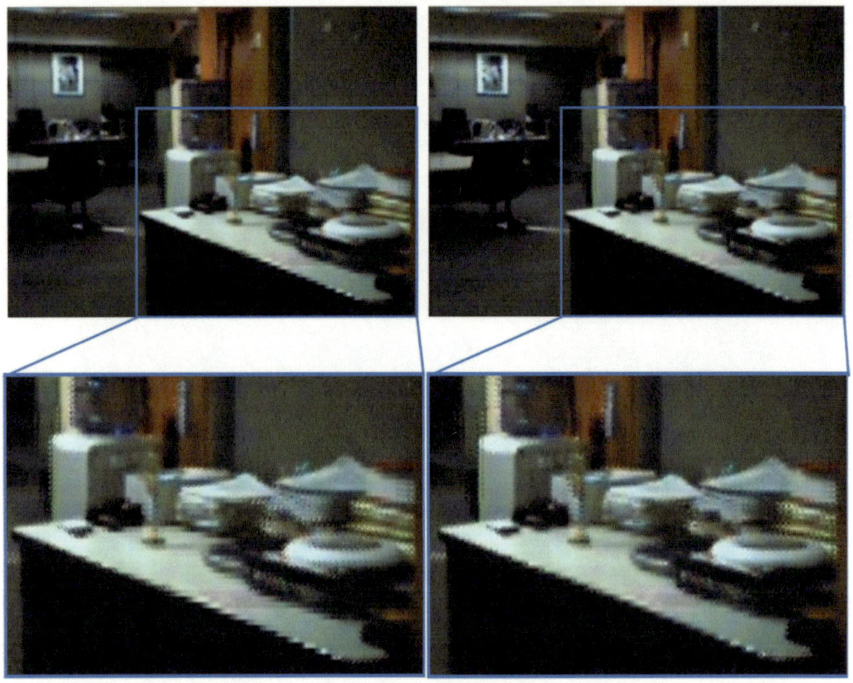

Figure 18. Complete and detailed view of a frame of *Water Cooler* sequence [22]. BSR (left); TS SR (right).

4. Conclusions

In conclusion, the main analyzed characteristics of the studied documents which combine SR and MC are shown in **Tables 3–5**:

http://dx.doi.org/10.5772/65442

Ref.	Multi-camera system		
	N°	Type	Arrangement
[5]	25	ProFUSION 25	5 × 5 array
[6]	9	CCD VCC-G20E20	3 × 3 array (3 C +6 I)
[7]	4	CCD Dragonfly	2 × 2 array (in PIC micro)
[8]	6–12	CCD cameras	Conical array (6 or 12 cam.)
[9]	2	Pulnix	Closely and overlapped
[10]	2	Logitech Quickcam	Flexible and overlapped
[11]	100	Cheap LR camera	Circularly shifted

Table 3. Multi-camera system.

Ref.	Image characteristics	
	Correspondence	Registration
[5]	One-shot mode	Two-parameter shift
[6]	Lenses adjustment and Blur uniformity	Preprocessing steps
[7]	Accurate trigger using PIC16F690	3D fundamental matrix
[8]	Planar checkerboard	Conical acquisition
[9]	Sequence to sequence alignment	2D homography
[10]	Harris feature points	2D homography
[11]	Continuous moments	Distributed acquisition

Table 4. Image characteristics.

Ref.	SR algorithm	Application	Limitations
[5]	Dense displacement estimation	Rendering	Grayscale cameras and vignetting
[6]	Bayesian multichannel	Rendering	Nonextensible MC system
[7]	Temporal: Point sampling	Rendering	No spatial resolution, only temporal resolution
[8]	3D mosaicing	Underwater	Non-real-time
[9]	POCS	Surveillance	Planar scene assumption and no tracking of the interest region
[10]	POCS + PSF	Rendering	Planar scenes and placement of cameras at a constant distance
[11]	-	Rendering	Restoration step to be improved and don't use "real-world" data

Table 5. SR Algorithm, applications, and limitations.

- *MC system:* Number, type, and position of cameras.
- *Image characteristics:* Correspondence and registration of images.

- *SR algorithm:* Algorithm used to perform the SR.
- *Application*: System use.
- *Limitations:* Not considered issues in the system.

As it can be noticed in the tables, there are limited approaches combining MC system and SR and what is more important, there are some issues which are almost always disregarded, such as:

- The implementation in MC systems of SR algorithms for real-time performance, using approaches as dedicated hardware or distributed systems. This is an important limitation for applications which require real-time solutions such as surveillance.
- The real-time self-reconfiguration of cameras in a camera array for SR applications, which has been used in the past for planning and control as a form of nonuniform sampling (or adaptive capturing) of image-based rendering scenes [4].
- The issue of SR of color images is another important research field. Although some color correction methods for multiview images have been introduced [25], monochrome processing by means of independently applying SR to every color channel is not optimal because it does not take into account the spectral correlation between the channels [26]. If the channels can be decorrelated using a transform like the *Karhunen Loeve Transform* (KLT) [27] or in a suitable color space, then the SR algorithm can be applied to every decorrelated channel separately and transformed back to the original domain or color space. The only reference found which analyzes this issue is the one proposed by Park et al. [6].
- The concept of learning-based SR [28, 29] has not been developed for MC applications. It exploits the prior knowledge between the HR examples and the corresponding LR examples through the so-called learning process. Most example-based SR algorithms usually employ a dictionary composed of a large number of HR patches and their corresponding LR patches, which may be useful for MC applications.

The study of the issues mentioned above is a clear field to research. The potential application of combining SR with a MC system is focused on research areas related to 3D mosaicing, surveillance applied to extreme conditions (underwater or blurred environments), and the improvement of more researched techniques such as medical imaging, video enhancement, remote sensing, or sporting events.

According to this review, it is shown that the exploitation of the spatial and temporal super-resolution is something novel which has been implemented by the authors. Section 3 presented a novel image enhancement SR technique integrated with an MC system to take advantage from the spatial and temporal correlations between the recorded sequences. Three different methods have been proposed: *temporal-spatial SR, spatial-temporal SR*, and *mixed SR*. Besides, three different preprocessing steps were introduced: *Full-Frame, Overlap* and *Overlap + Borders*. According to the results [22, 23], it has been shown that the *mixed SR* method with *Full-Frame* preprocessing outperforms the other methods.

http://dx.doi.org/10.5772/65442

Author details

Eduardo Quevedo[1,2*], Gustavo Marrero[1] and Félix Tobajas[1]

*Address all correspondence to: equevedo@iuma.ulpgc.es; eduardo.quevedo@plocan.eu

1 Institute for Applied Microelectronics, University of Las Palmas de Gran Canaria, Las Palmas, Spain

2 Oceanic Platform of the Canary Islands, Carretera de Taliarte, Las Palmas, Spain

References

[1] J. Tiang and K.-K. Ma. A survey on Super-Resolution imaging. Journal of Signal, Image and Video Processing. 2011;5(2):329–342.

[2] T. Goto, Y. Kawamoto, Y. Sakuta, A. Tsutsui, and M.Sakurai. Learning-based super-resolution image reconstruction on multi-core processor. IEEE Transactions on Consumer Electronics. 2012;(3):941–946.

[3] M. M. Islam, V. K. Asari, M. N. Islam, and M. A. Karim. Super-resolution enhancement technique for low resolution video. IEEE Transactions on Consumer Electronics. 2010;56(2):919–924.

[4] B. A. Stancil, C. Zhang, and T. Chen. Active multicamera networks: From rendering to surveillance. IEEE Journal of Selected Topics in Signal Processing. 2008;2(4):597–605.

[5] M. H. Fanaswala. Regularized Super-Resolution of Multi-View Images [dissertation]. Carleton University; 2009.

[6] J. Hyun Park, H. Mook Oh, and M. Gi Kang. Multi-Camera imaging system using Super-Resolution. In: The 23rd International Technical Conference on Circuits/Systems, Computers and Communications (ITC-CSCC), Shimonoseki; 2008.

[7] A. Agrawal, M. Gupta, A. Veeraraghavan, and S. G. Narasimhan. Optimal coded sampling for temporal super-resolution. In: IEEE Conference on Computer Vision and Pattern Recognition (CVPR); 2010.

[8] P. Firoozfam. Multi-Camera Imaging for 3-D Mapping and Positioning; Stereo and Panoramic Conical Views [dissertation]; 2004.

[9] G. Caner, A. Murat Tekalp, and W. Heinzelman. Super-Resolution recovery for Multi-Camera surveillance imaging. In: International Conference on Multimedia and Expo, Baltimore, MD; 2003.

[10] M. Directo, S. Shirani, and D. Capson. Wireless camera network for image Super-Resolution. In: Canadian Conference on Electrical and Computer Engineering, Ontario; 2004. DOI: 10.1109/CCECE.2004.1345204

[11] L. Baboulaz and P.Dragotti. Distributed acquisition and image Super-Resolution based on continuous moments from samples. In: International Conference on Image Processing; Atlanta, GA. 2006. pp. 3309–3312. DOI: 10.1109/ICIP.2006.312880

[12] A. Agrawal and Y. Xu. Coded exposure deblurring: Optimized codes for PSF estimation and invertibility. In: IEEE Conference on Computer Vision and Pattern Recognition; 20–25 June 2009; Miami, FL. IEEE. pp. 2066–2073. DOI: 10.1109/CVPR.2009.5206685

[13] J. Heikkilä. Pattern matching with affine moment descriptors. Pattern Recognition. 2004;37(9):1825–1834. DOI: 10.1016/j.patcog.2004.03.005

[14] W. D. Reynolds and D. S. Campbell. A scalable video stabilization algorithm for multi-camera systems. In: 6th IEEE International Conference on Advanced Video and Signal Based Surveillance; 2–4 Sept. 2009; Genova. pp. 250–255. DOI: 10.1109/AVSS.2009.91

[15] E. Shechtman, Y. Caspi, and M. Irani. Space-time super resolution. IEEE Transactions on Pattern Analysis and Machine Intelligence. 2005;27(4):531–545. DOI: 10.1109/TPAMI.2005.85

[16] A. J. Patti, M. I. Sezan, and A. M. Tekalp. Superresolution video reconstruction with arbitrary sampling lattices and nonzero aperture time. IEEE Transactions on Image Processing. 1997;6(8):1064–1076. DOI: 10.1109/83.605404

[17] B. K. Gunturk. High-resolution image reconstruction from multiple differently exposed images. IEEE Signal Processing Letters. 2006;13(4):197–200. DOI: 10.1109/LSP.2005.863693

[18] E. Eren, M. I. Sezan, and A. M. Tekalp. Robust, object-based high-resolution image reconstruction from low-resolution video. IEEE Transactions on Image Processing. 1997;6(10):1446–1451. DOI: 10.1109/83.624970

[19] E. S. Lee and M. G. Kang. Regularized adaptive high-resolution image reconstruction considering inaccurate subpixel registration. IEEE Transactions on Image Processing. 2003;12(7):826–837. DOI: 10.1109/TIP.2003.811488

[20] M. K. Park, M. G. Kang, and A. K. Katsaggelos. Regularized Super-Resolution image reconstruction considering innacurate motion information. SPIE Optical Engineering. 2007;46(11):1–12.

[21] S. L. Wood, H.-B. Lan, M. P. Chritstensen, and D. Rajan. Edge detection performance in super-resolution image reconstruction from camera arrays. In: IEEE Digital Signal Processing Workshop & 4th IEEE Signal Processing Education Workshop; 24–27 Sept. 2006; Teton National Park, WY. pp. 38–43. DOI: 10.1109/DSPWS.2006.265427

[22] E. Quevedo, J. de la Cruz, G. M. Callicó, F. Tobajas, and R. Sarmiento. Video enhancement using spatial and temporal super-resolution from a multi-camera system. IEEE

Transactions on Consumer Electronics. 2014.;60(3):420–428. DOI: 10.1109/TCE.2014.6937326

[23] E. Quevedo, J. de la Cruz, L. Sánchez, G. M. Callicó, and F. Tobajas. Super resolution with adaptive macro-block topology applied to a multi camera system. IEEE Transactions on Consumer Electronics. 2015;61(2):230–235. DOI: 10.1109/TCE.2015.7150598

[24] B. M. Smith, L. Zhang, H. Jin, and A. Agarwala. Light field video stabilization. In: IEEE International Conference on Computer Vision; Sept. 29 2009–Oct. 2 2009; Kyoto, Japan. pp. 341–348. DOI: 10.1109/ICCV.2009.5459270

[25] F. Shao, G. Jiang, M. Yu, and Y.-S. Ho. Highlight-detection-based color correction method for multiview images. ETRI Journal. 2009;31(4):448–450.

[26] M. K. Ng and N. K. Bose. Mathematical analysis of super-resolution methodology. IEEE Signal Processing Magazine. 2003;20(3):62–74. DOI: 10.1109/MSP.2003.1203210

[27] B. Hunt and O. Kubler. Karhunen-Loeve multispectral image restoration, part I: Theory. IEEE Transactions on Acoustics, Speech and Signal Processing. 1984;32(3):592–600. DOI: 10.1109/TASSP.1984.1164363

[28] S. C. Jeong and B. C. Song. Fast super-resolution algorithm based on dictionary size reduction using k-means clustering. ETRI Journal. 2010;32(4):596–602.

[29] G. Anbarjafari and H. Demirel. Image super resolution based on interpolation of wavelet domain high frequency subbands and the spatial domain input image. ETRI Journal. 2010;32(3):390–394.

Chapter 6

Novel Approaches for Regional Multifocus Image Fusion

Long Chen, Junwei Duan and C. L. Philip Chen

Additional information is available at the end of the chapter

http://dx.doi.org/10.5772/65076

Abstract

Image fusion is a research topic about combining information from multiple images into one fused image. Although a large number of methods have been proposed, many challenges remain in obtaining clearer resulting images with higher quality. This chapter addresses the multifocus image fusion problem about extending the depth of field by fusing several images of the same scene with different focuses. Existing research in multifocus image fusion tends to emphasis on the pixel-level image fusion using transform domain methods. The region-level image fusion methods, especially the ones using new coding techniques, are still limited. In this chapter, we provide an overview of regional multi-focus image fusion, and two different orthogonal matching pursuit-based sparse representation methods are adopted for regional multi-focus image fusion. Experiment results show that the regional image fusion using sparse representation can achieve a comparable even better performance for multifocus image fusion problems.

Keywords: image fusion, multifocus, region, image segmentation, sparse representation

1. Introduction

The depth of field is usually limited in current imaging systems using conventional sensors like CCD cameras. Hence, the image we obtained is usually only partly in focus, and the objects in focus are captured more sharply and clearer. However, to accurately analyze the images, having all objects in focus is desired [1]. Multifocus image fusion is an effective approach to extend the depth of field by combining several images of the same scene with different focuses and to provide a better view for human perception. The function of multifocus image fusion is illustrated in **Figure 1**. The white boxes in the source images indicate the regions in focus.

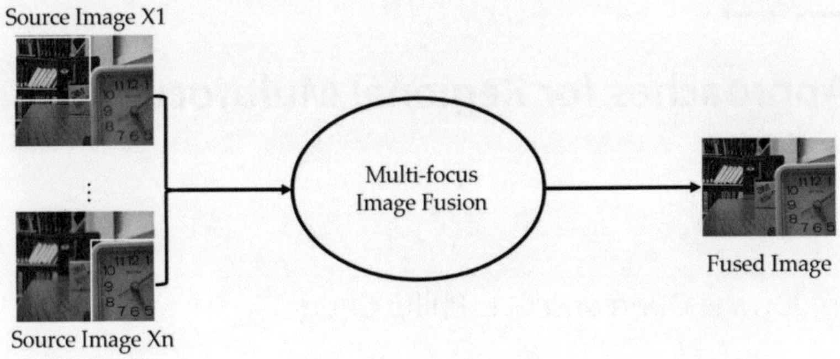

Figure 1. The function of multifocus image fusion.

In recent years, the technique of multifocus image fusion has been broadly used in various application fields such as biochemical analysis [2], medical image processing [3], remote sensing [4], and other areas [5]. Many novel multifocus image fusion methods have been proposed, and they can be categorized into the pixel-level fusion methods and the region-level fusion methods. In pixel-level image fusion, source images are usually fused by considering the pixel-wise features to make the decision of fusion. There are several advantages for pixel-level image fusion, such as extracting full of original information in the source images and easy to implement. However, the pixel-level image fusion is sensitive to noise, which will cause the wrong pixel choosing from corresponding source images. Recently, many multiscale transform-based pixel-level image fusion methods are very popular because these methods can keep more sharpness and edge information in source images. The benefits of different transforms, such as discrete wavelet [6], curvelet [7], contourlet [8], and so on, have been well explored. However, due to the pixel-level coefficients selection and less considerations of spatial information, some artifacts may be found in the fused images.

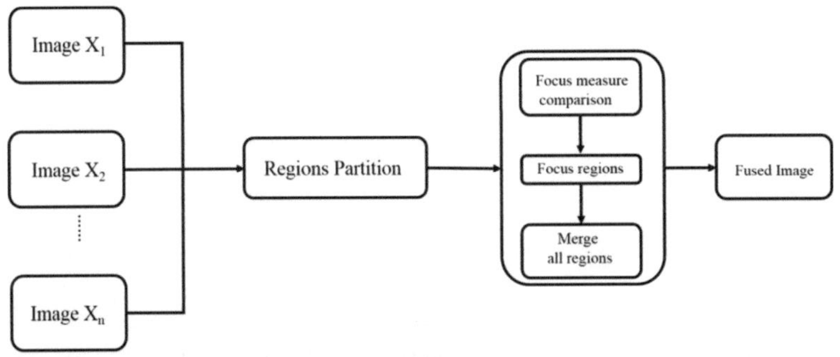

Figure 2. The general process of region level multifocus image fusion.

To address the weaknesses mentioned above and employ more spatial information in images, the manner of fusion can be changed from pixel by pixel to region by region. Few regional multifocus image fusion methods have been proposed. For instance, Omar et al. have proposed a region-based image fusion method using a combinatory Chebyshev-ICA method [9]. Li et al. have proposed a regional image fusion method using spatial frequency [10]. Regional multifocus image fusion usually contains the following steps: the image segmentation/partition and the fusion/merging of different regions. The general process of region-level multifocus image fusion is illustrated in **Figure 2**. Each source image is initially partitioned in some way to produce a set of regions. Various properties of these regions can be calculated and used to determine which regions from which source images are to be included in the fused image. This has advantages over pixel-level methods as more semantic fusion rules can be considered based on regional features in the image. Finally, the selected regions in focus are combined into the fused image.

The regional multifocus image fusion is the major contents of this chapter. In the following section, we first introduce on how to express the image patches using two kinds of sparse representation algorithms: orthogonal matching pursuit (OMP) algorithm and simultaneous orthogonal matching pursuit (SOMP) algorithm. Besides, how to calculate the focus measure using the obtained sparse coefficients is also described. Second, two regional multifocus image fusion schemes based on different sparse representation algorithms are given in Section 3, and the corresponding fusion processes are introduced. Experiments are conducted based on some source image pairs with different depths of field. To evaluate the performance of the new methods, we conduct the comparison of some state-of-art methods and provide the fusion results in Section 4. Finally, the conclusion and future work are given in Section 5.

2. Sparse representation theory and clarity measure

As shown in **Figure 2**, one important module in regional multifocus image fusion is the focus measure (this is also important in pixel-by-pixel fusion). Many coding schemas for images such as wavelet and EMD have been used for this purpose [11, 12]. Here we use more recently proposed coding schema, i.e., the sparse representation.

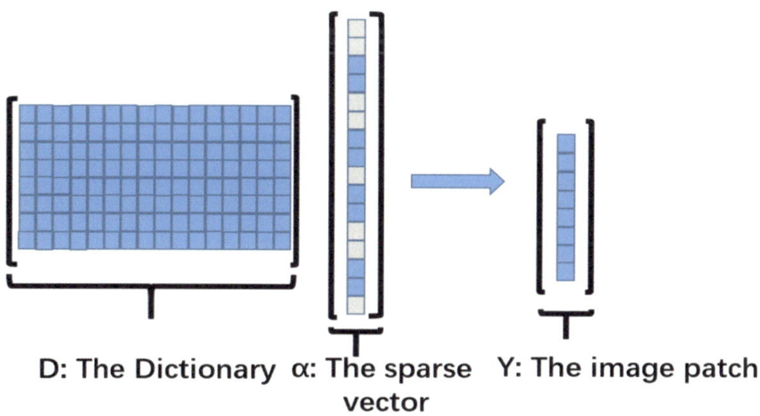

Figure 3. The spare representation of an image patch.

As an extension to wavelet transform (WT), sparse representation has become a popular tool widely used in image or signal processing tasks such as compressed sensing [13], image denoising [14], image classification [15], and face recognition [16]. In sparse representation, the image patches in original image are usually represented as linear combinations of a "few" atoms from an overcomplete dictionary [17]. **Figure 3** shows the sparse linear model. In this model, an image patch can be expressed by a sparse vector $\boldsymbol{\alpha}$, and

$$y = \sum_{n=1}^{N} p_n d_n = DP \tag{1}$$

where the overcomplete dictionary is $D = \{d_1, d_2, \ldots, d_N\}$ and the number of atoms is N. There are many methods to generate the overcomplete dictionary, such as K-SVD [18] and discrete cosine transforms (DCTs), and they can be directly created from some images by learning [19]. According to the dictionary D, the image signal can be represented by the sparse coefficient $\mathbf{P} = \{p_1, p_2 \ldots, p_N\}$.

The number of the non-zero entries in coefficient P is $\|P\|_0$. According to the sparse representation theory, the smaller is $\|P\|_0$, the sparser the image patch can be represented. Therefore, we need to minimize the $\|P\|_0$, which can be formulated as follows:

$$\min \|P\|_0 \quad \text{subject to} \quad \|DP - y\| < \varepsilon \tag{2}$$

where ε means the global tolerance of error. We can solve the optimization problem in Eq. (2) by greedily testing the possible combinations of columns of y [20]. In such kind of greedy algorithms, the orthogonal matching pursuit (OMP) is widely used, and we refer the readers to Ref. [21] for details of the OMP algorithm.

Unlike the OMP algorithm that works on signals (image patches) separately, if we fix the dictionary D to be used in representing several signals at the same time, we are attempting to derive the sparse coefficients for several signals simultaneously by solving the following optimization problem,

$$\hat{P} = \arg\min_{P} \|P\|_{row,0} \quad \text{subject to} \; \|DP - Y\|_F^2 < \varepsilon \tag{3}$$

where P means the sparse coefficients for a set of signals (image patches Y) and ε is the error tolerance. $\hat{P}$ is the spare representation of image patches Y. The assumption that the several image patches are sparse represented by the dictionary simultaneously is valuable to the multifocus image fusion problem because the image patches at the same location of different source images are regarded as perceptions of the same objects. The optimization problem in Eq. (3) can be solved by another greedy algorithm called simultaneously orthogonal matching pursuit (SOMP); its details can be found in Ref. [22].

In multifocus image fusion, some clarity measures should be used to see the image pixel/region in focus or not. Therefore, no matter which sparse representation algorithm we adopt to obtain the sparse coefficients, how to use the derived coefficients to define the clarity measure is an important step for multifocus image fusion.

When we have the sparse coefficient P_i for one image patch i, we can calculate the information embedded in this coefficient by summarizing all the absolute values of elements in P_i. More specifically, the information level in this patch is $F_i = \|P_i\|$, here $\|\cdot\|$ is the Manhattan norm of P_i. Considering the out-of-focus patch will be smoother than the in-focus patch, the information or details contained in the out-of-focus patch will be in lower level. So the information level defined by Manhattan norm can be regarded as a decent indicator or clarity measure on if the patch is in focus or not [23].

By window sliding technique, each source image can be reshaped into a series of image patches. And then each image patch can be changed into a vector, which can be denoted by sparse coefficients. Assuming that the overcomplete dictionary contains T atoms and each source image can be divided into r patches, we can get all the vectorized patches as follows:

$$V = [d_1, d_2, \dots d_T] \begin{bmatrix} \mathrm{p}_1(1) & \dots & p_r(1) \\ \vdots & \ddots & \vdots \\ p_1(T) & \dots & p_r(T) \end{bmatrix} \tag{4}$$

where P is the sparse coefficient matrix.

$$P = [p_1, \dots, p_r] = \begin{bmatrix} p_1(1) & \dots & p_r(1) \\ \vdots & \ddots & \vdots \\ p_1(T) & \dots & p_r(T) \end{bmatrix} \tag{5}$$

In the following, we calculate the Manhattan norm of the vectors as the clarity measure. The metric is also applied in Ref. [24], and we call them the activity levels or clarity levels of responding patches.

$$F = \left[\|P_1\|_1, \dots, \|P_r\|_1\right] \tag{6}$$

where $\|P_i\|_1$ is the Manhattan norm.

3. Regional image fusion using sparse representation

In traditional sparse representation-based image fusion methods, the spatial information of source images is less considered because we only calculate the sum of absolute sparse coefficients as the activity level of image patch and apply the choose-max fusion rule pixel by pixel. This may lead to ringing effects-related distortions in the fused image. On the contrary, in the regional image fusion approach, the source images are first partitioned by an image segmentation method, and then according to different sharpness measures, the sharp regions are used to construct the fused image. A lot of image segmentation algorithms such as normalized cuts [25], watershed-based segmentation [26], and others [27] have been proposed. Currently, most of image segmentation algorithms are quite complicated and time consuming.

In traditional regional multifocus image fusion, less consideration on the effects of focus in source images may increase the risk of bad segmentation in some images because the features of in-focus and out-of-focus pixels sometimes are very similar. Using region-by-region selection, if the in-focus and the out-of-focus pixels are segmented in the same region, the traditional regional image fusion approach cannot avoid to get some out-of-focus pixels in the final fused image, and the clarity level of the fusion result will be decreased. In the following subsections, to alleviate this weakness of traditional regional image fusion, we provide two new approaches with more considerations on the clarity information in the image segmentation step.

3.1. Regional multifocus image fusion using OMP algorithm

The first new regional multifocus image fusion approach is shown in **Figure 4**. This method is also viable for the case of fusing more than two source images, but here we just use two source

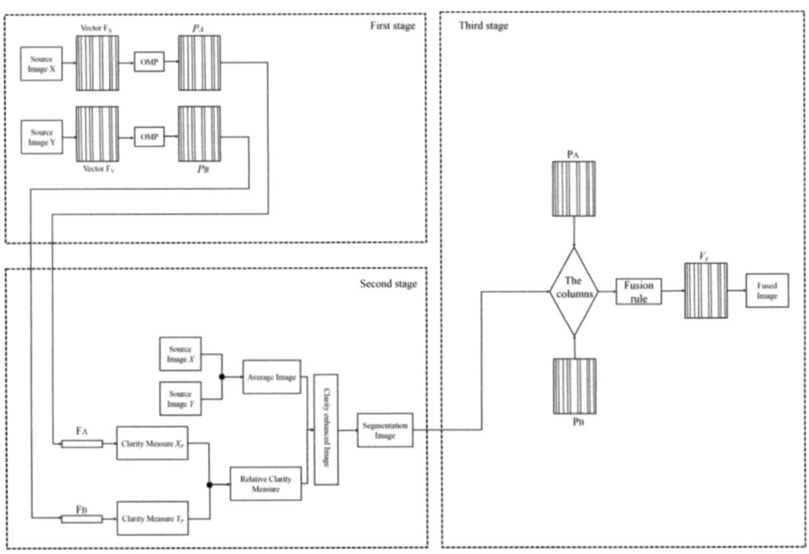

Figure 4. The schematic diagram of the regional multifocus image fusion using OMP.

images for simplicity. This approach includes a new operation before the image segmentation step. That is, after obtaining the clarity information from sparse coefficients, we produce a new clarity enhanced image for further image segmentation by linearly combining the average of source images and the clarity information. We detail the three stages of the first proposed approach in the following subsections.

3.1.1. Clarity measure based on sparse representation

To obtain the sparse coefficients P_X and P_Y, OMP algorithm is adopted in the first stage of fusion process [24]. Next, by Eq. (6), the clarity levels of the source image patches F_x and F_Y can be calculated with the sparse coefficients P_X and P_Y. Then we can get the clarity level images X_P and Y_P, in which, by averaging the clarity levels of all the patches that cover the pixel, the clarity level of a pixel at a specific location is obtained. Finally, the relative clarity level images X_P' and Y_P' can be obtained as follows:

$$X_p' = X_p / (X_p + Y_p) \tag{7}$$

$$Y_p' = Y_p / (X_p + Y_p) \tag{8}$$

3.1.2. Segmentation based on clarity enhanced image

The clarity enhanced image is constructed by the relative clarity measures X_P', Y_P', and the source images. Here, we normalize the source images into the interval [0, 1] and denote them as X' and Y'. The clarity enhanced image ZZ is obtained by

$$XX = \exp\left[(1-\beta)\log X' + \beta \log X_p'\right] \tag{9}$$

$$YY = \exp\left[(1-\beta)\log Y' + \beta \log Y_P'\right] \tag{10}$$

$$ZZ = \left(XX + YY\right)/2 \tag{11}$$

where β is used to adjust the contribution of the relative clarity measure and the original information of source images. The clarity enhanced image ZZ is segmented to many regions by normalized cut algorithm.

The image to be segmented is usually generated by simply averaging of source images in traditional regional multifocus image fusion. By adding the focus information to the source images, it is also considered as the feature in the segmentation process and the segmentation results get lower possibility of having in- and out-of-focus pixels in one segment, and the risk of incorrect segmentation is decreased.

3.1.3. *Regional image fusion*

After the stage of image segmentation, we obtain the partition of ZZ. So we divide the normalized images X' and Y' into the homogenous regions according to the segmentation results over ZZ. In regions of the corresponding position of source images, we calculate the mean value of clarity level of each region of X' and Y', compare the means and use the choose-max-mean rule to select the regions in focus. With the selected regions, the fused sparse coefficient matrix P_F can be obtained by using the corresponding column vectors of P_A and P_B. According to Eq. (12), the vectors of the image patch in the fused image can be calculated as follows:

$$V_F = P_F D \tag{12}$$

where P_F is the fused sparse coefficient matrix and D is the overcomplete dictionary.

Finally, each vector in V_F is reshaped into a patch. And all the image patches are put into the fused image according to their corresponding positions in source images. The final fused image is obtained by averaging all the recovered patches.

3.2. Regional image fusion using SOMP algorithm

In this subsection, we introduce the second regional multifocus image fusion approach using sparse representation. In classical sparse representation, OMP algorithm is usually used to obtain the sparse coefficients by solving the related non-convex optimization problem. Different from OMP, the dictionary in SOMP can be used for decomposing several image patches simultaneously. More specifically, for a location, we can extract one patch from each of the source images. Then, these patches are to be rebuilt by some sparse set of atoms from the dictionary simultaneously. Because the patches in different source images contain the same

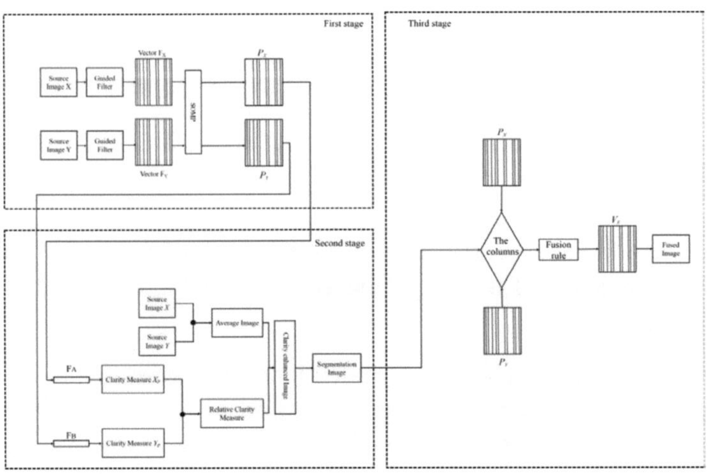

Figure 5. The schematic diagram of the regional multifocus image fusion using SOMP.

visual information in one location, obtaining sparse coefficients together is more advantageous. Combing SOMP and the regional image fusion schema in previous subsection, a new region-based multifocus image-fusion method using the guided filter and greedy analysis is proposed here [28]. The illustrative scheme program of this method is shown in **Figure 5**.

There are also three stages in this scheme. In the first stage, guided filter is adopted for enhancing the details of source images and then we obtain the sparse coefficients using SOMP algorithm. By doing this, more accurate sparse coefficients are obtained from images with details sharpened by guided filter. In addition, the filter enhanced edge information is introduced into the image to be segmented and enhances the segmentation results eventually. The remaining two stages in this fusion approach are the same as the ones in our first proposed approach.

3.2.1. Guided filter and image fusion

Guided filter is proposed by He et al. in 2010 [29]. For the purpose of edge preserving, guided filter has been demonstrated better than bilateral filter, which is also used for detail enhancement. Li et al. have proposed a novel guided filtering-based weighted averaging image fusion method using spatial consistency [30]. As we know, the more feature information the processed images have, the clearer fused image can be obtained. **Figure 6** shows the process of guided filtering. Here, we just introduce this filter briefly.

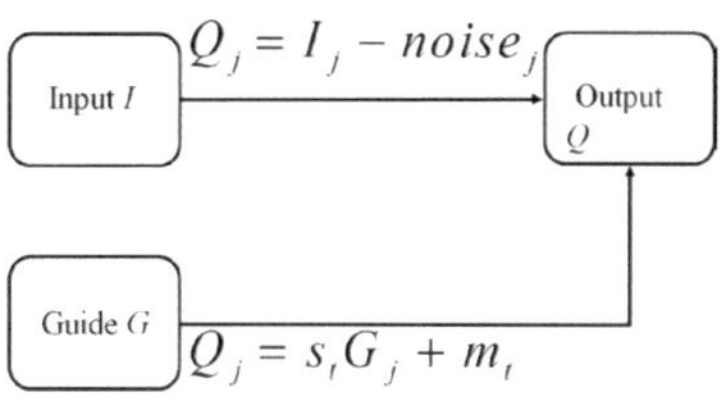

Figure 6. Guided filter.

Mathematically, the guided filter uses a local linear model as follows:

$$Q_j = s_t G_j + m_t, \forall j \in w_t \tag{13}$$

where Q is the output of guided filter, G is the image used to guide the filtering process, w_t is the sliding window, and (s_t, m_t) is usually constants in w_t.

By taking the difference between the filter output and the filter input as cost function and minimizing it, we can get the best values (s_t, m_t) by a simple linear regression problem as follows:

$$E(s_t, n_t) = \sum_{i \in wt} ((s_t G_i + m_t - I_j) + \varepsilon s_t^2) \tag{14}$$

Here, to avoid that the value of s_t is too large, we bring in a regularization parameter ε in Eq. (14). With the optimized (s_t, m_t), we can obtain the filtered image by averaging all the patches generated by Eq. (13). More details can be found in Ref. [29].

For the source images processed by guided filter, we apply sliding window to get a set image patches. For the same location in each image, the corresponding patches are simultaneously decomposed by the same subset of atoms using SOMP. Then taking the same steps as the ones in previous subsection, we use the obtained coefficients to calculate the clarity measure, obtain the clarity enhanced image, conduct the image segmentation, and fuse the image regionally according to the segmentation result.

4. Experiments and results

In this section, we will evaluate the performance of the proposed regional multifocus image fusion methods and compare them with following four methods. They are multifocus image fusion using DWT [31], multifocus image fusion using guided filtering [30], multifocus image fusion using sparse representation [20], and regional multifocus image fusion using spatial frequency [10]. For simplicity, we use DWT, GF, SR, and RIFSF to indicate these methods, respectively. Here, DWT-based method and GF-based method are pixel-level multifocus image fusion methods. SR-based method and RIFSF-based method are regional multifocus image fusion methods. The platform that we use to conduct the image fusion experiments is Matlab 2014b.

4.1. Data

The test images are obtained from Ref. [32]. Four pairs of source images are shown in **Figure 7**, which are named as "book," "balloon," "flower," and "leopard," respectively. There are different depths of focus in every pair of images.

(a) book (b) balloon (c) flower (d) leopard

Figure 7. Four pairs of multifocus source images.

4.2. Results

4.2.1. *Image segmentation results*

For simplicity, we call two fusion methods introduced in this chapter RIFOMP and RIFSOMP. Four other image fusion methods are compared with these two methods. The fusion results will be totally different if the setting parameters are different. So in order to do the comparison fairly, we use all the settings of parameters the same as the ones in the papers [10, 20, 30, 31]. In the proposed methods, after obtaining the image patches by window sliding technique, based on normalized cuts on clarity enhanced image, the corresponding segmentation results are shown in **Figure 8**. From the segmentation results, we can see that the in-focus and out-of-focus pixels are basically divided into different regions.

(a) book (b) balloon (c) flower (d) leopard

Figure 8. The results of image segmentation.

4.2.2. *Image fusion results*

Our multifocus image fusion is conducted based on segmentation results, and the fusion results for source images above are shown in **Figures 8–12**. The other method results are also listed for the purpose of comparison. From these figures, we can see that the fused images produced by DWT-based method are not so clear. Besides, there are incorrect region selections

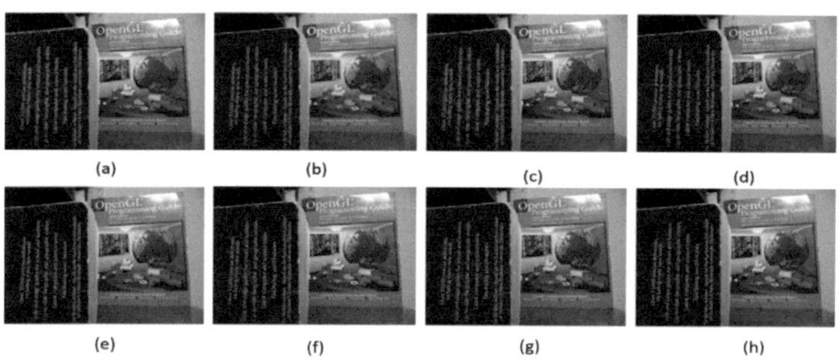

Figure 9. The image fusion results: (a) source image: book 1, (b) source image: book 2, (c) DWT, (d) GFF, (e) SR, (f) RIFSF, (g) RIFOMP, and (h) RIFSOMP.

in some fused images produced by the RIFSF-based method. For example, in **Figure 10(f)**, the boundary of balloon is blurred because of this problem. The results of other four methods are visually similar, so we further conduct the quantitative comparison according to several image quality indexes.

Figure 10. The image fusion results: (a) source image: balloon 1, (b) source image: balloon 2, (c) DWT, (d) GFF, (e) SR, (f) RIFSF, (g) RIFOMP, and (h) RIFSOMP.

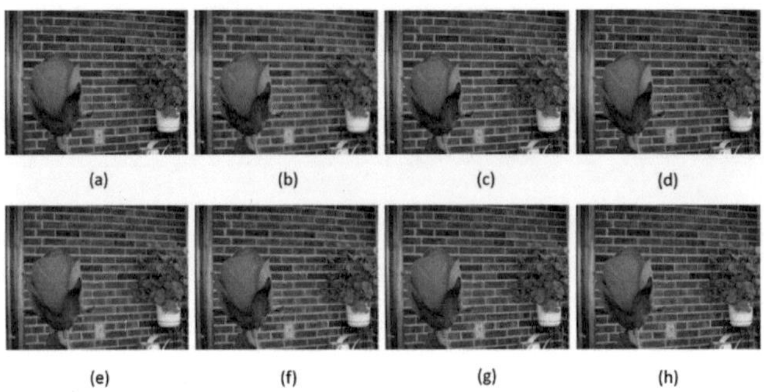

Figure 11. The image fusion results: (a) source image: flower 1, (b) source image: flower 2, (c) DWT, (d) GFF, (e) SR, (f) RIFSF, (g) RIFOMP, and (h) RIFSOMP.

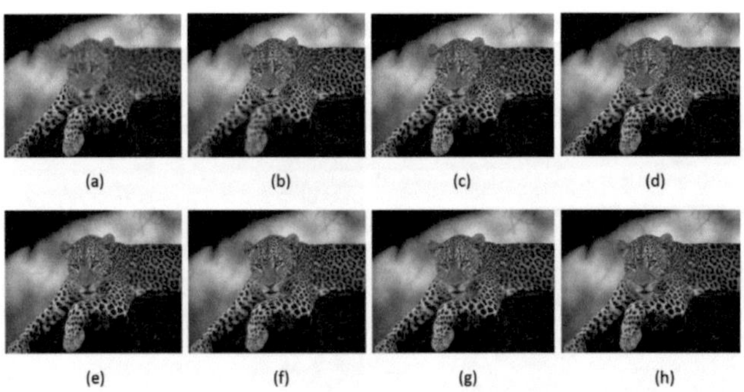

Figure 12. The image fusion results: (a) source image: leopard 1, (b) source image: leopard 2, (c) DWT, (d) GFF, (e) SR, (f) RIFSF, (g) RIFOMP, and (h) RIFSOMP.

4.3. Quantitative evaluation

Besides the subjective evaluation of the fusion results, the objective criteria are also used to evaluate the image fusion results quantitatively. Six popular performance criteria that we adopt are Petrovic metric ($Q^{AB/F}$) [33], mutual information (MI) [34], root mean square error (RSME) [35], peak signal-to-noise ratio (PSNR) [36], structure similarity measure (SSIM) [37], and correlation coefficient (CC) [38].

1. Petrovic metric ($Q^{AB/F}$): $Q^{AB/F}$ is used to evaluate that the edge information transferred from the source images to the fused image. Generally speaking, the larger the value of $Q^{AB/F}$ is, the better the fusion result is. The value of $Q^{AB/F}$ is always smaller than 1.

2. Mutual information (MI): MI is used to measure the dependence between the source images and the fused image. It is a good indicator of information shared by the fused image and the source images, therefore the higher the better.

3. Root mean square error (RMSE): RMSE is used to denote the difference of standard deviation between the fused and source images. A better image fusion result has a smaller RMSE value.

4. Peak signal-to-noise ratio (PSNR): PSNR is widely used to measure the similarity of multiple images (the source images and the fused image). If the value of PSNR is higher, the fusion result will be better.

5. Structure similarity measure (SSIM): SSIM is used to measure the structure distortion between the source images and the fused image. The higher the value of SSIM is, the lower structure distortion is and the better the fusion result is.

6. Correlation coefficient (CC): CC is often used to indicate the degree of correlation between the source images and the fused image. If the value of CC approaches 1, the correlation of the source images and the fused image is very strong.

According to these six measures, the comparison results are shown in **Table 1**. From this table, we can see the MI values of two proposed methods are better than the ones of others for source images "book," "balloon," and "flower." For the source image "leopard," the proposed method RIFSOMP is still the best. According to $Q^{AB/F}$, the two proposed methods also perform very well. For example, the RIFSOMP gets the best $Q^{AB/F}$ for image "balloon." We also list the average performance of each method in comparison. From the average performance in each criterion, we can safely say that the performance of two proposed regional methods is at least comparable to the best of other state-of-the-art methods and according to some specific performance indices such as MI and $Q^{AB/F}$, the proposed RIFSOMP is even superior to other methods in comparison. We conclude that the focus information is well preserved by our methods in the fused images, and there are no obvious artifacts in fusion results.

Source images	Quality measure	Method					
		DWT	GFF	SR	RIFSF	RIFOMP	RIFSOMP
Book	$Q^{AB/F}$	0.7715	0.7985	0.8044	0.7902	0.8009	0.8010
	MI	7.1809	8.9691	8.2072	9.2945	9.7756	9.7775
	RMSE	0.0377	0.0117	0.0124	0.0119	0.0109	0.0110
	PSNR	27.7426	37.9276	37.4354	37.8021	38.4568	38.4451
	SSIM	0.9145	0.9143	0.9242	0.9148	0.9232	0.9229
	CC	0.9850	0.9840	0.9861	0.9843	0.9857	0.9854
Balloon	$Q^{AB/F}$	0.8133	0.8218	0.8160	0.8007	0.8208	0.8220
	MI	10.1277	11.1296	10.3557	11.1252	11.1355	11.1632
	RMSE	0.0114	0.0056	0.0055	0.0055	0.0055	0.0056
	PSNR	32.1260	38.3339	38.4714	38.4370	38.3358	38.2833
	SSIM	0.9684	0.9689	0.9716	0.9685	0.9693	0.9687
	CC	0.9914	0.9917	0.9923	0.9911	0.9918	0.9915
Flower	$Q^{AB/F}$	0.6817	0.7270	0.7224	0.6933	0.7238	0.7240
	MI	5.0983	7.2740	5.6288	7.6310	7.8754	8.0319
	RMSE	0.0304	0.0109	0.0094	0.0103	0.0108	0.0108
	PSNR	25.5105	34.4559	35.7465	34.8986	34.5014	34.4631
	SSIM	0.9041	0.8921	0.9352	0.9069	0.8922	0.8907
	CC	0.9407	0.9275	0.9565	0.9387	0.9267	0.9256
Leopard	$Q^{AB/F}$	0.8302	0.8356	0.8378	0.8275	0.8348	0.8357
	MI	9.8038	10.8384	10.0490	10.9832	10.9083	10.9901
	RMSE	0.0364	0.0175	0.0116	0.0177	0.0174	0.0176
	PSNR	28.0629	34.3990	38.0155	34.3415	34.4489	34.3644
	SSIM	0.9036	0.9045	0.9629	0.9040	0.9058	0.9038
	CC	0.9881	0.9882	0.9949	0.9881	0.9884	0.9881
Average	$Q^{AB/F}$	0.7741	0.7957	0.7952	0.7779	0.7951	0.7957
	MI	8.0527	9.5528	8.5602	9.7585	9.9237	9.9907
	RMSE	0.1159	0.0114	0.0097	0.0114	0.0112	0.0113
	PSNR	28.3605	36.2791	37.4172	36.3698	36.4357	36.3890
	SSIM	0.9227	0.9200	0.9485	0.9236	0.9226	0.9215
	CC	0.9763	0.9729	0.9825	0.9756	0.9732	0.9727

Table 1. Quantitative assessments of different multifocus image fusion methods on different source images.

5. Conclusion and future work

As more advanced coding techniques appear, the fused image will be clearer by using regional multifocus image fusion methods. In this chapter, the general structure of regional multifocus image fusion is introduced. Regional multifocus image fusion methods using two different sparse representation algorithms, i.e., OMP and SOMP, are formulated. The experiments by proposed regional multifocus image fusion methods are conducted, and the experimental results demonstrate that the performance of regional methods using sparse representation is better than several state-of-the-art methods.

To further improve the regional image fusion's performance, two possible directions can be explored more. The first one is to apply other coding techniques like the group or structure sparse representations to get more robust clarity measures. The second future work can focus on the re-designing of the image segmentation approaches. We can embed the focus information directly in the segmentation procedures to obtain better partitions of images for the regional fusion. For example, the biased normalized cut [39] is a possible solution to embed the focus information as the bias in the classical normalized cut segmentation algorithm.

Author details

Long Chen, Junwei Duan* and C. L. Philip Chen

*Address all correspondence to: duanjunwei123@gmail.com

Faculty of Science and Technology, University of Macau, Macau

References

[1] Mansour Nejati, Shadrokh Samavi, and Shahram Shirani. Multi-focus image fusion using dictionary-based sparse representation. Information Fusion, 25:72–84, 2015.

[2] Raf Van de Plas, Junhai Yang, Jeffrey Spraggins, and Richard M Caprioli. Image fusion of mass spectrometry and microscopy: a multimodality paradigm for molecular tissue mapping. Nature Methods, 12(4):366–372, 2015.

[3] Zhaobin Wang and Yide Ma. Medical image fusion using m-pcnn. Information Fusion, 9(2):176–185, 2008.

[4] Giovanni Simone, Alfonso Farina, Francesco Carlo Morabito, Sebastiano B Serpico, and Lorenzo Bruzzone. Image fusion techniques for remote sensing applications. Information Fusion, 3(1):3–15, 2002.

[5] Tania Stathaki. Image fusion: algorithms and applications. 1st ed. Amsterdam: Elsevier; 2008.

[6] Gonzalo Pajares and Jesus Manuel De La Cruz. A wavelet-based image fusion tutorial. Pattern Recognition, 37(9):1855–1872, 2004.

[7] Myungjin Choi, Rae Young Kim, Myeong-Ryong Nam, and Hong Oh Kim. Fusion of multispectral and panchromatic satellite images using the curvelet transform. IEEE Geoscience and Remote Sensing Letters, 2(2):136–140, 2005.

[8] Qu Xiao-Bo, Yan Jing-Wen, Xiao Hong-Zhi, and Zhu Zi-Qian. Image fusion algorithm based on spatial frequency-motivated pulse coupled neural networks in nonsubsampled contourlet transform domain. Acta Automatica Sinica, 34(12): 1508–1514, 2008.

[9] Zaid Omar, Nikolaos Mitianoudis, and Tania Stathaki. Region-based image fusion using a combinatory chebyshev-ica method. In 2011 IEEE International Conference on Acoustics, Speech and Signal Processing (ICASSP), pages 1213–1216. IEEE, 2011.

[10] Shutạo Li and Bin Yang. Multifocus image fusion using region segmentation and spatial frequency. Image and Vision Computing, 26(7):971–979, 2008.

[11] Hui Li, BS Manjunath, and Sanjit K Mitra. Multisensor image fusion using the wavelet transform. Graphical Models and Image Processing, 57(3):235–245, 1995.

[12] David Looney and Danilo P Mandic. Multiscale image fusion using complex extensions of emd. IEEE Transactions on Signal Processing, 57(4):1626–1630, 2009.

[13] David L Donoho. Compressed sensing. IEEE Transactions on Information Theory, 52(4): 1289–1306, 2006.

[14] Huafeng Li, Yi Chai, Hongpeng Yin, and Guoquan Liu. Multifocus image fusion and denoising scheme based on homogeneity similarity. Optics Communications, 285(2): 91–100, 2012.

[15] Ke Huang and Selin Aviyente. Sparse representation for signal classification. In B. Schölkopf, J. C. Platt, and T. Hoffman, editors, Advances in Neural Information Processing Systems 19, pages 609–616. Cambridge: MIT Press, 2007.

[16] Richa Singh, Mayank Vatsa, and Afzel Noore. Integrated multilevel image fusion and match score fusion of visible and infrared face images for robust face recognition. Pattern Recognition, 41(3):880–893, 2008.

[17] Bruno A. Olshausen, David J. Field. Emergence of simple-cell receptive field properties by learning a sparse code for natural images. Nature, 381(6583):607–609, 1996.

[18] Michal Aharon, Michael Elad, and Alfred Bruckstein. K-SVD: an algorithm for designing overcomplete dictionaries for sparse representation. IEEE Transactions on Signal Processing, 54(11):4311–4322, 2006.

[19] Shu Kong and Donghui Wang. A dictionary learning approach for classification: separating the particularity and the commonality. In European Conference on Computer Vision, pages 186–199. Springer, 2012.

[20] Bin Yang and Shutao Li. Multifocus image fusion and restoration with sparse representation. IEEE Transactions on Instrumentation and Measurement, 59(4):884–892, 2010.

[21] Geoff Davis, Stephane Mallat, and Marco Avellaneda. Adaptive greedy approximations. Constructive Approximation, 13(1):57–98, 1997.

[22] Joel A. Tropp, Anna C. Gilbert, and Martin J. Strauss. Simultaneous sparse approximation via greedy pursuit. In Proceedings (ICASSP'05). IEEE International Conference on Acoustics, Speech, and Signal Processing, volume 5, page v/721–v/724. IEEE, 2005.

[23] Richard E. Wendell and Arthur P. Hurter, Jr. Location theory, dominance, and convexity. Operations Research, 21(1):314–320, 1973.

[24] Long Chen, Jinbo Li, and C. L. Philip Chen. Regional multifocus image fusion using sparse representation. Optics Express, 21(4):5182–5197, 2013.

[25] Jianbo Shi and Jitendra Malik. Normalized cuts and image segmentation. IEEE Transactions on Pattern Analysis and Machine Intelligence, 22(8):888–905, 2000.

[26] André Bleau and L. Joshua Leon Bleau and L Joshua Leon. Watershed-based segmentation and region merging. Computer Vision and Image Understanding, 77(3):317–370, 2000.

[27] Nikhil R. Pal and Sankar K. Pal. A review on image segmentation techniques. Pattern Recognition, 26(9):1277–1294, 1993.

[28] Junwei Duan, Long Chen, and CL Philip Chen. Region-based multi-focus image fusion using guided filtering and greedy analysis. In 2015 IEEE International Conference on Systems, Man, and Cybernetics (SMC), pages 2932–2937. IEEE, 2015.

[29] Kaiming He, Jian Sun, and Xiaoou Tang. Guided image filtering. In European conference on computer vision, pages 1–14. Springer, 2010.

[30] Shutao Li, Xudong Kang, and Jianwen Hu. Image fusion with guided filtering. IEEE Transactions on Image Processing, 22(7):2864–2875, 2013.

[31] Matilde Santos, Gonzalo Pajares, M Portela, and Jesús Manuel de la Cruz. A new wavelets image fusion strategy. In Iberian Conference on Pattern Recognition and Image Analysis, pages 919–926. Springer, 2003.

[32] Available from: http://home.ustc.edu.cn/~liuyu1/

[33] Mohammad Bagher Akbari Haghighat, Ali Aghagolzadeh, and Hadi Seyedarabi. Multi-focus image fusion for visual sensor networks in DCT domain. Computers & Electrical Engineering, 37(5):789–797, 2011.

[34] Guihong Qu, Dali Zhang, and Pingfan Yan. Information measure for performance of image fusion. Electronics Letters, 38(7):1, 2002.

[35] Wei Huang and Zhongliang Jing. Evaluation of focus measures in multifocus image fusion. Pattern Recognition Letters, 28(4):493–500, 2007.

[36] Nedeljko Cvejic, Artur Loza, David Bull, and Nishan Canagarajah. A similarity metric for assessment of image fusion algorithms. International Journal of Signal Processing, 2(3):178–182, 2005.

[37] Zhou Wang, Alan C Bovik, Hamid R Sheikh, and Eero P Simoncelli. Image quality assessment: from error visibility to structural similarity. IEEE Transactions on Image Processing, 13(4):600–612, 2004.

[38] Wenzhong Shi, ChangQing Zhu, Yan Tian, and Janet Nichol. Wavelet-based image fusion and quality assessment. International Journal of Applied Earth Observation and Geoinformation, 6(3):241–251, 2005.

[39] Subhransu Maji, Nisheeth K Vishnoi, and Jitendra Malik. Biased normalized cuts. In 2011 IEEE Conference on Computer Vision and Pattern Recognition (CVPR), pages 2057–2064. IEEE, 2011.

Section 4

Role of Artificial Vision in Mechanical Applications

Chapter 7

Artificial Vision for Manufacturing System

Mejia Ugalde Mario and Mejia Ugalde Ignacio

Additional information is available at the end of the chapter

http://dx.doi.org/10.5772/64611

Abstract

Artificial vision for manufacturing is a very important step when the process is automatic, so to improve productivity with high quality, this investigation presents a new method for manufacturing by applying artificial intelligence for tool selection; in the proposed method, a camera takes a picture and artificial program is applied to process the image and thus generate it to the size of the cutting tool. This chapter describes the development of a new method by programming using artificial vision to select the cutting tool. The experimental results show that the combination of artificial vision and programming is capable of selecting the correct tool.

Keywords: artificial vision, cutting tool, artificial intelligence, image, manufacture

1. Introduction

In recent years, artificial vision is impacting the manufacturing process due to the mass adoption in different lines of research such as robotics [1, 2], machining [3, 4], and automotive [5], among others. However, numerous variables affect the machining process, for example, tool materials, total error compensation, concepts of autonomous manufacturing, and process condition monitoring, among others. On the other hand, the computer vision for cutting condition effects as roughness (presented by Sarma et al. [6]), the prediction of cutting conditions (by Gadelmawla et al. [7], and path generation are included for milling Computerized Numerical Control (CNC) machines (by Eladawi et al. [3]).

At present, the development of a system capable of recognizing complex features for tool selection in commercial computer-aided manufacturing (CAM) transfers this task to the workers who do it based on their own experience, ability, and knowledge. The literature on automatic tool selection using image processing is minimal; on the other hand, simple and easy to implement algorithms are the core of this method [8].

2. Artificial vision in manufacture

This research presents a new technique based on artificial vision using image processing for automatic tool selection in operations of milling-turning manufacture.

The proposed method starts recognizing an image taken by a photographic camera. Then, different techniques of image processing are applied, such as binarization to convert the image of gray scale to black and white; after segmentation to reduce the contour or increase it if necessary; directional morphology to determine the magnitude, position, and direction of edge of the part; and finally, a structural element with the shape of the tool is moved to generate the trajectory and dimensions of the cutting tool [9].

3. Artificial vision in lathe

This research consists of eight steps for machining 2D objects mainly for two-axis lathe machines: in step 1, an image designed in CAD or taken from a camera is extracted and saved to a DXF file; the next step (step 2) consists of transforming the DXF file to the BMP file (image); in step 3, a binarization is applied to convert the image to grayscale; step 4 consists of labeling to separate the object of the picture; in step 5, the perimeter of the piece is obtained; in step 6, a partial derivative to obtain the gradient in the edge of the piece is applied; in step 7, a structure element with the shape of the tool is moved in the image; and finally, in steps 8 and 9, a condition is applied to determine if there is no intersection between the selected tool and the object to generate the selection of the tool and the trajectory [9].

The method for automatic selection of the tool consists in identifying when an element structure with the shape of the tool travels in each pixel on the edge of the part in the image. If there is an intersection between the cutting tool and the workpiece, then the diameter of the cutting tool is automatically changed until there is no intersection. These steps and the previous steps are shown in **Figure 1**, as well as in the following steps [9]:

Step 1. Generation of DXF file starting with a picture

The DXF file contains information of the piece inside the image (**Figure 2b**), while the CAD file is generated in 3D but it is exported in 2D (**Figure 2a**) [9].

Step 2. File transformations (DXF to BMP)

When different transformations are applied, it is necessary to know the dimensions of the piece and keep the precision nearest between the part in physical (length in mm) and the image (length in pixels), an analysis applied is shown in **Table 1** [9].

http://dx.doi.org/10.5772/64611

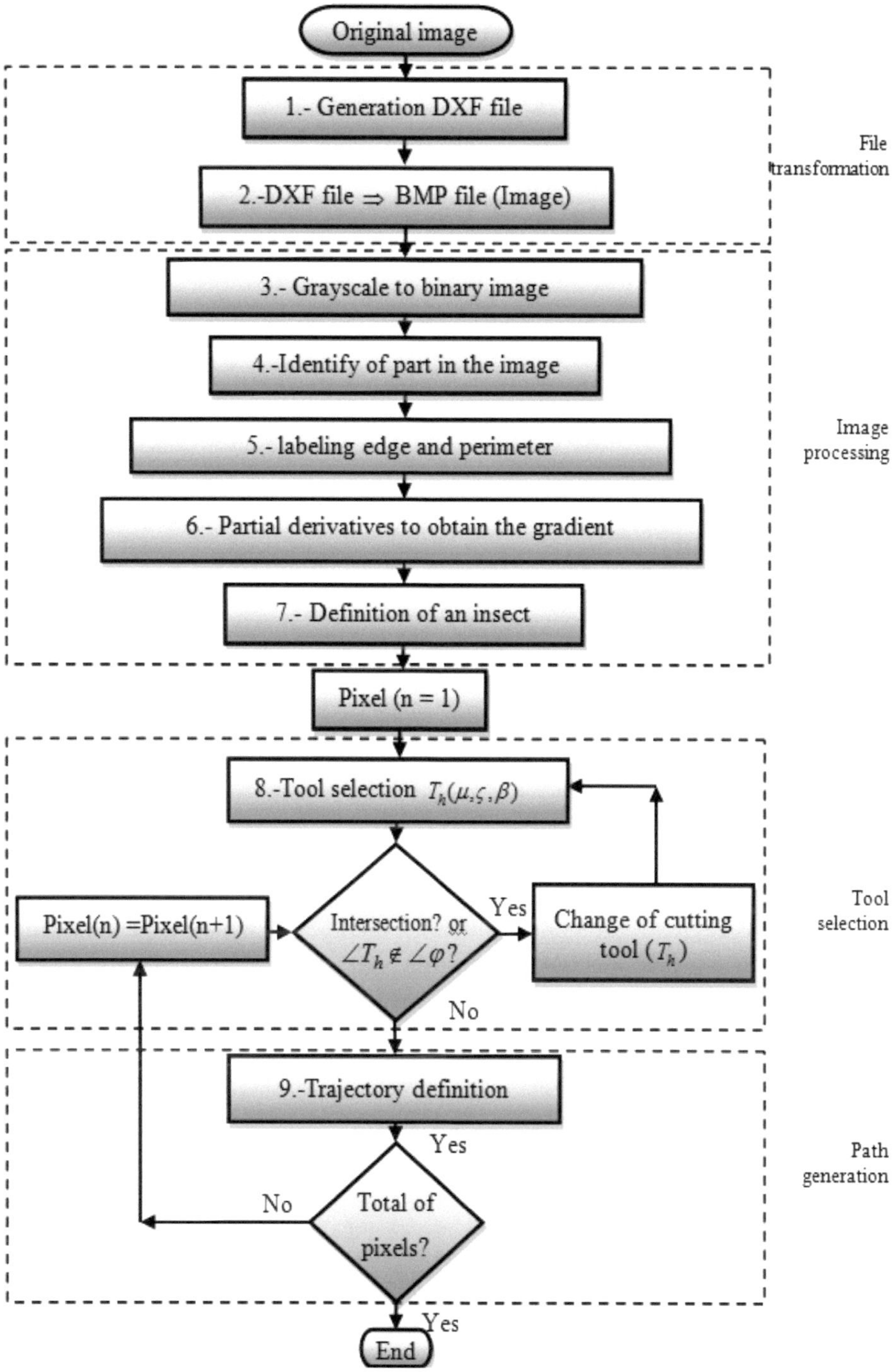

Figure 1. General diagram of the automatic cutting tool selection.

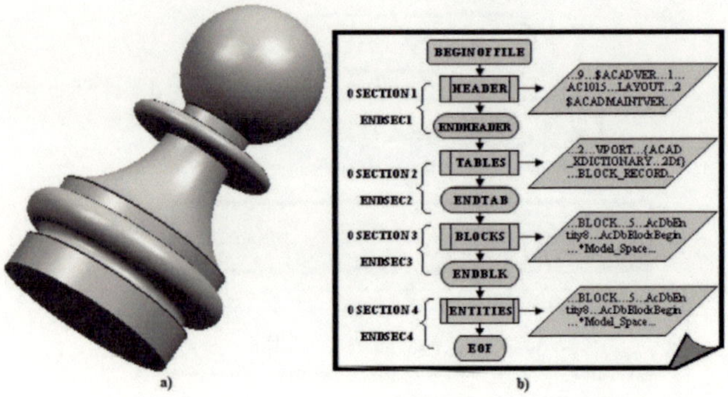

Figure 2. Principal file, (a) design from CAD and (b) DXF file [9].

Resolution	Scale	mm	Length (pixels)	Height (pixels)
800 × 600	4:3	1	15	11
3200 × 2048	25:16	1	62	40
5120 × 4096	5:4	1	100	80
7680 × 4800	16:10	1	151	94
10,000 × 10,000	1:1	1	196	196
50,800 × 50,800	1:1	1	1000	1000

Table 1. The resolution of this system.

The calibration value is also the resolution of this system and is approximately 1 μm. A method of data extraction [6] is applied to convert the DXF file to BMP file, as shown in **Figure 3(a)** and **(b)**. The same distance is then automatically determined in pixels in the image, and a calibration value is obtained by dividing the distance in millimeters by the distance in pixels to obtain a relation of mm per pixel:

$$\text{Re}\mathit{lation} = \frac{\text{distance}_{mm}}{\text{distance}_{pixel}} \tag{1}$$

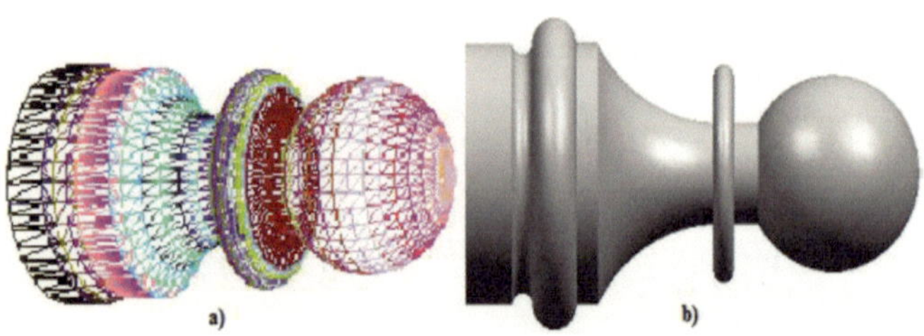

Figure 3. Files, (a) design without texture (Wire file) and (b) image (BMP file) [9].

All the dimensions are known in the DXF file. In order to find the directional gradient of the edge, image processing is applied.

Step 3. Grayscale to binary image

The workpiece λ^{τ} is a subset $\lambda^{\tau} \subset \mathbf{f}$ of the image $\mathbf{f}$, where it represents a matrix with m pixels to be stored in an array f in the following way:

$$\lambda^{\tau} \subset \mathbf{f} \Rightarrow \sum_{\tau=1}^{m} (\lambda^{\tau} = \mathbf{f}) \tag{2}$$

where m is the total number of pixels in the image and τ is the region of the image. After starting with the image that is shown in **Figure 3(b)**, a transformation (thresholding) is applied to convert the image of gray scale to binary using Eq. (3):

$$\sum_{i=1}^{n}\sum_{k=1}^{m}\left\{ if\ \mathbf{f}(i,k) > 128 \text{ then } \mathbf{f}^{B}(i,k) = 1\ else\ \mathbf{f}^{B}(i,k) = 0 \right\} \tag{3}$$

Each pixel has a value of 255 representing the largest tonality (white) and 0 when the minimum (black) cannot work with this whole range of colors. $\mathbf{f}(i,k)|_n^m$ (image in gray scale 0 multicolor) is needed only for two $\mathbf{f}^{B}(i,k)|_n^m$ (binary image), one for the piece (black) and the other for the rest of the image (white) [9].

Step 4. Labeling of the workpiece into of the image

Figure 4(a) shows the labeling of the image and the piece $\mathbf{e}(i,k)|_n^m$ (Eq. (4)). Be an image $\mathbf{f}_k \subseteq \mathbf{f}(i,k)|_n^m$ white and black in the binary space $\mathbf{f}^{B}$, where

$$\mathbf{e} = \bigcup_{k}^{\infty}\left\{ \forall \mathbf{f}_k \in \mathbf{f}^{B} \mid \left\langle if\ \mathbf{f}_k = 0 \text{ then } x_k = 0 \right\rangle \vee \left\langle if\ \mathbf{f}_k = 1\ then\ x_k = 1 \right\rangle \right\} \tag{4}$$

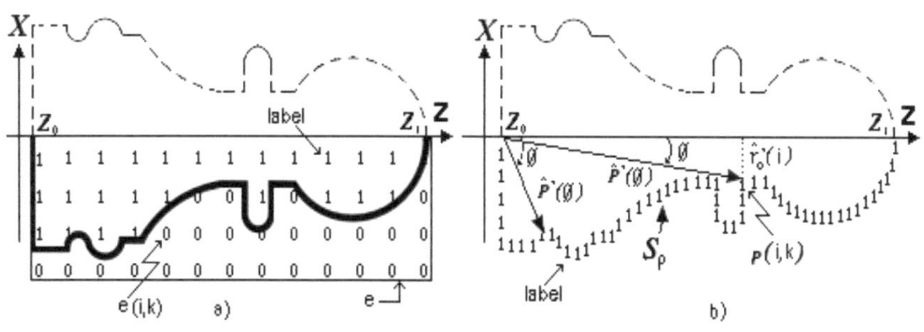

Figure 4. Labeling definition, (a) labeling of part and (b) labeling of perimeter [9].

Or it can also be written as Eq. (5):

$$\sum_{k=\frac{m}{2}}^{m}\sum_{i=0}^{n}\{\mathbf{e}(i,k)=[if\ \mathbf{f}(i,k)=1 \text{ then } \mathbf{f}_e(i,k)=1]\cup[if\ \mathbf{f}(i,k)=0 \text{ then } \mathbf{f}_e(i,k)=0]\} \tag{5}$$

where $\mathbf{f}_e(i,k)|_n^m$ is the labeling image saved in the image of the exit $\mathbf{e}(i,k)|_n^m$ of Eq. (5), taking half of the image $k=\frac{m}{2}$ on the axis Z. The directional classification of the edge for half of the image in the point $p(x,z)$ is presented in **Figure 3(b)**.

Step 5. Labeling edge and perimeter

The perimeter ($\hat{P}(\theta)$) can be obtained from the edge ($|\nabla f|$) of the image ($\mathbf{f}(i,k)|_n^m$) by Eq. (6):

$$\hat{P}(\theta)=2\int_{z_0}^{z_1}\sqrt{1+\hat{q}'}dz=\int_{0}^{2\pi}\sqrt{\hat{r}_o^2+\hat{r}'^2_0}d\theta \tag{6}$$

The vector $\hat{q}'(i,k)$ represents the partial derivative of the piece in the image $f(i,k)$ with respect to a frame of reference (($\hat{r}_0(i)$ and $\hat{r}_0'(k)$ are the radii) for each pixel ($p(i,k)$)) (see **Figure 4(b)**.

Another way to calculate an integral is the arithmetic sum of each pixel of the image represented with the symbol($\Sigma\mathbf{f}(i,k)|_n^m$) for a frame of reference (of z_0 to z_1), with the aim of finding the perimeter S_p [10] that represents the labeled edge, as shown in Eqs. (7) and (8) [9]:

$$\sum_{N=0}^{\infty}\{\ (\mathbf{E}_N(i,k)\Leftarrow\{\mathbf{p}(z,P(z)),\{N=N+1\vee z=N\}\ \} \tag{7}$$

$$S_p=\sum_{k=\frac{m}{2}}^{m-2}\sum_{i=1}^{n-1}\left\{\prod_{N=1}^{m-2}\langle if\ \mathbf{E}_N(i,k)=1 \text{ then } \mathbf{f}(i,k)\Leftarrow\mathbf{E}_N(i,k),\ else\,\mathbf{f}(i,k)\Leftarrow\mathbf{f}(i,k)\rangle\right\} \tag{8}$$

Figure 4(b) shows the labeling of the perimeter $S_{p'}$ in the edge of the piece for each point $p(i,k)$.

Step 6. Using partial derivatives to obtain the gradient

There are several methods to obtain the gradient (variations in intensity of pixels) (Eq. (9)), but among them the Sobel method is selected for its computational easeas is shown in Eqs. (10) and (11) [11], the gradient generates directional vectors, orientation of the piece, and direction of the contour of the workpiece:

$$\nabla \boldsymbol{f} = \text{gradient} \quad \mathbf{f} = \begin{cases} \boldsymbol{G}_x = \dfrac{\partial}{\partial x}\mathbf{f}(x,z) = \dfrac{\partial}{\partial x}\hat{\boldsymbol{i}} = \dfrac{\partial}{\partial x}\hat{\boldsymbol{u}}_1 \\ \boldsymbol{G}_z = \dfrac{\partial}{\partial z}\mathbf{f}(x,z) = \dfrac{\partial}{\partial z}\hat{\boldsymbol{k}} = \dfrac{\partial}{\partial z}\hat{\boldsymbol{u}}_2 \end{cases} \tag{9}$$

Therefore,

$$\boldsymbol{G}_x = \sum_{i=1}^{n-1}\sum_{k=1}^{m-2}\left\{ \boldsymbol{Edge\_x}(i,k) = \sum_{z=-1}^{1}\sum_{x=-1}^{1} \mathbf{e}(x,z)\mathbf{M}_x(z+2,x+2) \right\} \tag{10}$$

$$\boldsymbol{G}_z = \sum_{i=1}^{n-1}\sum_{k=1}^{m-2}\left\{ \boldsymbol{Edge\_z}(i,k) = \sum_{z=-1}^{1}\sum_{x=-1}^{1} \mathbf{e}(x,z)\mathbf{M}_z(z+2,x+2) \right\} \tag{11}$$

Here, $\mathbf{M}_x$ and $\mathbf{M}_z$ are the transformation matrices to generate the edge applied to the image. The vector gradient represents the maximum change of intensity for the point $p(i, k)$.

The magnitude ($|\nabla f|$) and direction ($\angle \nabla f$) are given by Eqs. (12) and (13), respectively,

$$|\nabla f| = \sqrt{G_x + G_z} \tag{12}$$

$$\angle \nabla f = \tan^{-1}\frac{G_z}{G_x} \tag{13}$$

Figure 5(a) illustrates the vector direction of the edge of the part sample.

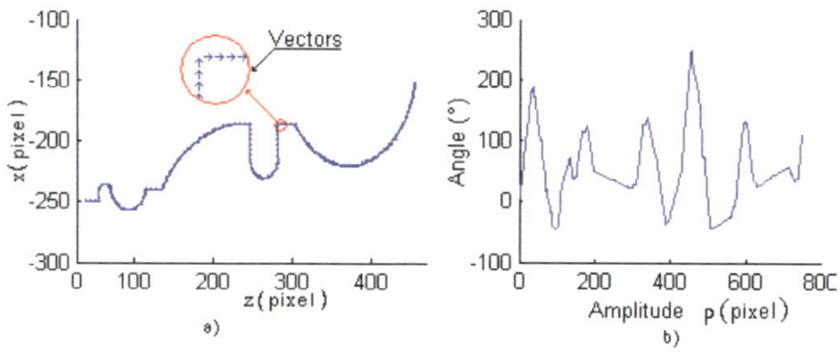

Figure 5. Vectors of part, (a) direction vector of part and (b) magnitude of edge direction [9].

Figure 5(b) shows the directional angles according to the trajectory of the edge, when the gradient is applied to binary image in the part.

The magnitude and direction of the edge are saved in the variable $Maq(i,k)$ using Eq. (14) to generate the dimension of structural element:

$$\sum_{k=m}^{\frac{m}{2}-1}\sum_{i=1}^{n-1}\left\{\text{if exist edge then}\left\{\mathbf{Maq}(i,k) <= \begin{Bmatrix} |\nabla f|(i,k)\text{"magnitude"} \\ \angle\nabla f(i,k)\text{"direction"} \end{Bmatrix}\right\}\right. \tag{14}$$

Step 7. Automatic tool selections

The workspace is considered according to the size of the piece but it is necessary to consider other collisions as the turret with the part, these will be considered in future issues [10]. **Table 2** shows the common cutting tool, the dimensions of the cutting tool are obtained from manuals and introduced into the software to be converted into structural elements with the length, orientation, and radius of the nose, this part is shown in **Figure 6(a)**. Among the common dimensions are those of 15°, 35°, and 45°, with 9525 mm requiring 36 pixels, 2540 requiring a mesh of 25.5 square units of pixels, and the structural element requiring 414 pixels, see **Figure 6(a)** [9].

Tool for turning			**Type**	$\mu(°)$	**Size (mm)**			
Name	**Letter**	**Shape**			ζ	β	FL	φ
1. Right	R	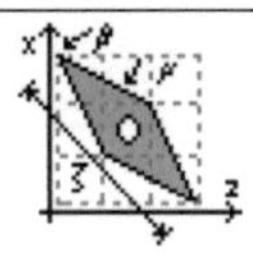	External Internal	35 125	19.049	0.406	– –	– –
2. Left	L	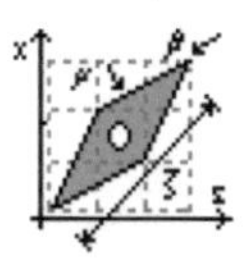	External Internal	197 19	19.0496	0.406	– –	– –
3. Neuter	N	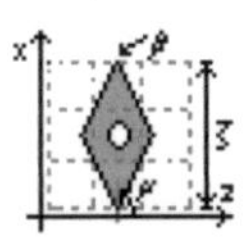	External Internal	90 93	12.699	0.507	– –	– –
4. Knife	K	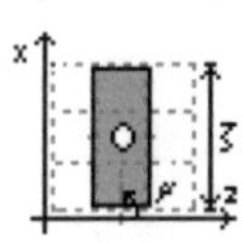	External Internal	90 95	12.699	–	– –	– –
5. Drilling	D	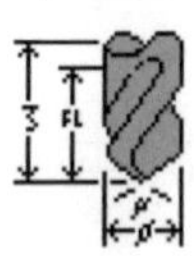	External Internal	60	44.449	–	38.099	12.699
6. Holder	H	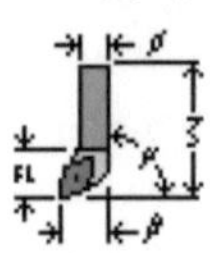	S16R PCLNR-L 09	95	71.118	20.141	20.319	19.989

Table 2. Common inserts (structural element).

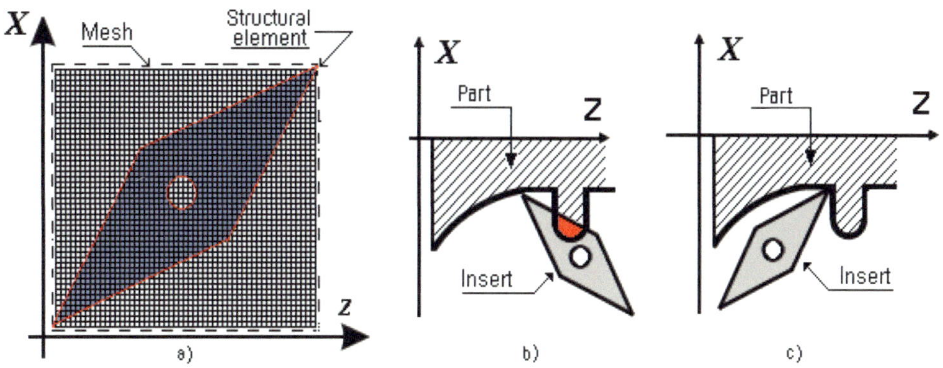

Figure 6. (a) Structural element for right insert, (b) incorrect insert and (c) correct insert [9].

There are several conditions for machining between them and it is necessary to determine if the cut is internal or external, and whether it is an insert right ($180° \leq \angle\nabla f < 270°$) or left ($270° \leq \angle\nabla f < 360°$). The common are those that are situated in the last two quadrants, the first two quadrants are generally used for internal machining. Eq. (15) generates the movements of the structural element through the image; the angle marks the start of the selection of the cutting tool in machining $\mathbf{Maq}(i,k) = 1$ [9].:

$$\sum_{k=m}^{\frac{m}{2}-1} \sum_{i=1}^{n-1} \{ if\ \mathbf{Maq}(i,k) = 1\ then\ select\ insert \{ \boldsymbol{\mu}(i,k) \Leftarrow \angle\nabla f(angle\ of\ edge) \} \} \tag{15}$$

where μ is the dimension for cutting tool presented in Eq. (16):

$$\sum_{k=m}^{\frac{m}{2}-1} \sum_{i=1}^{n-1} \left\{ if\ \mathbf{Maq}(i,k) = 1 then\ \boldsymbol{\mu}(i,k) is \begin{cases} left\ \text{insert},\ if\ 17.5° \leq \mu(i,k) < 45° \\ right\ \text{insert},\ if\ 107° \leq \mu(i,k) < 180° \\ neuter\ \text{insert},\ if\ \mu(i,k) = 90° \\ knife,\ if\ \mu(i,k) = 90° (up\ and\ down) \end{cases} \right\} \tag{16}$$

Table 2 shows the common inserts that are generated in structural elements. **Figure 6(a)** illustrates a structural element generated with pixels to be moved through the contour so that the contour matches the nose radius of the tool. The number of pixels in a line according to the used resolution of 800 × 600 is five pixels; the evaluation is taken from reference [9]. Second, the pixels that are represented the line in **Figure 6(a)** are used only to demonstrate the method; the pixels processed are the inner using centroid method.

When a structural element passes through the edge of the workpiece, it is necessary to know if this insert is correct, free of intersection, if there is intersection, and if another insert is treated. The structural element (**Figure 6b**) is displaced through all the images, when a structural element (**Figure 6b**) collides (**Figure 6c**), other structural element is chosen automatically, this process is determined in the software itself. The technique for automatic tool selection may be to change the radius, length, or angle of the insert according to the inserts, obtained from handbooks [9].

After the correct holders and inserts have been selected to work on each area, many changes in cutting tools are probably required. The number of changes can be reduced by ordering the changes with the next procedure (Eq. (17)):

$$\sum_{i=1}^{n-1}\sum_{j=1}^{m-2}\left\{\begin{array}{l} if\left\{(\mathbf{S}_P(i,j)=1)\ and\ \sum_{h=-1}^{1}\sum_{\psi=-1}^{1}\lambda[i+\psi][j+1]=1\right\} \\ then\,\mathbf{Tray}\,(i,j)\Leftarrow\lambda[i+\psi][j+1]\end{array}\right\} \tag{17}$$

To determine the tool path, each pixel should share information with eight neighbors and follow the path of the perimeter (edge S_P) in the mesh $\lambda[i+\psi][k+1]$.

Step 8. Generation of trajectory

Figure 7(a) illustrates the method of zig using one way, but there are other methods of creating paths such as zigzag of two paths (back and forth), zig with contour, which follows only the path of the edge of the piece widely used for finishing and roughing at the same time; the follow-periphery that has the function to be used only for finishing; the trochoidal profile is used in special cases when the piece has peaks, elevations, or very long inclinations; and on the other hand, the generation of trajectory is used only for rough cutting. To generate the trajectories, a structural element with the shape of the cutting tool with angle μ, lengthς, and noise angle β is displaced through all the images from right to left.

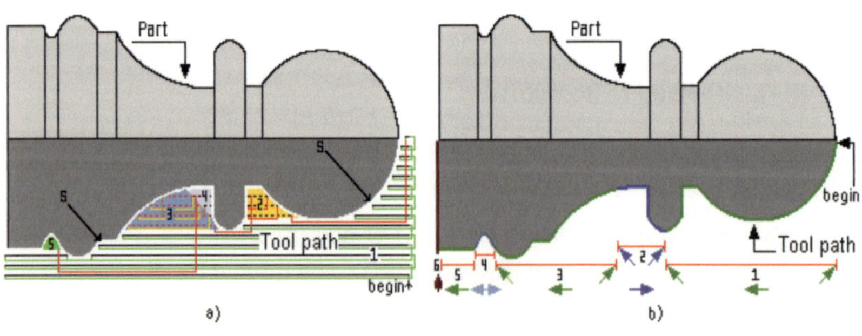

Figure 7. Tool selection (final piece), (a) rough turn (zig) and (b) finish turn (zig with contour) [9].

Finally, to move the tool in the image, it is necessary to use a counter ($k=0, i=i+1$) with the total number of pixels m. This method is obtained by Eq. (18) and is displayed is **Figure 7(a)** [9]:

$$\sum_{k=m}^{\frac{m}{2}-1}\sum_{i=1}^{n-1}\left\{\mathbf{Move\_Tray}(i,k)=\mathbf{f}(i,k);\left\{\ if\,\mathbf{f}(i,k)=\mathbf{Tray}(i,k)=1\text{ then }k=k+1\ \right\}\right\} \tag{18}$$

Machining time is given by Eq. (19):

$$T = \sum_{i=1}^{n} \frac{L_i}{v_i} \tag{19}$$

4. Results in lathe

With the proposed method, an image can be directly taken by a camera or other devices for automatic tool selection. The use of an image generated from DXF file is to compare the structural elements (part and tool) in pixels using PI; the original dimensions from DXF file are used to compare them if the design comes from CAD file. This new method, which reduces the complex, complicated, and difficult to understand mathematical algorithms, shows an easy simulated viewing for selecting cutting tool. To show the method for automatic selection of the tool, two pieces were used, the results are presented in **Table 2**. The generation of trajectories is shown in **Figure 7(a)** and **(b)**, and the selection of the tool in **Table 3** for the first piece.

Rough turn		Finish turn	
Area	**Type**	**Line**	**Type**
1	L	1	L
2	L	2	R
3	L	3	L
4	R	4	N
5	N	5	R
6	–	6	K

Table 3. Selected inserts for part of **Figure 7**.

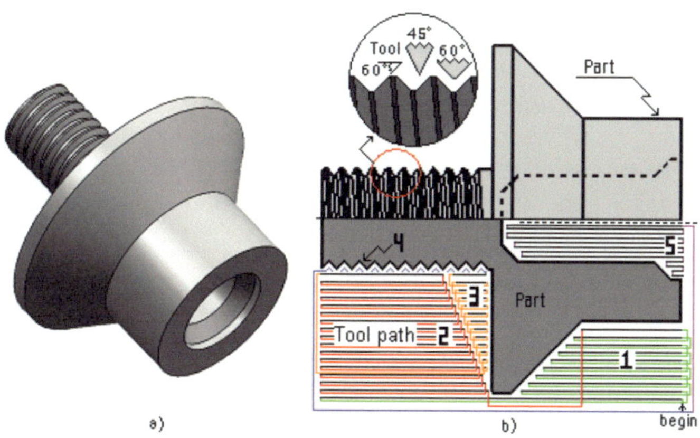

Figure 8. Tool selection, (a) final piece and (b) thread and rough turn (zig) [9].

Table 3 shows the results of the selected inserts by applying the proposed method. Where the numbers represent the area for each insert, and L, R, or N represents the types of inserts more common than before which was proposed relative to its size.

The second example is presented in **Figure 8**. The selected cutting tools are presented in **Table 4**, where an existing thread machining is represented by the number four and an internal machining is labeled number five.

Rough turn		**Finish turn**	
Area	**Type**	**Line**	**Type**
1	L	1	L
2	L	2	–
3	R	3	R
4	M12_×_1.25	4	–
5	D/L	5	D/L

Table 4. Cutting tool selection for second example.

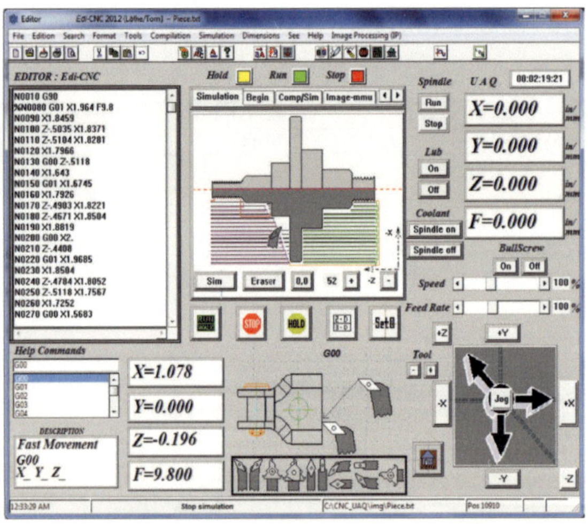

Figure 9. Final software for tool selection [9].

The developed software is shown in **Figure 9**. It was developed in Microsoft Visual C++ 2010 and tested in 2D images generated in any CAD software and exported to DXF file.

5. Conclusions

In this work, a new method for automatic tool selection using techniques of image processing for computer numerical control lathe machines has been presented. The proposed methodology has been implemented in images generated by CAD software and exported to DXF file. The resolution of this system is determined as approximately 1 μm.

From this, it is clear that this methodology can be implemented in commercial CAM software in order to systematize the lathe CNC process. The novelty of this article is the use of image processing to automatically generate the selection of the cutting tool, the design of the part can be from a photograph taken from a camera or other device or directly from a CAD.

6. Artificial vision in mill

A 2.5D solid model can be defined as a cut with a series of 2D tool paths at different Z slices of a 3D solid model. Nowadays, a large percentage of pieces used in the industry have a shape of contours, where the base face is a plane denominated by 2.5 axis. Automatic tool selection in milling operation is one of the important steps of process planning. Moreover, at present, the commercial computer-aided manufacturing software transfers this task to the worker who does it based on its own experience, ability, and knowledge. Considerable articles have reported about the variables that affect the milling process such as material piece selection [7, 12], tool selection [7], cutting conditions [7], tool materials [12], tool sequence [13], cutting fluids tool selection [12], tool path [6], and control and identification, among others.

The tool selection, task commonly made by a human operator, is an important aspect in machining processes, since if the tool selected is incorrect, it can produce dimensional errors in workpiece, possible crashes, and consequently, reject the piece. In this way, some researches based their principles on the selection of the tool for machining 2.5D parts as in the case of Ahmad et al. [13], who present an optimization algorithm for the problem of tool sequence [8]. Or the method proposed by Lim et al. [14] who used experimental algorithms using mathematical Boolean to determine the optimal setoftools in pockets with the integration of CAD/CAM.

In the same way, Hemant et al. [15] developed an algorithm for the tool selection used by Veeramani tool, although using dynamic programming, human intervention is necessary because of its mathematical complexity [4]. The tool selection using image processing based on the shape is a new method in the literature, the core of this research issimple and easy to implement algorithms [8].

Although the image processing plays a very important role when the images are manipulated inside the morphology (opening operation), the main research is the defects by Tunák et al. [16], the cutting conditions by Sarma et al. [7] and Gadelmawla et al. [3], and the path generation by Eladawi et al. [6, 8].

The contribution of this research is the easy way to simulate the cutting path, automatic tool selection, easy method for 2.5 axis machining in operation of milling, reduction of errors, and not requiring prior knowledge. The novelty of this work is the use of morphology based on the image processing applied for the automatic tool selection. The advantages of this method are: easy to implement, eliminates the decisions and errors when the tool is selected [8].

7. Introductions

Application of directional morphology in the tool and the workpiece with the sole aim of finding the selection of the cutters for 2.5-axis machining in the bibliography is a new proposal. The method begins by taking the mesh of a 3D object exported to a DXF file (Mejia et al. [8]) or an image taken by a camera. To manipulate this file, it is necessary to extract the coordinates, lengths, and positions of the pixels generated on the frontier of the piece on the surface. The pixels are discretized on the edge of the piece to obtain normal vectors and stored in a text file. The file data gives the necessary information about the orientation of tool when it passes through that place. The dimensions of the tools are stored and discretized; these were extracted from the handbook more common in the industry. The resolution of the system depends on the size of the tool and the complexity of the piece. To improve the algorithm, it is necessary to reduce the size of the pixels, after the pixels of the tool are displaced on the frontier of the piece. Each movement of the tool is inspected if there is no collision.

The image processing techniques used are: (a) morphological operations: using erosion and dilation [17, 18], these methods reduce or increase the contour of the workpiece; (b) binary image: the pixels that contain a gray scale $\mathbf{f}(i,j)$ are converted to black and white $\mathbf{f}^B(i,j)$; (c) direction vectors of piece: Sobel model is the common operator because it has better performance and is easy to use [19]; (d) extracting piece: the common method is labeling (scan mask) to register images; (e) Software CAD-CAM-CAE: these are the systems that graphics, designs, and simulates, respectively; (f) 2.5D models: the images in the present article are 2.5D model. These models are from a single 2D image having a manual axis that is the axis *Z*; and (g) structural elements: the cutting tool is represented in pixels, because a greater number of pixels to represent the cutting tool improves accuracy [8].

The work published by Bithika and Asit [18] applies mathematical morphology to detect manufacturing defects. It is an example of the application of image processing, using such techniques for measuring the effect of cutting speed on the surface roughness, which is another example that provides a new strategy in manufacturing, as presented by Sarma et al. [7].

8. Methodology

This research consists of six steps for machining 2D and 2.5D objects mainly for 2.5-axis lathe machines, an image designed in CAD or taken from a camera is extracted and saved to a DXF file, after transforming the DXF file to the BMP file (image), a binarization is applied to convert the image to grayscale, the labeling to separate the object of the picture, the perimeter of the piece is obtained, a partial derivative to obtain the gradient in the edge of the piece is applied, in step seven, a structure element with the shape of the tool is moved in the image, finally, a condition is applied to determine if there is no intersection, using mathematical morphology, especially erosion and dilation to generate automatic tool selection and tool path as it is shown in **Figure 10** [8].

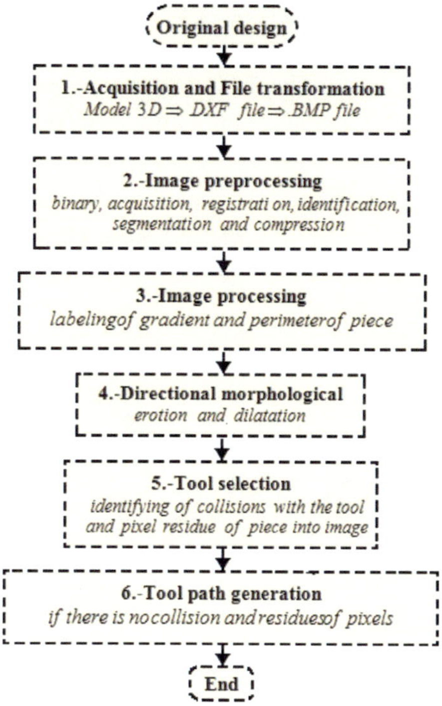

Figure 10. General diagram of the automatic cutting tool selection [8].

Step 1. Generation of DXF file starting with a picture

The DXF file (**Figure 11b**) contains information of the piece inside the image (**Figure 11a**), the CAD file is generated in 3D but it is exported in 2D.

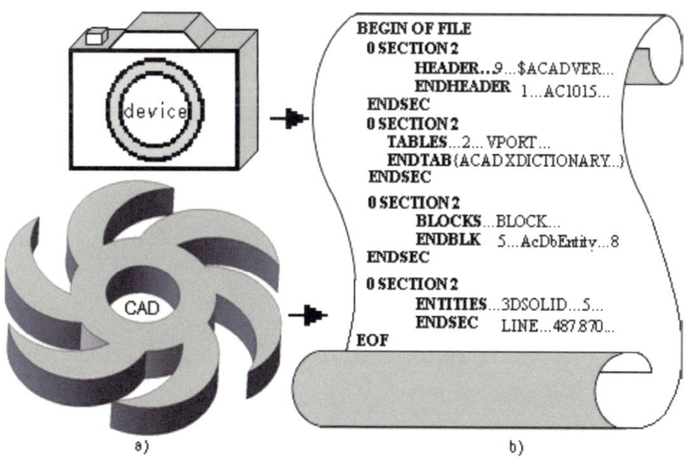

Figure 11. Original files, (a) design from CAD or camera and (b) DXF file [8].

When different transformations are applied (DXF to BMP), it is necessary to know the dimensions of the piece and keep the precision nearest between the part in physical (length in mm) and the image (length in pixels), an analysis is applied, the calibration value of this system is in micrometer, the adjustment parameters for 1 mm of 800×600 (scale 4:3, 15×11 pixels) and 50,800×50,800 (scale 1:1, 1000×1000 pixels) [8].

The archive DXF file contains the necessary information about the part that is necessary when the DXF file is converted to a BMP file, as shown in **Figure 12(a)** and **(b)**. The calibration is the relation between the distance in millimeters ($\text{distance}_{\text{mm}}$) and the relation of millimeters per pixel (Relation (mm per pixel)).

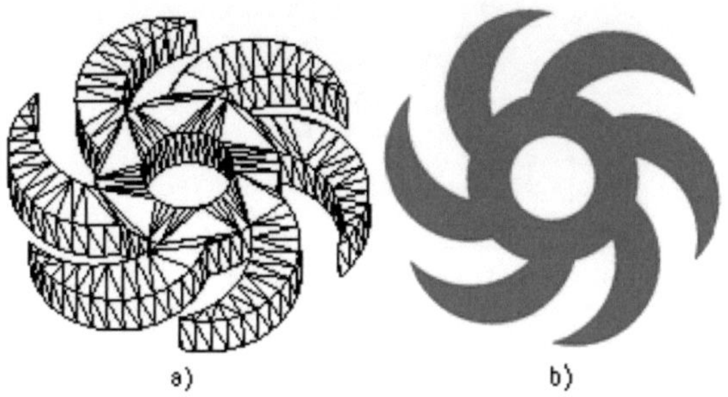

Figure 12. Files, (a) design without texture (Wire file) and (b) image (BMP file) [8].

Step 2. Image preprocessing

Binary image: a binary image ($(\mathbf{f}^B(i,j)|_n^m)$) in 2.5D is a subset χ_D of $\Re^3$ if $\{0, 1\}^{2.5}$ represents the set of functions as $\chi_D \subset \Re^3$ in the set {0, 1}, so that any binary image can be represented by a characteristic function $\chi_D : \Re^3 \rightarrow \{0, 1\}$. After starting with the image, a transformation (thresholding) is applied to convert the image of gray scale to binary using

$$\sum_{i=1}^{n}\sum_{k=1}^{m}\left\{ if \begin{pmatrix} \mathbf{f}(i,j) > T(\text{object pixels}) & \Rightarrow A_1 = \mathbf{f}(i,j) \\ \mathbf{f}(i,j) \le T(\text{background pixels}) & \Rightarrow A_2 = \mathbf{f}(i,j) \end{pmatrix} \text{then } \mathbf{f}^B(i,j) \right\} \tag{20}$$

where $\mathbf{f}^B(i,j)$ is equal to

$$\sum_{i=1}^{n}\sum_{k=1}^{m}\left\{ \mathbf{f}^B(i,j) = \frac{\text{Average value of } A_1 + \text{Average value of } A_2}{2} \right\} \tag{21}$$

where $\mathbf{f}(i,k)|_n^m$ is the image in gray scale (image matrix of $n\,x\,m$ pixels) and $f^B(i,j)\,|_n^m$ is the result of the transformation of gray scale into a binary image.

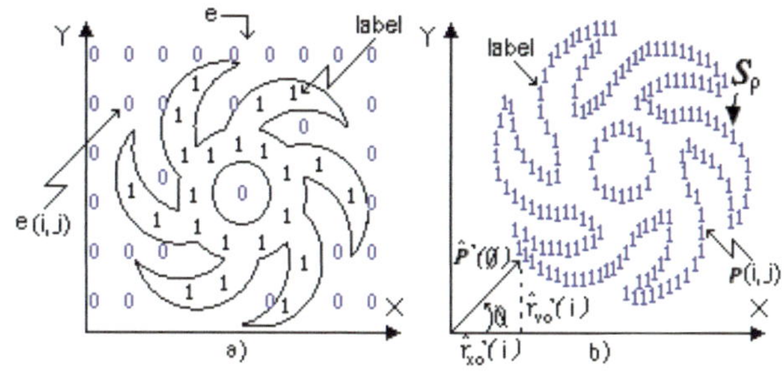

Figure 13. Labeling definition, (a) labeling of piece and (b) labeling of perimeter [8].

Step 3. Image processing

Detection and labeling of gradient and perimeter in the edge of the piece: The following step is the binary label, or limitation, of the piece $\mathbf{e}(i,k)|_n^m$, see **Figure 13(a)** (Eq. (22)). Be an image $\mathbf{f}_k \subseteq \mathbf{f}(i,k)|_n^m$ white and black in the binary space $\mathbf{f}^B$

$$\sum_{j=1}^{m}\sum_{i=1}^{n}\left\{\mathbf{e}(i,j)=\begin{cases}\mathbf{f}(i,j)=1\Rightarrow \mathbf{f}_e(i,j)=1\\ \mathbf{f}(i,j)=0\Rightarrow \mathbf{f}_e(i,j)=0\end{cases}\right\} \tag{22}$$

where $(\mathbf{f}(i,j)|_n^m)$ is the labeling image saved in the image of exit $e(i,j)\,|_n^m$ of Eq. (22). The directional classification of the edge for half of the image in the point $p(x,y)$ is presented in **Figure 13(b)**.

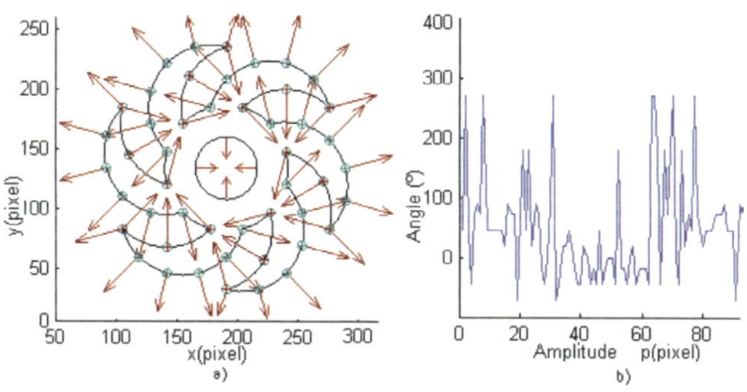

Figure 14. Vectors of piece, (a) direction vector of piece and (b) magnitude of edge direction [8].

Perimeter of the piece: The perimeter $(\widehat{P}(\theta))$ can be found by applying an edge $(|\nabla f|)$ into the image $(f(i,j)\,|_n^m)$ to provide information about the shape of the object, and the labeled perimeter S_p can be defined as the position vector for the edge. **Figure 14(b)** presents the result of the trajectory of the labeled perimeter S_p represented with label "1" in the point $p(i,j)$ of the image.

Figure 14(a) and **(b)** show the direction vectors in the contour of the workpiece when image processing is applied.

The magnitude ($|\nabla f|(i,j)$) and direction ($\angle\nabla f(i,j)$) of the labeling gradient and perimeter ($\angle\nabla f(i,j)$) of the edge are saved in the variable $\mathbf{Maq}(i,j)$ to generate the dimension of structural element:

$$\left\{\forall \boldsymbol{S}_p(i,j) \in f(x,y) : \exists \begin{pmatrix} |\nabla f|(i,j) \wedge \\ \angle\nabla f(i,j) \end{pmatrix} \subset \mathbf{Maq}(i,j)\right\} \tag{23}$$

Therefore,

$$\mathbf{Maq}(i,j) = \int_{j=1}^{j=m-1} \int_{i=1}^{i=n-1} \left[\left(|\nabla f|(i,j)\right) \wedge \angle\left(\nabla f(i,j)\right)\right] dx\,dy \tag{24}$$

Step 4. Directional morphology

Directional morphologies to generate size of tool, erosion, and dilation are fundamental operations in morphological image processing, defined for binary images. To grayscale images and to complete lattices, dilation (δ) and erosion (ε) are formed by a structural element.

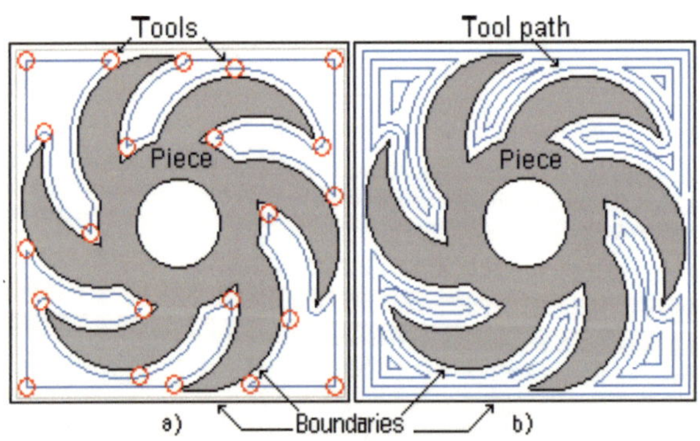

Figure 15. Directional morphology, (a) tool size dilatation and (b) tool path dilatation [8].

Dilation allows thinning of the contour of the part in the image $\mathbf{f}(i,j)$, using a structural element $b(i,j)$, which is developed in Eq. (25), see **Figure 15**:

$$(A \oplus B)(w,q) = \max\left\{\mathbf{f}(w-i,q-j) + b(i,j)\right\} \tag{25}$$

Such that $(w\text{-}i,q\text{-}j) \in D_{A'}$ $(i,j) \in D_B$

With D functions with respect to A and B [4].

Eqs. (26) and (27) represent fundamental operations of dilation $A \oplus B$, where A contains all pixels and B is a structural element of cutting tool with $\hat{B}$ reflected in B a variation of s:

$$A \oplus B = \left\{ s \mid (\hat{B})_s \cap A \neq \Phi \right\} \tag{26}$$

Equivalently,

$$A \oplus B = \left\{ s \mid ((\hat{B})_s \cap A) \subseteq A \right\} \tag{27}$$

Dilation is a joining of the translations of one picture for each pixel of an image B, called structural element as

$$A \oplus B = \bigcup_{b_i \in B} \mathbf{A}_{b_i} \tag{28}$$

Therefore

$$\sum_{i=1}^{n-1} \sum_{j=1}^{m-1} \left| \left\{ if \begin{bmatrix} ((f(i,j) == 0)) \delta\delta ((f(i,j-1) == 1) \mid\mid f(i- \\ 1,j) == 1 \mid\mid f(i,j+1) == 1 \mid\mid f(i+1,j) == 1 \end{bmatrix} \Rightarrow f(i,j) \Leftarrow 1 \right\} \right| \tag{29}$$

$$(A \Theta B)(w,q) = \min \left\{ \mathbf{f}(w+i, q+j) - b(i,j) \right\} \tag{30}$$

Such that

$$(\mathrm{w} + \mathrm{i}, \mathrm{q} + \mathrm{j}) \in \mathrm{D}_{\mathrm{A}}, (i,j) \in D_B \tag{31}$$

With D functions with respect to A and B [8].

Eqs. (32) and (33) represent fundamental operations of erosion ($A \,\theta\, B$), and inverse operation to dilation:

$$(A \Theta B) = \left\{ s \mid (B)_s \subseteq A \right\} \tag{32}$$

$$(A\Theta B)=\{p \mid B_p \subseteq A\} \tag{33}$$

The set of edges reduction, elimination of white dots, and the expansion of the small black dots of an image B are called erosion:

$$A\Theta B=\bigcap_{b_i \in B} \mathbf{A}_{b_i} \tag{34}$$

Therefore

$$\sum_{i=1}^{n-1}\sum_{j=1}^{m-1}\left|\left\{ if \begin{bmatrix} ((f(i,j)==1))\delta\delta((f(i,j-1)==0)\mid\mid f(i- \\ 1,j)==0\mid\mid f(i,j+1)==0\mid\mid f(i+1,j)==0 \end{bmatrix} \Rightarrow f(i,j)\Leftarrow 0\right\}\right| \tag{35}$$

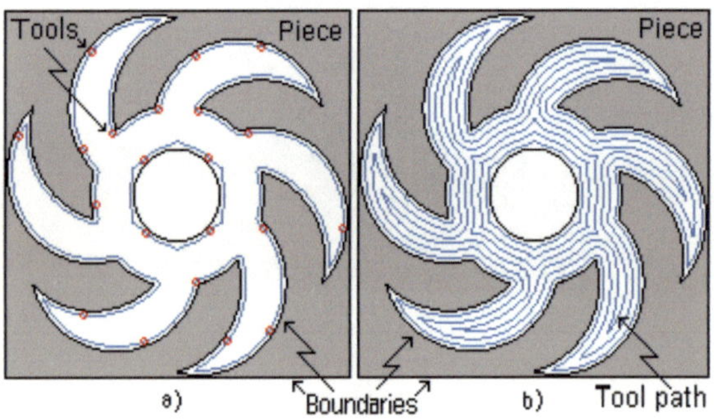

Figure 16. Directional morphology, (a) tool size erosion and (b) tool path erosion [8].

Modifying Eqs. (29) and (35) of directional morphology to generate the structural element of insert and tool path using the workspace boundaries, edge, and the perimeter function of the piece generating Eq. (39) and as results provided by **Figures 16** and **8**:

$$\sum_{i=1}^{n-1}\sum_{j=1}^{m-1}\left\{SE_1(i,j)=\sum_{a=-2}^{2}(i,j+a)\right\} \tag{36}$$

$$\sum_{i=1}^{n-1}\sum_{j=1}^{m-1}\left\{SE_2(i,j)=\sum_{b=-2}^{2}(i+b,j)\right\} \tag{37}$$

$$\sum_{i=1}^{n-1}\sum_{j=1}^{m-1}\left\{\sum_{h=n-4}^{n}\left(SE_{n-2}(i,j)=\sum_{c=-1}^{1}\sum_{d=-1}^{1}(i+c,j+d)\right)\right\} \tag{38}$$

http://dx.doi.org/10.5772/64611

$$SE = \sum_{i=1}^{n-1}\sum_{j=1}^{m-1}\left\{\{SE_1(i,j)\} \cup \{SE_2(i,j)\} \cup \ldots \cup \left\{\sum_{h=n-4}^{n}\left(SE_{n-2}(i,j)\right)\right\}\right\} \tag{39}$$

$$if\left\{(SE_{n-2}) == \left((SE_1)\ or\,(SE_2)\right) then\ \text{eliminate}\ (SE_{n-2})\right\} \tag{40}$$

where (SE_1) is the first piece of structural element and (SE_1) is given by

$$SE_1 = \sum_{a=-2}^{2}(i, j+a) = (i, j-2) \cup (i, j-1) \cup (i, j) \cup (i, j+1) \cup (i, j+2) \tag{41}$$

Step 5. Automatic tool selections

Table 5 shows the most common cutting tool. The dimensions of the cutting tool are obtained from manuals and introduced into the software to be converted into structural elements with the length, orientation, and radius of the nose, this part is shown in **Figure 16(a)**. Among the common dimensions are those of 15°, 35°, and 45°, with 9525 mm needing 36 pixels, 2540 requiring a mesh of 25.5 square units of pixels, and the structural element having 414 pixels, see **Figure 17(a)** [8].

Tool for milling		**Type**	**Size (mm)**						
Name	**Shape**		*D*	*d*	*L*	*l*	*FI*	*Sd*	ϕ(°)
Ballnose	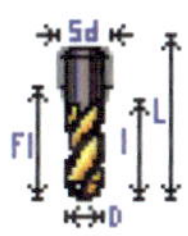	Milling	0.016	0.016	40.149	15.181	20.417	0.016	0.009
			0.200	0.199	20.149	15.181	17.417	0.210	0.099
Endmill		Drilling	0.150	0.015	20.149	14.181	16.417	0.015	0.749
Conic	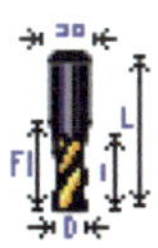		0.099	0.099	25.149	14.181	20.417	0.100	0.049
		Milling	0.049	0.049	15.149	7.181	12.417	0.050	0.025
Corner			0.009	0.005	10.149	5.181	7.4173	0.010	0.005
Dovetail	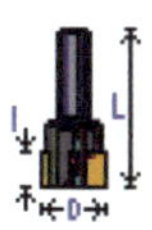		0.309	0.309	30.000	19.999	22.999	0.400	0.200
Chamber			0.349	0.349	40.149	15.181	20.417	0.350	0.210
Counter		Facing	0.399	0.399	45.149	10.181	15.417	0.380	0.230
Holder			0.599	0.599	25.149	10.181	15.417	0.390	0.250

Table 5. Common cutting tool (structural element) used.

The cutting tools are shown in **Table 5**, where D is the diameter, d is the tip diameter, L is the major length, l is the minor length, FI is the usable length, Sd is presetting, and φ is the corner radius of the cutting tool. The tool is generated from handbooks; although, a real insert as the drilling cutting tool with a diameter of 5.56 mm (D, 21 pixels) requires a structural element as a tool of $\pi(20)^2$ pixels. For more details see **Figure 17(a)**.

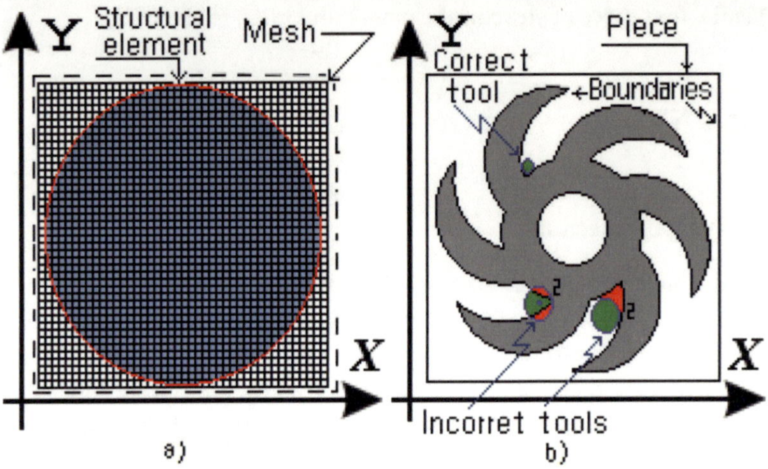

Figure 17. Tool selection, (a) structural element and (b) incorrect tool and correct tool [8].

The conditions for machining to determine the cutting tool are given by Eq. (42) that generates the movements of the structural element through the image, and the angle labels the start of the selection of the cutting tool in machining $\mathbf{M}(i,k)=1$ [9]..

$$\sum_{j=m}^{m-1}\sum_{i=1}^{n-1}\{if\ \mathbf{M}(i,j)=1\ then\ select\ \ insert\{\boldsymbol{\mu}(i,j)\Leftarrow diameter\}\} \tag{42}$$

The structural element (**Figure 17a**) is designed to create a trajectory using Eq. (42). To check the intersection (**Figure 17b**), it is necessary that the pixels have the same coordinates. The design of the software to create the automatic tool selection is developed in Microsoft Visual C ++ 2010, generating a matrix with coordinates (i, j) of the image.

After the correct holders and inserts have been selected to work in each area, many changes in cutting tools are probably required. The number of changes can be reduced by ordering the changes with the next procedure:

$$\sum_{i=1}^{n-1}\sum_{j=1}^{m-2}\left\{\begin{array}{l} if\left\{(\boldsymbol{S}_p(i,j)=1)\ and\ \sum_{h=-1}^{1}\sum_{\psi=-1}^{1}\lambda[i+\psi][j+1]=1\right\} \\ then\ \mathbf{Tray}\,(i,j)\Leftarrow\lambda[i+\psi][j+1] \end{array}\right\} \tag{43}$$

To determine the tool path, each pixel should share information with eight neighbors and follow the path of the perimeter (edge S_p) in the mesh $\lambda[i + \psi][k + 1]$.

Step 6. Generation of trajectory

In the present article, zig and zig with contour were developments to generate the trajectories. A structural element with the shape of the cutting tool, with diameter D and longitude, is displaced through all images from right to left. If there is no intersection between the structural element and the edge of the piece, other tool is selected [8].

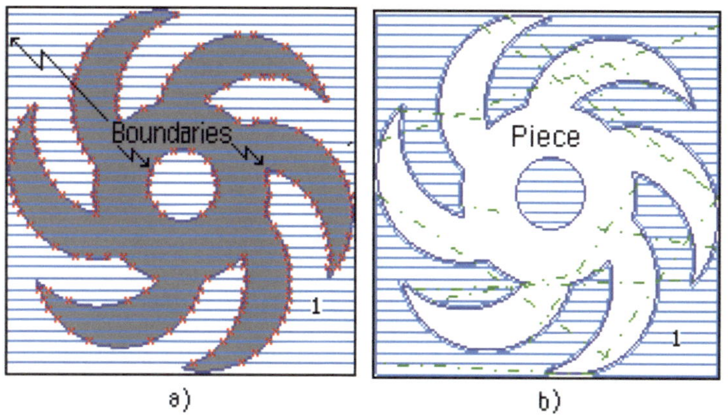

Figure 18. Tool selection (final piece), (a) boundaries identification and (b) rough milling (zig) [8].

Finally, to move the tool in the image, it is necessary to use a counter ($k = 0$, $i = i + 1$) with the total number of pixels m. This method is obtained by Eq. (44) and is displayed in **Figure 18(a)** and **(b)** [8]:

$$\sum_{j=m}^{m-1}\sum_{i=1}^{n-1}\left\{\mathbf{Maq}(i,j) \Leftarrow \mathbf{f}(i,j); \left\{ \ if\, \mathbf{f}(i,j) = \mathbf{Tray}(i,j) = 1 \text{ then } j = j+1 \ \right\}\right\} \tag{44}$$

9. Results in mill

A new method is presented for tool selection using directional morphology. To validate the method, three examples were proposed.

Figure 19(a) and **(b)** depict machining with tools CB and C with labels "4" and "3," respectively. **Figure 20** shows four selected tools, using pocket in zigzag with contour, applying dilation because the machining is external. After this, in **Figure 19(c)**, the machined area (labeled with "2") can be seen. In the same way, the piece finally machined with a B tool is shown in **Figure 19(d)**. **Figure 19(e)** depicts the final workpiece obtained. In **Table 6**, parameters of cutting tool selected by the proposed method can be seen.

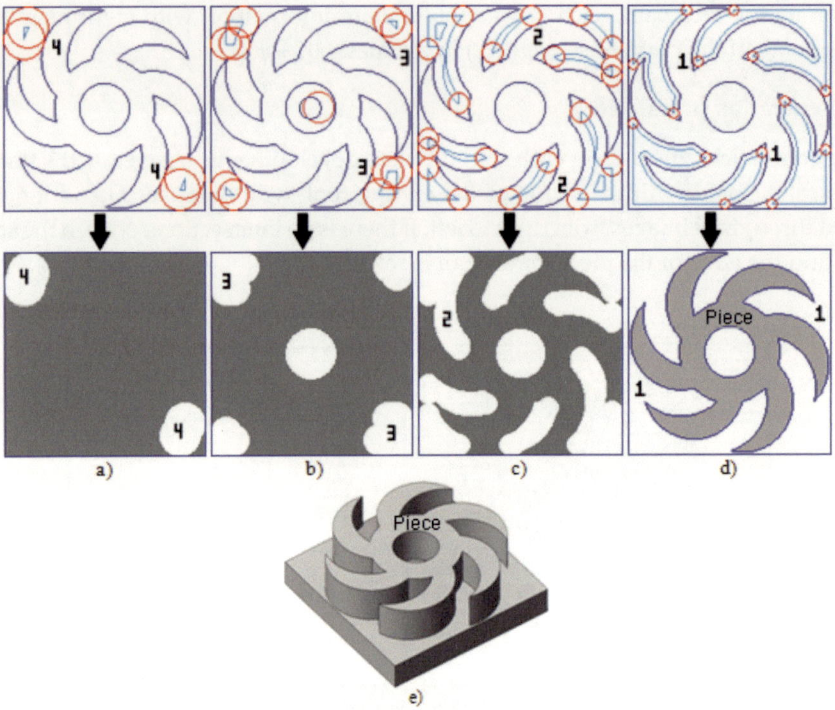

Figure 19. Tool selection for first piece based in residues of pixels [8].

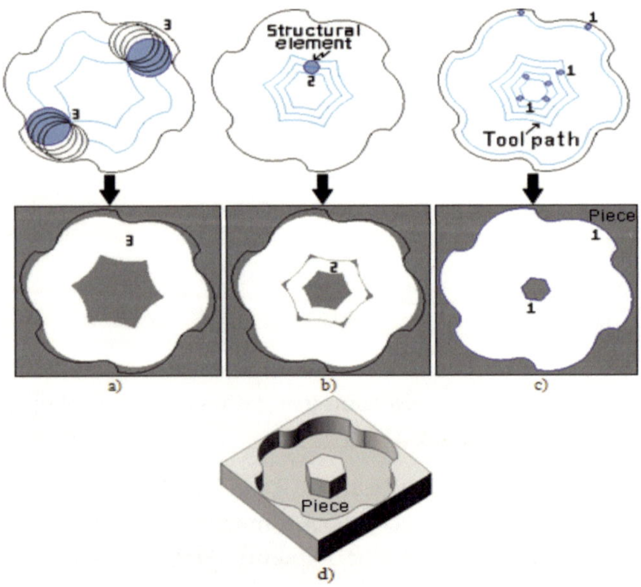

Figure 20. Tool selection for second piece using zigzag with contour [8].

Rough milling			Finish milling
Area	**Type**	**D (mm)**	**D (mm)**
1	B	–	0.0157
2	C	0.1500	–
3	C	0.3499	–
4	CB	0.3999	–

Table 6. Selected tools for the first piece.

The second piece is shown in **Figure 20**. In this case, the piece is machined using zigzag with contour and boundaries. An erosion operation, to automatically select the tool, applied to the surface to remove pixels is internal by the geometry desired. The three contours and approximations of machining with different tools marked with labels "3," "2," and "1" are depicted in **Figure 20(a)**, **(b)**, and **(c)**, respectively. Finally, **Figure 20(d)** depicts the machined piece. **Table 7** shows the parameters of the three different tools selected by the method (see **Table 8**).

Figure 21 shows the rough mill with the last piece using zig with contour. **Figure 21(a)–(c)** with their respective tool selections. **Figure 21(d)** shows the finish milling and **Figure 21(e)** the final piece.

Rough milling			Finish milling
Area	**Type**	**D (mm)**	**D (mm)**
1	B	–	0.0157
2	C	0.2000	–
3	C	0.3999	–

Table 7. Selected tools for second piece.

Rough milling			Finish milling
Area	**Type**	**D (mm)**	**D (mm)**
1	B	–	0.0157
2	C	0.0499	–
3	C	0.1500	–
4	D	0.5999	–

Table 8. Selected tools for third example.

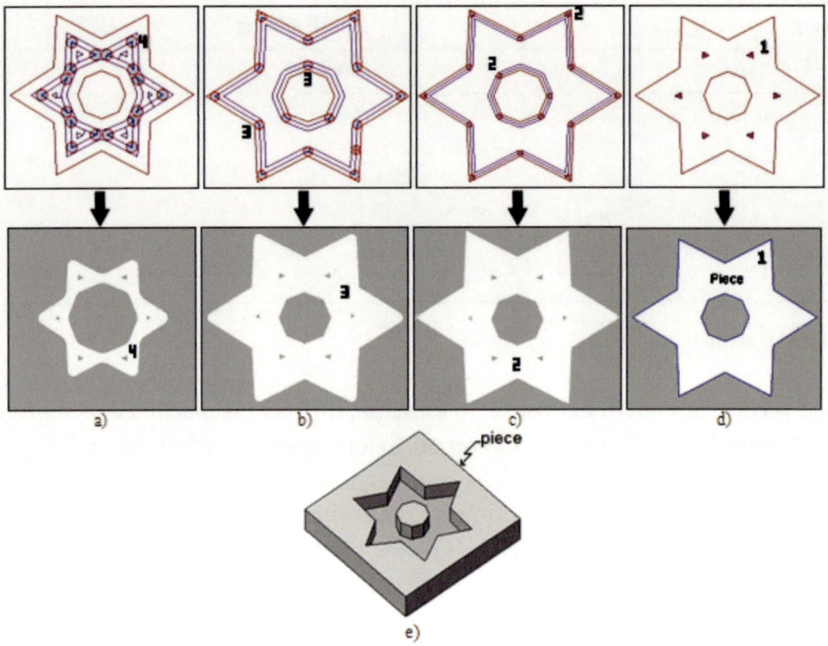

Figure 21. Tool selection for third piece (rough mill using zig with contour) [8].

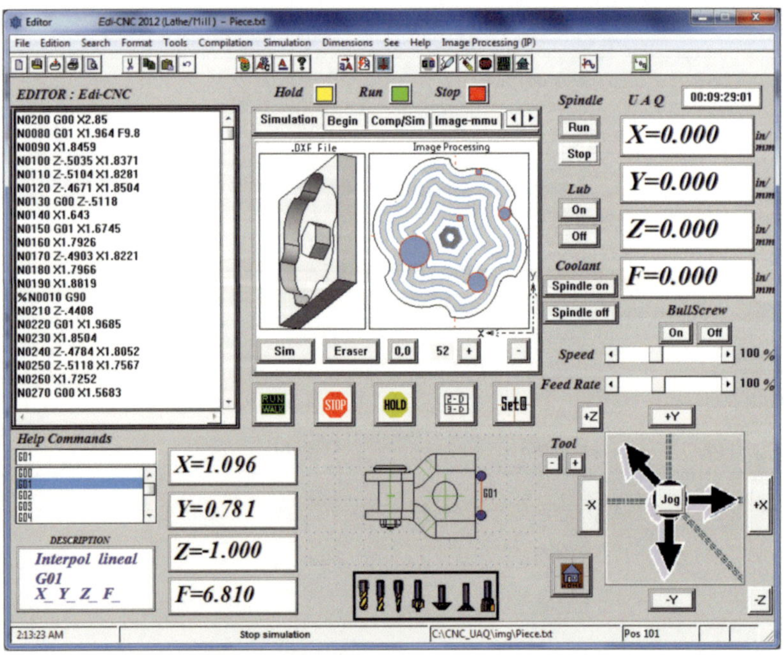

Figure 22. Final software for automatic tool selection [8].

Figure 22 shows the software developed in Microsoft Visual C ++ 2010 for the automatic tool selection.

10. Conclusions of mill

Image processing for manufacturing three-dimensional models that require movements in three axes based on the directional morphology to detect collisions when the workpiece and the tool are moving is a new method in the literature. The automatic selection of cutting tool and the generation of tool paths to manufacture pieces in three-axis machining have been presented. The advantages of this method arefast and easy-to-implement programming, the proposed method can correctly select cutting tool; traditional methods of morphology as dilation and erosion in conjunction with edge piece to create tool dimensions and automatic tool selection are used. In order to diminish the possible error in boundary obtaining, a DXF file was used to compare and correct it when an image is utilized with a resolution of 1 μm.

Author details

Mejia Ugalde Mario* and Mejia Ugalde Ignacio

*Address all correspondence to: mmu92@hotmail.com

Engineering Faculty, Autonomous University of Queretaro, San Juan of Rio, Queretaro, Mexico

References

[1] Perez Paina G., Araguas G., Gaydou D., Steiner G., and Rafael Canali L., RoMAA-II, an open architecture mobile robot. Lat Am Trans IEEE (Revista IEEE Am Lat). 2014; 12(5): 915–921.

[2] Jimenez Moreno R. and Brito M., Path planning for a mobile robot in a 3D environment. In 2014 IEEE Biennial Congress of Argentina (ARGENCON), 2014; 125–129.

[3] Gadelmawla E.S., Eladawi A.E., Abouelatta O.B., et al., Application of computer vision for the prediction of cutting conditions in milling operations. , Part B: J Eng Manuf. 2009; 223: 791–800.

[4] Al-Kindi G. and Zughaer H., An approach to improved CNC machining using vision-based system. Mater Manuf Process. 2012; 27(7): 765–774.

[5] Boix E., Ferrer A., Fernandez S., and Sellart X., Vehicle guiding system through image processing in crash and misuse tests. In Proc SAE-China Congress 2014: Selected Papers. 2015; 411–424.

[6] Eladawi A.E., Gadelmawla E.S., Elewa I.M., et al., An application of computer vision for programming computer numerical control machines. Proc IMechE, Part B: J Eng Manuf. 2003; 217: 1315–1324.

[7] Sarma P.M.M.S., Karunamoorthy L., and Palanikumar K., Surface roughness parameters evaluation in machining GFRP composites by PCD tool using digital image processing. J Reinf Plast Compos. 2009; 28: 1567–1585.

[8] Mejia-Ugalde M., Trejo-Hernandez M., Dominguez-Gonzalez A., Osornio-Rios R.A., and Benitez-Rangel J.P., Directional morphological approaches from image processing applied to automatic tool selection in computer numerical control milling machine. Proc IMechE, Part B: J Eng Manuf. 2013; 227: 1607–1619

[9] Mejia-Ugalde M., Dominguez-Gonzalez A., Trejo-Hernandez M., Morales-Hernandez L.A., and Benitez-Rangel J.P., New approach for automatic tool selection in computer numerically controlled lathe by applying image processing. Proc IMechE, Part B: J Eng Manuf. 2012; 226: 1298–1308.

[10] Mejia-Ugalde M., Dominguez-Gonzalez A., Trejo-Hernandez M., Morales-Hernandez L., Osornio-Rios R., and Benitez-Rangel J., Triangulation intersection approach from Poissons equation applied to automatic tool selection in computer numerical control mill-lathe. Proc IMechE, Part B: J Eng Manuf. 2014; 230: 722–731.

[11] Chen T.H., Chang W.T., Shen P.H., and Tarng Y.S., Examining the profile accuracy of grinding wheels used for microdrill fluting by an image-based contour matching method. Proc IMechE, Part B: J Eng Manuf. 2010; 224: 899.

[12] Siller H.R., Vila C., Rodriguez C.A., and Abellan J.V., Study of face milling of hardened AISI D3 steel with a special design of carbide tools. Int J Adv Manuf Technol. 2009; 40: 12–25.

[13] Ahmad Z., Rahmani K., and D'Souza R.M., Applications of genetic algorithms in process planning: tool sequence selection for 2.5-axis pocket machining. J Intell Manuf. 2010; 21: 461–470.

[14] Lim T., Corney J., Ritchie J.M., and Clark D.E.R., Optimizing tool selection. Int JProd Res. 2001; 39: 1239–1256.

[15] Ramaswami H., Shaw R.S., and Anand S., Selection of optimal set of cutting tools for machining of polygonal pockets with islands. Int J Adv Manuf Technol. 2011; 53: 963–977.

[16] Maros T., Vladimír B., and Testik M.C., Monitoring chenille yarn defects using image processing with control charts. Tex Res J. 2011; 81: 1344–1353.

[17] Mallik-Goswami B. and Datta A.K., Detecting defects in fabric with laser-based morphological image processing. TexRes J. 2000; 70: 758–762.

[18] Li J., Huang P., Wang X., et al. Image edge detection based on beamlet transform. J Syst Eng Electron. 2009; 20: 1–5.

[19] Tufoi M., Vela I., Marta C., et al. Optimization of withdrawing cylinder at vertical continuous casting of steel using CAD and CAE. Int J Mech. 2011; 5: 10–18.

Section 5

Efficient Video Coding-New Perspectives

Chapter 8

Fast Algorithm Designs of Multiple-Mode Discrete Integer Transforms with Cost-Effective and Hardware-Sharing Architectures for Multistandard Video Coding Applications

Chih-Peng Fan

Additional information is available at the end of the chapter

http://dx.doi.org/10.5772/64985

Abstract

In this chapter, first we give a brief view of transform-based video coding. Second, the basic matrix decomposition scheme for fast algorithm and hardware-sharing-based integer transform design are described. Finally, two case studies for fast algorithm and hardware-sharing-based architecture designs of discrete integer transforms are presented, where one is for the single-standard multiple-mode video transform-coding application, and the other is for the multiple-standard multiple-mode video transform-coding application.

Keywords: video coding, transform coding, fast algorithm, matrix factorization, hardware sharing, multiple modes, multiple standards

1. Introduction

Video-coding system has generally utilized block-based transform-coding skills to shrink the data rates by joining quantization and entropy coding. Among some block-based transforms, the discrete cosine transform (DCT) [1] and integer transforms have extensively been used to still image and video-coding specifications, such as JPEG [2], MPEG-1/2 [3, 4], MPEG-4 [5], H.264/AVC [6, 7], AVS [8, 9], VC-1 [10], VP8 [11], and HEVC [12]. Because integer transforms perform the low complexity and effective coding performance, the advanced video coding (AVC) in ITU-T H.264 [6, 7, 13, 14], which is also known as MPEG-4 part 10, applies integer transforms for transform process. The 4 × 4 and 8 × 8 transforms in [13, 14] were calculated exactly to prevent non-adaptation issues of inverse transforms for high-quality moving visual images. The VC-1 specification [10, 15, 16] employed 4 × 4 and 8 × 8 integer transforms, and it was developed by Microsoft Corporation and standardized by the Society of Motion Picture and Television Engineers (SMPTE). The 8 × 8 integer transform is utilized to obtain the high-coding performance in the Audio Video Coding Standard (AVS) for China [8, 9]. In [11], the VP8 video-coding standard was developed for Internet browser applications. The Joint Collaborative Team on Video Coding proposed the high-efficiency video coding (HEVC) specification [12]. By HEVC, the compression efficiency was greatly better than that achieved using the H.264/AVC high-profile-coding specification.

To support the single-standard H.264/AVC video coding, several transform architectures in [17–24] have been developed to approach the multiple transform modes in H.264. To support the single-standard H.265/HEVC video coding, several transform architectures in [25–32] have been developed to approach the multiple transform modes in HEVC. Besides, supporting multiple-standard functions in video coding has been an important issue in multimedia applications recently, such as H.264/AVC, MPEG-1/2/4, VC-1, AVS, and VP8 standards, and several transform architectures in [33–41] have also been developed to complete the multiple transform functions. Owing to the growth of multistandard video-coding applications, how to achieve low-computational complexities and implement by hardware-sharing-based cost-effective architectures simultaneously are interesting research topics for the VLSI design of video codecs.

2. Matrix decomposition preprocessing for fast algorithm and hardware-sharing-based designs

Based on the resemblance property, the 8 × 8 inverse integer transforms [41] in H.264/AVC, AVS, VC-1, VP8, MPEG-1/2/4, and HEVC specifications are revealed in Eq. (1), and **Table 1** depicts the coefficient values in the transforms.

$$C_{8\times8}=\begin{bmatrix} a & b & f & c & a & d & g & e \\ a & c & g & -e & -a & -b & -f & -d \\ a & d & -g & -b & -a & e & f & c \\ a & e & -f & -d & a & c & -g & -b \\ a & -e & -f & d & a & -c & -g & b \\ a & -d & -g & b & -a & -e & f & -c \\ a & -c & g & e & -a & b & -f & d \\ a & -b & f & -c & a & -d & g & -e \end{bmatrix} \quad (1)$$

Transform sizes	VC-1	AVS	VP8	MPEG-1/2/4	H.264/AVC	HEVC
4 × 4	√	√	√	N/A	√	√
8 × 8	√	√	N/A	√	√	√
16 × 16	N/A	N/A	N/A	N/A	N/A	√
32 × 32	N/A	N/A	N/A	N/A	N/A	√

Table 1. The transform modes in several video-coding standards [41].

In Eq. (1), it is decomposed by Eq. (2) as

$$C_{8\times8} = P_1 \cdot A_0 \cdot P_r. \tag{2}$$

In Eq. (2), A_0 is divided into two modules, $U_{4\times4}$ and $D_{4\times4}$, where $P_1 = \begin{bmatrix} 1&0&0&0&0&0&0&-1 \\ 0&1&0&0&0&0&-1&0 \\ 0&0&1&0&0&-1&0&0 \\ 0&0&0&1&-1&0&0&0 \\ 0&0&0&1&1&0&0&0 \\ 0&0&1&0&0&1&0&0 \\ 0&1&0&0&0&0&1&0 \\ 1&0&0&0&0&0&0&1 \end{bmatrix}$,

$$P_r = \begin{bmatrix} 1&0&0&0&0&0&0&0 \\ 0&0&1&0&0&0&0&0 \\ 0&0&0&0&1&0&0&0 \\ 0&0&0&0&0&0&1&0 \\ 0&1&0&0&0&0&0&0 \\ 0&0&0&1&0&0&0&0 \\ 0&0&0&0&0&1&0&0 \\ 0&0&0&0&0&0&0&1 \end{bmatrix}, A_0 = \begin{bmatrix} a&f&a&g&0&0&0&0 \\ a&g&-a&-f&0&0&0&0 \\ a&-g&-a&f&0&0&0&0 \\ a&-f&a&-g&0&0&0&0 \\ 0&0&0&0&-e&d&-c&b \\ 0&0&0&0&-d&b&-e&-c \\ 0&0&0&0&-c&e&b&d \\ 0&0&0&0&-b&-c&-d&-e \end{bmatrix}.$$

Thus

$$A_0 = U_{4\times4} \oplus D_{4\times4} \tag{3}$$

and $C_{8\times8}$ becomes

$$C_{8\times8} = P_1 \cdot (U_{4\times4} \oplus D_{4\times4}) \cdot P_r. \tag{4}$$

In (3), "⊕ " is the direct sum operator, and the two diagonal blocks $U_{4\times4}$ and $D_{4\times4}$ are processing in parallel. To cut down the computational operations and achieve effective hardware shares, the upper diagonal matrix $U_{4\times4}$ and the down diagonal matrix $D_{4\times4}$ are further decomposed into the cascaded multiplication form or the addition form of sparse matrices. After matrix factorizations, the chosen sparse matrices have the coefficients which are 1, −1, 0, or an integer, and an integer value can equal the combination of powers of two. Besides, zero factors in the chosen sparse matrices could be factorized as many as possible [42].

By Eq. (1), for VC-1 the values of the coefficient set {*a, b, c, d, e, f, g*} are {12, 16, 15, 9, 4, 16, 6}, and those for AVS are {8, 10, 9, 6, 2, 10, 4}. Next, those for MPEG-1/2/4 are {362, 502, 426, 284, 100, 473, 196}, and those for H.264/AVC are {8, 12, 10, 6, 3, 8, 4}. Finally, those for HEVC are {64, 89, 75, 50, 18, 83, 36}.

The general 4 × 4 inverse integer transform matrices [41] can be presented in Eq. (5) as

$$M_{4\times 4} = \begin{bmatrix} h & i & h & j \\ h & j & -h & -i \\ h & -j & -h & i \\ h & -i & h & -j \end{bmatrix}. \tag{5}$$

By Eq. (5), for VC-1 the values of the coefficient set {h, i, j} are {17, 22, 10}, and those for VP8 are {128, 167, 70}. Next, those for AVS-M are {2, 3, 1}, and those for H.264/AVC are {1, 1, 0.5}. Finally, those for HEVC are {64, 83, 36}.

3. Case study [32]: single-standard multiple-mode transform design

3.1. Hardware-sharing based 32 × 32 integer core transform for HEVC

The one-dimensional (1D) 32 × 32 inverse core transform for HEVC is described in [30]. By the symmetrical property, the 32 × 32 inverse core transform is presented as

$$H_{i32} = P_A \cdot C_{A1}, \tag{6}$$

where $C_{A1} = \begin{bmatrix} C_{11} & C_{12} \\ C_{21} & C_{22} \end{bmatrix}$, $P_A = \begin{bmatrix} I_{16x16} & -\tilde{I}_{16x16} \\ \tilde{I}_{16x16} & I_{16x16} \end{bmatrix}$, $\tilde{I}_{16x16} = \begin{bmatrix} 0 & 0 & \cdots & 0 & 1 \\ 0 & 0 & 0 & 1 & 0 \\ \vdots & \vdots & \iddots & 0 & \vdots \\ 0 & 1 & 0 & \vdots & 0 \\ 1 & 0 & \cdots & 0 & 0 \end{bmatrix}$, and $I_{16\times 16}$ is a 16 × 16 identity matrix. In Eq. (6), P_A is the butterfly-like postprocessing, and C_{A1} is the sparse matrix. By swapping each column of C_{A1}, it becomes

$$C_{A1} = C_{A2} \cdot P_{Ar}. \tag{7}$$

By Eqs. (6) and (7), H_{i32} becomes

http://dx.doi.org/10.5772/64985

$$H_{i32} = P_A \cdot C_{A2} \cdot P_{Ar}, \tag{8}$$

where P_{Ar} is the permutation matrix. In Eq. (7), C_{A2} is expressed by

$$C_{A2} = \begin{bmatrix} T_{A11} & 0_{16x16} \\ 0_{16x16} & T_{A22} \end{bmatrix} = T_{A11} \oplus T_{A22}, \tag{9}$$

where "⊕" means the direct sum operation, and then T_{A11} and T_{A22} are 16 × 16 matrices, which are revealed in [32]. The matrix P_{Ar} in Eq. (8) is expressed as

$$P_{Ar} = P(2,16), \tag{10}$$

where the permutation matrix $P(m, n)$ is defined in [43], and the notation "⊗" means the Kronecker product. In Eq. (9), A_{A22} is presented as

$$T_{A22} = T_{M1} + T_{N1}, \tag{11}$$

First, the lower half of C_{N1} is divided into sixteen 8 × 1 column vectors X_i, where $i = 0, 1, 2, \ldots,$ 15, and then T_{N1} becomes

$$T_{N1} = \begin{bmatrix} & 0_{8x16} & \\ - - - & - - - & - - - \\ X_0 \quad X_1 & \cdots & X_{15} \end{bmatrix}. \tag{12}$$

Second, the coefficients in a single column vector can be shared. The vector coefficient computations are achieved by integrating several base coefficients [32]. After realizing the column vectors of T_{N1}, the lower half of T_{N1} is factorized as an integration of eight 1 × 16 row vectors depicted as Y_i, where $i = 8, 9, \ldots,$ and 15, and T_{N1} becomes

$$T_{N1} = \begin{bmatrix} 0_{8x16} \\ --- \\ Y_8 \\ Y_9 \\ \vdots \\ Y_{15} \end{bmatrix}. \tag{13}$$

Adder tree structures are utilized to calculate the aggregate results for the row vectors Y_8–Y_{15} [32]. By the duplicate operations for T_{N1}, T_{M1} is presented as

$$T_{M1} = \begin{bmatrix} \hat{X}_0 \cdots \hat{X}_{15} \\ ----- \\ 0_{8x16} \end{bmatrix}, \tag{14}$$

where $\hat{X}_i$ is an 8 × 1 column vector, where $i = 0, 1, 2, \ldots,$ and 15. Then, T_{M1} becomes

$$T_{M1} = \begin{bmatrix} Y_0 \\ \vdots \\ Y_7 \\ --- \\ 0_{8x16} \end{bmatrix}, \tag{15}$$

where Y_i is a 16 × 1 row vector, where $i = 0, 1, \ldots,$ and 7. The realization of T_{M1} equals that of T_{N1}. Finally, the operations of T_{M1} and T_{N1} are merged to T_{A22}. The computational operations T_{A22} require 630 additions and 326 shift operations [32]. The matrix T_{A11} in Eq. (9), which is also denoted as H_{i16}, is the 1D 16 × 16 inverse core transform in HEVC [30].

3.2. Hardware-sharing-based 16 × 16 integer core transform for HEVC

The 16 × 16 integer core transform in [30] changes into

$$H_{i16} = P_B \cdot C_{B1}, \tag{16}$$

where $P_B = \begin{bmatrix} I_{8x8} & -\tilde{I}_{8x8} \\ \tilde{I}_{8x8} & I_{8x8} \end{bmatrix}$, and C_{B1} is revealed in [32]. By swapping each column of C_{B1}, it will be

$$C_{B1} = C_{B2} \cdot P_{Br}, \tag{17}$$

where $P_{\mathrm{Br}} = P(8,2)$. By Eqs. (16) and (17), H_{i16} is expressed by

$$H_{i16} = T_{A11} = P_B \cdot C_{B2} \cdot P_{Br}. \tag{18}$$

http://dx.doi.org/10.5772/64985

In Eq. (18), C_{B2} is presented as

$$C_{B2} = \begin{bmatrix} T_{B11} & 0_{8x8} \\ 0_{8x8} & T_{B22} \end{bmatrix} = T_{B11} \oplus T_{B22}, \tag{19}$$

and T_{B22} becomes

$$T_{B22} = T_{M2} + T_{N2}, \tag{20}$$

where $T_{M2} = \begin{bmatrix} -9 & 25 & -43 & 57 & -70 & 80 & -87 & 90 \\ -25 & 70 & -90 & 80 & -43 & -9 & 57 & -87 \\ -43 & 90 & -57 & -25 & 87 & -70 & -9 & 80 \\ -57 & 80 & 25 & -90 & 9 & 87 & -43 & -70 \\ 0 & 0 & 0 & 0 & 0 & 0 & 0 & 0 \\ 0 & 0 & 0 & 0 & 0 & 0 & 0 & 0 \\ 0 & 0 & 0 & 0 & 0 & 0 & 0 & 0 \\ 0 & 0 & 0 & 0 & 0 & 0 & 0 & 0 \end{bmatrix},$

$$T_{N2} = \begin{bmatrix} 0 & 0 & 0 & 0 & 0 & 0 & 0 & 0 \\ 0 & 0 & 0 & 0 & 0 & 0 & 0 & 0 \\ 0 & 0 & 0 & 0 & 0 & 0 & 0 & 0 \\ 0 & 0 & 0 & 0 & 0 & 0 & 0 & 0 \\ -70 & 43 & 87 & -9 & -90 & -25 & 80 & 57 \\ -80 & -9 & 70 & 87 & 25 & -57 & -90 & -43 \\ -87 & -57 & -9 & 43 & 80 & 90 & 70 & 25 \\ -90 & -87 & -80 & -70 & -57 & -43 & -25 & -9 \end{bmatrix}.$$

By the duplicate processed of T_{N1} in Section 3.1, T_{N2} turns into

$$T_{N2} = \begin{bmatrix} 0_{4x8} \\ ------ \\ U_0 \cdots U_7 \end{bmatrix}, \tag{21}$$

where U_i is an 8 × 1 column vector, where $i = 0, 1, 2, \ldots,$ and 7. Next, T_{N2} also is

$$T_{N2} = \begin{bmatrix} 0_{4x8} \\ --- \\ V_4 \\ \vdots \\ V_7 \end{bmatrix}, \tag{22}$$

where V_i is a 1 × 8 row vector, where i = 4, 5, 6, and 7. Adder tree schemes are applied to compute the summed outcomes of V_4–V_7 [32]. By the same processes of T_{M1} in Section 3.1, T_{M2} becomes

$$T_{M2} = \begin{bmatrix} \hat{U}_0 & \cdots & \hat{U}_7 \\ -- & -- & -- \\ & 0_{4x8} & \end{bmatrix}, \tag{23}$$

where $\hat{U}_i$ is a 4 × 1 column vector, where i = 0, 1, 2, …, and 7. Next, T_{M2} also is

$$T_{M2} = \begin{bmatrix} V_0 \\ \vdots \\ V_3 \\ --- \\ 0_{4x8} \end{bmatrix}, \tag{24}$$

where V_i is a 1 × 8 row vector, where i = 0, 1, 2, and 3. Then, adder trees are used to treat the row vectors V_0–V_3 [32]. Finally, the calculations of T_{M2} and T_{N2} are merged to T_{B22}. The computational operations of T_{B22} are 164 additions and 106 shift operations [32]. Meantime, the T_{B11} in Eq. (19), which is also denoted as H_{i8}, is the 1D 8 × 8 inverse core transform in HEVC [30].

3.3. Hardware-sharing-based 8 × 8 integer core transform for HEVC

The 8 × 8 integer transform in [30] is described as

$$H_{i8} = P_C \cdot C_{C1}, \tag{25}$$

where $P_C = \begin{bmatrix} I_{4x4} & -\tilde{I}_{4x4} \\ \tilde{I}_{4x4} & I_{4x4} \end{bmatrix}$, and $C_{C1} = \begin{bmatrix} 64 & 0 & 83 & 0 & 64 & 0 & 36 & 0 \\ 64 & 0 & 36 & 0 & -64 & 0 & -83 & 0 \\ 64 & 0 & -36 & 0 & -64 & 0 & 83 & 0 \\ 64 & 0 & -83 & 0 & 64 & 0 & -36 & 0 \\ 0 & -18 & 0 & 50 & 0 & -75 & 0 & 89 \\ 0 & -50 & 0 & 89 & 0 & -18 & 0 & -75 \\ 0 & -75 & 0 & 18 & 0 & 89 & 0 & 50 \\ 0 & -89 & 0 & -75 & 0 & -50 & 0 & -18 \end{bmatrix}$. After swapping each column in C_{C1}, it changes into

$$C_{C8} = C_{C2} \cdot P_{Cr}, \tag{26}$$

where $P_{Cr} = \begin{bmatrix} 1&0&0&0&0&0&0&0 \\ 0&0&1&0&0&0&0&0 \\ 0&0&0&0&1&0&0&0 \\ 0&0&0&0&0&0&1&0 \\ 0&1&0&0&0&0&0&0 \\ 0&0&0&1&0&0&0&0 \\ 0&0&0&0&0&1&0&0 \\ 0&0&0&0&0&0&0&1 \end{bmatrix}$. Based on Eqs. (25) and (26), H_{i8} is presented by

$$H_{i8} = T_{B11} = P_C \cdot C_{C2} \cdot P_{Cr}, \tag{27}$$

In Eq. (27), C_{C2} becomes

$$C_{C2} = \begin{bmatrix} T_{C11} & 0_{4x4} \\ 0_{4x4} & T_{C22} \end{bmatrix} = T_{C11} \oplus T_{C22}, \tag{28}$$

where $T_{C11} = \begin{bmatrix} 64 & 83 & 64 & 36 \\ 64 & 36 & -64 & -83 \\ 64 & -36 & -64 & 83 \\ 64 & -83 & 64 & -36 \end{bmatrix}$ and $T_{C22} = \begin{bmatrix} -18 & 50 & -75 & 89 \\ -50 & 89 & -18 & -75 \\ -75 & 18 & 89 & 50 \\ -89 & -75 & -50 & -18 \end{bmatrix}$.

In Eq. (28), T_{C22} is factorized as

$$T_{C22} = S_1 + S_2, \tag{29}$$

where $S_1 = \begin{bmatrix} -18 & 0 & 0 & 89 \\ 0 & 89 & -18 & 0 \\ 0 & 18 & 89 & 0 \\ -89 & 0 & 0 & -18 \end{bmatrix}$. Moreover, S_1 is expressed by

$$S_1 = Z_1 + (18 \cdot Z_2), \tag{30}$$

where $Z_1 = \begin{bmatrix} 0 & 0 & 0 & -1 \\ 0 & -1 & 0 & 0 \\ 0 & 0 & -1 & 0 \\ 1 & 0 & 0 & 0 \end{bmatrix}$ and $Z_2 = \begin{bmatrix} -1 & 0 & 0 & 5 \\ 0 & 5 & -1 & 0 \\ 0 & 1 & 5 & 0 \\ -5 & 0 & 0 & -1 \end{bmatrix}$. In Eq. (29), S_2 is presented as

$$S_2 = 25 \cdot Z_3, \tag{31}$$

where $Z_3 = \begin{bmatrix} 0 & 2 & -3 & 0 \\ -2 & 0 & 0 & -3 \\ -3 & 0 & 0 & 2 \\ 0 & -3 & -2 & 0 \end{bmatrix}$. By Eqs. (29)– (31), T_{C22} becomes

$$T_{C22} = Z_1 + (18 \cdot Z_2) + (25 \cdot Z_3). \tag{32}$$

In Eq. (32), the computations of T_{C22} require 36 additions and 28 shift operations [32]. The matrix T_{C11} in Eq. (28) is also the 1D 4 × 4 inverse core transform matrix in HEVC.

3.4. Hardware-sharing-based 4 × 4 integer core transform for HEVC

The 4 × 4 integer core transform matrix is indicated as

$$H_{i4} = P_D \cdot C_{D1}, \tag{33}$$

where $P_D = \begin{bmatrix} 1 & 0 & 1 & 0 \\ 0 & 1 & 0 & 1 \\ 0 & 1 & 0 & -1 \\ 1 & 0 & -1 & 0 \end{bmatrix}$ and $C_{D1} = \begin{bmatrix} 64 & 0 & 64 & 0 \\ 64 & 0 & -64 & 0 \\ 0 & -36 & 0 & 83 \\ 0 & -83 & 0 & -36 \end{bmatrix}$. By swapping each column of C_{D1}, it changes into

$$C_{D1} = C_{D2} \cdot P_{D2}. \tag{34}$$

where $P_{Dr} = \begin{bmatrix} 1 & 0 & 0 & 0 \\ 0 & 0 & 1 & 0 \\ 0 & 1 & 0 & 0 \\ 0 & 0 & 0 & 1 \end{bmatrix}$. From Eqs. (33) and (34), H_{i4} is described by

$$H_{i4} = T_{C11} = P_D \cdot C_{D2} . P_{Dr}. \tag{35}$$

In Eq. (34), C_{D2} is rewritten as

$$C_{D2} = T_{D11} \oplus T_{D22}. \tag{36}$$

In Eq. (36), T_{D11} becomes

$$T_{D11} = 64 \cdot Z_4, \tag{37}$$

http://dx.doi.org/10.5772/64985

where $Z_4 = \begin{bmatrix} 1 & 1 \\ 1 & -1 \end{bmatrix}$. In Eq. (36), T_{D22} is indicated by Z_5 and Z_6 as

$$T_{D22} = 36 \cdot Z_5 + 11 \cdot Z_6, \tag{38}$$

where $Z_5 = \begin{bmatrix} 2 & 1 \\ 1 & -2 \end{bmatrix}$ and $Z_6 = \begin{bmatrix} 1 & 0 \\ 0 & -1 \end{bmatrix}$. Thus, the computations of T_{D22} are 10 additions and 10 shift operations [32]. Based on Eqs. (35)– (38), H_{i4} is changed into

$$H_{i4} = P_D \cdot [(64 \cdot Z_4) \oplus (36 \cdot Z_5 + 11 \cdot Z_6)] \cdot P_{Dr}. \tag{39}$$

By the abovementioned discussions, the hardware modules of 4 × 4, 8 × 8, and 16 × 16 inverse core transforms are shared to implement H_{i8}, H_{i16}, and H_{i32}, respectively [32]. By sharing the hardware of H_{i4} in Eq. (39), the cost-effective design of the 8 × 8, 16 × 16, and 32 × 32 inverse core transforms is obtained progressively. First, the hardware-sharing-based eight-point inverse transform is presented as

$$H_{i8} = P_C \cdot \{H_{i4} \oplus [Z_1 + (18 \cdot Z_2) + (25 \cdot Z_3)]\} \cdot P_{Cr}. \tag{40}$$

Next, the hardware-sharing-based 16-point inverse transform is described as

$$H_{i16} = P_B \cdot \{H_{i8} \oplus [T_{M2} + T_{N2}]\} \cdot P_{Br}. \tag{41}$$

Finally, the hardware-sharing-based 32-point inverse transform is depicted as

$$H_{i32} = P_A \cdot \{H_{i16} \oplus [T_{M1} + T_{N1}]\} \cdot P_{Ar}. \tag{42}$$

In this section, the hardware-sharing transform architecture cuts down the hardware cost because the same submodules and coefficients of the transforms are extracted to be shared. **Figure 1** illustrates the architecture of the hardware-sharing-based inverse core transform design for 4 × 4/8 × 8/16 × 16/32 × 32 transforms [32].

3.5. Architecture comparison

The proposed 1D inverse core transform in [32] involves four inputs to sustain 4 × 4, 8 × 8, 16 × 16, and 32 × 32 transform modes. Several multiplexers are utilized to acquire the transform outputs of the 32 × 32 inverse core transform by the shared design of 4 × 4, 8 × 8, and 16 × 16 inverse core transforms [32]. **Table 2** lists the number of adders and shifters needed to calculate four modes of the 1D inverse core transform for HEVC. The developed architecture in [32] does not require any multiplier, and the fixed-coefficient multiplications are replaced with simple additions and shift operations. **Table 3** shows the comparison of three 16-point inverse transform designs. Compared with the previous works in [29] and [31], the applied architecture contains fewer adders. However, several more shifters are required. Compared with the cost of adders, the shifters need lower hardware expense. Thus, the used architecture decreases the hardware cost more efficiently than previous transform schemes do.

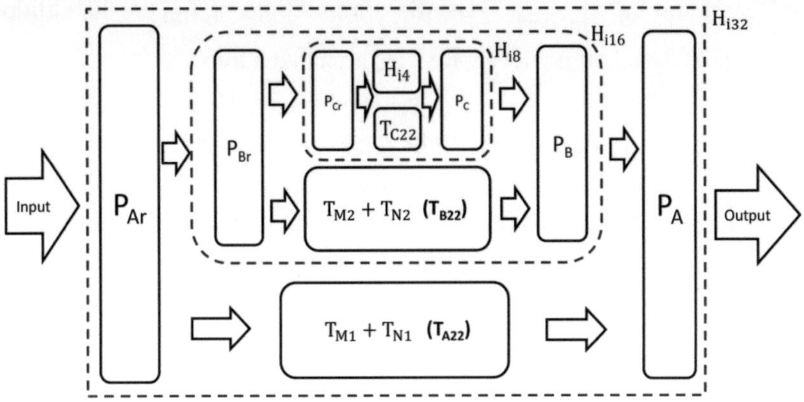

Figure 1. The hardware-sharing-based inverse core transform structure for HEVC.

Transform sizes	32 × 32	16 × 16	8 × 8	4 × 4
No. of shifters	256	93	40	11
No. of adders	461	146	64	10

Table 2. The 1D inverse transform architecture at different transform modes [32].

Designs	No. of shifters	No. of adders
Ahmed [29]	132	232
Haggag [31]	58	242
Design in Section 3.2	93	146

Table 3. Hardware comparison of three 1D 16-point transform designs [32].

4. Case study [41]: multiple-standard multiple-mode transform design

4.1. Hardware-sharing design for 8 × 8 transforms mode

For H.264/AVC, the transform matrix is employed as a foundation matrix for the multistandard hardware-sharing scheme. Based on Eq. (3), the cost of the upper diagonal matrix in Eq. (43) is eight adders and two shifters.

http://dx.doi.org/10.5772/64985

$$U_{4\times4\_AVC} = \begin{bmatrix} 8 & 8 & 8 & 4 \\ 8 & 4 & -8 & -8 \\ 8 & -4 & -8 & 8 \\ 8 & -8 & 8 & -4 \end{bmatrix} = 8 \cdot C_1 \cdot C_2, \tag{43}$$

where $C_1 = \begin{bmatrix} 1 & 0 & 0 & 1 \\ 0 & -1 & 1 & 0 \\ 0 & 1 & 1 & 0 \\ 1 & 0 & 0 & -1 \end{bmatrix}$, and $C_2 = \begin{bmatrix} 1 & 0 & 1 & 0 \\ 0 & -0.5 & 0 & 1 \\ 1 & 0 & -1 & 0 \\ 0 & 1 & 0 & 0.5 \end{bmatrix}$. For AVS, the upper diagonal matrix $U_{4\times4\_\mathrm{AVS}}$ in Eq. (44) costs 10 adders and four shifters.

$$U_{4\times4\_AVS} = \begin{bmatrix} 8 & 10 & 8 & 4 \\ 8 & 4 & -8 & -10 \\ 8 & -4 & -8 & 10 \\ 8 & -10 & 8 & -4 \end{bmatrix} = 8 \cdot C_1 \cdot (C_2 + C_3), \tag{44}$$

where $C_3 = \begin{bmatrix} 0 & 0 & 0 & 0 \\ 0 & 0 & 0 & 0.25 \\ 0 & 0 & 0 & 0 \\ 0 & 0.25 & 0 & 0 \end{bmatrix}$. In Eq. (45), the upper diagonal matrix $U_{4\times4\_\mathrm{VC1}}$ for VC1 needs 14 adders and eight shifters.

$$U_{4\times4\_VC1} = \begin{vmatrix} 12 & 16 & 12 & 6 \\ 12 & 6 & -12 & -16 \\ 12 & -6 & -12 & 16 \\ 12 & -16 & 12 & -6 \end{vmatrix} = 8 \cdot C_1 \cdot (C_4 + C_5 \cdot C_2), \tag{45}$$

where and $C_4 = \begin{bmatrix} 0 & 0 & 0 & 0 \\ 0 & 0 & 0 & 0.5 \\ 0 & 0 & 0 & 0 \\ 0 & 0.5 & 0 & 0 \end{bmatrix}$, and $C_5 = \begin{bmatrix} 1.5 & 0 & 0 & 0 \\ 0 & 1.5 & 0 & 0 \\ 0 & 0 & 1.5 & 0 \\ 0 & 0 & 0 & 1.5 \end{bmatrix}$. For HEVC, the 8×8 transform matrix is acquired by the AVS design in Eq. (44), and the design in Eq. (46) costs 16 adders and 12 shifters.

$$U_{4\times4_{HEVC}} = \begin{bmatrix} 64 & 83 & 64 & 36 \\ 64 & 36 & -64 & -83 \\ 64 & -36 & -64 & 83 \\ 64 & -83 & 64 & -36 \end{bmatrix} = 2 \cdot C_1 \cdot [32 \cdot (C_2 + C_3) - U_1], \tag{46}$$

where $U_1 = \begin{bmatrix} 0 & 0 & 0 & 0 \\ 0 & 2 & 0 & -1.5 \\ 0 & 0 & 0 & 0 \\ 0 & -1.5 & 0 & -2 \end{bmatrix}$. For MPEG-1/2/4, the upper diagonal matrix is factorized by

$$U_{4\times4\_MPEG} = \begin{bmatrix} 362 & 473 & 362 & 196 \\ 362 & 196 & -362 & -473 \\ 362 & -196 & -362 & 473 \\ 362 & -473 & 362 & -196 \end{bmatrix} = C_1 \cdot [256 \cdot (C_4 + C_5 \cdot C_2) - (U_2 + U_3)], \quad (47)$$

where $U_2 = \begin{bmatrix} 22 & 0 & 22 & 0 \\ 0 & 0 & 0 & 0 \\ 22 & 0 & -22 & 0 \\ 0 & 0 & 0 & 0 \end{bmatrix}$,and $U_3 = \begin{bmatrix} 0 & 0 & 0 & 0 \\ 0 & 4 & 0 & 39 \\ 0 & 0 & 0 & 0 \\ 0 & 39 & 0 & -4 \end{bmatrix}$. In Eq. (47), the parameter "22" of U_2 is implemented by $(C_5 \cdot C_5 \ll 4) - (C_1 \ll 1)$, where "$\ll 1$" is left shifting one bit, and the cost in Eq. (47) requires 28 adders and 26 shifters.

By Eq. (3), on the other side, the down diagonal matrix $D_{4\times4\_AVC}$ for H.264/AVC becomes Eq. (48), and it needs 17 adders and eight shifters.

$$D_{4\times4\_AVC} = \begin{bmatrix} -3 & 6 & -10 & 12 \\ -6 & 12 & -3 & -10 \\ -10 & 3 & 12 & 6 \\ -12 & -10 & -6 & -3 \end{bmatrix} = 8 \cdot U_4 \cdot (D_4 + D_5) \cdot (D_2 + U_3), \quad (48)$$

where $U_4 = \begin{bmatrix} 1 & 0 & 0 & 0 \\ 0 & 1 & 0 & 0 \\ 0 & 0 & 1 & 0 \\ 0 & 0 & 0 & -1 \end{bmatrix}$, $D_4 = \begin{bmatrix} -1 & -1 & 1 & 0 \\ 1 & 0 & 1 & -1 \\ -1 & 1 & 0 & -1 \\ 0 & 1 & 1 & 1 \end{bmatrix}$, $D_5 = \begin{bmatrix} -0.5 & 0 & 0 & 0 \\ 0 & 0 & 0.5 & 0 \\ 0 & 0.5 & 0 & 0 \\ 0 & 0 & 0 & 0.5 \end{bmatrix}$,

$D_2 = \begin{bmatrix} 0.25 & 0 & 0 & 0 \\ 0 & 0.25 & 0 & 0 \\ 0 & 0 & -0.25 & 0 \\ 0 & 0 & 0 & 0.25 \end{bmatrix}$, $U_3 = \begin{bmatrix} 0 & 0 & 0 & -1 \\ 0 & 0 & 1 & 0 \\ 0 & 1 & 0 & 0 \\ 1 & 0 & 0 & 0 \end{bmatrix}$.

For AVS, the $D_{4\times4\_AVS}$ matrix becomes (49), and D_4 and D_5 are shared with the design in Eq. (48), and then U_3 and U_4 are also partially shared with the scheme in Eq. (48). In Eq. (49), it costs 24 adders and 12 shifters

$$D_{4\times4\_AVS} = \begin{bmatrix} -2 & 6 & -9 & 10 \\ -6 & 10 & -2 & -9 \\ -9 & 2 & 10 & 6 \\ -10 & -9 & -6 & -2 \end{bmatrix} = 4 \cdot U_4 \cdot (D_4 + D_5) \cdot D_3 \cdot (D_1 + U_3), \tag{49}$$

where $U_3 = \begin{bmatrix} 0 & -1 & 0 & 0 \\ 0 & 0 & 0 & -1 \\ 1 & 0 & 0 & 0 \\ 0 & 0 & 1 & 0 \end{bmatrix}$, $D_3 = \begin{bmatrix} 1 & 0 & 0 & 0 \\ 0 & -1 & 0 & 0 \\ 0 & 0 & -1 & 0 \\ 0 & 0 & 0 & 1 \end{bmatrix}$, and $D_1 = \begin{bmatrix} 1.5 & 0 & 0 & 0 \\ 0 & 1.5 & 0 & 0 \\ 0 & 0 & -1.5 & 0 \\ 0 & 0 & 0 & 1.5 \end{bmatrix}$.

For VC-1, the $D_{4\times4\_VC1}$ matrix is factorized by Eq. (50), and the design requires 21 adders and 12 shifters

$$D_{4\times4\_VC1} = \begin{bmatrix} -4 & 9 & -15 & 16 \\ -9 & 16 & -4 & -15 \\ -15 & 4 & 16 & 9 \\ -16 & -15 & -9 & -4 \end{bmatrix} = 8 \cdot U_4 \cdot (D_4 \cdot D_6 + D_5) \cdot (D_2 + U_3), \tag{50}$$

where $D_6 = \begin{bmatrix} 1.5 & 0 & 0 & 0 \\ 0 & 1.5 & 0 & 0 \\ 0 & 0 & 1.5 & 0 \\ 0 & 0 & 0 & 1.5 \end{bmatrix}$. For HEVC, the $D_{4\times4\_HEVC}$ matrix is expressed by Eq. (51), and it expends 44 adders and 20 shifters

$$D_{4\times4\_HEVC} = \begin{bmatrix} -18 & 50 & -75 & 89 \\ -50 & 89 & -18 & -75 \\ -75 & 18 & 89 & 50 \\ -89 & -75 & -50 & -18 \end{bmatrix} = D_{4\times4\_AVS} \cdot 9 + [4 \cdot (U_5 \cdot D_1 + U_6) - U_7], \tag{51}$$

where $U_5 = \begin{bmatrix} 0 & 0 & -1 & 0 \\ 0 & 0 & 0 & 1 \\ 1 & 0 & 0 & 0 \\ 0 & 1 & 0 & 0 \end{bmatrix}$, $U_6 = \begin{bmatrix} 0 & -1 & 0 & 0 \\ 1 & 0 & 0 & 0 \\ 0 & 0 & 0 & -1 \\ 0 & 0 & 1 & 0 \end{bmatrix}$, $U_7 = \begin{bmatrix} 0 & 0 & 0 & 1 \\ 0 & 1 & 0 & 0 \\ 0 & 0 & 1 & 0 \\ -1 & 0 & 0 & 0 \end{bmatrix}$. For MPEG-1/2/4, based on $D_{4\times4\_AVS}$, the $D_{4\times4\_MPEG}$ matrix is presented by Eq. (52), and the design costs 48 adders and 32 shifters

$$D_{4\times4\_MPEG}=\begin{bmatrix}-100 & 284 & -426 & 502\\ -284 & 502 & -100 & -426\\ -426 & 100 & 502 & 284\\ -502 & -426 & -284 & -100\end{bmatrix}=D_{4\times4\_AVS}\cdot 50+[16\cdot(U_5\cdot D_1+U_6)+2\cdot U_7]. \tag{52}$$

4.2. Hardware-sharing design for 4 × 4 transforms mode

For AVS-M, the matrix $M_{4\times4\_AVS}$ is presented by (53), and it spends 10 adders and six shifters

$$M_{4\times4\_AVS}=\begin{bmatrix}2 & 3 & 2 & 1\\ 2 & 1 & -2 & -3\\ 2 & -1 & -2 & 3\\ 2 & -3 & 2 & -1\end{bmatrix}=C_1\cdot(2\cdot C_2+U_8), \tag{53}$$

where $U_8=\begin{bmatrix}0&0&0&0\\0&0&0&1\\0&0&0&0\\0&1&0&0\end{bmatrix}$. For VC-1, $M_{4\times4\_VC1}$ is expressed by Eq. (54), and the design requires 14 adders and 12 shifters

$$M_{4\times4\_VC1}=\begin{bmatrix}17 & 22 & 17 & 10\\ 17 & 10 & -17 & -22\\ 17 & -10 & -17 & 22\\ 17 & -22 & 17 & -10\end{bmatrix}=C_1\cdot(16\cdot C_2+U_9), \tag{54}$$

where $U_9=\begin{bmatrix}1&0&1&0\\0&-2&0&6\\1&0&-1&0\\0&6&0&2\end{bmatrix}$. For VP8, all coefficients in 4 × 4 transform matrix are multiplied by 128 to get integer values, and it costs 18 adders and 14 shifters

$$M_{4\times4\_VP8}=\begin{bmatrix}128 & 167 & 128 & 70\\ 128 & 70 & -128 & -167\\ 128 & -70 & -128 & 167\\ 128 & -167 & 128 & -70\end{bmatrix}=C_1\cdot(128\cdot C_2+U_{10}), \tag{55}$$

where $U_{10} = \begin{bmatrix} 0 & 0 & 0 & 0 \\ 0 & -6 & 0 & 39 \\ 0 & 0 & 0 & 0 \\ 0 & 39 & 0 & 6 \end{bmatrix}$. The matrix $U_{4\times4\_AVC}/8$ equals the 4 × 4 inverse transform matrix in H. 264/AVC. In addition, the matrix $U_{4\times4\_HEVC}$ equals the 4 × 4 inverse transform matrix in HEVC. Thus, several multiplexers are used to share the hardware between the submatrices to decrease hardware cost.

4.3. Architecture comparison

The applied hardware-sharing-based 1D multistandard inverse integer transform scheme has two inputs, which sustain 4 × 4 and 8 × 8 transform modes. The hardware blocks of processing the 4 × 4 inverse transforms are shared with that of the upper diagonal matrix $U_{8\times8}$. Thus, several multiplexers are utilized for $U_{8\times8}$ to compute the 4 × 4 inverse transforms without additional operations. For the multistandard applications, the hardware-sharing architecture of the fast 1D 4 × 4 and 8 × 8 inverse integer transforms is illustrated in [41]. The shifters are also realized by wiring. Compared with the individual designs without hardware shares, **Table 4** depicts that the used scheme in [41] decreases the number of shifters and adders by 50 and 75%, respectively.

Different 1D inverse integer transform modes	No. of adders	No. of shifters
Individual designs without hardware shares	336	180
Hardware-sharing-based design in Section 4	82	90
Reduction of cost	**75%**	**50%**

Table 4. Hardware comparison between two architectures [41].

To implement the discussed architecture, a cell-based VLSI design flow is utilized to design, simulate, and verify the cost-effective hardware-sharing architecture. For fair comparisons among different transform structures, the normalized mode gain, which is required to normalize the gate counts, is described as follows: By matrix dimensions and without missing generality [40], the normalized mode gains defined for the 32 × 32, 16 × 16, 8 × 8, and 4 × 4 inverse integer transform matrices are 16, 4, 1, and 1/4, respectively.

The hardware-sharing-based design in Section 3 supports 4 × 4, 8 × 8, 16 × 16, and 32 × 32 inverse transform modes for HEVC. Thus, the normalized mode gain of the design is 21.25 (i.e., 16 + 4 + 1 + 0.25). Similarly, five 8 × 8 and five 4 × 4 inverse transform functions are provided by the hardware-shared design in Section 4. Therefore, the normalized mode gain is assigned by 6.25 (i.e., 5 + 1.25) [41]. Afterwards, the normalized gate counts are defined by [40, 41]

$$Normalized\ gate\ counts = {}^{Gate\ counts}\!\big/_{Normalized\ mode\ gain}. \tag{56}$$

Table 5 shows the hardware cost comparisons among different 1D multiple transform architectures, which includes single-standard multiple-mode [32] and multiple-standard multiple-mode [41] transform designs.

Architecture	Ahmed et al. [29]	Hardware-sharing based-design in Section 3	Shen et. al. [26]	Martuza et. al. [28]	Qi et al. [36]	Wang et al. [38]	Hardware-sharing-based design in Section 4
Gate counts	144.8K	115.7 K	134.8 K	39.4 K	18 K	23.06 K	27.4 K
Normalized mode gain	21.25	21.25	25.75	5	3.5	4.5	6.25
Normalized gate counts	6.81 K	5.44 K	5.23 K	7.88 K	5.14 K	5.12 K	4.38 K
Supporting modes	Single-standard Multiple-mode	Single-standard Multiple-mode	Multiple-standard Multiple-mode	Multiple-standard Multiple-mode	Multiple-standard Multiple-mode	Multiple-standard Multiple-mode	Multiple-standard Multiple-mode
Supporting standards/ Transforms	**HEVC**: 4 × 4, 8 × 8, 16 × 16, 32 × 32 modes	**HEVC**: 4 × 4, 8 × 8, 16 × 16, 32 × 32 modes	**H.264/AVC, VC-1**: 4 × 4,8 × 8 modes **MPEG-1/2/4, AVS**: 8 × 8 mode; **HEVC**: 4 × 4, 8 × 8, 16 × 16, 32 × 32 modes	**H.264/ AVC, VC-1, AVS, HEVC**: 4 × 4, 8 × 8 modes	**H.264/AVC, VC-1**: 4 × 4, 8 × 8 modes; **MPEG-1/2/4**: 8 × 8 mode	**H.264/ AVC;, VC-1**: 4 × 4, 8 × 8 modes; **MPEG-1/2/4, AVS**: 8 × 8 mode	**H.264/AVC, VC-1, HEVC**: 4 × 4, 8 × 8 modes; **MPEG-1/2/4, AVS**: 8 × 8 mode; **VP8, AVS-M**: 4 × 4 mode

Table 5. Hardware cost comparisons among different 1D multiple transform architectures [32, 41].

5. Conclusion

For the single-standard multiple-mode transform design, this chapter discussed the 4 × 4, 8 × 8, 16 × 16, and 32 × 32 inverse core transforms in HEVC with a cost-effective and hardware-efficient design. By the symmetrical characteristics of the elements, the core transform matrices were factorized into several submatrices. Thus, the hardware of the $(N/2) \times (N/2)$ inverse core transform was shared with that of the $N \times N$ inverse core transform for $N = 32$, 16, and 8. Compared with the direct design without hardware shares, the applied transform scheme in Section 3 decreased the hardware cost of adders and shifters by 32 and 36%, respectively. Besides, for VLSI implementation, the design in Section 3 requires less normalized gate counts than the design does in [29].

For the multiple-standard multiple-mode transform design, this chapter also discussed the fast algorithm and hardware-sharing-based design of 4 × 4 and/or 8 × 8 inverse transforms among H.264/AVC, VC-1, HEVC, MPEG-1/2/4, AVS, and VP8 for multistandard video decoders. By only shifters and adders, the decomposition scheme of matrices was used to develop the hardware-shared scheme. The used structure in Section 4 decreased the number of shifters and adders by 50 and 75% more than the individual fast algorithm-based implementation did. Besides, for VLSI implementation, the design in Section 4 requires less normalized gate counts than the designs do in [26, 28, 36, 38].

Acknowledgements

This work was supported by Ministry of Science and Technology, Taiwan, R.O.C. under Grant MOST 105-2221-E-005-078.

Author details

Chih-Peng Fan

Address all correspondence to: cpfan@dragon.nchu.edu.tw

Department of Electrical Engineering, National Chung Hsing University, Taichung, Taiwan, ROC

References

[1] J. R. Rao and P. Yip, Discrete Cosine Transform: Algorithms, Advantage, Applications, New York, NY: Academic, 1990.

[2] ISO/IEC JTC 1/SC 29/WG 1—Coding of Still Pictures, 2009.

[3] ISO/IEC 11172-2 MPEG-1 Video Coding Standard, Information Technology—Coding of Moving Pictures and Associated Audio for Digital Storage Media at up to about 1,5 Mbit/s – Part 2: Video, 1993.

[4] ISO/IEC 13818-2 MPEG-2 Video Coding Standard, Information Technology—Generic Coding of Moving Pictures and Associated Audio Information: Video, 1995.

[5] ISO/IEC 14496-2 MPEG-4 Video Coding Standard, Information Technology—Coding of Audio-Visual Objects – Part 2: Visual, 2004.

[6] T. Wiegand and G. Sullivan, Draft ITU-T Recommendation and Final Draft International Standard of Joint Video Specification, (ITU-T rec. H.264/ISO/IEC 14496-10 AVC, presented at Joint Video Team (JVC) of ISO/IEC MPEG and ITU-T VCEG), 2003.

[7] Iain E. G. Richardson, H.264 and MPEG-4 Video Compression—Video Coding for Next-generation Multimedia, John Wiley & Sons, 111 River Street, Hoboken NJ07030-5774, New Jersey, United States, 2003.

[8] W. Gao, C. Reader, F. Wu, Y. He, L. Yu, H. Lu, S. Yang, T. Huang, and X. Pan, AVS—The Chinese Next-Generation Video Coding Standard, National Association of Broadcasters (NAB) Conference, 2004.

[9] L. Yu, S. Chen, and J. Wang, Overview of AVS video coding standards, Signal Processing: Image Communication, vol. 24, issue 4, pp. 247–262, April 2009.

[10] SMPTE, Standard for Television: VC-1 Compressed Video Bitstream Format and Decoding Process, SMPTE 421M-2006.

[11] J. Bankoski, P. Wilkins, and Y. Xu, Technical overview of VP8, an open source video codec for the web, IEEE International Conference on Multimedia and Expo (ICME), pp. 1–6, July 11–15, 2011.

[12] M. T. Pourazad, C. Doutre, M. Azimi, and P. Nasiopoulos, HEVC: the new gold standard for video compression: How does HEVC compare with H.264/AVC ?, IEEE Consumer Electronics Magazine, vol. 1, pp. 36–46, July 2012.

[13] H. S. Malvar, A. Hallapuro, M. Karczewicz, and L. Kerofsky, Low-complexity transform and quantization in H.264/AVC, IEEE Transactions on Circuits and Systems for Video Technology, vol. 13, no. 7, pp. 598–603, July 2003.

[14] S. Gordon, D. Marple, and T. Wiegand, Simplified use of 8x8 transforms—updated proposal and results, JVT-K028, 11th Meeting, Munich, Germany, March 2004.

[15] S. Srinivasan, P. Hsu, T. Holcomb, K. Mukerjee, S. L. Regunathan, B. Lin, J. Liang, M. C. Lee, and J. Ribas-Corbera, Windows media video 9: overview and applications, Signal Processing: Image Communication, vol. 19, issue 9, pp. 851–875, October 2004.

[16] S. Srinivasan and S. L. Regunathan, An overview of VC-1, Proceedings of the SPIE, Visual Communications and Image Processing (VCIP), Beijing, China, vol. 5960, pp. 720–728, July 2005.

[17] T. C. Wang, Y. W. Huang, H. C. Fang, and L. G. Chen, Parallel 4x4 2D transform and inverse transform architecture for MPEG-4 AVC/H.264, IEEE International Symposium on Circuits and Systems, vol. 2, pp. 800–803, 2003.

[18] Z. Y. Cheng, C. H. Chen, B. D. Liu, and J. F. Yang, High throughput 2-D transform architectures for H.264 advanced video coders, IEEE Asia-Pacific Conference on Circuits and Systems, pp. 1141–1144, December 2004.

[19] K. H. Chen, J. I. Guo, and J. S. Wang, A high-performance direct 2-D transform coding IP design for MPEG-4 AVC/H.264, IEEE Transactions on Circuits and Systems for Video Technology, vol. 16, no. 4, pp. 472–483, April 2006.

http://dx.doi.org/10.5772/64985

[20] G. A. Su and C. P. Fan, Cost effective hardware sharing architecture for fast 1-D 8x8 forward and inverse integer transforms of H.264/AVC high profile, IEEE Asia Pacific Conference on Circuits and Systems, pp. 1332–1335, November 2008.

[21] T. T. T. Do and T. M. Le, High throughput area-efficient SoC-based forward/inverse integer transform for H.264/AVC, IEEE International Symposium on Circuits and Systems, pp. 4113–4116, May 2010.

[22] W. Hwangbo and C. M. Kyung, A multi-transform architecture for H.264/AVC high-profile coders, IEEE Transactions on Multimedia, vol. 12, no. 3, pp. 157–167, April 2010.

[23] M. L. Hsia and Oscal T. C. Chen, Low-complexity inverse integer transform in H.264/AVC, IEEE International Conference on Multimedia & Expo, pp. 826–830, July 2010.

[24] M. Nadeem, S. Wong, and G. Kuzmanov, Inverse integer transform in H.264/AVC intra-frame encoder, Sixth IEEE International Symposium on Electronic Design, Test and Application, pp. 228–233, 2011.

[25] R. Jeske, J. C. de Souza, G. Wrege, R. Conceicao, M. Grellert, J. Mattos, and L. Agostini, Low cost and high throughput multiplierless design of a 16 point 1-D DCT of the new HEVC video coding standard, Conference on Programmable Logic (SPL), pp. 1–6, March 2012

[26] S. Shen, W. Shen, Y. Fan, and Xiaoyang Zeng, A unified 4/8/16/32-point integer IDCT architecture for multiple video coding standards, IEEE International Conference on Multimedia and Expo (ICME), pp. 788–793, July 2012.

[27] W. Zhao, T. Onoye, and T. Song, High-performance multiplierless transform architecture for HEVC, IEEE International Symposium on Circuits and Systems (ISCAS), pp. 1668–1671, 2013.

[28] M. Martuza, K. A. Wahid, Implementation of a cost shared transform architecture for multiple video codecs, Journal of Real-Time Image Processing, vol. 10, no. 1, pp. 151–162, March 2015.

[29] A. Ahmed, M. U. Shahid, and A. Rehman, N point DCT VLSI architecture for emerging HEVC standard, VLSI Design, volume 2012, Article ID 752024, pp. 1–13, 2012.

[30] Joint Collaborative Team—Video Coding, CE10: Core transform design for HEVC, JCTVC-G495, Geneva, Switzerland, 21–30, November 2011.

[31] M. N. Haggag, M. El-Sharkawy, and G. Fahmy, Efficient fast multiplication-free integer transformation for the 2-D DCT H.265 standard, IEEE International Conference on Image Processing, pp. 3769–3772, September 2010.

[32] C. W. Chang, H. F. Hsu, C. P. Fan, C. B. Wu, and Robert C. H. Chang, A fast algorithm-based cost-effective and hardware-efficient unified architecture design of 4×4, 8×8, 16×16, and 32×32 inverse core transforms for HEVC, Journal of Signal Processing Systems, vol. 82, no. 1, pp. 69–89, 2016.

[33] S. Lee and K. Cho, Architecture of transform circuit for video decoder supporting multiple standards, Electronics Letters, vol. 44, no. 4, pp. 274–275, February 2008.

[34] C. P. Fan and G. A. Su, Efficient low cost sharing design of fast 1-D inverse integer transform algorithms for H.264/AVC and VC-1, IEEE Signal Processing Letters, vol. 15, pp. 926–929, December 2008.

[35] G. A. Su and C. P. Fan, Low-cost hardware sharing architecture of fast 1-D inverse transforms for H.264/AVC and AVS applications, IEEE Transactions on Circuits and Systems, Part II, vol. 55, no. 12, pp. 1249–1253, December 2008.

[36] H. Qi, Q. Huang, and W. Gao, A low-cost very large scale integration architecture for multistandard inverse transform, IEEE Transactions on Circuits and Systems, Part II, vol. 57, no. 7, pp. 551–555, July 2010.

[37] Y. K. Lai and Y. F. Lai, A Reconfigurable IDCT architecture for universal video decoders, IEEE Transactions on Consumer Electronics, vol. 56, no. 3, pp. 1872–1879, August 2010.

[38] K. Wang, J. Chen, W. Cao, Y. Wang, L. Wang, and J. Tong, A reconfigurable multi-transform VLSI architecture supporting video codec design, IEEE Transactions on Circuits and Systems II: Express Briefs, vol. 58, no. 7, pp. 432–436, July 2011.

[39] K. Wahid, M. Martuza, M. Das, and C. McCrosky, Resource shared architecture of multiple transforms for multiple video codecs, 24th Canadian Conference on Electrical and Computer Engineering (CCECE), pp. 000947–000950, 2011.

[40] C. P. Fan, C. W. Chang, and S. J. Hsu, Cost effective hardware sharing design of fast algorithm based multiple forward and inverse transforms for H.264/AVC, MPEG-1/2/4, AVS, and VC-1 video encoding and decoding applications, IEEE Transactions on Circuits and Systems for Video Technology, vol. 24, no. 4, pp. 714–720, April 2014.

[41] C. W. Chang, H. F. Hsu, and C. P. Fan, High-efficiency multiple 4x4 and 8x8 inverse transform design with a cost-effective unified architecture for multistandard video decoders, 2014 IEEE Asia Pacific Conference on Circuits & Systems, Okinawa, Japan, pp. 507–510, November 2014.

[42] C. W. Chang, Fast algorithm based cost-effective and hardware-sharing architecture designs of multiple-mode discrete integer transforms for multi-standard video Codecs, Ph.D. dissertation, National Chung Hsing University, Taiwan, 2015.

[43] http://en.wikipedia.org/wiki/Kronecker_product

Chapter 9

Implementation of Video Compression Standards in Digital Television

Branimir S. Jaksic and Mile B. Petrovic

Additional information is available at the end of the chapter

http://dx.doi.org/10.5772/64833

Abstract

In this paper, a video compression standard used in digital television systems is discussed. Basic concepts of video compression and principles of lossy and lossless compression are given. Techniques of video compression (intraframe and interframe compression), the type of frames and principles of the bit rate compression are discussed. Characteristics of standard-definition television (SDTV), high-definition television (HDTV) and ultra-high-definition television (UHDTV) are given. The principles of the MPEG-2, MPEG-4 and High Efficiency Video Coding (HEVC) compression standards are analyzed. Overview of basic standards of video compression and the impact of compression on the quality of TV images and the number of TV channels in the multiplexes of terrestrial and satellite digital TV transmission are shown. This work is divided into six sections.

Keywords: MPEG-2, MPEG-4, HEVC, SDTV, HDTV, UHDTV

1. Introduction

Video compression technology is technology which allows you to record video in such a way that they take up less memory space and allows for the video to be a little different from the original, when playing. Reducing data (data compression) is possible because the image contains redundant (same) information [1]. Compression is the process of reducing the number of bits that are used to encode individual picture elements.

In digital television, parameters for digital video signal with compression and without compression are given by recommendation ITU-R BT.601 [2]. In broadcasting, transmission with lower speed requires less bandwidth and transmitter with lower power. Recording signals, using compression, reduces the required capacity of storage media, and it is directly proportional to the size of compression. For archival purposes that significantly reduces the required space and cost of the archive.

Techniques for accomplishing a reduction in the video size are mostly confined to compress individual frames of content and techniques of writing changes and differences between frames. Videos are usually composed of three types of frames: I-frames (*intra-frames*), P-frames (*predicted-frames*) and B-frames (*bidirectional-frames*). The difference between different types of frames is only in the write mode and read mode (the interpretation). During the playing (displaying), each frame is shown as a normal image regardless of recording technique of the video format. Intraframe or spatial compression is technique in the video compression for reducing the size of individual frames. Interframe or temporal compression is a video compression technique that achieves a reduction in size of similar series of frames [3].

The development of digital telecommunications allows the use of high-definition television (HDTV) besides standard-definition television (SDTV). HDTV is a technology that offers significantly higher quality of picture and sound than the traditional display technology did (analog PAL, NTSC, SECAM, SDTV and digital). Since the resolution is higher, the image is sharper, less blurry and the content is closer to reality. HDTV offers smoother movement, detailed and more vibrant colors, and there is a very high-quality multichannel sound that makes viewing experience even better. **Table 1** shows the basic characteristics of the primary digital TV standards.

DTV	Resolution	Aspect ratio	Number of frames per second
HDTV	1920 × 1080	16:9	25p, 30p, 50i
	1280 × 720	16:9	25p, 30p, 50i
SDTV	720 × 576	16:9	25p, 30p, 50i
	720 × 576	4:3	25p, 30p, 50i

Table 1. Primary DTV standards.

HDTV offers two quality signals: 720 and 1080 are the basic tags, which can be added to either the letter "i" or the letter "p", which means the ways of drawing the image (i = *interlaced*—draws every other line; p = *progressive*—draws the line-by-line). The "heights" of image are 720 and 1080, and the width is 1280 or 1920 pixels. The number of images per second is specified next to the tag, for example. 720p50 indicates a resolution of 1280 × 720, progressively rendering images and 50 frames per second [4].

Without compression, digital video signal would contain an enormous amount of data. For example, the standard digital video signal according to CCIR standards has 25 frames per second, resolution of 720 × 576 pixels, and each pixel is represented by 24 bits (3 bits for each color component). Transmission of uncompressed video signals requires channel capacity of 216 Mb/s. Video-definition HDTV signal requires six times bigger channel capacity of about 1.5 Gb/s. In multimedia systems, problems occur during the storage of digital video signal.

http://dx.doi.org/10.5772/64833

That is why different algorithms are used to compress video signals. Compression ratio depending on the algorithm used for compression (MPEG-2, MPEG-4, etc.) can be different. The required bit rate for MPEG-2 standard used to transfer HD signal is about 20 Mb/s, and for SDTV, resolution 720 × 576, line is about 4 Mb/s. If we are using the MPEG-4 standard then for the same quality, twice lower is required signal strength. European broadcasters mainly use MPEG-2 standard, although lately MPEG-4 standard is increasingly used [5, 6].

Table 2 shows the flows of compressed television signals that are used in practice in a broadcast, obtained from the MPEG-2 and MPEG-4 standards.

Standards for video compression	TV video resolution	Bit rates compressed video signals (Mb/s)
MPEG-2	SDTV	2–4
	HDTV	15–20
MPEG-4	SDTV	1.5–2
	HDTV	6–8

Table 2. The flows of compressed video/audio signals for certain standards.

Ultra-high-definition television (UHDTV) includes 4K UHDTV (2160p) and 8K UHDTV (4320p), which represents the two digital video formats proposed by NHK Science & Technology Research Laboratories and approved by the International Telecommunications Union (ITU). Minimum resolution of this format is 3840 × 2160 pixels [7]. Digital TV program consists of three components: video, audio and service data as shown in **Figure 1**.

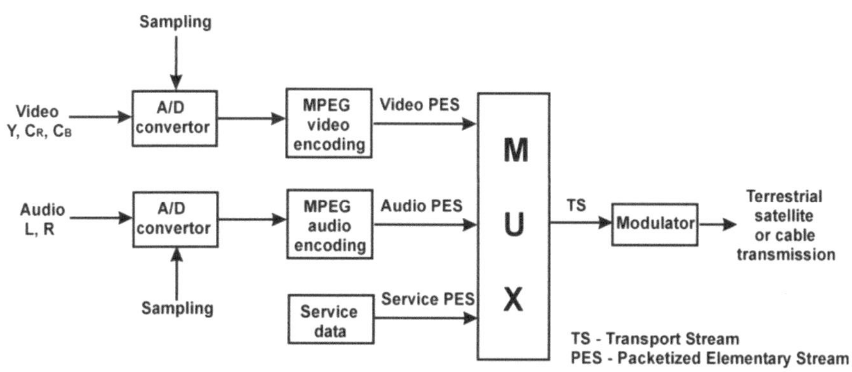

Figure 1. Components of digital television.

Service information, which contains additional information such as teletext and specific information of network, including an electronic program guide (EPG), is generated in digital form and does not require coding. Encoders compress the data by removing irrelevant or redundant parts of the image and sound signals and perform a reduction operation to produce separate video and audio packets of elementary streams.

In 1990, due to the need for storage and playback of moving images and sound in digital format for multimedia applications on various platforms, ISO has formed an expert group called Motion Picture Experts Group (MPEG).

In order to enable the interconnection of equipment from different manufacturers, standards for compression and transmission of video signals are defined. Among them, the best known are H.261, H.263 and H.264 for videoconferencing transmission, videophone and distribution of digital material via the web, as well as the MPEG standards (MPEG-1, MPEG-2, MPEG-4, MPEG-7, MPEG-21), which are intended for standardization of multimedia systems and digital television.

2. MPEG-2 standard

2.1. The principles of the MPEG-2 standard

Other standard developed by the MPEG group is ISO/IEC IS 13818: Generic Coding of Moving Pictures and Associated Audio, so-called MPEG-2 standard. It is aimed to professional digital television [8, 9], adopted in 1999, produced on the disadvantages of the standard MPEG-1. It is compatible with MPEG-1 standard, using the same tools and adding some new.

Basic innovations with the MPEG-2 standard are as follows: an increased bit rate, picture formats with and without thinning, scalability of quality and time, improved methods of quantization and coding, etc. Since it is primarily designed for TV signal compression, MPEG-2 standard allows the use of both types of image scanning: progressive scanning and scan by line spacing. In the compression process, all three types of pictures can be coded as *I*, *P* and *B* pictures. Standard encoder structure comprises a mixture of *I*, *P* and *B* frames in a way that *I* frame appears after every 10–15 frames, and two *B* frames between two adjacent *I* frame. Usually, a group of pictures (GOP) has one *I* frame or more *P* and *B* frames.

2.2. Profiles and levels MPEG-2 standard

Since the complete syntax of the MPEG-2 standard is complex and difficult for practical implementation on a single silicon chip, the MPEG-2 standard defines five subsets of the full syntax, called profiles, which are designed for a variety of applications. These are simple (simple) profile, main (main) profile, signal-to-noise ratio (SNR) scalable profile, spatial scalability (spatial scalable) and high profile (high) profile. Later, another is created, 4:2:2 profile, and definition of another (multiview) profile is in progress.

The profile is defined by four levels, which regulate the choice of available parameters during the hardware implementation. The levels determine the maximum bit rate, and according to the bit rate the speed of transmission of TV programs and resolutions of the system are chosen, and they are, on the other hand, determined by the number of samples per line, number of lines per image and the number of frames per second. There are four levels: high level (HL) H14L (H 1440 level), main level (ML) and low level (LL) [2]. Parameter limitations by levels are shown in **Table 3** [3].

http://dx.doi.org/10.5772/64833

Level	Maximum pixel number	Maximum line number	Maximum frames/s
Low level	352	288	30
Main level	720	576	30
H 1440 level	1440	1152	60
H 1920 level	1920	1080	60

Table 3. Limits of parameters in the levels of MPEG-2 standard.

Simple profile is designed to simplify the transmitter encoder and receiver decoder, with reductions in binary rate (transfer speed), and the inability bidirectional prediction (*B* pictures do not exist) supports only *I* and *P* prediction. As such it is suitable only for low-resolution terrestrial television. The maximum bit rate is 15 Mb/s.

The main profile is the optimal compromise between compression ratio and price. It supports all three types of prediction *I, P, B,* which automatically leads to the complexity of the encoder and decoder. Main profile supports all four levels, with a maximum bit rates of 4, 15, 60 and 80 Mb/s, for low, main, high-1440 and 1920 high level, respectively. The majority of broadcast applications are scheduled for operation in the main profile. Terrestrial digital TV uses the *main profile and main level* (MP and ML). SNR scalable supports profile only for low and main levels with a maximum bit rate of 4 and 15 Mb/s, respectively.

Spatially scalable profile supports only high-1440 level with a maximum flow rate of 60 Mb/s, of which 15 Mb/s is part of the base layer. It allows the transfer of basic image quality depending on the spatial resolution (spatial) or quantization accuracy, with addition of supporting information (enhanced layer). This allows simultaneous broadcasting of a program in elementary and higher resolution, so that in case of difficult reception conditions the signal of lower quality can be received (lower resolution) instead of higher. They are intended for extended-definition TV (EDTV).

High profile (also known as professional) is designed for later use with hierarchical coding for applications with extremely high definition (HDTV—high-definition TV) in format sampling 4:2:2 or 4:2:0. High profile supports the main, high-1440 and 1920 high level, with a maximum flow rates of 20, 80 and 100 Mb/s, respectively. The flow of the base layer is 4, 20 and 25 Mb/s, respectively.

4:2:2 profile has been introduced to allow working with color images in 4:2:2 format, which is necessary for studio equipment. Although, during the development of MPEG-2 standard, studio uses have not been taken into account, it showed that the MPEG-2 standard is suitable for this purpose. 4:2:2 profile has allowed the use of existing tools for coding and in studio applications, which requires a higher bit rate.

Multiview profile (MVP) is introduced in order to enable efficient coding of two video sequences derived from two cameras which are recording the same scene, and which are set at a slight angle (stereovision). This profile also uses existing tools for encoding, but with a new purpose. There is also reverse compatible decoder which means a higher level still can play lower level profile, while compatibility in the opposite direction is not possible. Present stage of development uses a combination profile and level of main profile at main level. Maximum number of pixels that can theoretically be transmitted by MPEG-2 encoder is 16,383 × 16,383 = 22,657,689.

2.3. MPEG-2 transport stream

Video and audio encoders transmit signal in the main stream. Raw uncompressed audio and video parts of the signal, known as presentation units, are located in the encoder for receiving video and audio access units. Video access unit can be I, P and B coded picture. Audio access units are containing encoded information for a few milliseconds of sound window: 24 ms (layer II), and 24 or 8 ms in the case of the layer III. The video and audio access units form the elementary streams in a respective manner. Each *elementary stream* (ES) is then divided into packets to form a video or audio *packetized elementary stream* (PES). Service and other data are similarly grouped into their PES. PES packets are then divided into smaller 188-bit transport packages [2, 10].

To gain access to the transfer of MPEG-2 signal, data streams must be multiplexed. With multiplexing, the following is obtained:

- portable data stream (TS = *transport stream*)—designed to transmit signals to terrestrial, cable and satellite connections,
- programming data stream (PS = *program stream*)—designed for storing digital data on DVD or other storage space.

Multiplexing of audio and video signals is necessary in order to enable their joint transmission, and properly decode and display. The multiplexing hierarchy determined by MPEG-2 standard can be divided into:

- basic data stream (ES = *elementary stream*),
- packetized basic data stream (PES = *packetized elementary stream*),
- portable (TS) or program data stream—PS (**Figure 2**).

Programming flow obtained by multiplexing includes packages resulting from one or more elementary streams belonging to one program. It can contain one stream of the video signal, and more data streams of an audio signal.

All packages have certain common components that are grouped into three parts: header, data and control data [10, 11].

Packets of the program stream have a variable length, which causes difficulties when the decoder needs to recognize the exact beginning and the end of the package. To make this possible, the packet header contains information of the length of the package. PES packet can vary in length up to a maximum of 64 KB, while the typical length is about 2 KB. The part that follows the header contains the access unit as parts of the original elementary stream. At the same time, there is no obligation to equalize the start of access units with a start of information part (payload). According to that a new access unit can start at any point in the information part of PES packets, there is also the possibility that a few small access units can be contained in one PES packet.

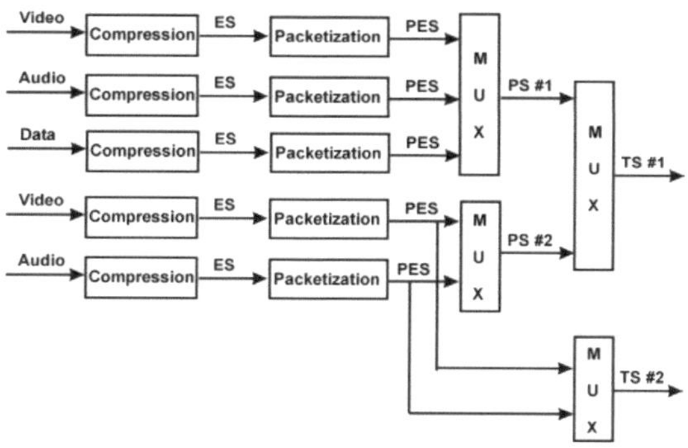

Figure 2. Obtaining transmission and programming data flow.

The most important components of the header are as follows:

- starting prefix code (3 bits),
- starting code of a flow (1 bit),
- start time stamp,
- PTS (33 bits),
- decoding time stamp (DTS; 33 bit).

PTS and DTS cannot be included in each PES packet, as long as they are being involved in at least 100 ms in the transport data stream (DTV), or every 700 ms in the programming data stream (DVD). DTS indicates the time required for deleting or decoding access unit. Within the headers, some other fields that contain important parameters are included, such as the length of the PES packet, the length of the header and whether the PTS and DTS fields are present in the package. Among this, there are several other optional fields, a total of 25, which can be used to transfer additional information about packetized elementary stream, such as the relative priority and copyright information.

3. MPEG-4 standard

3.1. General characteristics of the MPEG-4 standard

MPEG-4 is a generic standard for coding audiovisual information, and it was presented in 1998 under the label ISO/IEC 14496 [12]. In this standard, video and audio signals are characterized by interactivity, high degree of compression, and universal access, and this standard has a high level of flexibility and expandability.

The algorithms that are implemented in MPEG-4 standard represent scene as a set of audio-visual objects, among which there are some hierarchical relations in space and time. In all previous standards for compression of video, image has been seen as a unified whole. In this standard, we are meeting with the concept of video object, thereby to distinguish two types of visual objects—natural and synthetic visual objects.

At the lowest hierarchical level are primitive media objects, such as, for example, static images (fixed background scenes), visual objects (a person who speaks no background), and audio facilities (voice of the speaker). This approach brings an increase in compression ratio, increased interactivity and enables the integration of objects' different nature such as natural image or video, graphics, text and sound.

MPEG-4 standard has inherited the MPEG-2 standard. Each MPEG standard consists of several parts (Parts). Each part covers a certain aspect and area of use. Thus, for example, MPEG-4 Part 2 is used for video coding (such as DivX and Quicktime 6), MPEG-4 Part 10/H.264 represents an Advanced Video Coding (AVC), and it is used in areas with high-definition content such as HD broadcasting and storage, HD formats such as HD-DVD and Blue-ray discs [13]. MPEG-4 Part 3 Advanced Audio Coding (AAC) is a part for high-quality audio coding.

The first inheritor to MPEG-2 format was MPEG-4 Part 2, which is published by ISO in 1999. As in the case of the MPEG-2, coding efficiency is strictly related to the complexity of the source material and the encoder implementation. MPEG-4 Part 2 is defined for applications in the field of multimedia in small bit rates, but it is in further expanded for applications in the field of broadcasting. Formal subjective evaluation has shown that the gain of the efficient coding with MPEG-4 Part 2, compared to the MPEG-2, is between 15 and 20%. For Digital Video Broadcasting (DVB) applications, this gain is not enough to justify the destabilization and destruction of MPEG-2 codec (which are used by DVB systems)—considering that the MPEG-4 Part 2 is not compatible with MPEG-2.

3.2. Image formats in MPEG-4 standard

Following the example of MPEG-2 standard, MPEG-4 standard supports both ways scanning images, progressive and interlaced scanning. Spatial resolution of luminance component can be expressed in blocks ranging from 8 × 8 pixels, up to 2048 × 2048 pixels. For presentation of video signal in color, this standard is using a conventional Y Cb Cr color coordinate system with weighing 4:4:4, 4:2:2, 4:1:1 and 4:2:0. Each component is represented with 4–12 bits per image pixel. Different temporal resolution is supported, as well as an infinitely variable number of frames per second [2].

As it was the case in the previous MPEG standards, the macroblock presents basic unit in which data of video signal are transmitted. Macroblock contains coded information about the shape, motion and texture (color) of the pixels. There is a wide range of bit rate from 5 Kb/s to 38.4 Mb/s, but it is optimized for use in three ranges of bit rate: <64 Kb/s, 64 Kb/s to 384 Mb/s and 384 Kb/s to 4 Mb/s. Also are supported constant bit rate and variable bit rate.

Each video object can be coded in one or more layers, which allows it variable resolution (scalability) encoding. Also, each video object is discretized in time so that each time samples

http://dx.doi.org/10.5772/64833

representing a video object plane (VOP) [2, 13, 14]. Time samples of video object are grouped into group of video object planes (GOV).

3.3. MPEG-4.10 (H.264/AVC) standard

Previous video coding standards such as MPEG-2 and MPEG-4 Part 2 have been established and are used in the areas of videoconferencing over mobile TV and broadcasting TV content in standard/high definition, up to the application of very high quality, such as applications for professional digital video recorders and digital cinema—digital images on the big screen. But with the spread of digital video applications and its use in new applications such as advanced mobile TV or broadcast HDTV signal, requirements for effective representation of the video image are increased to the point where the previous standards for video coding cannot keep pace.

The new MPEG-4 Part 10 (MPEG-4.10) standard of video compression is the result of efforts of the Joint Video Team (JVT), which includes members of the Video Coding Expert Group (VCEG) and the Motion Picture Experts Group (MPEG), which is the reason for naming it twice (H.264 and MPEG-4.10). Standard is also commonly referred to as H.264/Advanced Video Coding (AVC).

This standard, registered under the number ISO-IEC14496-10, provides a significant increase in compression efficiency in regard to MPEG-2 (gain of at least 50%) [12]. This efficiency is of particular importance for high-definition television (HDTV), which in the MPEG-2 requires a bit rate of at least 15–18 Mb/s.

H.264 showed significant improvement in coding efficiency, a significant improvement when it comes to resistance to errors, as well as increased flexibility and area of use compared to their predecessors. A change was added in the MPEG-4.10 (H.264/AVC), the so-called FRExt (FREkt) amendment, which further extended the area of use to areas such as mobile TV, internet broadcasting, distribution and professional studio and postproduction [15]. **Table 4** [16] shows the usage scenarios and compression in bits supplied with the H.264 codec, and **Table 5** [16] shows the characteristics of the H.264 standard level.

Using	Resolution and frame rates	Bit rate
Mobile content (3G)	176 × 144, 10–24 fps	70–180 Kb/s
Internet/standard definition	640 × 480, 24 fps	2–3 Mb/s
High definition (HDTV)	1280 × 720, 25p, 30p	7–8 Mb/s
Full high definition (full HDTV)	1920 × 1080, 25p, 30p	10–12 Mb/s

Table 4. Different scenarios of use H.264 standard.

H.264 consists of two layers: layer for video encoding, designed for effective representation of video coding layer (VCL) and network-flexible layer network abstraction layer (NAL), which converts VCL video content in formats suitable for transmission over a variety of transport layers or storage media.

H.264 level	Resolution	Frame rate	Max. compressed bit rate (non-FRExt profile) maximum	Maximum number of reference frames
1	QCIF	15	64 Kb/s	4
1b	QCIF	15	128 Kb/s	4
1.1	CIF or QCIF	7.5 (CIF)/30 (QCIF)	192 Kb/s	2 (CIF)/9 (QCIF)
1.2	CIF	15	384 Kb/s	6
1.3	CIF	30	768 Kb/s	6
2	CIF	30	2 Mb/s	6
2.1	HHR (480i or 576i)	30/25	4 Mb/s	6
2.2	SD	15	4 Mb/s	5
3	SD	30/25	10 Mb/s	5
3.1	1280 × 720p	30	14 Mb/s	5
3.2	1280 × 720p	60	20 Mb/s	4
4	HD formats (720p or 1080i)	60p/30i	20 Mb/s	4
4.1	HD formats (720p or 1080i)	60p/30i	50 Mb/s	4
4.2	1920 × 1080p	60p	50 Mb/s	4
5	2k × 1k	72	135 Mb/s	5
5.1	2k × 1k or 4k × 2k	120/30	240 Mb/s	5

Table 5. Levels of H.264 standard.

3.4. The concept of video coding layer (VCL)

Video coding layer (VCL) for MPEG-4.10 (H.264/AVC) codec is in a some way similar to the previous video codecs such as MPEG-2 [15]. **Figure 3** shows a block diagram of coder.

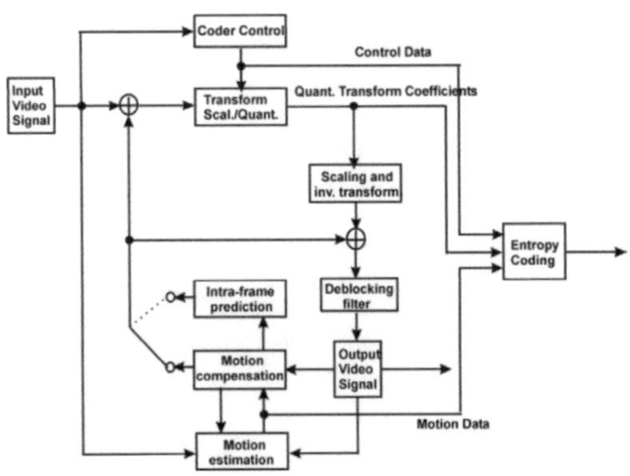

Figure 3. Structure of H.264 video coder.

The coded video sequence in the H.264 consists of a series of encoded pictures. The coded image may represent either the entire frame or one field, as was the case with the MPEG-2

http://dx.doi.org/10.5772/64833

codec. Overall, it can be considered that the video frame comprises two fields: the field at the top and the field at the bottom. If the both fields of a given frame were taken at various time points, the frame is called interlaced scan frame; otherwise, it is called a progressive scan frame.

4. H.265/HEVC standard

4.1. General principles of HEVC standard

Thanks to the evolution of technology, which has enabled us to have a resolution of video material from 4K and higher reality, the evolution of video coding is inevitable, so it can keep up the step. HEVC/H.265 video coding (*High Efficiency Video Coding*) [17], is the fruit of cooperation between ISO/IEC Moving Picture Experts Group (MPEG) and ITU-T Video Coding Experts Group (VCEG) standardization organization, which brings better performance than the previous coding standards, as well as H.264/AVC, and the biggest advantage of the new standard is up to 50% more efficient compression compared to H.264 and support for 8K UHD resolution. This means that the video material of the same quality will occupy at half encoding less space with HEVC than the H.264/AVC coding, thanks to better algorithms and analysis of the video material which eventually brings better coding efficiency.

Direct predecessor of this standard is H.264/MPEG-4 Advanced Video Coding (AVC). HEVC seeks to replace its predecessor by using a generic syntax that could be customized to newer emerging applications. He wants to achieve several goals, such as code efficiency, adaptability to different systems of transport, resilience on errors and implementation with parallel processing in a multiprocessor's architecture.

4.2. The data structure in H.265/HEVC standard

H.265/HEVC is a hybrid video coding algorithm based on blocks. The basic coding algorithm is a hybrid of intraprediction, interprediction and transformational coding. For representation of a color video signal, H.265/HEVC standard uses YCbCr color space in format 4:2:0. Each sample of the individual components of the color space is represented with a resolution of 8–10 bits per sample, in coding and decoding. Video image is progressively scanned in a rectangular format dimensions W × H, where W represents a width, H height of the image for the luma component. Chrominance components for color format 4:2:0 are scanned in a rectangular format dimensions W/2 × H/2 [17, 18].

H.265/HEVC standard has kept hybrid architecture of previous coding MPEG standard for video encoding. A significant difference in approach lies in the fact that the previous H standards—video coding are based on macroblocks, H.265/HEVC standard for encoding uses the adaptive quadtree structure based on Coding Tree Unit (CTU). Basically, the quadtree structure is composed of various blocks and units.

A block is defined as a matrix of samples of different sizes, while the unit includes a luma block and corresponding chrominance blocks together with the syntax necessary for their coding. With the further division of structure coding units are obtained and also the coding blocks.

Decoding of quadtree structure does not represent a significant additional burden because it can easily be switch into a hierarchical structure by using z-scan. Predictable modes for interframe encoded CU are using non-square PU, which requires the necessary support for decoding in the form of additional logic in the decoder which performs multiple conversions between the raster scan, and the scan-scan. In terms of preserving the speed of bit rates, with the encoder side, there is a simple algorithm to analyze the structure of the tree to determine the optimal share of the blocks [7]. CTU sizes are 16 × 16, 32 × 32 and 64 × 64 pixels.

4.3. Profiles, levels and layers

Profile is defined by a set of coding tools or algorithms which, if used, ensure compatibility of the output coded bit stream with standard applications that belong to this profile, or have similar functional requirements. Level refers to the limitations of the current stream bits that define memory and resource requirements of the decoder. These restrictions are maximum number of samples and the maximum number of samples per second that can be decoded (sample rate), the maximum image size, maximum bit rate (how many bits can decoder spend per second of video record), minimum compression ratio, size of the buffer memory and so on. In HEVC standard, only for the purposes of diversity from some applications, in bit rate and buffer memory, which are used to store the encoded image (control flow information), were defined two layers: a basic "Main" and demanding "High". Currently, the draft of HEVC has defined a single profile "Main" and expectation is more defined profiles. Goal is to reduce the number of profiles, so that there will be maximum compatibility between devices, and also, due to the fact that sometimes services are separated, for example, for broadcasting TV signals, mobile services and video on demand, the goal is convergence to devices that will support all of them together.

4.4. UHDTV

Ultra-high-definition television (UHDTV or UHD) includes 4K UHDTV (2160p) and 8K UHDTV or Super Hi-Vision (4320p), which are two digital video formats proposed by NHK Science & Technology Research Laboratories and defined and approved by the International Telecommunication Union (ITU) [17].

Full high definition (FHD) indicates that the image with 1920 pixels set in the 1080 lines. UHD includes twice the number of pixels and lines in its basic version, which can be called a Quad Full HD because it has four times more pixels than Full HD. Basically, there are two UHD resolution, 3840 × 2160 and 7680 × 4320 for easier identification is often called the first UHD-1 (4K) and the other UHD-2 (8K).

Number of 3840 pixels in one row consist UHD 4K, while Full HD consist from 1920 lines. The point is that the nomenclature "No. K" it was taken from formats works with theatrical distribution; on the other side, UHD starts to use as commercial term. When you see a movie that has a 2K resolution film, it will be 2048 pixels' resolution in 1080 lines, and in the case of 4K projection, it will be a resolution of 4096 × 2160 pixels [19].

UHD brings many benefits, but also the kind of disadvantages like any new technology, especially in its beginning. The benefits of higher resolution logically have a greater amount of information on the screen and therefore a more realistic view, especially on the diagonals that are larger than 140 cm (55″) and where full HD resolution loses the impression of high sharpness. This is why manufacturers have presented the first UHDTVs in diagonals of 84″ (213 cm) that they would now be available in smaller dimensions—140 cm (55″) and 165 cm (65″). UHD on smaller diagonals does not have much sense because the density of information is too large and the average viewing distances further details cannot be seen in relation to the full HD content.

Many parameters have effect on the realism of images, and among them resolution is not most important element. Number of pixels has a smaller impact on how we experience the image of other parameters, such as increased dynamic range, the range and depth of color, as well as the number of frames per second. UHD used Rec. 2020 standard color range in contrast to the definition used by Rec. 709 standard. Rec. 2020 defines a bit depth of either 10 bits per sample or 12 bits per sample. Rec. 2020 specifies the following frame rates: 120p, 119.88p, 100p, 60p, 59.94p, 50p, 30p, 29.97p, 25p, 24p, 23.976p [18]. **Table 6** [18] provides an overview of the main characteristics of images in HDTV, 4K and 8K UHDTV.

	HDTV	4K UHDTV	8K UHDTV
Pixels × number of lines	1280 × 720 p 1440 × 1080 i 1920 × 1080 p(i)	3840 × 2160	7680 × 4320
Mpixels/frame	0.922 1.6 2.1	8.3 Progressive	33.2 Progressive
Aspect ratio	16:9	16:9	16:9
Frame rate	25, 50, ... fps 30 fps +24 fps	25, 50, ... fps 30, 60, 120 fps +24 fps	25, 50, ... fps 30, 60, 120 fps +24 fps
Bit depth	8 or 10 bits	10 or 12 bits	10 or 12 bits
Viewing distance	3 × H (30°)	1.5 × H (60°)	0.75 × H (100°)

Table 6. The characteristics of different digital TV formats.

5. Comparison of compression standards for terrestrial SDTV and HDTV transmission

In the period from May 15 to June 16, 2006, in Geneva, held a Regional Conference on Radio Communications (RRC-06), organized by the International Telecommunication Union (ITU), with the aim of establishing a new international agreement and the associated frequency plan for the digital broadcasting of radio and television programs. The conference RRC-06 Final Act were adopted (Final Acts) which contain a new agreement Geneva 2006 (GE06), which enables the introduction of complete digital terrestrial television broadcasting in the planning zone. All European countries have pledged that no later than June 17, 2015, the switch to digital broadcasting of radio and television signals, and perform analog switch off (ASO). In many countries, it is already implemented as ASO [20].

European countries have adopted the standard Digital Video Broadcasting-Terrestrial (DVB-T) and DVB-T2. The first concepts DVB-T were adopted in 1993, and the first final version in 1997. It involves the transmission of digitized audio and video content via terrestrial broadcasting technology in the VHF and UHF band using conventional system transmitter and corresponding receiver [21].

DVB-T2 is an enhanced version of the DVB standard for terrestrial broadcasting. Compared with DVB-T, DVB-T2 offers a significantly lower sensitivity to noise and interference and provides 30–50% greater flow of data which is particularly suitable for HDTV [22].

Video compression standards of DVB-T standards used in different countries are shown in **Table 7** [23]. The number of national multiplex (MUX) is given, local and regional non-represented. When digital terrestrial TV transmission started and year ASO was executed are presented. Data were collected from the official websites of national regulatory agencies and providers of digital terrestrial transmission.

Country	MUX	DVB standard		Start	ASO
		DVB-T	DVB-T2		
Andora	6	MPEG-2	–	2005	2007
Austria	6	MPEG-2	MPEG4 for pay TV and HD	2004	2010
Belgium	2	MPEG-2	–	2002	2011
Bulgaria	3	MPEG-4	–	2004	2013
Croatia	5	MPEG-2	MPEG-4 for pay TV	2002	2010
Cyprus	4	MPEG-4	–	2010	2011
Czech Republic	3	MPEG-2	MPEG-4 for experimental HD	2000	2012
Denmark	6	MPEG-4	MPEG-4 for pay TV	2003	2009
Estonia	4	MPEG-4	MPEG-4 for HD	2004	2010
Finland	9	MPEG-2	MPEG-4	1999	2007
France	8	MPEG-2	MPEG-4 for pay TV and HD	2005	2011
Germany	5	MPEG-2	–	2002	2008
Hungary	3	MPEG-4	–	2004	2013
Ireland	2	MPEG-4	–	2006	2012
Italy	22	MPEG-2, MPEG-4	MPEG-4 tests	1998	2012
Latvia	7	MPEG-4	–	2002	2010
Lithuania	5	MPEG-4	–	2003	2012
Luxemburg	4	MPEG-2	–	2002	2010

Country	MUX	DVB standard		Start	ASO
		DVB-T	DVB-T2		
Macedonia	7	MPEG-4	–	2004	2013
Netherlands	5	MPEG-2	–	1998	2006
Norway	5	MPEG-4	–	1999	2009
Poland	3	MPEG-4	–	2001	2013
Portugal	1	MPEG-4	–	2009	2012
Slovakia	4	MPEG-2, MPEG-4	MPEG-4 tests	2009	2012
Slovenia	2	MPEG-4	–	2001	2010
Spain	8	MPEG-2, MPEG-4	–	1999	2010
Sweden	7	MPEG-2, MPEG-4	MPEG-4	1999	2007
Switzerland	4	MPEG-2	–	2000.	2008
United Kingdom	6	MPEG-2	MPEG-4 for HD	1998.	2012
Albania	10	MPEG-2, MPEG-4	MPEG-4 for HD	2004	–
Belarus	3	MPEG-4	MPEG-4 for pay TV	2004	–
Greece	8	MPEG-2, MPEG-4	–	2006	2015
Iceland	3	MPEG-2	MPEG-4	2005	2015
Moldova	2	MPEG-4	MPEG-4	2003	2015
Montenegro	1	MPEG-4	MPEG-4	2014	2015
Romania	3	MPEG-4	MPEG-4 adopted	2005	2015
Russia	2	–	MPEG-4	2005	–
Serbia	1	–	MPEG-4	2005	2015
Turkey	1	–	MPEG-4	2006	–
Ukraine	4	–	MPEG-4	2007	–

Table 7. Video compression standards of digital terrestrial TV transmission in Europe.

From **Table 2**, it can be seen that countries that have moved completely to digital broadcasting mainly used DVB-T standard, or used in parallel and DVB-T2, while countries that are transitioning to digital transmission opted for the DVB-T2 standard. A small number of countries using DVB-T standard include MPEG-2 compression, mainly for free-to-air (FTA). Compression standard MPEG-4, due to savings in capacity, mainly used for encrypted channels, i.e., pay TV and HDTV. An increasing number of countries that use the DVB-T standard are planning to in the near future switch to an enhanced DVB-T2 standard.

6. Application of compression standards for UHDTV

6.1. 4K UHDTV via satellite

Number of UHD content is not large, but their number is growing rapidly. Many cameras are now able to record materials and above 4K resolution, such as RED Epic camera which can record approximately 5K resolution or 5120 × 2700 pixels, as well as the Sony F65 8K camera recording at a resolution of 8192 × 4320 pixels. The first 4K UHD facilities were available over broadband services (Netflix and YouTube) to 2013 and in 2014 started the first experimental TV channels that broadcast 4K UHD controversial content. Sporting events in 2012, 2013 and 2014 were the first UHD content broadcast via satellite. Pioneers in the distribution of 4K UHDTV are the Japanese public broadcaster NHK and KBS Korean TV [24]. The leading satellite companies took part in the distribution of UHD Eutelsat, SES Astra, Measat, Eutelsat, and Hispasat. Although in tests carried out with video H.264/AVC, HEVC is mainly used today. **Table 8** [25] provides an overview of the number of SDTV, HDTV and 4K UHDTV that may be received from the satellite to the various transmission parameters.

Satellite transmission	Carrier data rate (Mbps)	Number of channels		
		SDTV (p25/p30)	HDTV (p25/p30)	4K UHDTV (p50/p60)
DVB-S, QPSK, FEC 3/4	38	4–5 in MPEG-2	4–5 in MPEG-4	–
DVB-S2, 8PSK, FEC 5/6	72	24 + in MPEG-4	7–9 in MPEG-4 14–18 in HEVC	2–5 in HEVC
DVB-S2, 16APSK, FEC 2/3	79	–	7–9 in MPEG-4 15–19 in HEVC	1 in MPEG-4 3–5 in HEVC
DVB-S2X, 16APSK, FEC 3/4	83	–	8–10 in MPEG-4 16–20 in HEVC	1 in MPEG-4 3–5 in HEVC
DVB-S2X, 16APSK, FEC 135/180	99	–	9–12 in MPEG-4 19–24 in HEVC	1 in MPEG-4 3–6 in HEVC

Table 8. Number of satellite SSTV, HDTV and 4K UHDTV channels for the various transmission parameters.

6.2. 4K UHDTV in digital terrestrial television (DTT)

Initial tests 4K UHDTV in digital terrestrial television systems were carried out in 2012 in Japan and South Korea by KBS and NHK still using unstandardized HEVC video compression. Later tests were done in other countries. **Table 9** [26] gives the basic test characteristics of 4K UHDTV in digital terrestrial television (DTT) networks in the world.

Technicolor has successfully conducted tests to broadcasting terrestrial 4K UHDTV content. Broadcasting used American ATSC 3.0 standard, trough Sinclair Broadcast transmitter [27]. Technically speaking, this is the world premiere of the use of scalable HEVC (SHVC) video coding, MPEG-H compression standards, as well as MMT MPEG A/V standards. The test was performed in the Sinclair Broadcast experimental facility. The new technology allows you to receive signals via conventional antenna, as well as through mobile and tablet devices.

Based on technological profiles and the typology of the various countries, the report predicts that the demand of end users and the transition to the new standards take between 3 and 12 years old. Markets that were among the first to adopt new technologies will likely take between three and six years to the current broadcasting possibilities of yarn on a combination of DVB-

http://dx.doi.org/10.5772/64833

T2 MPEG4/HEVC, SDTV/HDTV/UHDTV (4K). The third profile that refers to the HDTV/UHDTV (4K/8K) is supposed to happen between 2023 and 2030. The report says that the DTT platform is currently threatened due to scarcity of radio spectrum, as well as plans for the redistribution of 700 MHz range, which will reduce the available capacity by an average of 30%.

Country	Multiplex capacity (Mbit/s)	Signal bit rate (Mbit/s)	Video encoding standard	Picture standard
Republic of Korea	<35.0	25–34	HEVC Main 10	3840 × 2160p 60 frames/s 8 bits or 10 bits/pixel
France	40.2	22.5 17.5	HEVC	3840 × 2160p 50 frames/s 8 bits/pixel
Spain	36.72	35	HEVC	3840 × 2160p 50 frames/s 8 bits/pixel
Sweden	31.7	24	HEVC	3840 × 2160p 29.97 frames/s 8 bits/pixel
United Kingdom	40.2	Variable (35)	HEVC	Mixture of 3840 × 2160p 50 frames/s and 3840 × 2160p 59.94 frames/s 8 or 10 bits/pixel
Czech republic	–	–	HEVC	3840 × 2160p

Table 9. Overview of the characteristics 4K UHDTV tested in the DTT.

In addition to broadcast 4K UHDTV channels in satellite and terrestrial digital networks during 2015 in the world has launched several UHDTV services in Internet Protocol Television (IPTV) and Over-The-Top (OTT) systems.

6.3. 8K UHDTV

Besides the ultra HD format, there is also Super Hi-Vision 8K for whose development and promotion are in charge of the Japanese public broadcaster NHK. Super Hi-Vision format was able to show 120 frames per second and a resolution of 7680 × 4320 pixels which corresponds to the format of 32 megapixels. This format offers four times the resolution of 4K format and 16 times higher than HD. **Table 10** [26] gives the basic test characteristics of 8K UHDTV in DTT networks in the world.

Country	Multiplex capacity (Mbit/s)	Signal bit rate (Mbit/s)	Video encoding standard	Picture standard
Japan	91.8	91.0	MPEG-4 AVC/H.264	7680 × 4320p 59.94 frame/s 8 bits/pixel
Republic of Korea	50.47	50.0	HEVC	–

Table 10. Overview of the characteristics 8K UHDTV tested in the DTT.

Digital Video Broadcasting Consortium in July 2014 adopted the basic parameters UHDTV transmission, and defined development plan of distribution UHDTV in stages, as shown in **Table 11** [25].

	4K UHDTV—Phase 1	4K UHDTV—Phase 2	8K UHDTV
Deployment	2015	2018	2020
Resolution	3840 × 2160	3840 × 2160	7680 × 4320
Frame rate	p50/p60	p100/p120	p100/p120
Dynamic range	HDR preferred	HDR mandatory	HDR mandatory
Color space	Rec. 2020	Rec. 2020	Rec. 2020
Color sampling	4:2:0, 4:2:2	4:2:0, 4:2:2	4:2:0, 4:2:2, 4:4:4
Color bit depth	10 bits	10/12 bits	10/12 bits
Video encoding	HEVC Main 10	HEVC Main 10	HEVC Main 10
Audio format	5.1	Beyond 5.1	Object based
Audio codec	Open	TBD	Next-generation audio codec
Viewing angle	66°	66°	100°
Viewing distance	1.5 picture height	1.5 picture height	0.75 picture height

Table 11. Development plan of distribution UHDTV.

7. Conclusion

The advantages brought by compression of the TV signal are as follows: reducing the frequency range of telecommunication channel which transmits TV signal, reducing the memory capacity required for recording images (storing images), access to data is reduced because the faster skips over the material, provided a data transfer in real time, it reduces the needed RAM memory and hardware becomes less expensive and leads to the miniaturization of hardware in the television. By reducing the number of bits, less power is required to broadcast; for example, if the transmitter of the same power is broadcasting analog and digital signal, for digital reception antenna of smaller diameter is required.

To ensure reliable communication between users who use equipment and software from different manufacturers, standardization of methods of compression was carried out. So today, depending on the quality and use (television, multimedia services, videoconferencing, video telephony, etc.), there are several standards (JPEG, MPEG-1, MPEG-2, MPEG-4, H.261, H.263, H. 264, H.265, etc.).

Since it is a new technology that just catches the "momentum" toward global use, UHD is the future of television. Also, UHD offers the ultimate user experience and creates opportunities for the entire industry. 4K and 8K services will stimulate the growth of broadband, as well as the expansion of TV services in emerging markets. Consequently, the compression standard for TV in the near future will be HEVC/H.265.

Acknowledgements

This work was done within the Erasmus Plus Capacity-Building projects in the field of Higher Education: "Implementation of the Study Program—Digital Broadcasting and Broadband Technologies (Master Studies)", Project No. 561688-EPP-1-2015-1-XK-EPPKA2-CBHE-JP.

Author details

Branimir S. Jaksic* and Mile B. Petrovic

*Address all correspondence to: branimir.jaksic@pr.ac.rs

Faculty of Technical Sciences, University of Pristina, Kosovska Mitrovica, Serbia

References

[1] K. F. Ibrahim, Newnes Guide to Television and Video Technology, First edition, Elsevier, Linacre House, UK, 2007.

[2] ITU-R BT.601-7: Studio encoding parameters of digital television for standard 4:3 and wide-screen 16:9 aspect ratios, ITU – International Telecommunication Union, Geneva, Switzerland, 2011.

[3] M. Petrović, Televizija, Faculty of Technical Sciences, Kosovska Mitrovica, Serbia, 2007, ISBN 978-86-80893-16-7, COBISS. SR-ID 138726156.

[4] S. Pechard, M. Carnec, P. Le Callet, D. Barba, From SD to HD television: effects of H. 264 distortions versus display size on quality of experience, IEEE International Conference on Image Processing, Atlanta, USA, pp. 409–412, 2006.

[5] J. M. Fernandez, J. Capdevila, R. García, S. Cabanillas, S. Mata, A. Mansilla, Single frequency networks for digital video broadcasting, URL: http://h30357.www3.hp.com/whitepapers/retevisionsfn.pdf.

[6] M. Cominetti, A. Morello, M. Visintin, Digital multi–programme TV/HDTV by satellite, EBU Technical Review, 1993, URL: http://tech.ebu.ch/docs/techreview/trev_256cominetti.pdf.

[7] S. Marcotte, The Road to UHDTV, Miranda Technologies, Qubeck, Canada, 2012.

[8] ISO/IEC SC29/WG11, MPEG-2 System Group 13818–1, Information Technology – Generic Coding of Moving Pictures and Associated Audio: Part 1 Systems, International Organization for Standardization, Geneva, Switzerland, 1995.

[9] ISO/IEC SC29/WG11, MPEG-2 13818-2, Information Technology – Generic Coding of Moving Pictures and Associated Audio: Part 2 Video, International Organization for Standardization, Geneva, Switzerland, 1995.

[10] D. Hoffman, G. Fernando, V. Goyal, M. Civanlar, RTP Payload Format for MPEG1/MPEG2 Video, The Internet Engineering Task Force – IETF, Fremont, USA, 1998.

[11] H. Benoit, Digital Television – Satellite, Cable, Terrestrial, IPTV, Mobile TV in the DVB Framework, Third Edition, Elsevier, Burlington, MA, USA, 2008.

[12] ISO/IEC SC29/WG11, MPEG-4 System Group 14496-1 Doc. N2739, Part 1 Systems/PDAM1, March 1999.

[13] O. Auro, MPEG-4 systems: overview, Signal Processing: Image Communications, Vol. 15, pp. 281–298, 2000.

[14] Z. Bojkovic, D. Milovanovic, Audiovisual integration in multimedia communications based on MPEG-4 facial animation, Circuits, Systems and Signal Processing, Vol. 20, pp. 311–339, 2001.

[15] H. Kalva, Delivery MPEG-4 Based Audio-Visual Services, Kluwer, Boston, MA, 2001.

[16] K. R. Rao, D. N. Kim, J. J. Hwang, Video Coding Standards: AVS China, H.264//MPEG-4 PART 10, HEVC, VP6, DIRAC and VC-1, Springer, Dordrecht Heidelberg, London, UK, 2014.

[17] Recommendation ITU-R BT. 2020-1(06/2014): Parameter values for ultra-high-definition television systems for production and international programme exchange BT Series Broadcasting service (television), ITU – International Telecommunication Union, Geneva, Switzerland, 2014.

[18] G. Cox, An Introduction to Ultra HDTV and HEVC, ATEME, Paris, France, July 2013.

[19] R. Salmon, Higher Frame Rates, DVB Scene, No. 44, September 2014.

[20] DVB (Digital Video Broadcasting) Project website: http://www.dvb.org.

[21] History of the DVB Project – DVB Standards and Specifications, Ver. 11.0, DVB Project, Geneva, Switzerland, August, 2008.

[22] Framing structure, channel coding and modulation for terrestrial television, European Standard (EN) 300 744 V1.5.1, European Telecommunications Standards Institute (ETSI), Valbonne, France, November 2004.

[23] B. Jaksic, M. Petrovic, M. Smilic, B. Gvozdic, A. Markovic, Terrestrial Digital Transmission of the High-Definition Television in Europe, Proceedings of the 23 International

http://dx.doi.org/10.5772/64833

Electrotechnical and Computer Science Conference ERK 2014, Portorož, Slovenia, 20–24 September 2014, pp. A: 61–64. ISSN: 1581–4572; 23.

[24] Ultra HD distribution, World Broadcasting Unions International Satellite Operations Group (WBU-ISOG) Forum, Rio de Janeiro, Brazil, November 4–6, 2013.

[25] A. Wong, UHD with AsiaSat, AsiaSat, Hong Kong, August 2015.

[26] B. Jaksic, M. Petrovic, I. Milosevic, R. Ivkovic, S. Bjelovic, UHDTV into terrestrial and satellite systems, Proceedings of International Scientific Conference "UNITECH 2015", Gabrovo, Bulgaria, 20–21 November 2015, pp. II112–II118. ISSN 1313-230X.

[27] Broadband TV News website: http://www.broadbandtvnews.com.

Chapter 10

Optimized Scalable Image and Video Transmission for MIMO Wireless Channels

Amin Zribi, Clency Perrine and Yannis Pousset

Additional information is available at the end of the chapter

http://dx.doi.org/10.5772/64924

Abstract

In this chapter, we focus on proposing new strategies to efficiently transfer a compressed image/video content through wireless links using a multiple antenna technology. The proposed solutions can be considered as application layer physical layer (APP-PHY) cross layer design methods as they involve optimizing both application and physical layers. After a wide state-of-the-art study, we present two main solutions. The first focuses on using a new precoding algorithm that takes into account the image/video content structure when assigning transmission powers. We showed that its results are better than the existing conventional precoders. Second, a link adaptation process is integrated to efficiently assign coding parameters as a function of the channel state. Simulations over a realistic channel environment show that the link adaptation activates a dynamic process that results in a good image/video reconstruction quality even if the channel is varying. Finally, we incorporated soft decoding algorithms at the receiver side, and we showed that they could induce further improvements. In fact, almost 5 dB peak signal-to-noise ratio (PSNR) improvements are demonstrated in the case of transmission over a Rayleigh channel.

Keywords: APP-PHY cross-layer design, image and video coding, multiple-input multiple-output (MIMO), link adaptation, soft decoding, unequal power allocation (UPA), unequal error protection (UEP), adaptive modulation

1. Introduction

During the past decade, there has been exponential growth in various visual multimedia applications demand over wirelessly connected devices. Maintaining good visual quality for these applications is the central concern of service providers and system designers. Then, there is a critical need for efficient algorithms that guarantee good user visual quality after transmission over corrupted, bandwidth-limited, and non-static wireless links.

The conventional communication model is based on layered components where the application layer (APP) focuses on how to efficiently compress the visual content and the physical layer (PHY) aims at transmitting the compressed stream with residual error rates. In this context, the multimedia research community efforts lead to emerging algorithms and standards for image and video compression [1]. On the other hand, wireless communication experts proposed new error correction and modulation methods combined with multiple antenna techniques (multiple-input multiple-output, MIMO) to decrease the error rates and enhance the system transmission capacity [2].

The aim of this chapter is to demonstrate that a joint optimization of the APP and PHY layers can improve substantially the system performance. Before presenting the main contributions, we give an overview of scalable image/video encoding and MIMO wireless communications, which are necessary to understand the rest of the chapter.

1.1. Scalable image and video coding

In communication theory, source coding is a basic operation that makes data compression because of the limitation in the channel capacity. In general, we apply lossless compression algorithms to reduce the redundancy and the correlation in the original data. Then, lossy compression can be applied to remove some useless information according to the human sensing behaviour. In this chapter, we mainly focus on visual content delivery, and we will treat the case of image and video source content.

1.1.1. Image and video source coding fundamentals

A static image contains many pixels that are correlated and redundant, and we speak about *spatial correlation*. The latter can be efficiently compressed based on three components: frequency domain transform, quantization, and entropy encoding. The most known frequency transforms used in image compression are the discrete cosine transform (DCT) and the discrete wavelet transform (DWT). Then, the quantization will assign a unique representation to a range of frequency. Finally, to compress the remaining redundancy between the quantized coefficients, entropy encoding makes lossless compression based on variable-length coding (VLC) or arithmetic coding (AC).

A video content can be seen as a time-evolving sequence of images. Then, we still have spatial correlation, and the three-phase image compression mechanism previously described is used for intra encoding where an image is compressed independently to the other ones. However, the neighbour pictures in a video have also many similarities, which we call *temporal correlation*. Then, to reach better compression rates, we can encode only the differences in the image with respect to a reference one. This is called inter compression, and the encoding process will involve motion estimation and compensation. Motion estimation will deliver the motion vectors between the current and the reference images, while motion compensation will help to compute the prediction error matrix.

http://dx.doi.org/10.5772/64924

To provide efficient delivery for different users with different quality requirements, while maintaining a single compression operation, scalable image/video encoders build a progressive stream with many quality layers. Every correctly decoded layer induces quality refinement in the reconstructed visual data. However, such a hierarchical structure induces different degrees of importance between the layers. In fact, if a layer is error corrupted, all the remaining layers will be useless for the reconstruction even correctly received. Then, the importance of a layer depends on its position within the stream. First layers are more important than the last layers. In the following, we will present some key image and video compression standards and focus on the scalable versions that will be used in the following.

1.1.2. Image compression standards

The first and most used image compression standard is Joint Photographic Experts Group (JPEG). The main advantage in JPEG is its simplicity; however, it remains non-efficient for high compression rates, and its compressed bitstream is very sensitive to transmission errors. In 2000, the JPEG committee proposed a new image compression standard called JPEG2000 [3]. This standard uses the wavelet transform DWT and delivers a scalable stream with rate-distortion optimized quality layers. After the DWT, the different sub-bands are quantized and split into precincts, which are also split into code-blocks. The scalable content is generated based on the DWT resolution level, and the bit-plane level using the embedded block coding with optimal truncation (EBCOT) algorithm. The latter involves two steps: *Tier 1* processing that makes the bit-plane processing and entropy encoding based on binary AC, and *Tier 2* that organizes the final bitstream. JPEG2000 considers segment and synchronization markers, which reduces the quality loss in the presence of transmission errors, but still not sufficient for severe wireless environments.

An extension of JPEG2000 is proposed in Part 11 for image compression dedicated to wireless multimedia applications: JPEG2000 Wireless (JPWL) [4]. This standard offers many tools to make the compressed bitstream more resilient against errors. One of these tools is the use of APP layer error correcting codes to protect the compressed data and the headers. The standard proposes the use of Reed Solomon (RS) codes over $GF(2^8)$ and gives a choice between many RS codes with different error-correction capabilities. JPWL allows also the use of unequal error protection (UEP) that assigns different RS codes to the different code-blocks according to their importance for image reconstruction. JPWL gives also some error-resilient features like defining the sensitivity of a code-stream and localizing residual. In this chapter, we focus on image transmission in mobile wireless environments, then a resilient image compression method is needed which justifies the use of JPWL.

1.1.3. Video compression standards

H264 Advanced Video Coding (H264/AVC) is one of the standards proposed by the Joint Video Team to enhance the rate-distortion performance and to form a bitstream structure suitable for network transport. Compared to its predecessors, H264/AVC considers the same concept (intra coding and inter prediction) but adds new tools like more precise motion estimation, image prediction based on many references, spatial prediction for intra pictures, and more efficient entropy encoding called context-adaptive binary arithmetic coding (CABAC). For better interoperability, three profiles are proposed in this standard. The *extended* profile considers error resilience techniques which make it more suitable for wireless applications. Recently, Joint Collaborative Team on Video Coding (JCT-VC) developed a successor for H264/AVC. The new standard is called HEVC for High Efficiency Video Coding. Compared to H264/AVC, HEVC doubles the data compression ratio at the same level of video quality.

However, H264/AVC and HEVC do not support scalability, and their application to variable rate systems is not guaranteed. In this context, scalable extensions were proposed. The main expectation of H264 Scalable Video Coding (H264/SVC) [5] is to support temporal, spatial, and quality scalability with similar coding efficiency as a H264/AVC. The temporal scalability is performed by the SVC codec by introducing the concept of hierarchical B-picture coding. Interlayer prediction mechanisms are also introduced for spatial scalability, and quality scalability is performed using a medium-grain quality scalability (MGS). In this chapter, we mainly focus on scalable multimedia coding techniques, then we will consider the H264/SVC codec with quality and temporal scalability.

1.2. MIMO for wireless communications

As described, image and video codec designers aim at having the maximum compression rate under a given quality constraint. Some resilience techniques are applied to improve the reconstruction quality if some errors occurred. However, when we deal with wireless communications, the transmitted data are subject to many phenomena such as noise and large- and small-scale fading. The corrupted environment will degrade the reception quality, and consequently the user reconstructed quality will be bad. The second constraint imposed by the wireless channel is the limited bandwidth, sometimes not enough to transfer a multimedia content. Multiple antenna techniques, also called MIMO, exploit the time, frequency, and spatial diversity inherent to the wireless channel to increase the transmission rate. The gain induced by the MIMO technology motivated its integration in the recent wireless communication standards such as 802.11n WiFi, 4G LTE, and 802.16e WiMAX. This section is devoted to the description of the basics of the MIMO technology.

1.2.1. MIMO channel modelling

Let us consider a MIMO system with n_t transmitting antennas and n_r receiving antennas. The link between a transmitting antenna *i* and a receiving antenna *j* is characterized by its complex gain denoted h_{ji}. Then, every receiving antenna *j* will have the contribution of the signals transmitted by the n_t antennas as:

$$y_j = \sum_{i=1}^{n_t} h_{ji} s_i + n_j \tag{1}$$

http://dx.doi.org/10.5772/64924

where s_i is the symbol transmitted by the antenna i, and n_j is the noise component. Finally, the general system can be formulated by a matrix operation as:

$$\mathbf{y} = \mathbf{H}\,\mathbf{s} + \mathbf{n} \tag{2}$$

where **y, s,** and **n** vectors represent, respectively, the received signals, the transmitted signals, and the noise components. The matrix **H** is called the channel matrix because it describes the gain of all the links between the transmitting and receiving antennas. Estimating the channel matrix **H** delivers the channel state information (CSI) that can be exploited by the encoder or the decoder as detailed in the next paragraph.

1.2.2. Open-loop and closed-loop MIMO systems

The MIMO system is called open-loop when the CSI is only exploited at the decoder to improve the demodulation and decoding performance. We distinguish two main categories in this context. The first is spatial multiplexing where the information is multiplexed on the different antennas, which helps improve the system capacity. The second type aims at improving the system resiliency by exploiting the space and time diversity. This can be achieved if the antennas transmit different versions of the same information at different times. We notice that these two strategies imply a quality capacity trade-off. Then, some hybrid optimized versions were proposed to have the best compromise [6].

Closed-loop MIMO (CL-MIMO) systems take advantage of a feedback channel that makes possible the use of the CSI at the transmitter. In fact, the channel information enables precoding that jointly optimises the transmitter and the receiver operations. Hence, the system can reach the best resilience and capacity improvements since multiplexing and diversity are now optimized at the transmitter. Moreover, the CL-MIMO precoder virtually subdivides the multiple antenna channels into independent parallel single antenna channels.

Many precoding techniques can be found in the literature [6]. However, the most used ones are linear precoders that optimize the transmitting power to reach a quality criterion (maximum capacity, lower error rates, maximize the signal-to-noise ratio…). If the precoding matrix is diagonal, we call it a diagonal precoder. The optimization process [7] generates an equivalent diagonal matrix for **H**, which means an equivalent virtual channel with multiple independent single antenna channels. Moreover, based on precoding, we can assign different powers to these virtual subchannels. This strategy will be called unequal power allocation (UPA) and cannot be applied in the case of open-loop MIMO (OL-MIMO) since the transmitter does not have access to the CSI. These advantages motivated the use of CL-MIMO technology with linear precoding in this chapter.

We notice that MIMO systems require a multipath propagation environment for spatial diversity. However, this will introduce inter-symbol interference (ISI), which justifies the use of the orthogonal frequency-division multiplexing (OFDM) modulation. The latter divides the wide band into many narrow band subchannels, which reduces the ISI phenomena. All the MIMO systems described in the following rely on OFDM modulation.

1.2.3. MIMO receivers

In MIMO systems, each receiving antenna collects different interfering signals coming from the transmitting antennas. In order to reconstruct the source symbols, we need to separate them. Many decoding techniques can be applied like zero-forcing, successive interference cancellation, minimum mean-square error estimation, and maximum likelihood. The latter delivers the best performance with the minimum possible error rates. In the case of Gaussian distributed noise, the ML delivers the estimate s as:

$$\hat{\mathbf{s}} = \arg\min_{\mathbf{s}} \| \mathbf{y} - \mathbf{H}\, \mathbf{s} \| \tag{3}$$

The problem with the ML decoding is its prohibitive complexity that grows exponentially with n_t. However, in this work, we will consider it with linear MIMO precoding generating independent single antenna channels, which reduces significantly its complexity.

1.3. Context and outline of the chapter

We described in the previous subsections the developments made by two different research communities in the fields of image/video compression and MIMO wireless communications. We also justified the chosen standards and technologies in this work and emphasized the need for a joint optimization of compression and transmission operations. Indeed, the multimedia compressed data are very sensitive to transmission errors, and the source encoder cannot take into account the fluctuating behaviour of the wireless channel. On the other hand, the MIMO transmission strategies do not care about the content, i.e. important and less important streams are transmitted in the same way. During the last years, APP layer image/video compression, and PHY layer wireless communications, began to converge to guarantee a dynamic access to the multimedia services over corrupted channels. However, the convergence of the multimedia world and the mobile communications raised new questions. How can we satisfy users with heterogeneous scenarios and using wireless channels varying in space and time? How can we improve the end-user visual quality without affecting the wireless system rate? The aim of the proposed book chapter is to answer these issues by proposing APP-PHY cross-layer algorithms based, respectively, on link adaptation and soft decoding. The details and the contributions of the chapter will be provided in the next section after the description of the state-of-the-art.

The chapter is organized as follows. Section 2 provides a state-of-the-art study where the main contributions dealing with the joint design of image/video compression and transmission are studied. Section 3 provides the main contributions of the chapter. After presenting the used channel models, we give the simulation results for image and video optimized transmission over MIMO channels. Then, a soft-input decoding method will be presented and investigated for JPWL image transmission. Finally, Section 4 concludes the paper and gives open directions for future work.

http://dx.doi.org/10.5772/64924

2. APP-PHY cross-layer design: state-of-the-art

In the previous section, we demonstrated the need for a joint optimization of the image/video compression and wireless communication operations. This requirement motivated researchers and academia to develop new APP-PHY cross-layer algorithms. Some of them optimized the error-correcting coding process; others focused on the modulation, or on the MIMO precoding. In this chapter, we target to optimize all the operations for a better reconstruction quality. To better illustrate the framework of our contribution, a description of the main state-of-the-art algorithms in the context of APP-PHY cross-layer design is provided.

2.1. Joint source-channel coding (JSCC)

Motivated by the well-known Shannon [8] separation theorem, the communication system designers have conceived separately source and channel coding. However, in most practical applications, it is impossible to fulfil the theorem requirements like unconstrained block lengths and unconstrained coding and decoding delays. Joint source/channel (JSC) coding and decoding techniques have emerged as a pragmatic approach. First solutions in this context tried to integrate some resilience modes into the source coding, which results in compression efficiency loss [9]. Other solutions tried to exploit the residual redundancy remaining after source coding to improve the decoding performance. Being the last block in every image/video compression scheme, many works focused essentially on the entropy encoding operations such as variable-length coding (VLC) and arithmetic coding (AC).

Motivated by the efficiency of the error-correcting codes, many researchers focused on developing new entropy decoding algorithms that exploit the code properties to enhance the system decoding performance like in [10, 11] for VLC and in [12] for AC. Then, a change was marked by the development of soft-input soft-output (SISO) channel decoders used in the very efficient turbo codes. JSC research community focused on developing SISO decoders for entropy codes. First solutions, inspired by the convolutional codes, modelled the entropy encoder by a finite-state machine or a trellis to apply conventional SISO channel decoding algorithms. The case of VLC was treated in the study of Wang et al. [13] and Park and Miller [14], and decoding methods for AC were considered in the study of Grangetto et al. [15] and Bi et al. [16]. Later contributions took benefit from the existing SISO decoders and applied iterative JSC decoding [17–19]. In Refs. [17] and [18], the authors considered specific trellis constructions, but their complexity becomes intractable for long source sequences. Recently, a new SISO entropy decoding was proposed for VLC [19] and AC [20]. The proposed algorithm was inspired from the Chase II decoding first used in turbo block codes and showed a good complexity-performance trade-off compared to trellis-based methods. In the present chapter, a soft-input decoding method will be needed to enhance the reconstruction quality of an image JPWL codec. Hence, we will consider the Chase decoder [19, 20] for soft-input arithmetic decoding. More details are provided in Section 3.4.

2.2. Unequal error protection (UEP)

In many studies, authors focused on optimizing the source and channel coding operations. This still can be considered as a JSC coding method, but where the source and the channel encoding and decoding algorithms remain unchanged. In fact, we just optimize their parameters to achieve a target constraint. We showed in Section 1.1 that the scalable image/video compressed bitstream contains information with different levels of importance. Hence, applying equal error protection implies the same correction performance for important and less important information, which is not accurate. It is more suitable to apply unequal error protection where important parts are more protected than less important ones.

Many solutions focused on applying UEP to JPEG2000 compressed streams since it provides scalability. Then, first quality layers have to be more protected than the last quality layers. In Refs. [21] and [22], the authors proposed different strategies for JPEG2000 stream headers protection and the application of UEP using RS codes on the different JPEG2000 quality layers. Substantial improvements in terms of image peak signal-to-noise ratio (PSNR) were demonstrated, which motivated their integration in the JPWL standard. The application of UEP to video transmission was investigated in [23] where different rate-compatible punctured convolutional (RCPC) codes were used to protect the MPEG-2 compressed video packets. We notice that these schemes assign different codes to the streams without guaranteeing rate-distortion optimality. To reach such a property, optimization process has to be included. In this context, a rate allocation process was introduced in [24] to minimize the distortion of a reconstructed JPEG2000 image. In Ref. [25], the authors derived an optimal wireless JPEG2000 compliant error correction rate allocation scheme for robust streaming of images and videos. In Ref. [26], the authors used the scalability property of the H264/SVC encoder to apply convenient UEP strategy. Even efficient, the proposed strategies considered a static channel with fixed parameters; then, we have no guarantee to obtain the same results in a MIMO varying wireless environment. Some works [27, 28] focused on optimizing the JPEG2000 compression and protection processes for open-loop MIMO systems. Extending these UEP results to the case of closed-loop MIMO systems can be very advantageous. Moreover, we will have another freedom degree that we can optimize to guarantee efficient rate-distortion trade-off. This will be the topic of the next subsection where unequal power allocation methods are described.

2.3. Unequal power allocation (UPA)

We can also improve the transmission quality of the more important packets in the compressed stream by improving their signal-to-noise ratio (SNR). For a given channel, this can be achieved by allocating more transmission power to them. Under a maximum power constraint, low transmission power will be assigned to the less important packets. This unequal power allocation (UPA) strategy can also improve significantly the image/video reconstruction quality.

In this framework, many researchers [29–32] proposed to allocate dynamically the power to the different packets according to their contribution in the quality improvements. While contributions proposed in Refs. [29, 30] focused on JPEG2000 image content, the authors in

Ref. [32] designed a UPA strategy for a scalable video content. These contributions were proposed for single antenna systems, and the extension to high capacity MIMO systems can be gainful. Hence, in Refs. [33] and [34], the authors focused on optimizing OL-MIMO space-time diversity exploiting systems to improve the image reconstruction quality. A novel precoding scheme capable of integrating both channel and source characteristics in order to achieve the desired prioritized spatial multiplexing was proposed in [35] for H264/SVC compressed-video transmission.

We recall that in CL-MIMO systems, we can construct, based on the channel matrix, equivalent independent single antenna subchannels with different propagation properties. Then, the image/video transmission can be optimized more efficiently to achieve the best quality at the receiver. In this chapter, we consider that the encoder knows the CSI, and we present a quality-constrained precoding method.

2.4. Hierarchical and adaptive modulations

As scientists focused on optimizing error correction in UEP, or transmit power in UPA, many other proposals treated the modulation process. The principle is the same: efficiently assign modulation methods to the different compressed information according to their contribution to the quality improvement.

In hierarchical modulation [36], each constellation point is assigned to a base layer and an enhancement layer streams. The bit-symbol mapping is made in a sense where the distance between the points with different base-layer bits is larger than that for the enhancement layer bits. Hence, in bad channel conditions, the base layer stream will be more resilient and can be decoded with low errors, and the base quality is guaranteed. If the channel is fair, we will be also able to decode the enhancement-layer stream and have better quality.

Another simple strategy can be considered to apply dynamic modulation that assigns different resiliency levels to the compressed data, which is adaptive modulation. Actually, using high-order modulation results in a better spectral efficiency, but higher error rates. Then, if we need to have low error rates for a very important information transmission with a noisy-channel, we can just use low-order modulation. While UEP and UPA strategies tend to guarantee a required user quality for a low channel SNR, adaptive modulation can help to improve the spectral efficiency for a channel with high SNR. This motivated the development of hybrid strategies where the described schemes can be optimized for a better system efficiency.

2.5. Contributions: hybrid optimized strategies

When the target is to deliver an image or video content over a wireless link, the system designer should take into account that the channel is varying. Hence, we should move from a static design to an adaptive one. To this aim, many link adaptation algorithms based on a hybrid optimization of the previously described methods were proposed. UEP was combined with hierarchical modulation in [37] in the case of equal power OFDM-MIMO wireless transmission. In Refs. [38] and [39], the authors proposed UPA strategies combined with adaptive modulation, respectively, for non-compressed and compressed image transmission, but the error correction scheme remains static. In Ref. [40], a link adaptation strategy where coding, modulation, and power are all optimized according to the channel CSI is proposed; however, the strategy does not take into account the content structure. The link adaptation strategy proposed by Houas et al. [41] considers an OFDM single antenna system where the modulation and error protection tasks are optimized based on the channel subcarrier status under a constrained JPEG2000 image quality.

In this chapter, we introduce a new paradigm where we develop a core system optimizing all the operations based on UEP, UPA, and adaptive modulation to achieve the best-reconstructed image/video quality, given the channel status. Moreover, we provide soft-input source and channel decoding to reduce the error rates at the receiver and consequently improve the user experience.

The chapter contributions are threefold. First, we show how the optimization of the system parameters (image/video compression and wireless transmission) can be very advantageous to guarantee a good quality-of-service (QoS) even the channel is varying. We also demonstrate that this is possible by using scalable techniques such as UEP, UPA, adaptive modulation, and scalable compression. Second, we demonstrate the efficiency of the proposed optimization procedure for JPWL image compressed data and for H264/SVC video compressed content. Third, we show that using soft decoding methods for the demodulator, the channel decoder, and the JPWL image decoder can provide significant quality gains while keeping the same throughput. The results are provided based on simulation results of the visual objective and subjective quality. This seminal chapter resumes many results [42, 43] developed in the XLIM-RESYST team of University of Poitiers, France, and some of them [44] were under a cooperation with the SYSCOM laboratory in Tunisia.

3. Solutions for optimized image and video transmission

3.1. Channel model

In this chapter, we consider two different channel models to run simulations: a statistical channel and a realistic channel. At large, the statistical channel model is used to emphasize the performance as a function of a given SNR, whereas the realistic channel model gives more details about the propagation environment of a given scenario with fluctuating transmission conditions.

The communication wireless channel induces random disturbances due to the thermic additive noise and low and large-scale fading, respectively, caused by obstacles and multipath propagation. These random phenomena can be described based on statistical models. In the following, we consider a Rayleigh fading channel where the elements of the channel matrix follow a Rayleigh distribution. The noise is modelled by the well-known additive white Gaussian noise (AWGN). In the case of a single antenna system, if we transmit a binary phase-shift keying modulated sequence $\mathbf{c} = (c_1, \ \ldots, \ c_n)$ over a Rayleigh channel, we will receive a sequence $\mathbf{r} = (r_1, \ \ldots, \ r_n)$ whose elements are $r_i = \alpha_i . c_i + b_i$ where α_i is random Rayleigh distributed coefficients and b_i represents random AWGN samples.

To have a more realistic approximation for the propagation environment, we consider a three-dimensional (3D) ray-tracing simulator [45] to provide the impulse responses of a realistic channel. The transmission environments used in this chapter take into account the user mobility and the existence of obstacles, and will be presented later. Then, the channel alternates between bad, medium and good states. In the case of realistic channel simulations, the CSI is obtained based on an estimate of the channel with a training sequence.

3.2. Compressed image transmission application

In this section, we focus on image transmission over CL-MIMO wireless systems. As previously specified, we consider the error-resilient scalable JPWL image compression standard. Two contributions are presented. The first considers equal error protection, and a fixed modulation scheme with a new CL-MIMO context-based precoder (CBP) optimized to reach the best reconstruction quality. In the second step, the precoder will be introduced into a link adaptation scheme where UEP, adaptive modulation, UPA, and source coding are optimized given the channel status to reach a better quality.

3.2.1. Context-based precoding for JPWL image transmission

In this part, we suppose that the channel coding and modulation are static. However, the power allocation will be optimized. The system model treated in this part is depicted in **Figure 1** and aims at transmitting the compressed data using a precoded MIMO system. After diagonalization, the equivalent channel matrix, given by the CSI, will have b virtual independent single antenna channels with different SNRs. Then, the scalable JPWL encoder will be asked to generate b quality layers that should be transmitted across the b virtual channels. Naturally, the first quality layer, which is the most important, will be assigned to the highest SNR subchannel. Then, according to their importance order, every quality layer will be assigned to a specific subchannel. The JPWL standard includes $\mathrm{RS}(N, K)$ error correcting codes that assign an encoded N-symbols codeword to every K-symbol input message, resulting in a $t = \left\lceil \frac{N-K}{2} \right\rceil$

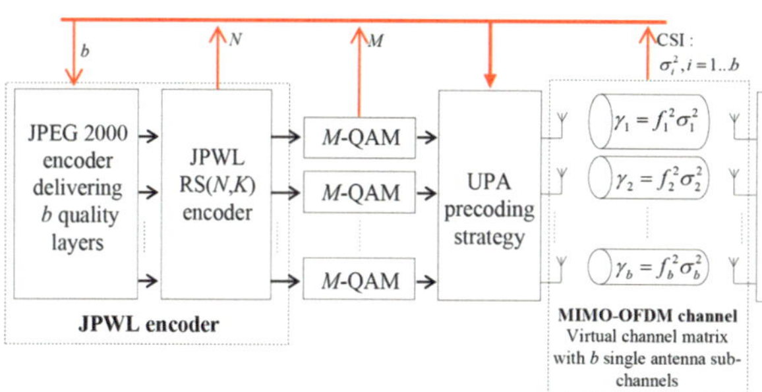

Figure 1. System model for JPWL image transmission over CL-MIMO system using UPA based on the CBP algorithm. Source coding, error correction, and modulation are not optimized.

symbol correction capacity. The encoded bit-sequence will be then modulated based on M-QAM, which assigns to every n bits one of the $M = 2^n$ modulation symbols. Finally, the CBP power allocation operation has to compute the power assigned to every quality layer i to reach a source target bit error rate denoted BER^t given the RS code and the modulation parameters, and eventually the channel CSI.

With scalable image coding, a quality layer can enhance the reconstruction quality under the condition that it and its previous quality layers were correctly received. Otherwise, it will be useless. Then, the proposed power allocation strategy works hierarchically: every quality layer i transmitted on a subchannel i should take enough power to achieve the bit-error rate (BER) target constraint. However, we should take into account that we have a maximum power P_0 to not exceed, and that the error rates depend on the modulation and channel coding parameters. For every subchannel $i \in \{1, ..., b\}$, the precoding coefficient f_i is evaluated in four steps:

The target source BER BER^t is defined after RS error correction; then, we have to compute the corresponding BER before correction denoted B, which depends on the RS code correction capacity as:

$$BER^t \geq \frac{1}{n}\sum_{j=t+1}^{N} \frac{j}{N}\binom{N}{j}(n.B)^j(1-n.B)^{N-j} \quad (4)$$

Given the modulation order M and the noise power of the subchannel i denoted σ_i^2, we can determine the needed power precoding coefficient f_i to achieve the needed BER B as:

$$f_i^2 = \frac{2(M-1)}{3\sigma_i^2}\left[erfc^{-1}\left(1 - \frac{B\sqrt{M}\log_2 M}{2\left(\sqrt{M}-1\right)}\right)\right]^2 \quad (5)$$

Finally, we have to check if the remaining power P_R can satisfy the precoding result. Hence, if $f_i^2 \geq P_R$, we still have power to transmit the quality layer i with the requested BER target; then, we have to update the remaining power to $P_R = P_R - f_i^2$. Then, we iterate the same process for the next layers. However, if this condition does not hold, i.e. $f_i^2 < P_R$, we will assign all the remaining power to the current quality layer $f_i^2 = P_R$ that will be transmitted with no guarantee to reach the target BER.

To investigate the efficiency of the CBP precoder, we run simulations where an image is transmitted for every receiver position in the trajectory given in **Figure 2** where the red blocks are buildings. The receiver is supposed to move along a path of 138 m at a speed of 5 m/s. The channel gain shows four different areas with different channel states. We consider a MIMO 4 × 4 channel where the diagonalization results in a maximum of $b = 4$ subchannels. Then, the

JPWL source encoder will compress the test image "Monarch" and deliver four quality layers with 0.25 bits per pixel (bpp) each. We use an equal error protection method with a fixed RS(37,32) code and a fixed *M*-QAM modulation with $M = 4$.

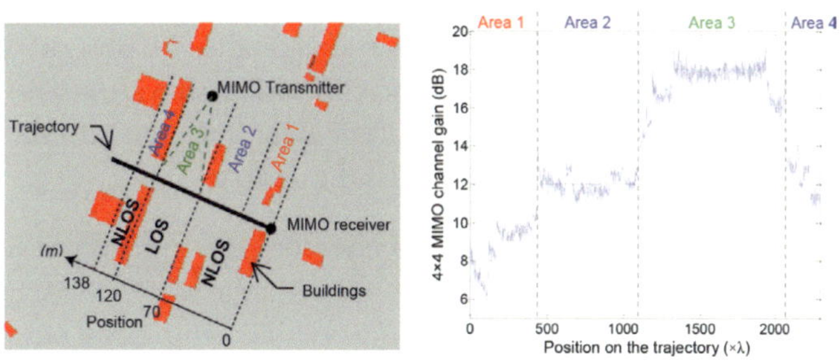

Figure 2. The wireless propagation environment (left) and the corresponding variation of the MIMO channel gain by position (right) for JPWL image transmission.

Figure 3 shows the PSNR results as a function of the receiver position for different precoding strategies. For better readability, we present the mean value over 20 samples with a sliding window for all the schemes. The presented precoding methods have the same principle with different optimization constraints. While water filling (WF) aims at maximizing the channel capacity, minimum mean square error (MMSE) tends to minimize the mean square error $E\left[\|\boldsymbol{y} - \boldsymbol{s}\|^2\right]$, and MBER stands for minimizing the BER. E-d_{min} is a non-diagonal precoder that focuses on maximizing the distance between the constellation points. All these precoders are compared to the proposed CBP precoder that aims at maximizing the image quality by exploiting the hierarchical structure of the JPWL compressed stream.

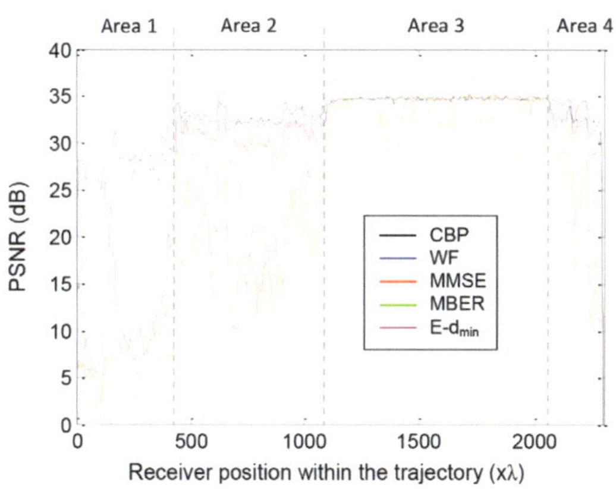

Figure 3. PSNR evolution as a function of the receiver position for different 4 × 4 CL-MIMO precoding strategies in the case of "Monarch" image with 4-QAM modulation and RS(37,32) channel code.

The PSNR results show that the different precoders involve different performance according to the channels status. For the first area, where the channel is very corrupted, all the precoders dispatch the power between the different layers which induces a quality loss. CBP is the best in this area, since it allocates approximately all the power to transmit correctly the first quality layer, which results in a mean PSNR of almost 28 dB. For medium channel states (areas 2 and 4), the CBP remains more efficient than the other precoders, even for certain positions where the E-d_{min} is better. The E-d_{min} gain with respect to the CBP is more clear for the low corrupted channel (area 3), and this is justified by the non-diagonality of this precoder that allows transmitting the four quality layers. However, the CBP will assign almost all the power to the three first quality layers. In the following, we will consider link adaptation strategies, and the CBP performance will be improved substantially for this area.

To better show the gains induced by the CBP precoder for high-to-medium corrupted channel state, we present in **Figure 4** the reconstructed images and the corresponding PSNRs to study the visual quality for the position index 2259. The results confirm the efficiency of the CBP precoder compared to the conventional MIMO precoders in the case of JPWL image transmission. However, the question remains for the area 3 where the channel is fair, and the CBP performance can be improved. To this aim, we propose in the next paragraph a link adaptation process based on optimized UEP and adaptive modulation.

Figure 4. Visual quality for the 4 × 4 CL-MIMO precoding strategies in the case of "Monarch" image with 4-QAM modulation and RS(37,32) channel code. The results correspond to the position index 2259 in area 4.

3.2.2. Optimized CBP and link adaptation for JPWL image transmission

In the previous part, we presented a system where the source rate, modulation, and error correction are static and independent from the channel state which is not accurate. In this paragraph, we will use link adaptation techniques as presented in **Figure 5**. The main difference compared to **Figure 1** remains in the new joint optimization block using the CSI as input to deliver the number of subchannels to use $L \leq b$, and, for each ith quality layer, the best configuration for the source coding rate R_{Si}, the correction capacity of the RS code given by N_i, and the corresponding modulation order M_i. The optimization process [42] makes independent tree-based exhaustive search for every subchannel. The objective is to minimize distortion under three main constraints, which are the rate constraint, the target BER quality to guarantee, and the maximum power to not exceed.

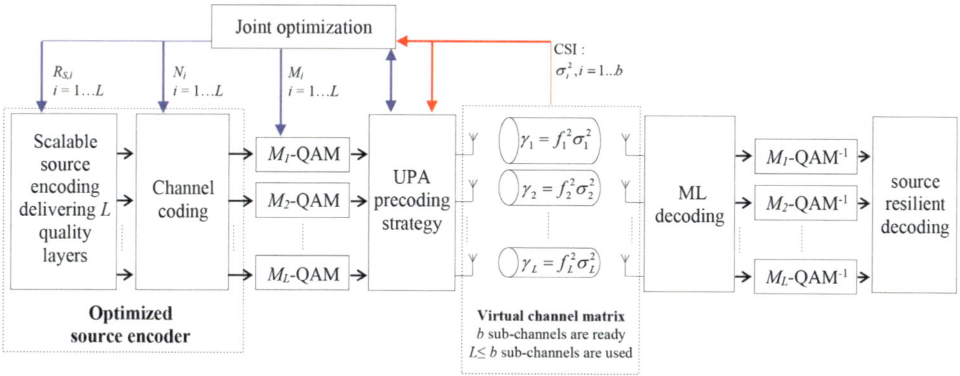

Figure 5. System model for scalable content transmission over CL-MIMO system using UPA based on the CBP algorithm and link adaptation techniques based on UEP, adaptive modulation, and variable rate source encoder.

Now, we run simulations to investigate the gains induced by the link adaptation technique in the case of 4 × 4 MIMO for the same realistic channel. We also assume the same channel estimation process. The reference static configuration for the test image "Monarch" 768 × 512 pixels considers a JPWL encoder generating four quality layers having each a constant rate of 0.125 bpp. The error correcting code is a RS(37,32), and the modulation is 4-QAM. The link adaptation optimized system always considers a 4 × 4 MIMO and can choose dynamically the number of subchannels to use $L \in \{1, 2, 3, 4\}$, the modulation order for each subchannel $M_i \in \{4, 16, 64\}$, the corresponding RS encoded sequence length $N_i \in \{37, 38, 40, 43, 45\}$, and source encoding rate R_{Si}. The power limitation is set to $P_0 = 1$, the objective BER to achieve is $BER^t = 10^{-9}$, and the rate is constrained by a maximum of 512 OFDM symbols per subchannel. We recall that we always apply the CBP precoding process of the previous paragraph, which is activated after fixing all the system configurations.

Figure 6 provides the PSNR results for the static and the optimized CBP strategies as a function of the receiver position index. We can see that the link adaptation induces remarkable improvements in terms of reconstructed image quality. Moreover, almost a 1 dB mean PSNR gain can be achieved for the intermediate channel state at the areas 2 and 4. The improvements are even more significant when the channel is under good conditions. This is justified by the fact that the link adaptation will allow the use of high order modulations with low redundancy, and consequently higher source coding rates and better quality. The mean PSNR gain can reach 5 dB. We demonstrated that using APP-PHY cross-layer design by optimizing all the system blocks according to the channel status can enhance remarkably the reconstructed image quality. Now, we propose to investigate if this efficiency remains when dealing with scalable video transmission.

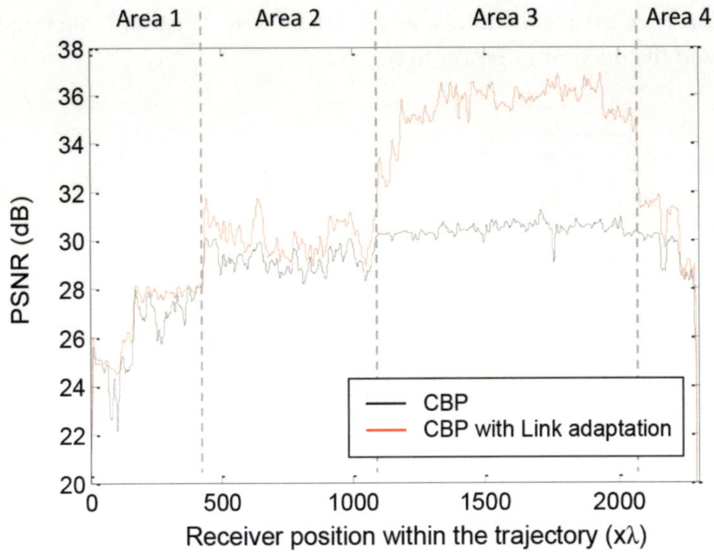

Figure 6. PSNR evolution as a function of the receiver position for 4 × 4 CL-MIMO with CBP precoding and link adaptation strategies in the case of "Monarch" image.

3.3. Compressed video transmission application

In this section, we propose to extend the link adaptation with the CBP MIMO precoding algorithms to scalable H264/SVC video transmission application. In fact, this standard generates three scalability layers. The first deals with temporal scalability where bi-directional (B) frames are adaptively appended to a base layer group of pictures (GOP) which means variable frame-rates. The second is spatial scalability which aims at satisfying users with different displaying capacities by generating many resolutions for every frame. The last is the quality scalability which transports complementary data in different layers to produce videos with distinct quality levels. This scalability is mainly based on implementing distinct quantization parameters for each layer. H.264/SVC supports three distinct quality scalability modes which are fine, medium, and coarse grain scalabilities (GS). While coarse GS (CGS) makes a prediction process for each quality layer, the medium GS (MGS) increases efficiency using a flexible prediction unit, where base and enhancement layers can be referenced. Finally, the compressed stream has a hierarchical structure, and we can apply the CBP with the link adaptation as described previously.

The studied system model is the same as in **Figure 5** with a H264/SVC source encoder. Simulations are operated on the "Foreman" 176 × 144 resolution test video. The source encoder generates a base quality layer, with three CGS quality enhancement layers. For a better scalability, we also consider subquality layers computed by the MGS process. The compressed bit-streams are then protected using a rate-compatible punctured convolutional (RCPC) channel code, then modulated with M-QAM where M is adaptively optimized. Finally, the CBP precoding is applied for the 4 × 4 MIMO channel UPA. To approach the reality, a realistic channel depicted in **Figure 7** is considered with the corresponding channel gain. The receiver is supposed to move through a path of 20 m at a 5 m/s speed. We can see that we have two channel states: the first part has a poor non-line-of-sight (NLOS) channel, then by the end we have a relatively reliable status with LOS propagation.

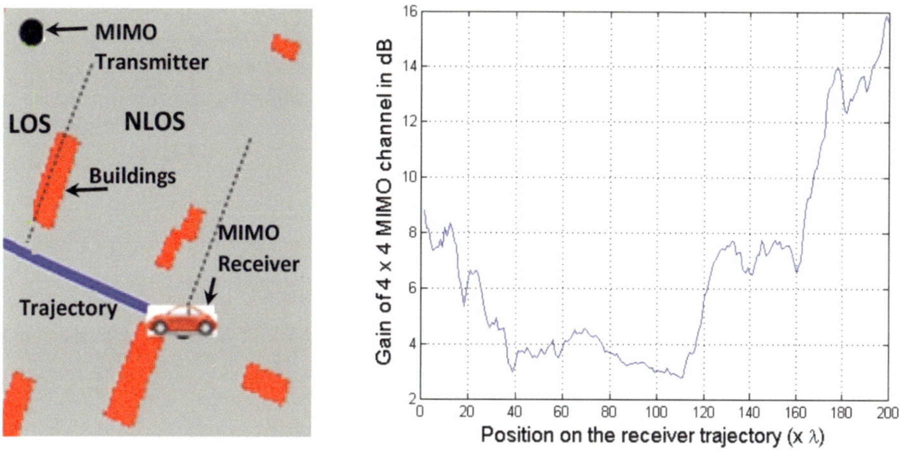

Figure 7. The wireless propagation environment (left) and the corresponding variation of the MIMO channel gain by position (right) for H264/SVC video transmission.

Figure 8 presents the simulation results for CBP precoding with and without link adaptation. In fact, the considered system uses an APP-PHY cross layer design based on UEP, adaptive modulation, UPA, and variable rate source coding. The optimization core selects for each subchannel the good RCPC code rate among the set $R \in \left\{\frac{4}{5}, \frac{2}{3}, \frac{1}{2}, \frac{1}{3}, \frac{1}{4}\right\}$, the modulation order $M \in \{4, \;\; 16, \;\; 64\}$, and the source coding rate and applies CBP precoding with a BER target $B = 10^{-9}$ to guarantee reliability for the more important quality layers. All this process aims at maximizing the user video quality under the constraints: maximum power $P_0 = 1$, equivalent overall transmission rate, and a minimum required QoS. The figure shows that applying CBP with link adaptation (red curve) is always better than using static CBP whatever the modulation order and coding rate. In fact, all the presented results have the same maximum rate. Using static CBP with $M = 16$ and $R = \frac{1}{4}$ results in very high error rates especially for the NLOS area, which degrades remarkably the image quality. Then, the system using the lowest order modulation, with the RCPC code rate $R = \frac{1}{2}$, is more robust and makes better error correction, which justifies its efficiency in a very noisy channel state. However, when the channel is fair, this configuration loses its efficiency because of its low spectral efficiency, and the high redundancy level. The CBP with link adaptation delivers a minimum PSNR quality of 34 dB, which is very acceptable, and can reach 37 dB for a good channel state. The results confirm that making joint optimization of the system parameters is also advantageous for scalable video transmission. Finally, sample frames are provided in **Figure 9** to show these video quality improvements.

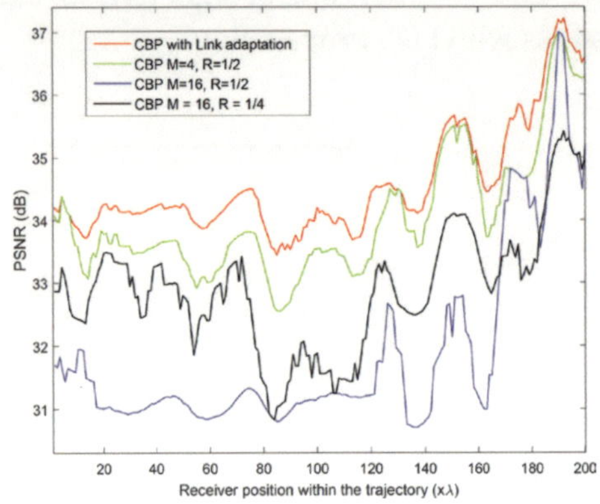

Figure 8. PSNR evolution as a function of the receiver position for 4 × 4 CL-MIMO with CBP precoding and link adaptation strategies in the case of "Foreman" video.

Figure 9. Example of reconstructed frames for Foreman video for CBP precoding with link adaptation ((a) and (c)) compared to a static scheme with 16-QAM modulation and rate 1/2 channel code ((b) and (d)).

3.4. Soft-decoding methods for image transmission

As specified in Section 2.1, joint source channel decoding is also a good solution to improve the image/video reconstruction quality. While CBP and link adaptation focused on how to transmit efficiently the image/video compressed information, soft decoding algorithms can enhance the quality of the reconstructed data without introducing extra redundancy. The aim of this section is to improve the performance of JPWL image transmission over highly corrupted noisy channels.

We focus on a system where the image is compressed with a JPEG2000 encoder, then protected by a RS code, and finally modulated and transmitted on single antenna noisy channel. Unlike conventional hard decoding methods, no decision has to be made on the received samples. The latter gives an extra information about the decision reliability, which can be exploited to further improve the system decoding performance. Algorithms that exploit such extra information are called soft decoding methods. To achieve a maximum gain, soft decoding methods will be used for RS decoding and JPWL arithmetic decoding.

Let us consider a statistical Rayleigh fading channel with binary-phase shift keying (BPSK) modulation. Based on the channel soft outputs, we can apply soft-input RS decoding using the well-known Chase decoder. Since we need also to make soft-input arithmetic decoding, the RS decoder should deliver an estimate for the probabilities of its decoded sequence elements. This can be made using a soft-input soft-output (SISO) RS decoder. The most used RS SISO decoder is the Chase II algorithm [46] where different test sequences are built by switching all the binary combinations over the q_{RS} least reliable bits. After decoding all the test sequences, the decoded sequence **d** will be the one having the minimum Euclidian distance with reference to the received sequence. Finally, soft outputs are computed bit-by-bit based on the difference between **d** and the valid competing sequence. We notice that increasing q_{RS} results in a better decoding performance and also a more accurate soft-outputs computation, but higher complexity.

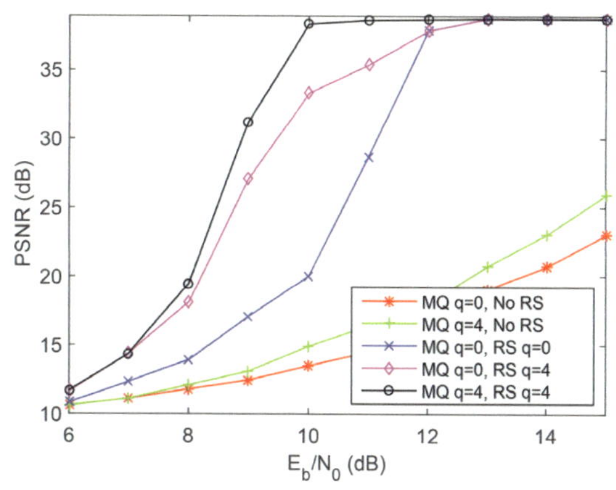

Figure 10. PSNR evolution as a function of the signal-to-noise ratio for the JPWL image transmission over a Rayleigh channel with soft decoding algorithms.

We recall that the JPEG2000 encoder uses two main components after the wavelet transform and quantization. *Tier 2* arranges the compressed stream, and *Tier 1* makes lossless arithmetic compression using MQ encoder. Then, we will have to re-arrange the reliabilities delivered by the RS SISO decoder to reconstruct the MQ-decoder soft inputs. A soft-input decoding can be applied based on a modified Chase decoder. The main differences between the RS and the MQ Chase decoding operations reside in the error detection mechanism. While RS Chase decoder focuses on valid code-words based on redundancy, the MQ decoder uses the variable-length encoding property to detect invalid sequences. Finally, the decoded sequences will be used to reconstruct the original image.

To investigate the proposed decoder performance, we use the grayscale test image Lenna 512 × 512 pixels. The latter is compressed with a JPEG2000 encoder to a D_s bpp source rate. The obtained packets are then protected using a RS(37,32), to achieve an overall rate of 1 bpp. When received with no errors, the image reconstruction leads to a maximum PSNR of 39.3 dB. However, in the case of corrupted channels, the results should depend on the SNR.

Figure 10 presents the evolution of the mean reconstructed image PSNR as a function of the channel SNR for different decoders having equivalent 1 bpp overall rate. It is obvious that the results are better for an increasing SNR, but the curves are not the same. Moreover, if no RS channel coding is used (green and red curves), the system performance is very low; however, the soft-input arithmetic decoding induces almost a 3 dB PSNR improvement. Using the error-correcting RS code with hard decoding (blue curve) improves the system performance remarkably. Indeed, using the soft decoding algorithms can make extra improvements. In fact, when applying soft-input RS decoding while keeping hard MQ decoding, we can achieve almost a 12 dB gain at $E_b/N_0 = 10$ dB. Furthermore, using soft decoding algorithms for RS and MQ decoding can further improve the image quality by 5 dB at the same SNR. Finally, **Figure 11** provides sample reconstructed images for a signal-to-noise ratio of $\frac{E_b}{N_0} = 10 \;\; dB$ for conventional hard decoding and the presented soft decoding methods. It is obvious that the PSNR gain is also justified by a remarkable visual quality improvement.

Hard input decoding
PSNR = 21.45 dB

Soft input decoding
PSNR = 38.71 dB

Figure 11. Examples of the reconstructed images in the case of hard and soft decoding.

We investigated in this section the main improvements we can reach by using soft decoding algorithms for a single antenna system. The next steps include the extension of these results to a CL-MIMO system using CBP precoding with link adaptation, which is under investigation.

http://dx.doi.org/10.5772/64924

4. Conclusions and future work

In this chapter, we showed that cross-layer APP-PHY design could be very advantageous to guarantee a good image/video quality even after transmission over a highly corrupted and varying MIMO wireless channel. We demonstrated that this is possible by making accurate optimization of different scalable techniques such as UEP, UPA, adaptive modulation, and scalable image/video compression. Moreover, we established the efficiency of the proposed optimization procedure for JPWL image compressed data, and for H264/SVC video compressed content. Finally, we emphasized that using soft decoding methods can provide remarkable quality gains while keeping the same throughput.

Future work includes the extension of the optimization process to more general networks including cooperative communication and wireless multimedia sensor networks. On the other hand, the proposed contributions are validated for JPEG2000 and H264 encoders, and they can be generalized to new standards like HEVC.

Acknowledgements

The authors like to thank Julien Abot, Samy Kambou, and Marwa Mhamdi for their collaboration and original contributions in making this seminal book chapter.

Author details

Amin Zribi[1*], Clency Perrine[2] and Yannis Pousset[2]

*Address all correspondence to: amin.zribi@gmail.com

1 Higher Institute of Communication Technologies (IsetCom), Tunis, Tunisia & Signal and Communications Department, Telecom Bretagne, Brest, France

2 XLIM RESYST Team, University of Poitiers, France

References

[1] Chakrabarti I, Batta KN, Chatterjee SK. Introduction to scalable image and video coding. In Motion Estimation for Video Coding 2015 (pp. 85–108). Springer International Publishing, Switzerland.

[2] Kim H. Wireless Communications Systems Design. John Wiley & Sons, USA; 2015 Oct 1.

[3] ISO/IEC 15444-1 / ITU-T T.800. JPEG 2000 Image Coding System: Core Coding System. 2002.

[4] ISO/IEC 15444-11:2007. JPEG 2000 Image Coding System—part11: Wireless JPEG 2000. May 2007.

[5] Schwarz H, Marpe D, Wiegand T. Overview of the scalable video coding extension of the H. 264/AVC standard. IEEE Transactions on Circuits and Systems for Video Technology. 2007; 17(9):1103–20.

[6] Biglieri E, Calderbank R, Constantinides A, Goldsmith A, Paulraj A, Poor HV. MIMO Wireless Communications. Cambridge University Press, UK; 2007 Jan 8.

[7] Berder O. Optimisation et stratégies d'allocation de puissance des systèmes de transmission multi-antennes. Ph.D. Dissertation, Bretagne Occidentale University. Dec 2002.

[8] Shannon CE. A mathematical theory of communication. ACM SIGMOBILE Mobile Computing and Communications Review. 2001 Jan; 5(1):3–55.

[9] Redmill DW, Kingsbury NG. The EREC: an error-resilient technique for coding variable-length blocks of data. IEEE Transactions on Image Processing. 1996 Apr; 5(4): 565–74.

[10] Sayood K, Borkenhagen JC. Use of residual redundancy in the design of joint source/ channel coders. IEEE Transactions on Communications. 1991 Jun; 39(6):838–46.

[11] Hagenauer J. Source-controlled channel decoding. IEEE Transactions on Communications. 1995 Sep; 43(9):2449–57.

[12] Boyd C, Cleary JG, Irvine SA, Rinsma-Melchert I, Witten IH. Integrating error detection into arithmetic coding. IEEE Transactions on Communications. 1997 Jan 3; 45(1):1–3.

[13] Wang Z, Wu X, Dumitrescu S. Fast length-constrained MAP decoding of variable length coded Markov sequences over noisy channel. In Communications, 2004 IEEE International Conference (vol. 1, pp. 542–546).

[14] Park M, Miller DJ. Joint source-channel decoding for variable-length encoded data by exact and approximate MAP sequence estimation. IEEE Transactions on Communications. 2000 Jan; 48(1):1–6.

[15] Grangetto M, Cosman P, Olmo G. Joint source/channel coding and MAP decoding of arithmetic codes. IEEE Transactions on Communications. 2005 Jun; 53(6):1007–16.

[16] Bi D, Hoffman MW, Sayood K. State machine interpretation of arithmetic codes for joint source and channel coding. In Data Compression Conference (DCC'06) 2006 Mar 28 (pp. 143–152). IEEE.

[17] Guyader A, Fabre E, Guillemot C, Robert M. Joint source-channel turbo decoding of entropy-coded sources. IEEE Journal on Selected Areas in Communications. 2001 Sep; 19(9):1680–96.

[18] Zribi A, Zaibi S, Pyndiah R, Bouallègue A. Low-complexity joint source/channel turbo decoding of arithmetic codes with image transmission application. In Proceedings of the Data Compression Conference. 2009 Mar (p. 472).

[19] Zribi A, Pyndiah R, Zaibi S, Guilloud F, Bouallegue A. Low-complexity soft decoding of Huffman codes and iterative joint source channel decoding. IEEE Transactions on Communications. 2012 Jun; 60(6):1669–79.

[20] Zaibi S, Zribi A, Pyndiah R, Aloui N. Joint source/channel iterative arithmetic decoding with JPEG 2000 image transmission application. EURASIP Journal on Advances in Signal Processing. 2012 Dec 1; 2012(1):1–3.

[21] Natu A, Taubman D. Unequal protection of JPEG2000 code-streams in wireless channels. In Global Telecommunications Conference, 2002. GLOBECOM'02. IEEE 2002 Nov 17 (Vol. 1, pp. 534–538). IEEE.

[22] Nicholson D, Lamy-Bergot C, Naturel X, Poulliat C. JPEG 2000 backward compatible error protection with Reed-Solomon codes. IEEE Transactions on Consumer Electronics. 2003 Nov; 49(4):855–60.

[23] Huang CL, Liang S. Unequal error protection for MPEG-2 video transmission over wireless channels. Signal Processing: Image Communication. 2004 Jan; 19(1):67–79.

[24] Thomos N, Boulgouris NV, Strintzis MG. Optimized transmission of JPEG2000 streams over wireless channels. IEEE Transactions on Image Processing. 2006 Jan; 15(1):54–67.

[25] Agueh M, Diouris JF, Diop M, Devaux FO, De Vleeschouwer C, Macq B. Optimal JPWL forward error correction rate allocation for robust JPEG 2000 images and video streaming over mobile ad hoc networks. EURASIP Journal on Advances in Signal Processing. 2008 Dec 1; 2008(1):1–3.

[26] Khalek AA, Caramanis C, Heath RW. A cross-layer design for perceptual optimization of H. 264/SVC with unequal error protection. IEEE Journal on Selected Areas in Communications. 2012 Aug; 30(7):1157–71.

[27] Yu W, Safar Z, and Ray Liu KJ. Rate efficient wireless image transmission using MIMO-OFDM. Technical Report, Institute of Systems Research, University of Maryland, TR 2003-30, August 2003.

[28] Colda R, Perrine C, Cances JP, Vauzelle R, Palade T. Content-based image unequal error protection strategies for an open loop MIMO system. International Journal of Communications, Network and System Sciences. 2012; 5(1):72–80.

[29] Atzori L. Transmission of JPEG2000 images over wireless channels with unequal power distribution. IEEE Transactions on Consumer Electronics. 2003 Nov; 49(4):883–8.

[30] El-Tarhuni M, Hassan M, Sediq AB. A joint power allocation and adaptive channel coding scheme for image transmission over wireless channels. International Journal of Computer Networks & Communications. 2010 May; 2(3):85–99.

[31] Sabir MF, Sheikh HR, Heath RW, Bovik AC. A joint source-channel distortion model for JPEG compressed images. In International Conference on Image Processing, 2004 Oct 24 (Vol. 5, pp. 3249–3252).

[32] Ahmad Z, Worrall S, Kondoz A. Unequal power allocation for scalable video transmission over WiMAX. In IEEE International Conference on Multimedia and Expo 2008 Jun 23 (pp. 517–520). IEEE.

[33] Shayegannia M. JPEG2000 image transmission over frequency selective channels (Doctoral dissertation, Applied Science: School of Engineering Science).

[34] Sabir MF, Bovik AC, Heath RW. Unequal power allocation for JPEG transmission over MIMO systems. IEEE Transactions on Image Processing. 2010 Feb; 19(2):410–21.

[35] Liu Q, Liu S, Chen CW. A novel prioritized spatial multiplexing for MIMO wireless system with application to H. 264 SVC video. IEEE International Conference on Multimedia and Expo. 2010 Jul 19 (pp. 968–973).

[36] Jiang H, Wilford PA. A hierarchical modulation for upgrading digital broadcast systems. IEEE Transactions on Broadcasting. 2005 Jun; 51(2):223–9.

[37] Noh Y, Lee H, Lee W, Lee I. Design of unequal error protection for MIMO-OFDM systems with hierarchical signal constellations. Journal of Communications and Networks. 2007 Jun; 9(2):167–76.

[38] El-Tarhuni M, Hassan M, Bin Sediq A. A jointly optimized variable M-QAM and power allocation scheme for image transmission. Journal of Computer Networks and Communications. 2012 Feb 29(2012) :1–14; 2012.

[39] Sun Y, Xiong Z. Progressive image transmission over space-time coded OFDM-based MIMO systems with adaptive modulation. IEEE Transactions on Mobile Computing. 2006 Aug; 5(8):1016–28.

[40] Ohlmer E, Fettweis G. Link adaptation in linearly precoded closed-loop MIMO-OFDM systems with linear receivers. In 2009 IEEE International Conference on Communications. 2009 Jun 14 (pp. 1–6).

[41] Houas H, Fijalkow I, Baras C. Resources allocation for the transmission of scalable images on OFDM systems. In 2009 IEEE International Conference on Communications. 2009 Jun 14 (pp. 1–5). IEEE.

[42] Abot J, Olivier C, Perrine C, Pousset Y. A link adaptation scheme optimized for wireless JPEG 2000 transmission over realistic MIMO systems. Signal Processing: Image Communication. 2012 Nov 30;27(10):1066–78.

[43] Kambou S, Perrine C, Afif M, Pousset Y, Olivier C. Resource allocation based on cross-layer QoS-guaranteed scheduling for multi-service multi-user MIMO-OFDMA systems. Wireless Networks. 2016.

[44] Mhamdi M, Zribi A, Clency P, Pousset Y, Olivier C. Methodes de decodage a entrees ponderees pour la transmission d'images JPEG2000 Wireless sur des canaux fortement bruites. In GRETSI 2015.

[45] Y. Chartois, Y. Pousset, R. Vauzelle. A spatio-temporel radio channel characterization with 3D ray tracing propagation model in urban environment. Proceedings of the IEEE International Symposium on Personal, Indoor and Mobile Radio Communications. 2004.

[46] Pyndiah RM. Near-optimum decoding of product codes: block turbo codes. IEEE Transactions on Communications. 1998 Aug; 46(8):1003–10.

Chapter 11

Efficient Coding Tree Unit (CTU) Decision Method for Scalable High-Efficiency Video Coding (SHVC) Encoder

Chou-Chen Wang, Yuan-Shing Chang and Ke-Nung Huang

Additional information is available at the end of the chapter

http://dx.doi.org/10.5772/64847

Abstract

High-efficiency video coding (HEVC or H.265) is the latest video compression standard developed by the joint collaborative team on video coding (JCT-VC), finalized in 2013. HEVC can achieve an average bit rate decrease of 50% in comparison with H.264/AVC while still maintaining video quality. To upgrade the HEVC used in heterogeneous access networks, the JVT-VC has been approved scalable extension of HEVC (SHVC) in July 2014. The SHVC can achieve the highest coding efficiency but requires a very high computational complexity such that its real-time application is limited. To reduce the encoding complexity of SHVC, in this chapter, we employ the temporal-spatial and inter-layer correlations between base layer (BL) and enhancement layer (EL) to predict the best quadtree of coding tree unit (CTU) for quality SHVC. Due to exist a high correlation between layers, we utilize the coded information from the CTU quadtree in BL, including inter-layer intra/residual prediction and inter-layer motion parameter prediction, to predict the CTU quadtree in EL. Therefore, we develop an efficient CTU decision method by combing temporal-spatial searching order algorithm (TSSOA) in BL and a fast inter-layer searching algorithm (FILSA) in EL to speed up the encoding process of SHVC. The simulation results show that the proposed efficient CTU decision method can achieve an average time improving ratio (TIR) about 52–78% and 47–69% for low delay (LD) and random access (RA) configurations, respectively. It is clear that the proposed method can efficiently reduce the computational complexity of SHVC encoder with negligible loss of coding efficiency with various types of video sequences.

Keywords: video standards, video compression, high-efficiency video coding (HEVC), scalable high-efficiency video coding (SHVC), temporal-spatial correlation

1. Introduction

With the advanced researches of electronic technology, the panels of 4K × 2K (or 8K × 4K) high-resolution have become the main specification of large size digital TV in future. On the other hand, with rapid development of Internet and mobile devices, more and more people browse high-quality video content by smart phone or laptop, which greatly enrich people's lives. However, the currently state-of-the-art video coding standard H.264/advanced video coding (AVC) is difficult to support the video applications of high definition (HD) and ultrahigh definition (UHD) resolution. Therefore, a new video coding standard called high-efficiency video coding (HEVC) has been standardized by the Joint Collaborative Team on Video Coding (JCT-VC) jointly established by the ITU-T and ISO/IEC to satisfy the UHD requirement in January 2013, and the first edition of HEVC was approved as ITU-T H.265 and ISO/IEC 23008-2 by JCT-VC [1]. The goal of H.265/HEVC is to achieve roughly 50% bitrate reduction over H. 264/AVC while still maintaining video quality [2–6]. The HEVC adopts the quadtree-structured coding tree unit (CTU), and each CTU allows recursive splitting into four equal coding units (CUs) where each CU can have the prediction unit (PU) and transform unit (TU). The HEVC can achieve the highest coding efficiency but requires a very high computational complexity so that it is difficult to be used for real-time applications. On the other hand, traditional client-server video streaming has been unable to satisfy people's ever-growing demands for video applications using heterogeneous devices and networks including the Internet and mobile network nowadays. To overcome this problem, scalable video coding (SVC) can provide an attractive solution using a single bitstream to simultaneous serve various devices with different display resolution and image fidelities. Therefore, to upgrade the HEVC further used in heterogeneous access networks, the JVT-CT develops a scalable extension of HEVC (SHVC) and is finalized in July 2014 [7, 8]. SHVC mainly includes spatial scalability, temporal scalability and quality/signal-to-noise ratio (SNR) scalability. Based on the HEVC, the SHVC scheme supports multi-loop solutions by enabling different inter-layer prediction (ILP) mechanisms [9–12]. Although the SHVC can achieve the highest coding efficiency, it requires a higher computational complexity than HEVC standard. As a result, the very high encoding complexity of SHVC has become a main obstruction for the real-time services.

To reduce the computational complexity of the SHVC encoder, there are many fast methods with negligible losses of image quality have been proposed recently [13–17]. Tohidypour et al. reduced the coding complexity of spatial or SNR/quality/fidelity scalability in SHVC using an adaptive range search method according to statistical properties [13–16]. Bailleul et al. speeded up the encoding process in enhancement layer (EL) using a fast mode decision for SNR scalability in SHVC [16]. Qingyangl et al. also proposed a fast encoding method using maximum encoding depth based on the correlation between the base layer (BL) and EL for SNR scalability in SHVC encoder and greatly reduce encoding time in BL and EL, respectively [17]. Although these methods can reduce the complexity of the encoding process for SHVC in different level with different complexity calculation method, their methods are used only in the correlation of CU depth and modes existing in BL and EL. So, the complexity of the whole encoder still has the room to be further reduced.

To overcome the drawback of huge encoding computation in SHVC, we firstly propose a temporal-spatial searching order algorithm (TSSOA) to speed up the encoding procedure in BL. Second, we develop a fast inter-layer searching algorithm (FILSA) in EL to predict the CTU quadtree structure. There are five encoded temporal-spatial causal neighbouring CTUs are chosen to be predicted by the TSSOA in BL, which shows the searching priority order according to the correlation values which are determined by values of statistic. Due to the less data information and high correlation existing in residual image in EL, thus only three encoded inter-layer causal neighbouring CTUs are chosen to be predicted by the FILSA in EL.

2. SHVC background

HEVC can greatly improve coding efficiency by adopting hierarchical structures of CU, PU and TU. The CU depths can be split by coding quadtree structure of four level, and the CU size can vary from largest CU (LCU: 64 × 64) to the smallest CU (SCU: 8 × 8). The CTU is the largest CU. During the encoding process, each CTU block of HEVC can be split into four equally sized blocks according to inter/intra-prediction in rate-distortion optimization (RDO) sense. At each depth level (CU size), HEVC performs motion estimation and compensation (ME/MC), transforms and quantization with different size. The PU module is the basic unit used for carrying the information related to the prediction processes, and the TU can be split by residual quadtree (RQT) at maximally three level depths which vary from 32 × 32 to 4 × 4 pixels. The relationship of hierarchical CU, PU and TU coding structure of HEVC is shown in **Figure 1** [2–6].

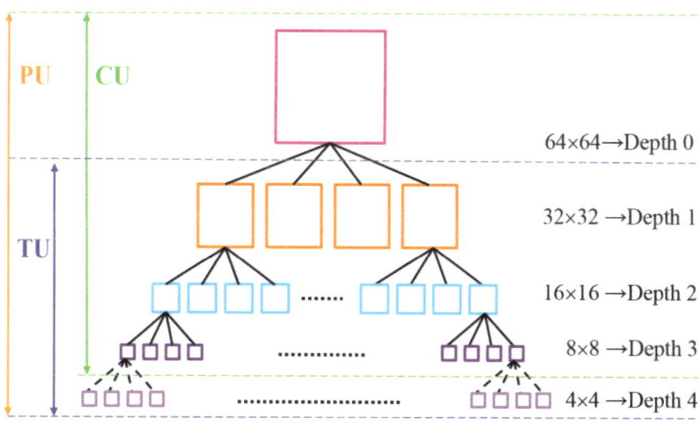

Figure 1. The relationship of hierarchical CU, PU and TU coding structure of HEVC [6].

In general, intra-coded CUs have only two PU partition types including 2N × 2N and N × N but inter-coded CUs have eight PU types including symmetric blocks (2N × 2N, 2N × N, N × 2N, N × N) and asymmetric blocks (2N × nU, 2N × nD, nL × 2N, nR × 2N) [4]. When only using symmetric PU blocks, H.265/HEVC encoder tests seven different partition sizes including SKIP, inter 2N × 2N, inter 2N × N, inter N × 2N, inter N × N, intra 2N × 2N and intra N × N for inter-slice as shown in **Figure 2**. The rate distortion costs (RDcost) have to be calculated by performing the PUs and TUs to select the optimal partition mode under all partition modes for each CU size. Since all the PUs and available TUs have to be exhaustively searched by rate-distortion optimization (RDO) process for an LCU, H.265/HEVC dramatically increased computational complexity compared with H.264/AVC [4, 5]. The optimization of the block mode decision procedure will result in the high computational complexity and limit the use of HEVC encoders in real-time applications. Since the coding procedure for HEVC is very complex, the coding procedure for SHVC is even more complex due to an extension of HEVC.

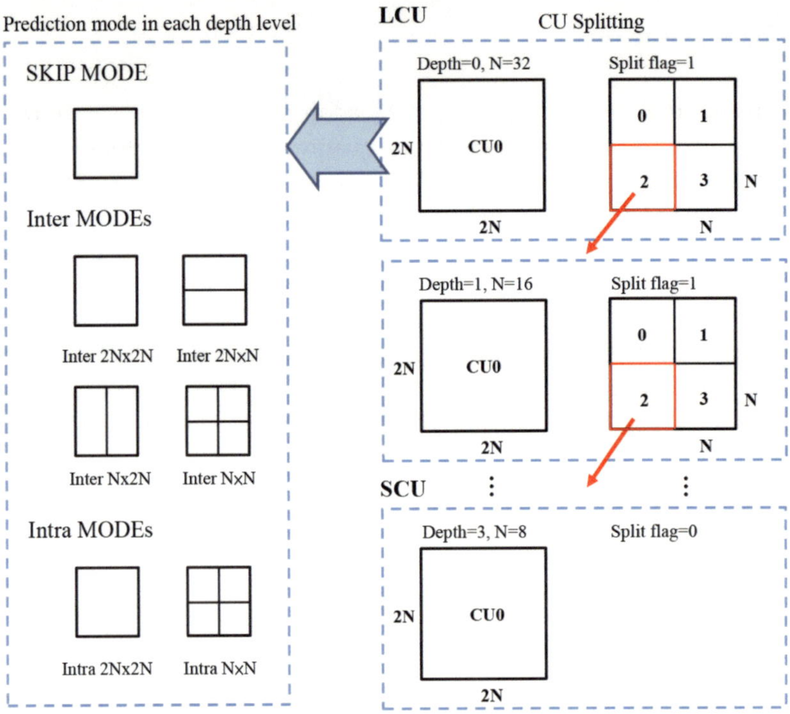

Figure 2. The architecture of quadtree structured CUs and PU partitioning [6].

Based on the HEVC, the SHVC scheme supports both single-loop and multi-loop solutions by enabling different inter-layer prediction (ILP) mechanisms [18, 19]. A typical architecture of two-layer SHVC encoder is shown in **Figure 3**. However, SHVC encoder allows one BL and more than one EL. **Figure 3** illustrates how the decoded BL picture is used for prediction in EL coding in a two-layer SHVC encoder. The input video of BL can be encoded or decoded with HEVC coding tools. The decoded picture of BL is processed by the ILP module before being sent to the decoded picture buffer (DPB) of EL. For the EL, the BL decoded picture which obtained by ILP is called as the inter-layer reference (ILR) picture. The ILP module performs inter-layer intra/residual prediction and inter-layer motion parameter prediction by upsampling calculations. Furthermore, the discrete cosine transform/quantization (DCT/Q) and inverse DCT/inverse quantization (IDCT/IQ) modules are further applied to inter-layer prediction residues for better energy compaction. The parameters used for such EL, shown as ILP information in **Figure 3**, are multiplexed together with BL and EL bitstreams to form an SHVC bitstream. For spatial scalability, the input high-resolution video sequence should be down-sampled to get the low-resolution video sequence, but for SNR scalability, BL and EL layer uses the same resolution video sequence. Therefore, there are larger redundancies between different layers for quality (SNR) scalability. From the Reference [18], we can find that the encoding complexity of HEVC is higher than that of H.264/AVC encoder. Therefore, the computational burden of SHVC encoder is expected to be several times more than HEVC encoder. Nowadays, it is an important topic to study how to reduce the computational complexity of SHVC to achieve real-time applications.

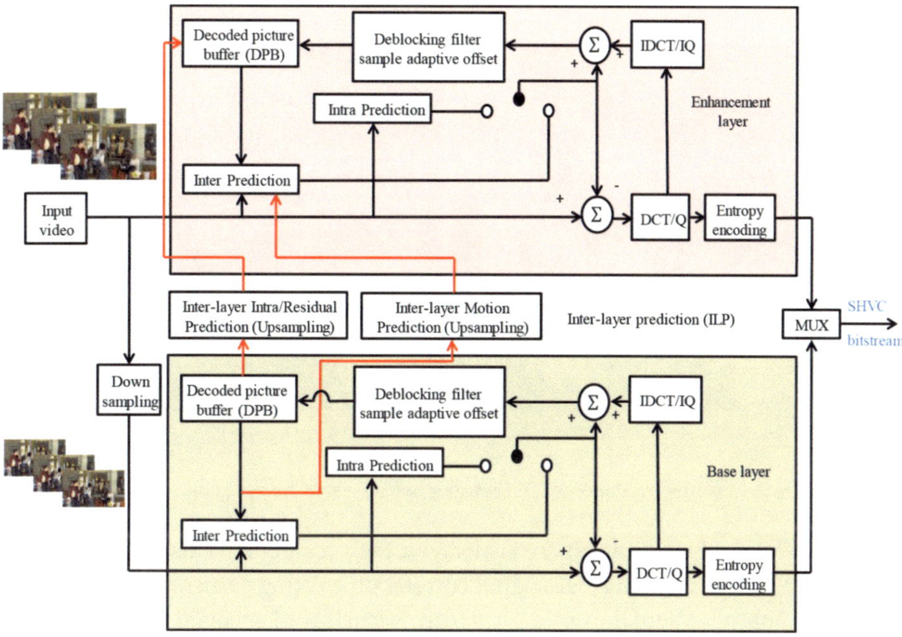

Figure 3. A typical architecture of two-layer SHVC encoder.

3. Proposed CTU decision method

Each layer encoding process in SHVC can be considered similar with HEVC, except for the enhancement layers using inter-layer prediction techniques. However, the computational complexity of the HEVC encoder increases dramatically due to its recursive quadtree representation to find the best CTU partition. Therefore, we can know that the computational complexity of SHVC encoder is more than HEVC encoder. Thus, we utilize the temporal-spatial correlation prediction in BL based on HEVC and inter-layer correlation prediction in EL to develop an efficient CTU decision method to speed up SHVC encoding process.

3.1. Temporal-spatial correlation in BL

As the frame rate highly increasing, the successive two frames have a stronger temporal-spatial correlation. **Figure 4** shows two certain frames of the test sequence encoded using low-delay (LD) configuration in BL by the SHVC reference software (SHM 6.0) [21]. As shown in **Figure 4**, the quadtree structures of the CTU in the current frame, for example **Figure 4** (A_0) and 4(A'_0), are the same as or similar to the split quadtree structures of the temporally co-located coded CTUs of the previous frame shown in **Figure 4**. On the other hand, there are also the same as or similar to the split structures of the spatial four neighbour CTUs in the current frame, for example **Figure 4**(B–E). **Figure 4** shows the corresponding five causal encoded neighbouring CTUs (A–E) of the current CTU(X) in the temporal-spatial direction.

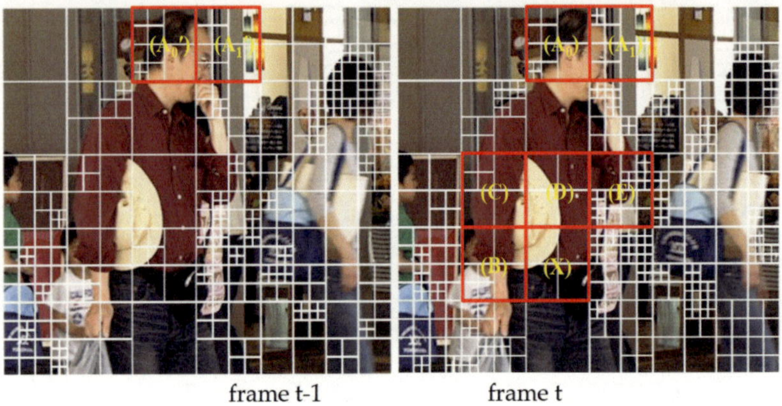

Figure 4. Examples of the quadtree structures of CTU between two successive frames in BL.

As observed and described above, there is always a high correlation existing encoded frames in BL. In order to show the temporal-spatial correlation existing successive frames in BL, we made statistical analysis about the optimal quadtree structure of encoded CTU in BLs. **Figure 5** shows the corresponding five causal encoded neighbouring CTUs (B_A~B_E) of the current CTU(X) in the temporal-spatial direction in BL, respectively.

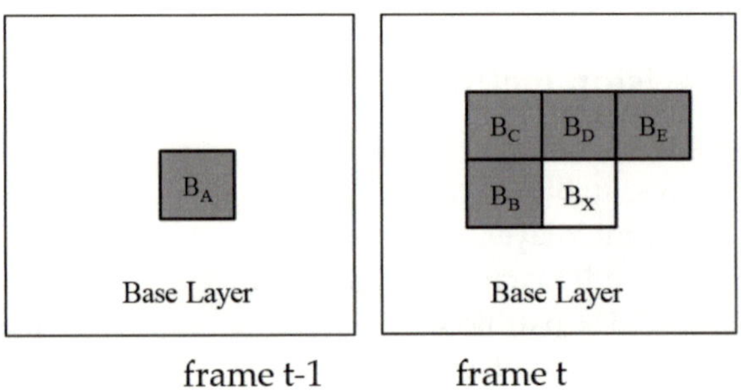

Figure 5. Corresponding five causal encoded neighbouring CTUs of the current CTU(X) in BL.

http://dx.doi.org/10.5772/64847

Table 1 shows the probability distribution of the same CTU quadtree between temporal-spatial neighbouring and current CTU in BL using quantization parameter QP_{BL} = 32 and 100 frames in the SHM 6.0. From **Table 1**, we can find that there is a high temporal-spatial correlation of quadtree exists between two successive frames. Thus, when encoding the current frame in BL, the current CTU can be predicted through the split quadtree structure of the co-located CTU in the reference frame and the split quadtree structure of the spatial four already encoded neighbouring CTUs in the current frame.

Sequence	$P(B_A = B_X)$%	$P(B_B = B_X)$%	$P(B_C = B_X)$%	$P(B_D = B_X)$%	$P(B_E = B_X)$%
Vidyo1	77.15	73.03	56.01	61.39	55.63
Vidyo3	76.07	70.09	55.59	61.59	55.02
Vidyo4	72.44	67.34	53.06	58.76	52.82
Kimono	33.71	30.55	22.49	27.51	22.13
ParkScene	35.80	36.81	29.67	34.60	29.10
Basketball	46.01	49.42	39.68	43.38	40.55
Cactus	52.69	48.57	39.69	45.35	40.43
BQTerrace	45.85	45.57	35.42	40.45	35.79
Average	**54.97**	**52.92**	**41.45**	**46.63**	**41.43**

Table 1. The probability distribution of the same CTU quadtree between temporal-spatial neighbouring and current CTU using QP_{BL} = 32.

3.2. Inter-layer correlation between BL and EL

As described in Section 2, there is always a strong inter-layer correlation when adopting layer-based encoding structure. In the same situation for SHVC, we can expect that there exists a high inter-layer correlation between BL and EL when using quality scalability configuration, which BL and ELs have the same resolution with different QP. In order to find the inter-layer correlation between BL and EL, we statistically analyse the split quadtree structures of encoded CTU in BL and EL with different video sequences. In this experiment, we find that there exists a high inter-layer correlation between BL and EL. The results we got are similar to temporal-spatial correlation in BL. **Figure 6** shows the examples of the quadtree structures of CTU between BL and EL in the same frame. As shown in **Figure 6**, the quadtree structures of the CTU in the BL, for example **Figure 6**(X_0) and (X_1), are the same as or similar to the split quadtree structures of the corresponding co-located coded CTUs, **Figure 6** (X'_0) and (X'_1) in the EL. **Figure 7** shows the corresponding six causal encoded neighbouring CTUs (E'_X, E_B~E_E) and CTU(B_A) of the current CTU(X) in the temporal-spatial direction in EL and in the inter-layer between EL and BL, respectively.

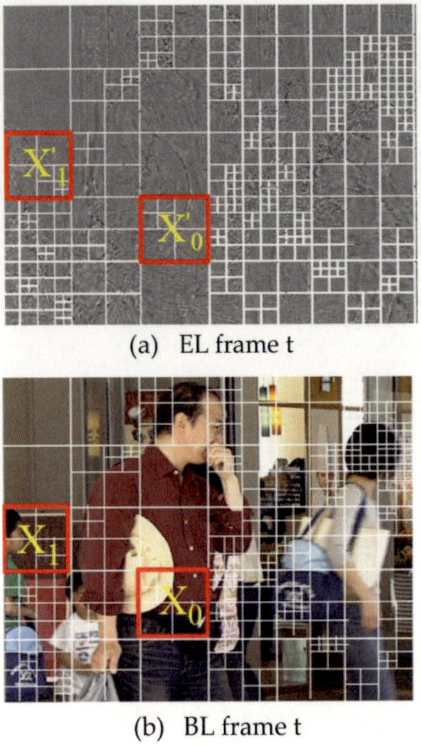

Figure 6. Examples of the quadtree structures of CTU between BL and EL in the same frame.

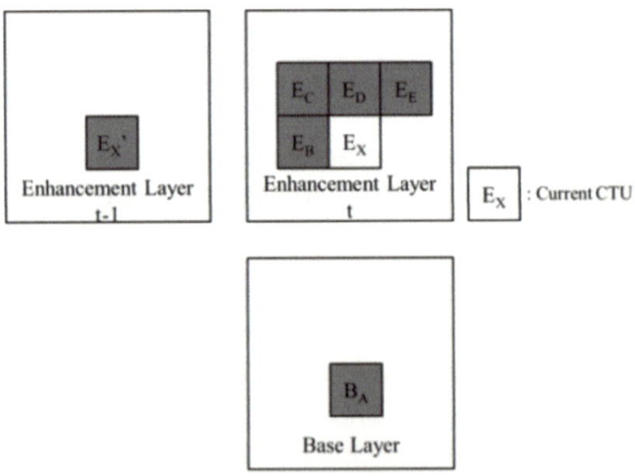

Figure 7. Example of the corresponding six causal encoded neighbouring CTU between BL and EL.

In the same procedure as BL, to show the inter-layer correlation existing in the same frame between BL and EL, we made statistical analysis about the optimal quadtree structure of encoded CTU between EL and BL. In addition, we also made statistical analysis for the temporal-spatial correlation existing successive frames in EL at the same time. **Table 2** shows the probability distribution of the same CTU quadtree between BL and EL using $QP_{(BL,\ EL)} = QP_{(32,\ 28)}$ in the SHM 6.0. In the same situation, we can find that there is a high inter-layer correlation exists between BL and EL. Since there is a high correlation between BL and EL, the encoded CTU quadtree of the BL frames can be utilized to speed up the process of selecting the best predicted CTU quadtree for the corresponding EL frames [20]. Besides, the already encoded neighbouring CTUs in the EL are valuable for predicting the quadtree of the current CTU. Therefore, the temporal-spatial neighbouring encoded CTUs in the EL and the inter-layer corresponding encoded CTU in the BL are used to predict the current CTU in EL. From **Table 2**, we can find that there is a higher inter-layer correlation exists between BL and EL except for temporal-spatial correlation in EL. In addition, we also find that the probability distributions of CTU(E_c), CTU(E_E) and CTU(E'_X) are almost the same and less than the others. For simplicity, when encoding the current frame in EL, the current CTU(X) can be interlayer predicted by the split quadtree structure of CTU in BL and then predicted through the split quadtree structure of the two split structure of the spatial already encoded neighbouring CTUs in EL.

Sequence	$P(B_A = E_X)$%	$P(E_B = E_X)$%	$P(E_C = E_X)$%	$P(E_D = E_X)$%	$P(E_E = E_X)$%	$P(E_{X'} = E_X)$%
Vidyo1	74.88	60.41	44.10	51.54	45.23	48.37
Vidyo3	74.03	61.53	44.50	51.74	44.23	46.84
Vidyo4	75.59	63.57	45.89	51.31	45.06	49.19
Kimono	32.52	32.18	24.06	27.95	23.38	26.58
ParkScene	41.45	27.53	21.56	26.35	19.77	23.67
Basketball	53.44	47.70	33.22	37.08	32.24	37.73
Cactus	54.31	43.69	35.40	41.09	35.93	36.51
BQTerrace	39.30	27.87	20.08	23.27	21.00	22.71
Average	**55.69**	**45.56**	**33.60**	**38.79**	**33.35**	**36.45**

Table 2. The probability distribution of the same CTU quadtree between inter-layer neighbouring and current CTU using $QP_{(BL,\ EL)} = QP_{(32,\ 28)}$.

3.3. Fast SHVC encoder using efficient CTU decision

3.3.1 Temporal-spatial searching order algorithm (TSSOA)

To speed up the encoding process of SHVC in BL, we propose a temporal-spatial searching order algorithm (TSSOA) which utilizes the characteristics of natural video sequence existing strongly temporal and spatial correlation. In this work, the five causal neighbouring encoded split quadtree structures of CTUs shown in **Figure 5**, on temporal-spatial direction, are firstly chosen as candidates for the current CTU encoding in BL. **Figure 8** shows the search priority order according to the sorted correlation values determined by experiments from **Table 1**. Block 1 represents the temporal neighbour, and blocks 2–5 denote spatial neighbours in horizontal, vertical, 45 and 135 diagonal directions. To determine whether a candidate split structure of the CTU is good enough for the current CTU, we check compute the RD cost using the predicted split structure. After the candidate split structure (one of blocks 1–5) is found, we check whether it is good enough for the current CTU by comparing its RD cost with a threshold (Thr). If it is less than the threshold, the candidate is good enough for the current CTU. Otherwise, it implies that the temporal-spatial correlation is low and a full recursive process is needed to find the optimal split quadtree structure of the current CTU.

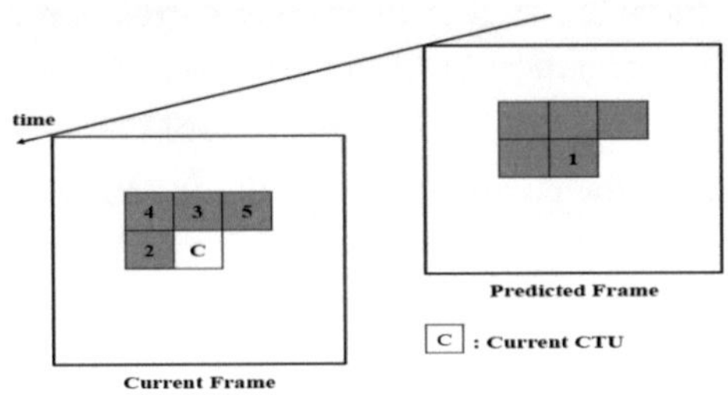

Figure 8. The search priority order.

The flow chart of the proposed TSSOA is shown in **Figure 9**.

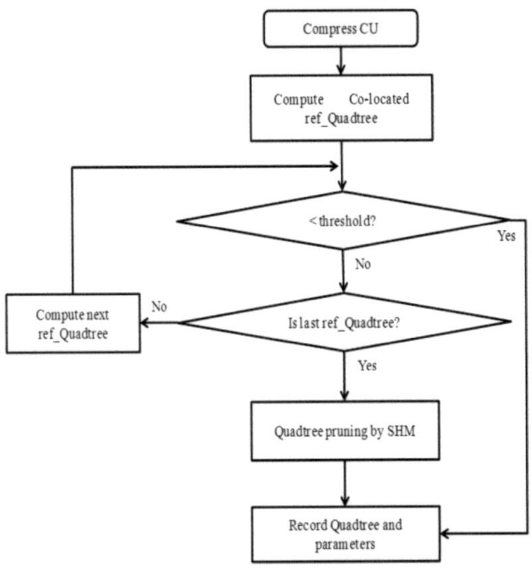

Figure 9. The flow chart of the proposed TSSOA.

The proposed TSSOA in the fast encoding for SHVC can be summarized as follows:

Step 1. Set a threshold (Thr) value according to QP.

Step 2. Encode the BL of SHVC using TSSOA. If the RDcost computed by priority order 1 is less than Thr, go to step 6. Otherwise, go to step 3.

Step 3. If it is last neighbouring CTU, go to step 5. Otherwise, go to step 4.

Step 4. Compute RDcost of next neighbouring CTU in the priority order (2–5), if the RDcost less than Thr, go to step 6. Otherwise, go to step 3.

Step 5. Use the original RDO module to prune the best CTU quadtree of the current CTU.

Step 6. Record the best CTU quadtree and corresponding parameters of BL.

3.3.2. Fast inter-layer searching algorithm (FILSA)

For fast EL encoding, we use the fast inter-layer searching algorithm (FILSA) between BL and EL to predict the split quadtree structure of CTU for the current CTU in EL. Due to the less data information and very high correlation existing in residual image in EL, thus only three causal neighbouring split quadtree structure of CTUs shown in **Figure 10** are chosen as the candidates. This is because we find that there is a highest inter-layer correlation existing CTU(B_A), CTU(E_B) and CTU(E_D). In other words, we eliminate CTU(E_C), CTU(E_E) and CTU($E_{X'}$) as candidates since their probability distributions are almost the same and less than the others. Therefore, when encoding the current frame in EL by FILSA, the current CTU(X) can be interlayer predicted by the split quadtree structure of CTU in BL and then predicted through the two split quadtree structure of the spatial already encoded neighbouring CTUs in EL. The FILSA determines that split quadtree structure of CTUs is the best candidate for the current CTU in EL, and it computes the RD costs from the predicted split quadtree of CTUs and selects the minimum RD cost as the best split quadtree of CTU(E_X). From our experiments, we can verify the encoding performance with negligible decrease when only utilizes three candidates as shown in **Figure 10**.

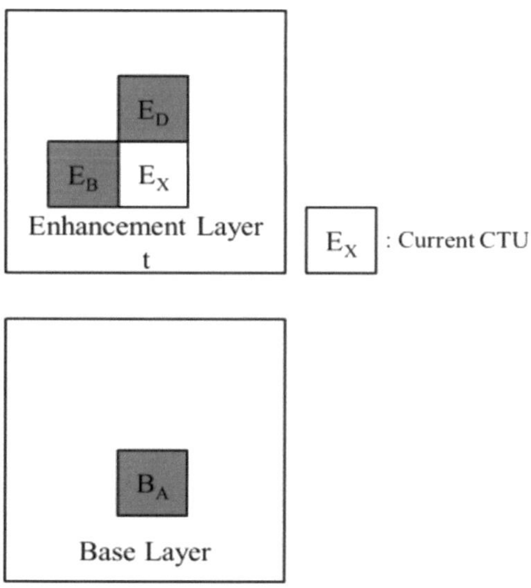

Figure 10. Three causal neighbouring split quadtree structure of CTUs as candidates.

3.3.3. Fast SHVC encoder

Based on the proposed TSSOA and FILSA in BL and EL encoding procedure, respectively, we can develop a fast SHVC encoder using efficient CTU decisions. First, we utilize the TSSOA to speed up the encoding procedure in BL. Second, we employ the FILSA to predict the CTU quadtree structure in ELs. Therefore, we can implement an early termination (ET) for split quadtree search using an efficient CTU decision method based on combining the proposed TSSOA and FILSA. The proposed SHVC encoder does not need to go through all the modes, thus significantly reducing the computational complexity. The flow chart of the proposed fast SHVC encoder is shown in **Figure 11**.

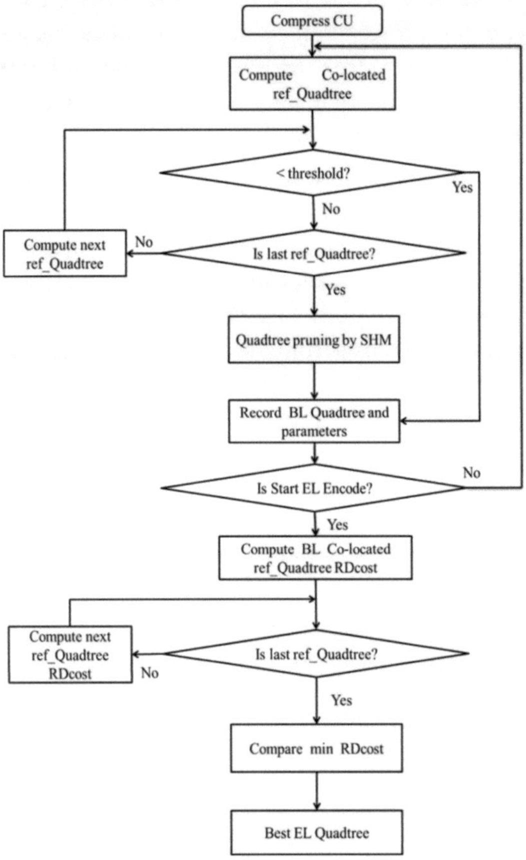

Figure 11. The flow chart of the proposed fast SHVC encoder.

4. Simulation results and discussion

For the performance evaluation, we assess the total execution time of the proposed method in comparison with those of the SHM 6.0 [21] in order to confirm the reduction in computational complexity. The system hardware is Intel (R) Core(TW) CPU i5-3350P @ 3.10 GHz, 8.0 GB memory, and Window XP 64-bit O/S. Additional details of the encoding environment are described in **Table 3**.

Test sequences	Class A (2560 × 1600): Traffic
	Class B (1920 × 1080): Kimono, ParkScene, Cactus, BasketballDrive and BQTerrace
	Class C (832 × 480): BasketballDrill, BQMall, PartyScene
Total frames	100 frames
Quantization parameter $QP_{(BL, EL)}$	(22, 20), (32, 28), (36, 32) and (40, 36)
Software	SHM 6.0
Scenario	Low delay (LD), random access (RA)

Table 3. Test conditions and software reference configurations.

The performance of our proposed complexity reduction method is compared with that of the unmodified SHVC encoder in terms of encoding time, impact on bitrate and peak signal-to-noise ratio of Y component (PSNRY). Note that for each video sequence, the encoding time is reported for the total time (BL + EL). The coding performance is evaluated based on ΔBitrate, ΔPSNRY and time improving ratio (TIR), respectively, which are defined in Eqs. (1–3) and described as follows:

$$\Delta\text{Bitrate} = \frac{\text{Bitrate}_{\text{proposed}} - \text{Bitrate}_{\text{SHM6.0}}}{\text{Bitrate}_{\text{SHM6.0}}} \times 100\%, \tag{1}$$

where the ratio of encoding bitrate reduction is represented by ΔBitrate, and $\text{Bitrate}_{\text{proposed}}$ and $\text{Bitrate}_{\text{SHM 6.0}}$ represent the encoding bitrate of the proposed method and the conventional method based on the SHM 6.0 reference software, respectively.

$$\Delta\text{PSNRY} = \text{PSNRY}_{\text{proposed}} - \text{PSNRY}_{\text{HM6.0}} \tag{2}$$

where ΔPSNRY is the ratio of encoding quality reduction, and $\text{PSNRY}_{\text{proposed}}$ and $\text{PSNRY}_{\text{HM 6.0}}$ represent the proposed method and the SHM 6.0, respectively.

$$\text{TIR} = \frac{\text{TIME}_{\text{proposed}} - \text{TIME}_{\text{SHM6.0}}}{\text{TIME}_{\text{SHM6.0}}} \times 100\% \tag{3}$$

where TIR is the ratio of encoding time reduction, and $\text{TIME}_{\text{proposed}}$ and $\text{TIME}_{\text{SHM 6.0}}$ represent the proposed method and the SHM 6.0, respectively. Encoding time is usually used to measure the computational complexity of the SHVC encoder, and thus, a TIR measurement is adopted to assess our proposed fast method.

The value of the threshold (Thr) for TSSOA is an important parameter in BL encoding, which affects the coding performance of the proposed algorithm. A lower value of means that more RDOs are performed to prune the best CTU quadtree, and thus, more time is spent to encode them and a closer quality to that of SHM 6.0 will be obtained. However, since the proposed fast algorithm is very desirable for achieving a real-time implementation of SHVC encoder, we focus on the improvement performance of encoding time. We have conducted several experiments with different values of Thr to study the effect of varying t on the resulting TIR for test sequences shown in **Table 3**. **Figure 12** shows the average curve of TIR vs. Thr_{QP} for $QP_{BL} = 32$ which indicates that the TIR is approximately the same for all ≥ 350,000. From our experiment results, we find that there are high dependent relationships existing resulting curves with various QPs. Since different QP_{BL}s could yield different average curves for TIR vs. Thr_{QP}, the thresholds are expected to be QP-dependent. Furthermore, it can be easily observed form our intensive experiments that there is a linear relationship between the threshold values and the various QP_{BL} values. To mathematically model this relationship which essentially performs polynomial fitting to approximate a linear function, a linear regress model is used to derive the formula as [20]

$$Thr_{QP} = (\lambda_{QP} - \lambda_{32}) \times 4350 + 350{,}000 \tag{4}$$

where $\lambda = 0.4845 \times 2^{(QP-12)/3}$ is defined in SHVC specification [5].

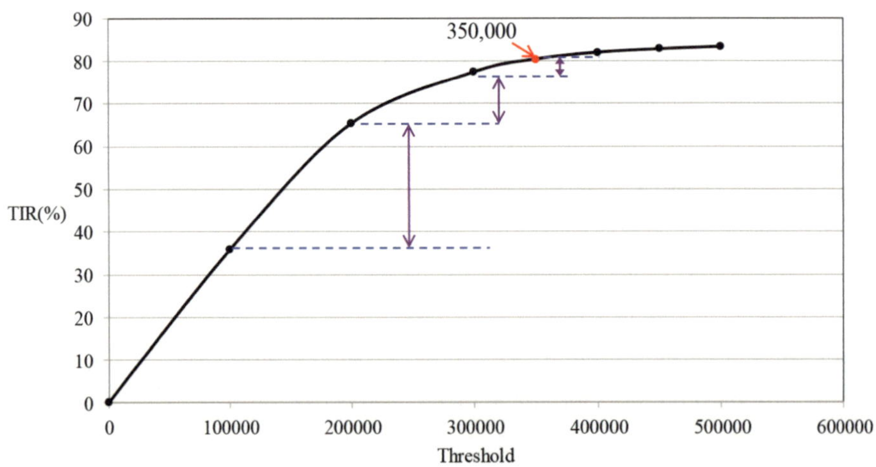

Figure 12. The average curve of TIR vs. Thr_{QP} for $QP_{BL} = 32$.

Tables 4–7 tabulate the performances obtained by testing the SHM 6.0 and the proposed method with different quantization parameter pairs when uses the random access (RA) and LD scenarios, separately. The simulation results show that the proposed algorithm can reduce the computational complexity of CTU quadtree pruning of SHVC about 34~71% when compared to SHM 6.0. From **Tables 4–7**, we find that the proposed fast SHVC encoder can further achieve an average TIR about 47~78%. In addition, we can observe that the encoding time improving is more efficient when the value of QP pairs increases. This is because the quantization error is too large that results in the lower temporal-spatial and inter-layer correlation. Furthermore, as can be seen in **Tables 4–7**, they also show that the TIR of CU module for Kimono and BasketballDrive sequences tested by different methods with different QP values has higher encoding reduction improvement. This is because backgrounds of these two sequences are slowly changed and the movements are rather homogenous.

$QP_{(22, 20)}$	RA			LD		
Sequence	**Proposed/SHM 6.0**			**Proposed/SHM 6.0**		
	ΔBitrate (%)	**ΔPSNRY (dB)**	**TIR (%)**	**ΔBitrate (%)**	**ΔPSNRY (dB)**	**TIR (%)**
Traffic	2.95	−0.17	−29.13	2.19	−0.13	−36.13
Kimono	0.90	−0.12	−62.27	0.76	−0.09	−64.45
ParkScene	1.04	−0.14	−42.41	0.92	−0.11	−46.62
Cactus	1.49	−0.15	−45.33	1.27	−0.09	−45.10
BasketballDrive	2.78	−0.18	−46.81	2.48	−0.15	−63.06
BQTerrace	2.09	−0.11	−42.24	1.86	−0.10	−50.62
BasketballDrill	0.34	−0.13	−50.64	0.28	−0.10	−55.63
BQMall	0.81	−0.11	−50.37	0.74	−0.10	−51.39
PartyScene	0.47	−0.13	−50.70	0.32	−0.09	−52.17
Average	**1.93**	**−0.14**	**−46.66**	**1.21**	**−0.11**	**−51.68**

Table 4. Comparison of the proposed method with SHM 6.0 using $QP_{(22, 20)}$.

$QP_{(32, 28)}$	RA			LD		
Sequence	**Proposed/ SHM 6.0**			**Proposed/ SHM 6.0**		
	ΔBitrate (%)	**ΔPSNRY (dB)**	**TIR (%)**	**ΔBitrate (%)**	**ΔPSNRY (dB)**	**TIR (%)**
Traffic	6.64	−0.21	−43.06	6.18	−0.17	−65.18
Kimono	1.87	−0.13	−71.26	1.38	−0.11	−78.61
ParkScene	3.62	−0.15	−62.06	3.34	−0.13	−56.95
Cactus	5.69	−0.17	−57.69	5.07	−0.15	−70.06
BQTerrace	5.96	−0.16	−56.64	5.46	−0.13	−58.60
Basketball	3.10	−0.13	−60.03	2.82	−0.11	−70.77
BQMall	2.81	−0.14	−58.96	2.74	−0.12	−64.49
PartyScene	2.21	−0.15	−58.52	1.97	−0.13	−44.06
Average	**4.28**	**−0.16**	**−59.96**	**3.88**	**−0.13**	**−65.18**

Table 5. Comparison of the proposed method with SHM 6.0 using $QP_{(32, 28)}$.

$QP_{(36, 32)}$	RA			LD		
Sequence	**Proposed/SHM 6.0**			**Proposed/SHM 6.0**		
	ΔBitrate (%)	**ΔPSNRY (dB)**	**TIR (%)**	**ΔBitrate (%)**	**ΔPSNRY (dB)**	**TIR (%)**
Traffic	5.98	−0.17	−52.32	5.71	−0.14	−65.77
Kimono	3.84	−0.11	−78.23	3.46	−0.09	−83.23
ParkScene	4.27	−0.12	−66.29	3.93	−0.10	−75.21
Cactus	5.14	−0.14	−65.36	4.83	−0.11	−66.22
BasketballDrive	7.53	−0.16	−76.68	7.21	−0.13	−81.00
BQTerrace	5.89	−0.11	−63.88	5.27	−0.09	−73.99
BasketballDrill	2.70	−0.13	−65.70	2.38	−0.13	−82.49
BQMall	3.87	−0.14	−58.77	3.40	−0.11	−66.90
PartyScene	4.02	−0.12	−61.34	3.77	−0.10	−67.13
Average	**5.14**	**−0.13**	**−65.73**	**4.44**	**−0.11**	**−73.55**

Table 6. Comparison of the proposed method with SHM 6.0 using $QP_{(36, 32)}$.

$QP_{(40, 36)}$	RA			LD		
Sequence	**Proposed/SHM 6.0**			**Proposed/SHM 6.0**		
	ΔBitrate (%)	**ΔPSNRY (dB)**	**TIR (%)**	**ΔBitrate (%)**	**ΔPSNRY (dB)**	**TIR (%)**
Traffic	8.04	−0.18	−63.00	7.13	−0.14	−77.74
Kimono	5.06	−0.14	−80.04	4.51	−0.12	−85.82
ParkScene	5.12	−0.13	−71.59	4.37	−0.11	−79.71
Cactus	7.33	−0.15	−72.93	5.88	−0.12	−78.36
BasketballDrive	8.26	−0.16	−75.92	7.43	−0.14	−82.27
BQTerrace	7.21	−0.15	−65.76	6.14	−0.15	−75.33
BasketballDrill	4.15	−0.14	−68.43	3.72	−0.13	−76.01
BQMall	4.86	−0.15	−60.40	4.06	−0.13	−69.86
PartyScene	4.22	−0.13	−66.15	3.49	−0.11	−74.52
Average	**6.03**	**−0.15**	**−69.36**	**5.19**	**−0.13**	**−77.74**

Table 7. Comparison of the proposed method with SHM 6.0 using $QP_{(40, 36)}$.

In summary, the results show the superiority of our proposed fast efficient CTU decision including TSSOA and FILSA over the state-of-the-art unmodified SHVC method.

5. Conclusions

In this chapter, we proposed a fast encoding method using temporal-spatial correlation and inter-layer correlation to reduce the encoding complexity for quality SHVC. In our scheme, the split quadtree information of the BL is utilized to facilitate the prediction of split CTU quadtree selection process in the ELs by avoiding redundant computations. Performance evaluations show that our approach results in significant SHVC coding complexity reduction (up to 77.74%, on average) while minimally hampering the overall bitrate.

Author details

Chou-Chen Wang*, Yuan-Shing Chang and Ke-Nung Huang

*Address all correspondence to: chchwang@isu.edu.tw

Department of Electronic Engineering, I-Shou University, Kaohsiung, Taiwan

References

[1] High Efficiency Video Coding. Rec. ITU-T H.265 and ISO/IEC 23008-2, 2013 file:///C:/Users/chchwang/Downloads/T-REC-H.265-201304-S!!PDF-E.pdf.

[2] Advanced Video Coding for Generic Audiovisual Services. ITU-T Rec. H.264 and ISO/IEC 14496 10, ITU-T and ISO/IEC, 2010 file:///C:/Users/chchwang/Downloads/T-REC-H.264-201201-S!!PDF-E.pdf.

[3] Joint Call for Proposals on Video Compression Technology. Kyoto, Japan, Document VCEG-AM91 of ITU-T Q6/16 and N1113 of JTC1/SC29/WG11, 2010 http://www.itu.int/oth/T4601000002/en.

[4] J. Ohm, W. J. Han and T. Wiegand, "Overview of the High Efficiency Video Coding (HEVC) Standard," IEEE Transactions on Circuits and Systems for Video Technology, vol. 22, no. 12, pp. 1649–1668, 2012.

[5] B. Bross, W. J. Han, J. R. Ohm, G. J. Sullivan and T. Weingand, "High Efficiency Video Coding (HEVC) Text Specification Draft 8," JCT-VC Document, JCTVC-J1003, 2012 http://phenix.it-sudparis.eu/jct/doc_end_user/current_document.php?id=6465.

[6] C. C. Wang, C. W. Tung and J. W. Wang, "An Effective Transform Unit Size Decision Method for High Efficiency Video Coding," Mathematical Problems in Engineering, vol. 2014, pp. 1–10, 2014.

[7] J. Boyce et al., Draft High Efficiency Video Coding (HEVC) Version 2, Combined Format Range Extensions (RExt), Scalability (SHVC), and Multi-View (MV-HEVC) Extensions, Document JCTVC-R1013_v6, Sapporo, Japan, 2014 http://phenix.int-evry.fr/jct/doc_end_user/current_document.php?id=9466.

[8] Reference Model for Mixed and Augmented Reality Defines Architecture and Terminology for MAR Applications (DOCX). MPEG. 2014-07-11. Retrieved 2014-07-26 http://mpeg.chiariglione.org/sites/default/files/files/meetings/docs/w14537_0.docx.

[9] G. J. Sullivan et al., "Standardized Extensions of High Efficiency Video Coding (HEVC)," IEEE Journal of Selected Topics in Signal Processing, vol. 7, no. 6, pp. 1001–1016, 2013.

[10] D. K. Kwon, M. Budagavi and M. Zhou, "Multi-Loop Scalable Video Codec Based on High Efficiency Video Coding (HEVC)," in Proceedings of the IEEE ICASSP 2013, pp. 1749–1753, 2013.

[11] J. Chen, J. Boyce, Y. Ye and M. M. Hannuksela, "Scalable High Efficiency Video Coding Draft 3," in Joint Collaborative Team on Video Coding (JCT-VC) Document JCTVC-N1008, 14th Meeting, Vienna, Austria, 2013.

[12] J. Boyce, Y. Ye, J. Chen and A. K. Ramasubramonian, "Overview of SHVC: Scalable Extensions of the High Efficiency Video Coding Standard," IEEE Transactions on Circuits and Systems for Video Technology, vol. 26, no. 1, pp. 20–34, 2015.

[13] H. R. Tohidypour, M. T. Pourazad and P. Nasiopoulos, "Adaptive search range method for spatial scalable HEVC," IEEE International Conference on Consumer Electronics (ICCE), pp. 191–192, 2014.

[14] H. R. Tohidypour, M. T. Pourazad and P. Nasiopoulos, "Content Adaptive Complexity Reduction Scheme for Quality/Fidelity Scalable HEVC," International Conference on Acoustics, Speech, and Signal Processing (ICASSP), pp. 1744–1748, Vancouver, Canada, May 2013.

[15] H. R. Tohidypour, H. R. Bashashati, M. T. Pourazad and P. Nasiopoulos, "Fast mode assignment for quality scalable extension of the high efficiency video coding (HEVC) standard: a Bayesian approach", Proceedings of the 6th Balkan Conference in Informatics (BCI), pp. 61-65, Thessaloniki, Greece, Sept, 2013.

[16] R. Bailleul, J. De Cock and R. Van De Walle, "Fast Mode Decision for SNR Scalability in SHVC Digest of Technical Papers," IEEE International Conference on Consumer Electronics (ICCE), pp. 193–194, 2014.

[17] G. E. Qingyangl and H. U. Dong, "Fast Encoding Method Using CU Depth for Quality Scalable HEVC," IEEE Workshop on Advanced Research and Technology in Industry Applications (WARTIA), pp. 1366–1370, 2014.

[18] L. Hahyun, K. J. Won, L. Jinho, C. J. Soo, K. Jinwoong and S. Donggyu, "Scalable Extension of HEVC for Flexible High-Quality Digital Video Content Services," ETRI Journal, vol. 35, no. 6, pp. 990–1000, 2013.

[19] D. K. Kwon, M. Budagavi, M. Zhou, "Multi-loop scalable video codec based on high efficiency video coding (HEVC)," International Conference on Acoustics, Speech, and Signal Processing (ICASSP), pp. 1749-1753, Vancouver, Canada, May 2013.

[20] David C. Lay, "Linear Algebra and Its Applications," 5th Edition, University of Maryland, College Park, Pearson Addison Wesley, 2016.

[21] https://hevc.hhi.fraunhofer.de/svn/svn_SHVCSoftware/tags/SHM-6.0/